Merchandising Math

Merchandising Math

A Managerial Approach

Doris H. Kincade, Ph.D.
Virginia Polytechnic Institute and State University

Fay Y. Gibson, M.S.
Industry Consultant

Ginger A. Woodard, Ph.D.
East Carolina University

Prentice
Hall

Upper Saddle River, New Jersey 07458

Library of Congress Cataloging-in-Publication Data

Kincade, Doris H.
    Merchandising math: a managerial approach/Doris H. Kincade, Fay Gibson, Ginger Woodard.
        p. cm.
    Includes index
    ISBN 0-13-099588-6
    1. Retail trade—Mathematics. 2. Merchandising. I. Gibson, Fay. II. Woodard, Ginger.
    III. Title

HF5695.5.R45K56 2004
510'.24'381—dc21   2003042549

Executive Editor: Gary Bauer
Managing Editor: Mary Carnis
Editorial Assistant: Natasha Holden
Marketing Manager: Leigh Ann Sims
Production Editor: Brian Hyland
Director of Production and Manufacturing: Bruce Johnson
Manufacturing Buyer: Ilene Sanford
Cover Design: Mary Siener
Design Director: Cheryl Asherman
Illustrator (Interior): Preparé
Composition: Preparé
Full-Service Project Management: Linda Zuk, WordCrafters Editorial Services, Inc.
Printer/Binder: Banta, Harrisonburg
Cover Printer: Phoenix Color Corp.

Pearson Education LTD.
Pearson Education Singapore, Pte. Ltd
Pearson Education, Canada, Ltd
Pearson Education–Japan

Pearson Education Australia PTY, Limited
Pearson Education North Asia Ltd
Pearson Educación de Mexico, S.A. de C.V.
Pearson Education Malaysia, Pte. Ltd

10 9 8 7 6 5 4 3 2 1
ISBN 0-13-099588-6

This book is dedicated to the inquiring young minds that inspired us to be better teachers. With our combined years of teaching experience, we estimate that this inspiration represents over 3,000 students who sat in our classrooms and listened to us teach merchandising math.

Brief Contents

Contents

Preface

This book is written for students who seek to be successful in retail, merchandising, and marketing, and who want to know the subject matter in more depth than what is necessary to simply find the solution to a problem. Such knowledge is the foundation to making good decisions, critical to the success of any business, and in turn, critical to the success of future careers. Possessing a solid understanding of merchandising math, making decisions based on sound principles backed with numeric explanation, and explaining decision processes to colleagues and bosses will be important every day in future merchandising careers. Companies can be saved or destroyed by the financial decisions made and the impact of those decisions on merchandising outcomes, especially those of product assortment and customer satisfaction. In this book, students are introduced to a broader knowledge about merchandising math and its application in day-to-day business transactions. With this knowledge, they will possess the aptitude to become skilled in and make decisions based on a variety of specialized programs.

In the past, many teachers, ourselves included, have used multiple books, drawn upon personal work experiences, created reams of worksheets, and designed hundreds of overheads and handouts to teach merchandising math. We were always searching for the book that would provide the right combination of background information, basic management decisions, mathematical formulas, explanation, and practice. From alumni, advisory boards and our own work experiences, we knew that few people in merchandising work in isolation; most work within organizations that expect teamwork and cross-functional networking. Even fewer people work with only numbers, and most work with problems, situations, and outcomes. To provide students with this integrated understanding, only this one book is needed—no more multiple book purchases, no more copies from the copy machine, no more extra exercises.

Formulas without explanations are merely mathematics; and management, marketing and merchandising processes without financial justification are merely theories. The two sides of the coin must merge for the student. With an understanding and a working knowledge of the formulas and their conceptual basis, the student will be able to work within any retail type, with any product classification, and for any size of business. When students memorize the formulas without understanding their application in a real-world work environment, they lack the ability to apply the information to new situations, to new products, or to new formats. With the approach that is provided in this book, students will understand why, how, and when to use this merchandising math information. They can work for a major chain that has its own hybrid computer system, a small, local store, or in any business in between and still understand the factors that must be considered in the financial decisions for the business.

This book is organized into four parts. The first part provides an overview of merchandising and retailing, with the basic spreadsheet format and pricing formulas used throughout the book. The next three parts follow the three-stage process of merchandising: planning, buying, and selling. To assist in the learning process, a student's solutions manual and a CD with test questions are available. For faculty, we provide a teaching manual including full solutions for all problems and transparency masters for several of the figures within the textbook.

In Part 1, "Introduction and Basics," Chapter 1 begins the study with the merchandising function within retail. This information is important for students who must understand the interrelated activities within retail and the importance of the team concept in merchandising. This foundation assists students, in later chapters, to perceive the impact of managerial decisions made in the merchandising function on the activities of other retail functions, such as operations, sales, and promotions. Chapter 2 presents the information on unit pricing and the elements of price. The student is introduced to the spreadsheet format of financial planning and the relationships between the basic elements of retail price, markup, and cost. Chapter 3 expands the basic price elements from one product unit to the store or business level. Chapter 4 expands a simple Profit and Loss statement into a complex statement that includes discussions of reductions, margins, and operations. This chapter also includes information about alterations, requirements of sales associates to wear company clothing, and other unique aspects of financial planning in the fashion industry.

Part 2, "Planning," begins with the broad scope of strategic planning. The basic process of strategic planning is described in Chapter 5, including the relationships of the P&L statement to the planning process and the role of the merchandising function in planning. The concepts in Chapter 5 are used extensively in subsequent chapters on planning sales, stock, and forecasting. Additionally, the value of an environmental scan and the collection of information, as described in Chapter 5, become evident to students through concepts and practice. Chapter 6 provides a unique view of sales planning from the perspective of both a continuing business and a new business. Chapter 6 also examines the various methods of planning stock, including discussions of turn, average stock, and the problems with fashion-oriented stock. Chapter 7 reveals the importance of stock to the merchandising process and the methods of determining appropriate stock levels. The presentation in Chapter 8 encourages students to compile the knowledge that they have acquired into developing the six-month spreadsheet. (Using this book, our students find that the six-month plan is easy to master. With texts we used previously, they struggled to assimilate a great deal of seemingly unrelated information.)

Part 3, "Buying," contains specific information and processes about the buying function within merchandising. For many students, these are their favorite chapters because we talk about the "real world" of buying: how buyers forecast (Chapter 9), how buyers organize the forecasting information (Chapter 10), what buyers do when they go to market (Chapter 12), and the specific number functions that are involved with determining open-to-buy and terms of the sale (Chapters 11 and 13). In this section, we provide exercises for the students to practice their forecasting skills and plan market trips. The chapter on assortment planning (Chapter 10) contains extensive and unique information not available in other merchandising texts about the organizational process of planning for buying. The merchandise classification system taught in this section enables the student as a future buyer to computerize the buying plan and prepare new buys to be entered into the computerized inventory systems used by most retail businesses. The balance, between the qualitative forecasting in Chapter 9 and the quantitative forecasting in Chapters 10 and 11, helps the student to understand the multiple-task role of the corporate and individual buyer.

Part 4, "Selling," completes the merchandising process. This part examines the floor functions of the buyer, and helps students bring closure to the class to understand more fully the interrelated functionality of merchandising and retailing. Buyers, merchandisers, department and store managers, and promotions personnel must work as a team to deliver the product to the consumer at the right price and the right time. Buying functions are closely related to inventory (Chapter 14), price adjustments including markdowns and other price adjustments (Chapter 15), and promotions, sales associates, and other methods of marketing communications between the retailer and the customer (Chapter 16). The information on price adjustments, especially markdowns, is presented in the context of the spreadsheet formats used for pricing as taught in Chapter 2. The student uses this chapter as a refresher on the information in Chapter 2 and is able to integrate the information from many concepts throughout the book into the managerial decisions used to make price adjustment decisions. The final chapter on marketing communications (Chapter 16) introduces the concepts of the various aspects of marketing communications, including promotions, sales, and public relations. The importance of these topics to the merchandising function is emphasized. This provides the student with an introduction, but not overlap, to this information for their subsequent courses in a retailing, business, or merchandising program.

We developed this book based on our combined experiences of teaching merchandising math, working as a buyer for a major retail corporation and a small privately owned apparel store, owning our own businesses, and working in both the fabric and apparel manufacturing segments of the fashion industry. We know first-hand the importance of financial decision making in the success of both small retail businesses and large multi-chain corporations. Doris Kincade was the owner of a family-owned and managed retail chain of dry cleaners/launderettes for ten years, worked for two years at Cone Mills, interned with Russell Corporation, and has been a Faculty Fellow with the Textile and Technology Corporation [TC]^2 since 1990. Fay Gibson was a buyer and then divisional merchandise manager for a partner group of Belk Stores for fifteen years, was the fashion director and trainer for a store group for Belk Stores, and was the owner/buyer of a ladies specialty store for seven years. We have been in the "real world" and have used what we know from that world to provide students with what they need to survive and thrive in business.

In addition, this book is the culmination of years of teaching at small schools, large universities, and major industrial corporations. Doris Kincade has taught merchandising math at Auburn University and Virginia Tech for more than twelve years, and taught merchandising courses prior to that for fourteen years at Peace College. Fay Gibson taught merchandising math and other merchandising courses for ten years at The University of North Carolina at Greensboro and has been a consultant or provided training for several Fortune 500 companies, Apparel Marts, and specialty retailers. Ginger Woodard has taught merchandising math and other merchandising courses at East Carolina for ten years, taught merchandising courses at Peace College for an additional seven years, and provided leadership for groundbreaking curriculum development for her area at East Carolina University.

Over the years, we have taught thousands of college students and hundreds of industry personnel. We have designed this book to help students think, to assist them with learning and practicing formulas, and to aid them in building merchandising knowledge as well as mathematical skills—a combination needed to succeed in business. We were inspired in writing this book by the thousands of students who asked questions in class, stayed after class for extra help, and either struggled with or loved merchandising math. Our combined years of teaching experience represent over 3,000 students who sat in our classrooms and listened to us teach merchandising math. With every semester of teaching—and for the three of us that represents about 85 semesters of merchandising math—we have refined the ideas in this book, developed exercises that assist with skill development, and organized the concepts to improve student learning.

Acknowledgments

We would like to express our appreciation to the following colleagues, who provided helpful reviews and suggestions while this book was being written: Joni V. Beach; Linda M. Cushman, Syracuse University; Laura D. Jolly, University of Tennessee; Lucy C. Lissard; and Mike Reisenauer, Lakeshore Technical College.

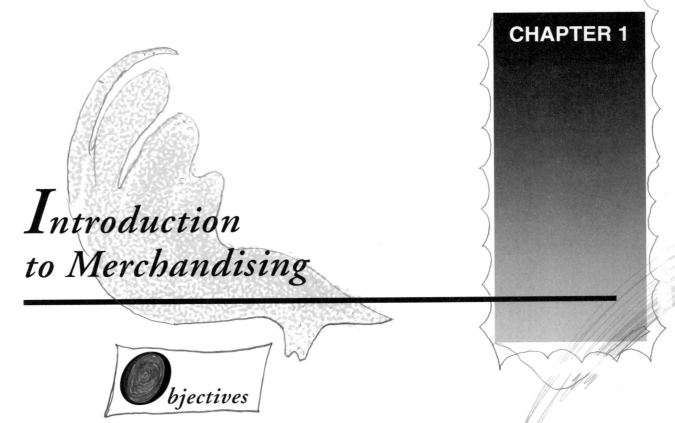

*I*ntroduction to Merchandising

*O*bjectives

After completing this chapter, the student will be able to

- describe the importance of retailing
- define the basic functions of retailing
- identify the types of retail organizations
- define merchandising
- explain the rights of merchandising
- compare and contrast the functions of merchandising, retailing, and marketing

Retailing is a major business in the United States and throughout the world that employs hundreds of thousands of people and involves many activities. The most important transaction in retailing is the one between the **consumer** (i.e., the final customer) and the retailer. For this transaction, the retailer purchases goods that are then resold to consumers for postpurchase use or final consumption. This exchange between retailer and consumer can occur through a variety of media: brick-and-mortar stores, television, catalog, computer, and telephone.

Brick-and-mortar stores are located along downtown streets, in shopping centers, and at strip centers. Some buildings are also free standing on out parcel lots near shopping centers, at busy intersections, or in low rent locations. In addition, some retail centers are located in remote areas without other nearby retail establishments or in areas proximate to vacation destinations or resort facilities. The brick-and-mortar stores are so called because the businesses are located in physical buildings; therefore, some people refer to owning these stores as **owning real estate**. These stores represent the aspect of the retail business to which the consumer or shopper must drive or walk for merchandise.

Other stores are **virtual stores**. The transactions for a virtual store are just as real as those exchanges in a brick-and-mortar store, but consumers visit the store via telephone or other electronic mode. In catalog, television, or Internet shopping, the consumer views the merchandise in pictures or on live models; however, the actual merchandise is not available for the consumer to touch or feel until delivery after the transaction.

E-commerce is the name given to the increasing number of transactions that occur over the Internet. Business-to-business transactions have been the main portion of e-commerce, but the number of retail e-commerce transactions between retailers and consumers are also increasing. Some of these electronic retail ventures represent new businesses and new brands or products, and some are expansions of the traditional brick-and-mortar stores. E-tailing is a term that is used for the retail businesses that utilize the Internet or other electronic formats for their consumer transactions. Retailers with brick-and-mortar stores who have expanded into electronic businesses are now known as click-and-mortar stores. When a business is composed of several retail types or outlets, the business is called a store group. Most store groups not only own real estate in strategic geographic locations, but also maintain Internet sites that reach consumers who cannot or do not wish to visit the physical store site. Through e-commerce, retailers have redefined the target market. The target market is no longer defined by geographic distance but is now defined by electronic access. Market share can be increased by penetrating into geographic locations in which the retailer does not own real estate.

E-commerce allows retailers to provide a wide range of services to their consumers; these services can be combined between click stores and brick stores. For instance, some click-and-mortar businesses permit consumers to buy products over the Internet and return any unwanted purchases to their nearest or most convenient brick-and-mortar location. This service is an added incentive that encourages the consumer to purchase additional products and provides the retailer with a competitive facet in an overstored retail environment. Clicks and bricks may also be combined with catalogs to reach even more potential consumers for a retail business. Retailers may offer a different assortment of products on the Internet or in catalogs than the assortment offered in the physical store. These retailers have the chance to customize the product offerings to provide a further incentive for consumers to shop with that retailer than to shop with competitive retailers. Through these multiple venues, a retailer can offer a variety of goods including unique or exclusive goods for selected consumers.

The retail transaction, or the activity of the consumer making a retail purchase, is near the end of a long pipeline of activities. With increased concern about the global environment, reuse or the resale of used merchandise and the recycling of used merchandise is a final segment that can be added to the pipeline. This pipeline or chain of activities contains the segments of raw materials production, product manufacturing, retailing, and consumer transactions. At each segment, value-added changes are made to the incoming supplies to provide goods and services to the next segment. The pipeline begins with the creation or production of raw materials. For apparel or home fashion items, these raw materials include fiber, fur, leather, plastic, and numerous other man-made materials. These materials are then made into woven, knit, or novelty fabrications, as well as findings and trimmings. During the product manufacturing process, these fabrications are transformed into finished products, called goods or merchandise. Retail buyers purchase these finished products for sale to the consumer. The retail buyer acts as the buying agent for the consumer; however, few buyers actually purchase items specifically for an individual consumer. Rather, the buyer purchases items for the retailer's customers (i.e., consumers) as a whole; therefore, knowing the characteristics of the consumer is a vital part of the retail buyer's job.

Retail

Retail is big business! The retail sector is one of the largest single employers in the United States. This sector includes very large businesses with stores throughout the United States and the world and very small businesses with one store servicing a small geographic area. The largest of the retail businesses are often studied by retail analysts and other retailers in all tiers of distribution. The practices and merchandising techniques of major retailers, including corporate culture, product offerings, pricing philosophies, and consumer- or community-centered approaches, are studied to provide guidance and other information for competitive and noncompetitive retail businesses.

The major goal of retailing is profit. To achieve this profit, the retailer must satisfy consumers. Satisfaction is the result of a retail transaction that meets or exceeds a consumer's expectation. When the retailer can achieve consumer satisfaction, consumers are more likely to (a) return to purchase more merchandise and (b) tell their neighbors, friends, and family about their good experience with the retailer. Therefore, satisfied consumers increase sales. Sales that are balanced with good management of purchases and expenses will generate profit. With continued sales, money to pay expenses, and profit, the retailer is able to stay in business.

Retailing is the distribution of goods to the final customer, or the activity of buying at wholesale from a manufacturer, wholesaler, or jobber and selling at retail to the consumer. Most manufacturers make one type of product, usually in large quantities. In contrast, the consumer usually wants only one item from one manufacturer. For most consumers, shopping and negotiating with many manufacturers would be too tiresome or expensive. Therefore, retailers provide this service for the consumer by shopping from manufacturers, wholesalers, or jobbers; pricing each individual item; and presenting an assortment of merchandise to the consumer. This procedure is called **breaking bulk**.

Retail Types

Retail organizations can be classified by numerous criteria, which are interconnected. Retail businesses can be classified by size, organizational structure, merchandise assortments, numbers of stores, price orientation, style orientation, location, use of store or nonstore methods of display, and numerous other criteria. A combination of criteria is generally used to classify businesses more adequately. The most common types of retail businesses are **mass merchandisers, department stores, specialty retailers** or limited line retailers, **mail order** or **catalog businesses**, and **discounters**. Within each classification, subclassifications exist to distinguish special attributes of a set of businesses from other businesses within that classification. For example, some department stores are identified as junior department stores, some as chain department stores, and others as specialty department stores. Specialty stores are categorized as "mom and pop" stores, chain stores, boutiques, and/or franchises. Within the discounter classification, businesses can be organized according to how they achieve the low price such as high-volume discounters, off-pricers, manufacturer's outlets or factory stores, warehouse clubs, and variety stores. (At warehouse clubs, consumers must pay a fee to belong to the club, and they must buy in bulk or large quantities. Variety stores are known for the array of low end, budget goods that they carry.)

Apparel and home fashions merchandise are a major part of the retail business and are sold by many of the top ten U.S. retail stores. These items can be found in home improvement stores, grocery stores, drug stores, and gasoline stations; even service businesses are involved in the selling of apparel merchandise. Restaurants, theaters, and other places of entertainment offer hats, shirts, and jackets that carry the logo of the business. Apparel sales account for a large percentage of some service businesses. Apparel retailing also affects the balance of trade in the world. Many of the apparel items sold in the United States are imported items. Decisions about the importation of apparel items become pivotal issues in discussions of world trade and political negotiations.

Retail Functions

The retailer performs four basic functions: merchandising, operations, promotions, and control. In addition, some retailers are responsible for a fifth function, personnel. All of these functions are necessary in facilitating the transaction between the retailer and the consumer.

Merchandising includes the activities of planning, buying, and selling of category-specific merchandise, including apparel and other fashion goods. The merchandising division in a store is often viewed as the "heart" or core of the retail store. With the buyer as the principle figure in the merchandising function, the merchandising division is first responsible for internal planning to ensure the acquisition of the appropriate merchandise mix and assortments for the retailer's consumer. The merchandise division also assists in developing a coordinated in-store merchandising program and product presentation to position the brand or image in a manner that will generate or increase (i.e., drive) sales. To accomplish this objective, the buyer is responsible for directing the creation of an organized visual presentation to maximize product presentation vehicles such as fixturing, signage, point-of-sale (POS) materials, and promotional and special events. The buyer is also responsible for inventory control and other functions for handling the merchandise; however, in a traditionally organized retail business, the sales associates assist with this function.

Operations involve the functions of store management. The physical plant of the store is controlled by this function. The store manager is the principle employee in the operations division. In some store groups, an operations manager, who is sometimes titled the assistant store manager, handles many of the operations or management functions. Store groups may increase in size of holdings until a second level of structure is needed. The stores are then organized into regional groups, and, within these groupings, the assistant store manager is then titled the store merchandise manager. This title is similar to, but not the same as, the general or divisional merchandise manager in the merchandising division who works in the corporate operations division. This store merchandise manager is responsible for housing of the merchandise, the in-store merchandise arrangement, the total package of the visual merchandise presentation (e.g., display and signage), and the overall appearance of the store's physical plant. This store merchandise manager is also responsible for scheduling sales associates to provide adequate floor coverage to optimize both sales per square foot and profit. Regardless of the title of the management positions, store management is responsible for the staffing, training, and compensating of store personnel; however, this set of activities is given to the personnel function if the store has that separate function or division. (Other activities, such as employee benefits, performance appraisals, and personnel records are also handled by personnel.) The store manager or operations manager is also responsible for the purchasing of supplies and equipment to operate the store, and for supervising store maintenance and housekeeping activities. Other operations activities include overseeing the receiving room for receiving and marking merchandise, and for checking merchandise against invoices and packing slips. Warehouse distribution and shipping are also functions of store management, unless the warehouse operations are under a separate function (usually in a separate location). Lastly, one of the most important activities supervised by store management is that of customer service.

The **promotions** function includes all of the public relations, publicity, and promotional activities of the store. The public relations manager or promotions manager is responsible for the public (i.e., potential customers) view of the store. This view, or the perceived store image, is created through promotions, advertisements, publicity, visual merchandise presentation, and special events staged by the store. Some promotional activities are designed to promote specific merchandise or to promote the store and the store's policies. Examples of these are sales and discounted merchandise. Other events are designed to promote goodwill in the community and to increase the public's awareness of the store. Benefits for charity, sponsorship of sporting events, and donations to underprivileged groups are examples of public relations for awareness and goodwill. The **promotions manager** is the key director of these promotional activities and may have assistants to work with the various aspects of this function. These individuals may include visual merchandising managers, advertising managers and artists, special events coordinators, public relations directors, fashion coordinators, and catalog managers. In some retail businesses, the promotions manager or publicity manager is also responsible for the activities of personal shoppers and fashion trainers.

The **control** function is the dollar function and is commonly called **financial control** or the accounting area. In addition to accounting, the record keeping tasks and merchandising statistics are maintained by financial control. Accurate and timely statistics, calculated by the financial control division, provide vital information for the merchandising division. These statistics provide information for the buyers to set parameters for planning, buying, and selling activities. Credit and collections activities are the responsibility of this function as well as inventory control and budgeting. Another task of financial control is paying vendor bills for both merchandise and store supplies. The principle employee serving in this capacity in a small store would be an **accountant**, and in a larger store, the function would be supervised by an account manager or **controller**.

Retail Organization

Exact responsibilities of each manager or employee are determined by individual stores or by the management of a chain of stores. The four functions (i.e., merchandising, operations, promotions, and control) overlap in activities because all of these functions have the goals of profit and consumer satisfaction. In addition, all functions are important to the selling of merchandise. For example, the buyer must work closely with the promotions manager to ensure that the right merchandise is available for a specific sale. The buyer must also work with the store manager to ensure that adequate numbers of sales associates will be on the floor for the sales promotion and that the sales associates are knowledgeable about the merchandise. The controller must be certain that the bills are paid for the merchandise so that the merchandise will arrive on time for the promotion.

Figure 1.1

Line and Staff
Organizational Chart.

An organizational chart is a visual model of the retail functions and the employees within each function, which provides an outline of the duties and responsibilities of the store employees. The charts establish the lines of authority and supervision for each employee and can be used to locate the position of any employee. As the retail organization grows in size, the charts reflect the specialization of functions and the development of a buying function that is separate from the selling function.

The traditional retail store was operated as a **line and staff organizational chart**. (See Figure 1.1.) Each employee was the supervisor of the next employee. The store manager was at the top of the chart and supervised the buyer, who in turn, supervised the department managers, who supervised the sales associates. Employees for promotions or control were staff functions and not in the straight line of command. This organizational structure is still used by many small, privately owned and operated retail businesses. In a very small store, the owner is often both the store manager and the buyer who would operate the store with only a few sales associates. The benefit of this organizational flow is the direct connection between selling and buying.

As retail businesses grew in the 1950s, 1960s, and 1970s, new organizational structures were developed for managing multiple functions of retail business. Four functions of retail began to specialize and each function established a hierarchy of employees and responsibilities. The fifth function, personnel, is separated from operations. Organizational charts began to widen into the **large store organizational chart**. (See Figure 1.2.)

The five functions of control, merchandising, promotions, personnel, and operations are represented in the large store organizational chart. The controller, the **general merchandise manager (GMM)**, the promotions manager, **personnel manager**, and store manager are key employees that report directly to general or top management. Each **divisional merchandise manager (DMM)** reports to the GMM and is responsible for supervising a group of buyers. Each DMM is responsible for a grouping of merchandise, and each buyer is responsible for a narrower assortment of merchandise or specific classification of merchandise. Most large chain stores have from five to eight DMMs, one each for women's wear, men's wear, young men's and boy's wear, children's attire, women's lingerie, shoes, and main floor merchandise, which may include ladies' accessories and cosmetics. For example, a DMM may be responsible for all of women's wear, and the buyers would individually buy for dresses, bridal, cocktail attire, coats, sportswear coordinates, or separates, which are divided into tops (e.g., sweaters, t-shirts, shirts, and blouses), bottoms (e.g., skirts, pants, and shorts), and swimwear. In some store groups, a large classification of merchandise such as separates may have buyers for subclassifications within separates. For example, the store grouping may have several sportswear buyers—a separate buyer for missy, juniors, bridge, designer, and women's or large sizes. These buyers select all merchandise clas-

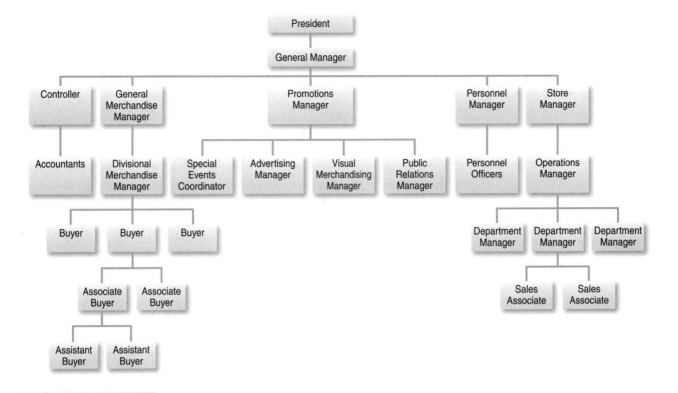

| Figure 1.2 | Large Store Organizational Chart. |

sifications housed in a specific department across all the stores. In this organizational structure, the buyer becomes an expert in a specific grouping of merchandise. The grouping may be determined by consumer lifestyle, design category, price range, or size. In the large store organization, a buyer selects the merchandise, but usually has no direct access to sales associates or promotions employees.

As a retail business expands and opens new **doors** or stores, the organization changes again, and a chain store organization develops with an associated **chain store organizational chart**. The chain store chart is similar to the large store chart except in the operations function. In the chain store organization, the store management vice president supervises the operations function and is responsible for the supervision of all **district managers (DM)**. Each district manager is responsible for the stores in a geographic district. Each store has a store manager, department managers, and sales associates. With the increased levels of organization, the buyer is further in organizational structure and often in geographic distance from the sales associates and has limited contact with the stores and the merchandise in the stores. With this separation of the buying and selling functions, new methods of electronic and video communication are helping buyers stay in contact with the stores, the sales associates, and the consumers.

Merchandising

The outcome of merchandising is a set of "rights," which are achieved through the merchandising process. The process includes the purchase of an appropriate assortment of goods, to ensure the profitable sale of those goods to a satisfied customer.

Simply stated, the process of merchandising is getting the **right goods in** the right silhouettes, sizes, and colors; at the **right price**; at the **right location**; for the **right consumers**. In addition, the **right time and the right quantity** of merchandise must be right for the retailer and for the consumer. Although these **rights of merchandising** can be stated simply, the coordination of activities to attain these rights simultaneously is very difficult for a merchandise manager. To succeed in satisfying the needs and wants of the right consumer, the activities in the merchandising function must be conducted with one part knowledge, one part experience, one part hard work, and even, one part good luck!

The *right goods* means the right merchandise for both consumer and retailers. For example, the right merchandise identified by a merchandise manager for one retailer might not be the right merchandise for another retailer in the same retail classification. For some retailers, the right merchandise may be seasonal merchandise such as heavy wool coats and gloves due to the specific geographic location. Meanwhile, for other retailers, basic trench coats and raincoats may sell in the store year-round. The quality of the merchandise may be another important feature for some retailers. Their target consumers may have specific expectations about workmanship, functional performance, and design aesthetics as related to the price for a valuable product. Other retailers may find that trendy merchandise might be part of their success in securing the right merchandise for the right consumer.

With the advanced technology available in business-to-business transactions, many merchandise managers are adding these product attributes to the databases they use for shopping and purchasing. Information about silhouette, size, and color can be identified and entered into databases for category-specific merchandise. This expanded use of computer technology helps the merchandise manager reach the ultimate goal of the right merchandise for the right customer at the right price in order to satisfy the consumer and make a profit.

Several factors, external and internal, can impact the ability of the retailer to obtain the merchandise at the *right price*. Pricing is a major factor in merchandising. Market trends, current domestic and global economic conditions, pricing and product offerings by the competition, and other external factors may influence the pricing of the merchandise assortment. Within the retail environment, last year's sales volume and markdown patterns can also affect potential pricing for this year.

To achieve the *right location* for the merchandise, the retail merchandiser must carefully organize the space within the store, in the catalog, or on the Web site for the right merchandise presentation. This right is important for the retailer to achieve the ultimate sales potential for the available space, be it real or virtual. Proper visual presentation as well as the combination of specific merchandise classifications must create an inviting retail environment for maximum sales potential. Artistic displays, appropriate usage of fixturing, proper signage, and organization and presentation of merchandise in print advertising, catalogs, and Web sites must be considered to develop the right location or place for each item and combination of items. The front of the store or the home page on a Web site is prime selling space. The location of floor space relative to store entrances and traffic paths, the buttons and links within a Web site, and the positioning of merchandise in a catalog are important considerations that are critical to the right place or location for specific types of merchandise. Retailers can track sales of merchandise and note locations to determine the right placement of the goods.

All of the rights of merchandising must be compatible with the *right consumer*. Consumers can be classified according to their needs and wants. What is demanded by one consumer during one purchase may not be a factor in the next purchase. In addition, preferences for the same type of product may vary from consumer to consumer. Meeting these demands is a difficult and ever-changing process for retailers. Because consumers have many options for obtaining their purchases, retailers must work hard to target the right consumer with the right product.

The *right time* of merchandise delivery is another important factor in all aspects and activities of the merchandising function. If goods, especially seasonal or fashion apparel products, arrive in the store too early, the retailer may be forced to house high inventory levels due to a lack of sales and low movement of stock. Keeping high inventory levels can create larger markdowns than anticipated and can reduce cash flow. On the other hand, if goods are received later than needed, a loss of sales resulting from consumer disappointment from low levels of stock, lack of desired merchandise, or unappealing merchandise assortments can occur. Late deliveries due to improper shipping may create unbalanced assortments and cause unexpected markdowns, low or no profits, and leftover and unwanted inventory.

The *right quantity* of merchandise is also important for the retailer and the consumer. The retailer must achieve a balance between the amount of inventory on hand at the beginning of a sales period and the amount of sales realized during that same period. In other words, the right quantities of specific merchandise assortments and classifications are necessary in meeting sales quotas for a specific period. These quantities are usually planned from the units and dollar volumes from the same season of the previous year with adjustments made for the new year. If a retailer orders too few goods, a loss of sales from lack of inventory may result. If the same retailer orders too much stock relative to consumer demands, excess and unsold inventories can lead to unplanned markdowns that reduce profit margins.

In addition to the activities of the merchandising function for the retailer, merchandising can also be a function of the manufacturing segment. With apparel products, the merchandiser working at the manufacturing segment is called the **apparel merchandiser** in contrast to the retail merchandiser who works at the retail segment.

Merchandise managers at manufacturing firms can select raw materials and request production of products that will be sold to retailers for their final customers. These merchandisers develop cohesive packages of merchandise that reflect the image of the manufacturer, the retailer, and the target consumer. This package is coordinated with the price structure of the related businesses, the available production facilities, sourcing capabilities, and labor structure in order to maintain the integrity of the desired design concepts as targeted to the right consumer. Throughout this text, the utilization of these rights in the merchandising process will be discussed in detail.

To achieve the rights of merchandising, the retailer conducts the merchandising process or a series of activities that can be grouped into three major steps: **planning the merchandise, buying the merchandise, and selling the merchandise.** The first step in merchandising, planning the merchandise, involves planning for future merchandise selections and assortments, evaluating current market conditions, and analyzing the past sales history of the retail business. In planning the merchandise, the buyer estimates customer demands and determines the quantity of stock needed to generate a level of sales activity. Planning begins with identifying the right consumer and matching the image of the business and the fashion image of the merchandise to the needs and wants of the consumer. The buyer is responsible for understanding the customer and uses market segmentation, consumer targeting, forecasting, and buying plans to plan the best assortment of merchandise. The buyer must forecast trends and adapt the information from those forecasts to meet the needs and wants of the consumer. In addition, buyers estimate consumer demand and determine quantity of stock needed to satisfy the demand for the desired level of sales activity.

Buying the merchandise requires the activities to obtain the right goods, which include, but are not limited to, comparison shopping, sourcing, and selecting goods. In this part of the merchandising process, the buyer works with manufacturers or **vendors**, either individually or within the market system. Negotiations on price, quantity, colors, styles, and delivery are part of obtaining or procuring the merchandise. Buying includes tasks of searching for the most appropriate or right merchandise to meet the needs and wants of the target consumer. The buyer then selects all of the vendors that are needed to fulfill the orders and to create a balanced merchandise mix. This assortment of vendors is called a **vendor matrix** or **retail matrix**. Buying may include trips to the manufacturer, trips to a market city, and/or selection from catalogs or sample merchandise in the central merchandising office. For buyers with Internet and other e-commerce capabilities, the selection may be from the manufacturer's Internet site with accompanying swatch books of fabric and color.

Selling the merchandise includes housing the merchandise, promoting the merchandise, and finally, selling the merchandise. The technique of storing, displaying, and promoting merchandise is of utmost importance to the total merchandising process. This merchandising step overlaps several store functions, such as promotions management, inventory management, store operations, and personnel management.

Housing the merchandise involves the areas of inventory control and distribution systems. Distribution systems can include the warehouse of the inventory and the shipping of the inventory between vendor and store, among multiple stores, and between vendor and consumer. Housing of merchandise also includes the trip that the merchandise takes from vendor, the presentation of the merchandise on the floor, and the trip that the merchandise takes from retailer to consumer. For a brick-and-mortar store, the merchandise will be received in the store, placed on the selling floor and in display spaces, and then sold to consumers. For catalog and Internet retailers, the merchandise is rarely housed at the site of the catalog or Web page creation; instead, images of the merchandise are displayed for the consumer. From those displayed images, the consumer makes a selection and places an order. The actual merchandise is then shipped directly to the consumer from a warehouse.

Promoting the merchandise is vital to achieve consumer acceptance and the final sale of the merchandise. This step of merchandising includes the promotions, final sale, and customer service after the sale. Promotional activities include visual presentation and displays, advertising in newspapers, banner strips on Web sites, television and radio spots, special events, and sales personnel training.

The actual sale of the merchandise is the final activity in this step. Managing both sales associates and the products is vital to the successful sale in order for the retailer to obtain the double goal of customer satisfaction and profit. Personal selling is important both for stores and for nonstores. Many catalog retailers have highly trained sales associates to help consumers with their telephoned purchases. Service after the sale is also an important aspect of promoting the merchandise and making the sale. Retailers must ensure that the products they sell will fulfill the promise of the promotion and will continue to satisfy the customer. Customer satisfaction may be enhanced through a partnership with the vendors. Vendors can supply information cards and toll-free phone numbers so that consumers can call directly to the source of the product for information and assistance with complaints. After the sale, support is vital to ensuring that the consumer is satisfied with the product, remains satisfied, and returns for more products.

Marketing

Marketing is the total set of activities for interaction between any supplier and any customer. This set includes the planning, pricing, promoting, and distributing of the goods and services for a profit. Marketing involves generating and sustaining the flow of goods from the raw material to the manufacturer to the retailer, and, finally, to the consumer. Each stage of the pipeline is facilitated by marketing activities. Underlying all of the marketing activities is the goal of customer satisfaction and ultimate profit for each segment in the pipeline. Marketing is used to facilitate transactions from business to business as well as business to consumer, exists beyond the retail segment, and can have a broader scope than merchandising. Finally, covering product development at both manufacturing and retailing, marketing can include functions of costing, product design, and management that are not usually included in the scope of merchandising.

*S*ummary

Marketing, merchandising, and retailing are sets of activities that are necessary to promote the profitable sale of merchandise to a consumer for that consumer's ultimate use and satisfaction. The type of retail business, the merchandise carried by retailers, and the number and jobs of the retail employees vary, but selling to the final consumer is the focus of all merchandising. The retail employees involved in these activities have overlapping functions, but one, single goal—profit through consumer satisfaction.

Key Terms

Accountant
Apparel merchandiser
Assistant store manager
Breaking bulk
Brick-and-mortar store
Buyer
Buying the merchandise
Catalog business
Chain store organizational chart
Click-and-mortar store
Consumer
Control (Financial)
Controller
Department store
Discounter
District manager (DM)
Divisional merchandise manager (DMM)

Doors
E-commerce
E-tailing
Financial control
General merchandise manager (GMM)
Housing the merchandise
Large store organizational chart
Line and staff organizational chart
Mail order business
Marketing
Mass merchandiser
Merchandising
Operations
Operations manager
Owning real estate
Personnel manager
Planning the merchandise

Promoting the merchandise
Promotions
Promotions manager
Raw material
Retail matrix
Reuse
Rights of merchandising:
    Right goods, right price, right location, right consumer, right time, right quantity
Selling the merchandise
Specialty retailer
Store group
Store manager
Store merchandise manager
Vendor
Vendor (Retail) matrix
Virtual store

Discussion Questions

1. What are retailing, marketing, and merchandising?
2. How are retailing, marketing, and merchandising related?
3. Why is retailing important to consumers?
4. How has the increased accessibility of electronic commerce changed retailing?
5. As a store grows, what are the problems involved with the separation between merchandising and operations?
6. How is the job of a buyer different in a small store than in a multistore chain?
7. What are the rights of merchandising?
8. What are the steps of merchandising?
9. How does the buyer work with promotions and operations in merchandising?
10. Why does the buyer need contact with the sales associates? with target customers?

Exercises

1. Access the Web site for the Department of Commerce. Investigate the categories of businesses within the retail industry sector.

2. Create an organizational chart for a small, "mom and pop" store, where the owner is also the buyer. Explain your chart.

3. Create an organizational chart for a chain store that has a buyer for women's, children's, shoes, men's, cosmetics, and jewelry departments.

4. Create an organizational chart for a large chain store that has three geographic regions and buyers for 10 categories of merchandise.

5. Find the Web site of several top retail stores. What do they include on their sites about jobs, internships, their organizational structure, their merchandise, and their history?

6. Examine a current store in your area that has the "right merchandise." Explain your selection by detailing what they have done correctly with each of the merchandising rights.

*R*etail Pricing

*O*bjectives

After completing this chapter, the student will be able to

- define the price elements of retail, cost, and markup
- calculate retail price from cost and markup
- use spreadsheets as a format for the retail, cost, and markup relationship
- identify types of markup
- identify methods for pricing decisions
- explain factors affecting the three price elements

Retail pricing is fundamental to the retail sale of merchandise, to the satisfaction of the consumer, and to the profitability of the business. For example, a buyer shops the market and selects a group of picture frames to be sold for the next season, and a retail price of $30.00 is assigned to each frame. The process seems simple, but the results have far-reaching implications on the well being of the store and its entire retail organization. With many items, the primary focus of the buyer's decision making is on the selection of the item based upon the style, color, size, and other features that will be in demand by the consumer. Style and color are the first characteristics noticed by the consumer when shopping for many items and are often the characteristics that give the item appeal when displayed in the store. In the market, the buyer will view a large variety of items with many characteristics. Selecting the right items for the store's target consumer is one of the keys to success in retail.

Determining which item will sell is a challenge for all who must forecast and buy for retail sales. Yet, the price of the item is equally important. The right item at the wrong price will not sell. Although assigning a retail price seems simple, it is as challenging as determining the right item. Pricing decisions involve three **retail price elements**: retail price, wholesale cost, and markup. Determining the right price includes a variety of activities: (a) understanding the retail price elements, (b) identifying the types of markup, (c) establishing a basis or method for all pricing decisions, and (d) examining factors affecting the three price elements.

Retail Price Elements

The retail price must contain the wholesale cost of the item and the markup assigned to the item. The wholesale cost of the item is generally called **cost of goods** or **cost**, a generic term that will be used regardless of the type of item that is purchased. In retailing, cost of goods is always used to refer to the wholesale cost. This cost is the price of the item charged by the wholesaler, manufacturer, or other distributor, and it represents the price that the retail buyer paid for the item. Cost of goods includes the invoice value of the item, which is also called the list price, the transportation, and often the cost of insurance to cover the merchandise while it is being shipped by the vendor or manufacturer to the retailer.

Markup includes operating expenses, retail reductions (i.e., markdowns, discounts, and shortages), and profit. Markup is the difference between the retail price and the cost of goods sold. As will be mentioned in the "methods of pricing" section, the markup may be established by one of several methods, for example, component addition, price lining, and market pricing. With the component addition method, markup is built from the value of needed expenses. In price lining and market pricing, markup is the result of the difference between cost and the established retail price. Markup may be set as a single amount for every item, regardless of type or classification of merchandise; however, a fixed or single markup is usually used only with like or similar items within a merchandise classification. Markup may also be fixed as equal to the cost of the merchandise. This method is known as a **keystone markup** or a markup that doubles the invoiced cost of the item to achieve the retail price. Alternatively, markup may vary across the same classifications and/or other merchandise categories. Markup, within one store, may be different for many items. Markup may also change for an item as the season and the level of sales change or during price adjustments such as markdowns, special promotions, or other price changes. Many methods are used to find markup, but the formula, which represents the relationship among the price elements, is the same in each situation. The formula for **retail dollars** is

$$\text{Retail \$} = \text{Cost \$} + \text{Markup \$}$$

Through algebraic changes, the retail dollars formula can be rewritten to solve for markup dollars and for cost dollars. The formula for **markup dollars** is

$$\text{Markup \$} = \text{Retail \$} - \text{Cost \$}$$

In addition, the formula for **cost dollars** is

$$\text{Cost \$} = \text{Retail \$} - \text{Markup \$}$$

If any two of the three retail elements (i.e., retail dollars, cost dollars, or markup dollars) are given, the other element can be identified. This situation of knowing only two of the three price elements could occur when the buyer wanted to have new merchandise at the same retail price as some previous merchandise. The buyer would know the needed markup and the retail price, and would need to determine what was the right cost for the new merchandise.

Sample Problems: Retail Price Elements

Problem 1

On a recent trip to the market, the buyer for a retail store purchased a group of shirts. Each shirt has a wholesale cost of $15.00. A keystone markup is used by the store; therefore, the markup on a shirt is $15.00. What is the retail price of the shirt?

Retail $ = Cost $ + Markup $

(Hint: Insert the values for cost and markup from the preceding situation.)

Retail $ = $15.00 + $15.00

Retail $ = $30.00

Problem 2

The same buyer purchased a group of candles at a cost of $13.50 per candle for a suggested retail price of $29.99 per candle. What is the necessary markup for one candle?

Retail $ = Cost $ + Markup $

(Hint: Through algebraic changes, formula can be rewritten to solve for markup $.)

Markup $ = Retail $ − Cost $

(Hint: Insert the values for cost and markup from the preceding situation.)

Markup $ = $29.99 − $13.50

Markup $ = $16.49

Problem 3

A buyer finds linen tablecloths at a cost of $50.00. A keystone markup will be used. What is the markup? What is the retail price?

(Hint: Keystoning means that the markup is the same as the cost.)

Retail $ = Cost $ + Markup $

Retail $ = $50.00 + $50.00

Retail $ = $100.00

Problem 4

Hoping to build multiple sales opportunities, another buyer for the same retail store purchased casual pants to coordinate with the shirts in Problem 1. The pants were retailed with a keystone markup on $48.00. What is the cost of each pair of pants?

Cost $ = Retail $ − Markup $

(Hint: Keystone is doubling the invoiced cost of the item. In this situation, calculate markup $ by finding one/half or 50% of the retail price.)

Cost $ = $48.00 − $24.00

Cost $ = $24.00

The retail price elements can also be viewed as percentages. Percentages are useful for making comparisons across items, across departments, and across stores. The retail price is the base of the relationship and represents 100% of the price. Using the retail price as a base is common for many retailers. The cost of goods can be used as a base, but this pricing situation is more common in manufacturing companies than for retailing companies. Traditionally, fashion goods manufacturers have focused their pricing methods on the component addition method because the cost of labor is an extremely important element in determining the overall cost of the item. For the work in this text, the percentages are expressed at two decimal places. This format is equivalent with the two decimals used for all dollar amounts. The formula for **retail price percentages** is

$$\text{Retail \%} = \text{Cost \%} + \text{Markup \%}$$

Sample Problems: Retail Price Elements as Percentages

Problem 1

A small picture frame is assigned the markup percentage of 45.30%, and the cost percentage is 54.70%. By applying the formula, a retail percentage of 100.00% can be confirmed.

$$\text{Retail \%} = \text{Cost \%} + \text{Markup \%}$$

(Hint: Insert the percentages from the aforementioned situation into the formula.)

$$\text{Retail \%} = 54.70\% + 45.30\%$$

$$\text{Retail \%} = 100.00\%$$

(Hint: By adding cost percentage and markup percentage, the retail percentage of 100% is confirmed.)

Problem 2

A sofa pillow with ruffles has a cost percentage of 38.80%. The retail percentage is known to be 100.00%. What is the markup percentage for this product?

$$\text{Retail \%} = \text{Cost \%} + \text{Markup \%}$$

(Hint: Using algebraic rules for solving equations, the percentage formula can be rewritten to solve for markup percentage. In this situation, Cost % is subtracted from both sides, and Cost % − Cost % results in a zero.)

$$\text{Retail \%} - \text{Cost \%} = (\text{Cost \%} - \text{Cost \%}) + \text{Markup \%}$$

(Hint: The resulting formula solves for Markup %. Further uses of this type of algebraic manipulation will not be discussed.)

$$\text{Markup \%} = \text{Retail \%} - \text{Cost \%}$$

(Hint: The percentages from Problem 2 can be inserted into the formula.)

$$\text{Markup \%} = 100.00\% - 38.80\%$$

$$\text{Markup \%} = 61.20\%$$

Problem 3

The standard markup percentage for the store is 45.50%. An umbrella is sold in the store at $50.00. What is the cost percentage of the umbrella?

(Hint: Retail percentage is 100%.)

$$\text{Retail \%} = \text{Cost \%} + \text{Markup \%}$$

(Hint: Using algebraic rules, the formula can be rewritten to solve for cost percentage.)

$$\text{Cost \%} = \text{Retail \%} - \text{Markup \%}$$

(Hint: Percentages from Problem 3 can be inserted into the formula.)

$$\text{Cost \%} = 100.00\% - 45.50\%$$

$$\text{Cost \%} = 54.50\%$$

In many situations for a company, the buyers, managers, and top administration will use both dollar amounts and percentages for the retail price elements in their study of the pricing situation. The consumer will not see this format. In those studies, the dollar values of cost and markup are expressed as percentages of the retail price. The retail price can be viewed as the base for the relationship among the three price elements, and markup and cost percentages are rates. With this relationship, retail prices, costs, and markups can be calculated from (a) industry standards or (b) percentages established by company policy.

Percentages are also used to make comparisons of cost and markups that are determined from different retail price bases. Consider the following example: The markup on a $48.00 dust ruffle is $21.00 and the markup on an $8.00 face cloth is $5.00. The dust ruffle appears to have the higher markup when comparing the markup dollar amounts, but if the percentages of markup are compared, the face cloth may have a higher, lower, or similar markup. The formula for calculating **markup percentage** (based on retail) when markup dollars and retail dollars are given is

$$\text{Markup \%} = \text{Markup \$}/\text{Retail \$} \times 100$$

The formula for calculating **cost percentage** (based on retail) when wholesale cost and retail price are given is

$$\text{Cost \%} = \text{Cost \$}/\text{Retail \$} \times 100$$

Sample Problems: Retail Price Elements as Percentages

Problem 1

Calculate the markup percentage on the dust ruffle with a markup of $21.00 and a retail price of $48.00.

$$\text{Markup \%} = \text{Markup \$}/\text{Retail \$} \times 100$$

$$\text{Markup \%} = \$21.00/\$48.00 \times 100$$

(Hint: In the application of another algebraic rule, the result of the ratio division must be multiplied by 100 to convert the decimal result to a percentage.)

$$\text{Markup \%} = 43.75\%$$

Problem 2

Calculate the markup percentage on the face cloth with a markup of $5.00 and a retail price of $8.00.

$$\text{Markup \%} = \text{Markup \$}/\text{Retail \$} \times 100$$

$$\text{Markup \%} = \$5.00/\$8.00 \times 100$$

$$\text{Markup \%} = 62.50\%$$

Which item, the face cloth or the dust ruffle, had the higher markup percentage? *Ans*: The face cloth!

Problem 3

A home furnishings buyer purchased a coverlet for $55.00 (at cost) and plans to retail it for $125.00. What is the markup percentage?

(Hint: The retail price dollars formula will first be needed to find the value of markup. So, use Markup $ = Retail $ − Cost $ and insert the known values from Problem 3.)

$$\text{Markup \$} = \text{Retail \$} - \text{Cost \$}$$
$$\text{Markup \$} = \$125.00 - \$55.00$$
$$\text{Markup \$} = \$70.00$$

> *(Hint: The markup percentage can be calculated with the markup percentage formula.)*

$$\text{Markup \%} = \text{Markup \$/Retail \$} \times 100$$
$$\text{Markup \%} = \$70.00/\$125.00 \times 100$$
$$\text{Markup \%} = 56.00\%$$

Problem 4

The cost of a blue vase is $12.00. The vase retails for $50.00. What is the cost percentage?

$$\text{Cost \%} = \text{Cost \$/Retail \$} \times 100$$
$$\text{Cost \%} = \$12.00/\$50.00 \times 100$$
$$\text{Cost \%} = 24.00\%$$

Frequently the buyer or merchandise planner will have a mixture of pricing information about a product. For example, the merchandise planner will know the anticipated retail price and will need to determine the potential markup dollars or cost percentage. The buyer may know the cost in dollar and the markup percentage and will need to determine the retail price. Although these combinations of variables in the **retail price relationship** can be confusing, the buyer or planner will be following a generic or basic format with each of these calculations. The basic format can be expressed with the *base dollars* always being the retail price and the *rate* being any percentage, for example, markup percentage or cost percentage. The *results* dollars from these calculations will be in correspondence to the rate. If the rate is markup percentage, the results are markup dollars. If the rate is cost percentage, the results are cost dollars. The rate and the results are considered a pair and must be the same variable, differing only in percentage or dollar format.

The basic formula for expressing this **retail price relationship** in both dollars and percentages is

$$\text{Results \$} = \text{Base \$} \times \text{Rate \%}$$

By inserting the terms for the price elements and through algebraic manipulation, the formula can be rewritten to solve for each retail element. The price relationship formula to find **cost dollars and percentage** is

$$\text{Cost \$} = \text{Retail \$} \times \text{Cost \%}$$

The price relationship formula to find **markup dollars and percentage** is

$$\text{Markup \$} = \text{Retail \$} \times \text{Markup \%}$$

Spreadsheets

The relationships among the three price elements can be best expressed in a spreadsheet-type format. **Spreadsheets**, written by hand or developed on a computer, are used by many companies to display financial information. Software for spreadsheet programs (e.g., Excel, dBase, Quattro Pro, and Lotus) is available for most computers. Although each program has some unique features, most of their basic operations are similar. Some retail companies may have their own proprietary software with computer programs written especially for that company, but regardless of how sophisticated a company's spreadsheet may appear, the basic format is usually the same. For pricing calculations, the price elements are shown on the rows of the spreadsheet, and the dollars and percentages are shown in the columns.

A spreadsheet for the dollars and percentages of the pricing elements could appear as the spreadsheet in Figure 2.1. This spreadsheet can be used for expressing the price relationship and calculating changes to that relationship.

Figure 2.1

Spreadsheet for
the Pricing Elements.

Elements	Dollars $	Percentages %
Retail		
− Cost		
= Markup		

After known values for each price element are entered into the appropriate cells, formulas are used in the remaining blank cells to complete the spreadsheet and determine the additional information needed. The use of a computer spreadsheet allows the decision maker to enter alternative values and rapidly make changes based on the results. Furthermore, information can be added to the spreadsheet over time, and adjustments can be made when prices change. The use of the spreadsheet also provides a ready source of information when past records are used in current buying decisions.

Sample Problem: Retail Price Elements in Dollars and Percentages

A tie has a markup of 38.80% and a retail price of $18.50. What is the markup in dollars for the tie? To use the spreadsheet format, follow these three steps:

Step 1. Write the spreadsheet format.

Elements	Dollars $	Percentages %
Retail		
− Cost		
= Markup		

Step 2. Insert the known values from the problem.

      Markup % = 38.80%

      Retail $ = $18.50

      (Remember: Retail % = 100%.)

Elements	Dollars $	Percentages %
Retail	$18.50	100.00%
− Cost		
= Markup		38.80%

Step 3. Use the relationship formula to solve for the unknown values.

Markup $ = Retail $ × Markup %

Markup $ = $18.50 × 38.80%

Markup $ = $7.18

Elements	Dollars $	Percentages %
Retail	$18.50	100.00%
− Cost		
= Markup	$7.18	38.80%

The relationship of dollars and percentages is very specific. When the retail dollars are known, markup percentage can be used to find markup dollars, and cost percentage can be used to find cost dollars. In the previous problem, markup dollars and markup percentages are now known, and retail dollars and percentages are known. To complete the spreadsheet and find the values for cost, additional calculations using the retail dollar formula, the retail percentage formula, and the relationship formula are used.

Sample Problem: Finding Cost when Retail and Markup Are Known

Using the spreadsheet from the previous problem, what are cost dollars and cost percentage?

Elements	Dollars $	Percentages %
Retail	$18.50	100.00%
− Cost		
= Markup	$7.18	38.80%

The following steps are used to solve this problem:

Step 1. Use the retail percentage formula.

Retail % = Cost % + Markup %

(Hint: Rewritten, this formula can be used to solve for cost percentage.)

Cost % = Retail % − Markup %

Cost % = 100.00% − 38.80%

Cost % = 61.20%

Enter the value into the spreadsheet.

Elements	Dollars $	Percentages %
Retail	$18.50	100.00%
− Cost		61.20%
= Markup	$7.18	38.80%

Step 2. Use the relationship formula.

Cost $ = Retail $ × Cost %

Cost $ = $18.50 × 61.20%

Cost $ = $11.32

Enter the value into the spreadsheet.

Elements	Dollars $	Percentages %
Retail	$18.50	100.00%
− Cost	$11.32	61.20%
= Markup	$7.18	38.80%

Step 3. Use the retail dollar formula to check the solution.

Retail $ = Cost $ + Markup $

Retail $ = $11.32 + $7.18

Retail $ = $18.50

(Hint: Small difference in value may appear due to rounding dollar amounts and percentages.)

The spreadsheet format may be used to calculate any of the missing values in the pricing relationship. For example, the buyer may have a preset markup (markup percentage) and a price point (retail dollars) that must be achieved. Before shopping for an item, the buyer must know the maximum cost that the item can have. The following problem provides an example of this situation.

Sample Problem: Finding Cost when Retail Price and Markup Percentage Are Known

A hand-painted box has a markup of 68.50% and a retail price of $48.50. What is the maximum cost in dollars that the buyer may pay for the box, and what is the markup dollar value?

Step 1. Use the spreadsheet format.

Elements	Dollars $	Percentages %
Retail		
− Cost		
= Markup		

Step 2. Enter the values from the problem.

Markup % = 68.50%

Retail $ = $48.50

(Remember: Retail % = 100%.)

Elements	Dollars $	Percentages %
Retail	$48.50	100.00%
− Cost		
= Markup		68.50%

Step 3. Find the percentage associated with the cost.

Retail % = Cost % + Markup %

Cost % = Retail % − Markup %

Cost % = 100.00% − 68.50%

Cost % = 31.50%

Elements	Dollars $	Percentages %
Retail	$48.50	100.00%
− Cost		31.50%
= Markup		68.50%

Step 4. Use the relationship formula.

Cost $ = Retail $ × Cost %

Cost $ = $48.50 × 31.50%

Cost $ = $15.28

Elements	Dollars $	Percentages %
Retail	$48.50	100.00%
− Cost	$15.28	31.50%
= Markup		68.50%

Step 5. Find the value of the remaining cell.

Retail $ = Cost $ + Markup $

Markup $ = Retail $ − Cost $

Markup $ = $48.50 − $15.28

Markup $ = $33.22

Elements	Dollars $	Percentages %
Retail	$48.50	100.00%
− Cost	$15.28	31.50%
= Markup	$33.22	68.50%

Using the same spreadsheet format, a retail buyer can also calculate retail dollars on specific items to reach a planned markup percentage goal. This goal is usually established by the buyer with the input from management, or by management alone, prior to the beginning of a new retail year. Markup is always reviewed before calculating buying plans and attending markets.

The retail dollar formula, when cost dollars and needed markup percentage are known, is

$$\text{Retail \$} = \text{Cost \$/Cost \%}$$

or

$$\text{Retail \$} = \text{Cost \$}/(100.00\% - \text{Markup \%})$$

Sample Problem: Calculating Retail Dollars when Cost Dollars and Markup Percentages Are Known

The buyer purchases a tote bag at the market for $75.00. Bags must have a 56.00% markup. What is the projected retail price if this markup in used?

Step 1. Use the spreadsheet format.

Elements	Dollars $	Percentages %
Retail	*170.45*	*100*
− Cost	*75*	*44*
= Markup		*56*

Step 2. Insert the known values from the problem.

Markup % = 56.00%
Cost $ = $75.00

(Remember: Retail % = 100%.)

Elements	Dollars $	Percentages %
Retail		100.00%
− Cost	$75.00	
= Markup		56.00%

Step 3. Calculate the percentage associated with the cost dollars.

Cost % = Retail % − Markup %
Cost % = 100.00% − 56.00%
Cost % = 44.00%

Elements	Dollars $	Percentages %
Retail		100.00%
− Cost	$75.00	44.00%
= Markup		56.00%

Step 4. Use the relationship formula to calculate retail dollars.

Cost $ = Retail $ × Cost %
Retail $ = Cost $/Cost %   *(Manipulate with algebra.)*
Retail $ = $75.00/44.00%
Retail $ = $170.45

Elements	Dollars $	Percentages %
Retail	$170.45	100.00%
− Cost	$75.00	44.00%
= Markup		56.00%

(Note: Many retailers would round or adjust the retail price to either $170.00 or $171.00 to bring the retail price within the desired price line.)

Step 5. Calculate the value of markup dollars (the remaining cell).

Markup $ = Retail $ − Cost $

Markup $ = $170.45 − $75.00

Markup $ = $95.45

Elements	Dollars $	Percentages %
Retail	$170.45	100.00%
− Cost	$75.00	44.00%
= Markup	$95.45	56.00%

With any method of price setting, the target consumer must be kept in mind because the objective of retailing is satisfying the target consumer. The retail price, regardless of how it is established, must seem appropriate to the consumer. While shopping, the consumer will observe an item and look at the price. The two factors, appearance (especially color) and price, must seem logical to the consumer. If the price is judged too high for the item, the consumer may refuse to buy. Some consumers may decide to wait for the item to be marked down, select a similar but lower cost item, or leave the store without making any purchases. Any of these three scenarios will result in less sales for the company. If the consumer judges that the price is too low, the consumer may question if the quality of the item is different from what is expected, if the item is mislabeled, or if the item has a hidden defect. For brand name products, the prestige of a brand can be damaged in the consumer's mind if the price seems to be too low or too high. Getting the consumer to perceive the price as right for the quality or value of the item is a very risky but vitally important retail decision.

Types of Markup

Markup, in general, is the difference between the cost of goods and retail price. Markup has a variety of specialized names that correspond to the uses and situations for each markup. **Individual markup** is the markup found on one item or one stock-keeping unit (SKU). For example, a pair of bookends has a retail price of $20.00 and a cost of $8.00; therefore, this item has a dollar markup of $12.00. The $12.00 represents an individual markup. When multiple units are considered together, the markup is a **gross markup**. If 15 pairs of bookends have individual markups of $12.00, the gross markup for the lot of bookends is $180.00. A gross markup may be calculated for multiple units in lots of merchandise, for an entire department, for all merchandise in a store, or for all merchandise in a company.

The formula for calculating **gross markup dollars** is

Gross markup $ = Markup A $ + Markup B $ + $\cdots$ + Markup X $

If the markup on each item is the same, the formula can be expressed as

$$\text{Gross Markup \$} = \text{Markup \$ per Unit} \times \text{\# of Units}$$

Sample Problem: Gross Markup

A store sells 22 coffee makers from the houseware section. Each coffee maker was from a well-known national brand and had a markup of $24.80. What is the Gross Markup dollars for the 22 appliances?

$$\text{Gross Markup \$} = \text{Markup \$ per Unit} \times \text{\# of Units}$$
$$\text{Gross Markup \$} = \$24.80 \times 22$$
$$\text{Gross Markup \$} = \$545.60$$

Most of the time, identical or similar items within a specific classification, such as brand name appliances, differ in cost when purchased at wholesale from each manufacturer or vendor. Sometimes private label merchandise has a lower wholesale cost and can have a higher markup than branded merchandise of the same or similar classification. For example, within the housewares department, several types of houseware items, such as toasters, coffee makers, and can openers with different costs and retail prices are purchased on one order form. Additionally, within any given store or department, numerous orders can be found with varying wholesale costs and various retail prices.

In each of these instances with multiple but diverse units within one purchase by the buyer, the retailer cannot calculate a single gross markup percentage by averaging markup percentages on individual items. Markup percentages can only be averaged when quantities are the same for every item or SKU. Markup percentage on individual items with varying costs and retail prices will differ from the markup percentage on the total group of items.

The next problem illustrates a method for determining markup percentage on a group of items with varying costs or retail prices.

Step 1. Calculate the retail price for each of the items
Step 2. Calculate total retail of all items
Step 3. Calculate total cost of all items
Step 4. Calculate the overall total cost and overall total retail
Step 5. Calculate total markup dollars
Step 6. Calculate markup percentage for total items or order(s)

Sample Problem: Markup Percentage on Group of Items with Varying Costs and Retail Prices

---

A buyer purchased the following items for a costume jewelry department. Each item will be retailed at a keystone markup plus $5.00. What is the gross markup dollars for the order? What is the markup percentage for the order?

Order Form for the Costume Jewelry Department

Item	Quantity	Wholesale Cost	Total Cost	Retail Price	Total Retail
Earrings	25	$15.00	375	35	875
Necklaces	15	$25.00	375	55	825
Pins	20	$18.50	370	42	840
Overall Total	60	58.50	1120	132	2540

QXWC   WCX2+5   QXR

Step 1. Calculate the total retail of the items.

(Hint: Keystone wholesale cost then add $5.00 to calculate retail for each item.)

Earrings	$15.00 × 2 (keystone)	= $30.00 + $5.00 = $35.00
Necklaces	$25.00 × 2	= $50.00 + $5.00 = $55.00
Pins	$18.50 × 2	= $37.00 + $5.00 = $42.00

Step 2. Insert costs, number of units, and retail price into order form.

Order Form for the Costume Jewelry Department

Item	Quantity	Wholesale Cost	Total Cost	Retail Price	Total Retail
Earrings	25	$15.00		$35.00	
Necklaces	15	$25.00		$55.00	
Pins	20	$18.50		$42.00	
Overall Total					

Step 3. Calculate the total retail dollars and insert the values into the spreadsheet.

Total Retail $ = # of Units × Retail $ per Unit

Earrings	25 × $35.00 = $875.00
Necklaces	15 × $55.00 = $825.00
Pins	20 × $42.00 = $840.00

(Note: When these calculations are done on a computer, the formula can be entered to multiply one cell [quantity] times another cell [retail price].)

Order Form for the Costume Jewelry Department

Item	Quantity	Wholesale Cost	Total Cost	Retail Price	Total Retail
Earrings	25	$15.00		$35.00	$875.00
Necklaces	15	$25.00		$55.00	$825.00
Pins	20	$18.50		$42.00	$840.00
Overall Total					

Step 4. Calculate the total cost dollars and insert the results into the spreadsheet.

Total Cost $ = # of Units × Unit Cost $

For example, earrings: 25 × $15.00 = $375.00

Order Form for the Costume Jewelry Department

Item	Quantity	Wholesale Cost	Total Cost	Retail Price	Total Retail
Earrings	25	$15.00	$375.00	$35.00	$875.00
Necklaces	15	$25.00	$375.00	$55.00	$825.00
Pins	20	$18.50	$370.00	$42.00	$840.00
Overall Total					

Step 5. Calculate the overall total cost and overall total retail.

(Hint: Sum the total cost and the total retail columns.)

Order Form for the Costume Jewelry Department

Item	Quantity	Wholesale Cost	Total Cost	Retail Price	Total Retail
Earrings	25	$15.00	$375.00	$35.00	$875.00
Necklaces	15	$25.00	$375.00	$55.00	$825.00
Pins	20	$18.50	$370.00	$42.00	$840.00
Overall Total			$1,120.00		$2,540.00

Step 6. Calculate the total markup dollars.

Total Markup $ = Total Retail $ − Total Cost $

Total Markup $ = $2,540.00 − $1,120.00

Total Markup $ = $1,420.00

Step 7. Calculate the total markup percentage.

Total Markup % = Total Markup $/Total Retail $ × 100

Total Markup % = $1,420.00/$2,540.00 × 100

Total Markup % = 55.91%

(Note: If the buyer were trying to achieve a markup percentage goal of 55%, the goal would be achieved on this order.)

Closely related to gross markup is **initial markup**, which is calculated using the initial or first retail price of all items at a point in time. This markup is based on gross sales and is used at the beginning of a selling period. Gross sales are all potential retail sales based on the initial retail prices. This initial markup covers adjustments for planned markdowns and other reductions that may occur later in the selling period. When an initial markup is based on actual retail sales for a period and not on initial retail prices, the markup is called a **gross margin**. Actual retail sales are also called **net sales** because gross sales have been adjusted for markdowns and for other losses.

The formula for calculating **gross margin dollars** is

Gross Margin $ = Net Sales $ − Cost of Goods Sold $

For a successful retail business, gross margin must be large enough to include the value of operating expenses, profits, and taxes.

Maintained markup is used to calculate the markups that can be achieved after adjusting for the charges of servicing the fashion goods. These charges can include alteration expenses and cash discounts. **Cumulative** or **average markups** are calculated for a group of items with different markups at a point in time. Cumulative markup is calculated after the beginning of each major delivery period or selling period. In this case, the cumulative markup includes the markup on the beginning inventory, which is usually at retail dollars and is based on book value of the inventory or actual physical inventory calculations. Cumulative markup is the difference between the total cost of purchases and total retail dollars of all merchandise in stock during a given time period. This markup is used to calculate a final markup when markups have changed over time. Gross, initial, maintained, and cumulative/average markups will be discussed in later chapters.

Methods for Pricing Decisions

The method used to determine price may be based on company policy, the judgment of top management, the classification of the merchandise, or the type of store in which the merchandise is being sold. For example, fashion goods usually have a higher markup than basic goods. National brands are sold at relatively the same retail price by most retailers within a particular geographic area, because the wholesale and transportation costs for the items are usually the same or very comparable for all of these retailers. Private label merchandise may be priced to help the retailer achieve a higher markup to compensate for markdowns, slow-selling merchandise, or poor selections from incorrect buying decisions. Private label merchandise may also be priced to reflect the best quality at the best available price for a specific product classification. In this case, the retail price is probably based on the firm's policy to utilize its private brand merchandise to build store traffic and store image and to maintain a substantial target customer base. Certain types or classifications of merchandise have a higher risk of theft and must be stored, merchandised, or displayed differently from most merchandise. Selling and visual presentation costs for merchandise such as jewelry and cosmetics, which are housed in glass display cases, are usually higher for the retailer. For these reasons, methods of determining price vary across store and merchandise classifications. The buyer may or may not have a choice in the selection of the method, but should have knowledge of the methods and the characteristics of the methods. Retail pricing methods include component addition, past records, price points, or market value.

Component addition builds the price of each item in the inventory from the cost of the item and the needed markup. This method is often used when a retailer is opening a new business and has limited past experience with pricing. A variation of this method, called **activity-based accounting**, is used to determine whether individual products, categories of merchandise, or departments are contributing their appropriate share of markup to the business. With component addition, the decision maker, the buyer or manager, examines what expenses must be covered by the retail price. A portion of the retail price for each item sold in the store must contribute to the income needed to cover the overall expenses of the store and to provide enough income for the desired profit. The retail price must also include enough money to cover the wholesale cost of the item.

Component addition can be a very exacting calculation or it can be a rule of thumb type calculation. For some stores, the markup is an automatic 50% of retail price. This 50% markup is called a keystone markup (as described earlier). Using a keystone markup, the cost of the item would be doubled to yield the retail price. In reality, keystone markup is rarely used for all items in the store. Even when the keystone markup is used as a starting point, the final or maintained markup for an item, a department, a store, or an entire company will be affected by losses and markdowns.

The amount of contribution from each item may vary depending on the type of merchandise and the activities needed to purchase, carry, or sell the merchandise. Some items contribute less to the overall income of the store because they are designed for promotional sales or as attention getters. When these items are sold at wholesale cost or below, they are called **loss leaders**. This pricing is designed to bring consumers into the store. Some retailers believe that loss leaders create a larger sales volume and entice consumers, once they are in the store, to buy higher priced items

that may have higher markups. With this technique, both markup and sales vo
are maintained or boosted. Other retailers are concerned that loss leaders can dam
the high fashion image of a store because price is often used by the consumer to eva.
uate the fashion or quality level of a store or item.

3 **Past records**, for a store with a sales history, provide a record of accomplishment for the sale of similar items. These records will include retail prices, numbers of items sold at the price, and adjustments that were made to the price throughout the season. Records will also indicate the number of unsold items. In the **past records method**, the historical retail records are used as a starting point for establishing current retail prices. The actual price must be adjusted for environment, market, product changes, inflation, competition, and style features. A pricing decision on current items is always somewhat different from any previous sale of a similar or even identical item. If a $30.00 shirt from one year is carried in the store the next year, the retail price may be adjusted upward to include dollars to provide for inflation, growth, or other changes in the store. On the other hand, the retailer may make a conscious decision to maintain the original retail price in hopes of building additional sales volume or store traffic that will offset the lower markup.

The position of the merchandise in regard to its stage in the product life cycle must be analyzed before establishing a new retail price. New items just appearing in the store and considered fashion forward can carry a higher retail price than items that have been in the store for a period or have been on the market for an extended period. (The items that have been sold over time may be entering the latter part of their product life cycle and demand for them may be diminishing.) The retailer must also consider whether a customer can recognize the item as part of last year's line. This recognition will diminish the retailer's image of being fashion forward.

Adjustments that are made to the past retail price are often made by estimations and overall merchandising judgment. Scientific or statistical data may not be available or simply not considered when setting new retail prices. Regardless of the method used, past records are always helpful as a point of comparison; however, the decision maker must remember that past records are not always indications of future sales and that fashion goods require that the pricing decision be a constantly evolving process.

4 **Price points**, or **price lines**, are levels used for groups of merchandise and are used by department stores and other stores with a wide variety of fashion goods to help the consumer discriminate among the similar items. The levels of price points are set at low, moderate, and high. Within one store, shirts may sell at each of three separate price points. These price points are established by starting with a price floor and subsequently increasing the price of similar, but more costly goods to higher and distinctly different price points. Fashion goods sold at separate price points must appear significantly different to the consumer. The styles of three price point shirts may be similar, but details will vary. A shirt at the lowest price point may have a fiber content of 50% polyester and 50% cotton with limited trim and plastic buttons. A shirt at the middle price point may be 100% cotton. The shirt at the top price point would be of 100% pima cotton and have eyelet trim with fabric-covered buttons.

Most department stores would house these shirts in separate departments based upon demographics, psychographics, lifestyles, and physical characteristics of the target consumer. In addition, the fashion awareness level of the consumer as well as the stage in which the merchandise falls on the fashion curve would be considered. Based upon fashion detailing, price, and size, the pima cotton shirt would probably be found in a Designer, Bridge, or Contemporary Department. The 100% cotton, middle price point, shirt would then be put in the Better Department, and the cotton/polyester blend shirt would be in the Moderate Sportswear Department. Price points for such items and other items in the store may be established at the corporate level for multiunit stores. This method is useful for stores that maintain a standardized image across store units.

Market pricing is often used for popular fashion goods and new items, or in highly competitive markets. The retail price is established by estimating the price desired by the target market. The question that retailers pose is "what will the market bear?" The retailer must determine what is the highest possible price that can be placed on an item and still have that item be attractive and buyable by the consumer. If the price is too high, the consumer will not purchase the item even if it is highly desirable from a fashion perspective. Knowing what is too high is a difficult process and requires market research, in-depth knowledge of the target consumer, and an excellent fashion sense by the retailer or buyer. On very new items, the retail price may be higher than the price will be later in the season because the item is projected to be very popular. In such a case, the consumer is expected to pay extra for the privilege of buying this item early in the season. Exclusive and unique fashion goods may also be priced higher than the more basic merchandise because the popularity of these items is subject to rapid change and the items are at risk for higher than usual markdowns later in the season. Overall, market priced items may have an average markup that is similar to the store average because of the high initial markup where some merchandise is sold and the lower final markup when the remaining merchandise is sold. The task of the retailer is to select a market price that will maximize the target market demand early in the selling season and leave very limited amounts of merchandise for drastic markdowns late in the season.

A higher markup on these trendy items also helps to offset the higher promotional and advertising costs needed to sell the more fashion forward merchandise. This method also requires a review of the company's marketing strategies. Market pricing may also be set by evaluating the prices of the competition. The retail price may be set higher, lower, or the same as the prices for similar items in the competitor's store. This decision is made relative to the strategic plan of the retailer and the positioning of the business. (See Chapter 5.) Determining markdowns and other aspects of pricing strategies are discussed in later chapters.

Determining the exact retail price for an item is an important step in selling merchandise. The retail price of an item affects its salability, the store's image, and the overall profitability of the store. The retail price of an item must be established before the merchandise is placed in the store, which further adds to the risky and speculative nature of the pricing decision. Although past records, current pricing policies, market conditions, expenses, and other factors are considered, the final decision in establishing a retail price must depend on the judgment of a person. Underlying all the previously described pricing methods is the need for the buyer or merchandiser who sets prices to possess knowledge of the item, the store, the market, and the consumer.

Factors Affecting the Three Price Elements

Retail price, cost of goods, and markup are affected by numerous factors in the business world. These retail price elements are interrelated; therefore, an adjustment in one element can cause the need for adjustments in one or two of the other elements. Decisions to make such changes should be carefully weighted for all the potential results. For example, a change in cost of goods can affect the retail price of those goods. If the cost of goods or markup must be adjusted upward, the retail price will have a corresponding rise to maintain the overall value. In **periods of inflation**, the rise in cost of goods is common as the manufacturer passes the increased costs of manufacturing to the retailer. The retailer may also have increased costs of doing business, such as wage increases and rent increases. The resulting rise in retail price could place the retail price of the item outside of the intended price line or higher than the ‾ of similar items at the competitor's stores.

For example, a brand name basketball with a $30.00 retail price, last season, had a wholesale cost of $15.00. The buyer found a cost increase of $4.00 at the next market. The new cost of the ball is $19.00. If markup dollars are kept constant for the next season, the ball has a new retail price of $34.00. If other brands of balls selling for $30.00 did not have a cost increase in the market, this ball may now be above the price point range for similar items. The buyer may wish to keep the brand name ball in the group of balls and must consider numerous factors before selecting a new retail price. The buyer has several options (a) lower the markup on this ball and raise the markup on other items, (b) raise the markup on all balls, or (c) keep the standard markup and hope the consumer will not be disturbed by a $4.00 price difference among similar items.

In **competitive markets** and periods of economic tension, consumers may not be willing to accept price increases. If the retail price must remain constant, either of the remaining price elements or both elements must experience a drop. For instance, consumers of apparel are becoming more demanding about price. Many consumers will not buy if the price is perceived as too high. As retailers review their pricing decisions, many buyers have had to seek lower priced merchandise. The lower priced merchandise may assist the retailer in achieving the desired retail price, but the lower priced merchandise may have a lower quality than previous items. The consumer is becoming more educated and may notice the drop in quality. This action can negatively affect the overall image of the store as well as the sales volume and profit. An alternative to changing merchandise is to lower markups. A lower markup can be achieved with lowering operating expenses or reducing profit.

An alternative action is to buy off-price, first quality merchandise up front or at the beginning of the season. In order to obtain larger orders or to build larger volume, manufacturers sometimes will offer off-price packages of current, first quality merchandise up front or when the buyer is placing a regular order for seasonal merchandise. Many times the amount of off-price merchandise that can be purchased by the retailer is based upon the dollar or unit amount of the initial season order that is placed at regular price. The off-price merchandise is usually offered to the retailer at 20% to 30% off the wholesale cost of the merchandise and may or may not be identical in style, color, or content as the other seasonal merchandise. Also, the off-price merchandise may or may not be delivered to the retailer at the same time as the initial order. Regardless of the time for shipping, the off-price goods can be retailed at the same retail price as the initial order, and the retailer will have a higher initial markup on this group of merchandise. The retailer can use the higher markup to offset the drop in sales volume created by higher wholesale costs and the resulting higher retail price of other items.

Retail price is related to **sales volume**. A rise in retail price will often lead to a drop in the overall sales volume. When retail prices rise, consumers tend to buy fewer items than when prices remain stable. If the store could sell 10 items at $30.00, the total sales would be $300.00, and the total markup may be $150.00. If the rise in cost of goods, as described previously, creates a new retail price of $34.00, the store may sell only seven items. The total sales would be $238. If the markup dollars per item remained at $15.00, the total markup would then be $105.00 for the seven items. This example illustrates how a rise in retail price could actually create a drop in the overall sales for the store. A drop in the sales volume can result in a drop in gross margin. This drop in margin can affect the amount of profit a store makes.

Profit can be made in two ways, many small markups or a few large markups. The large discount stores use the method of many small markups. They depend on high volume of sales for many, small, individual markups. The small stores or individual boutiques have higher individual markups, but have fewer sales. In a competitive market, the middle position of moderate markups with moderate number of sales is a difficult position for success. A clear store image and selection of desired merchandise is hard to maintain with this price structure. Department stores have used this moderate price structure and have found that their customers are being drawn away by retailers with lower retail prices.

Changes in retail price may also affect operating expenses and cost of goods. Items with high retail prices are associated, in the consumer's mind, with higher levels of service than items with lower retail prices. Consumers expect an upscale, high-fashion store to have high prices; new, expensive furnishings; and plenty of skilled sales associates. Most importantly, service in retail is directly associated with the number and qualifications of the sales associates. To provide excellent customer service, sales associates must be selected carefully and trained continually. Qualified sales associates will require higher wages than unqualified staff. Training requires both time and money. To maintain high levels of service, the markups on items must be large enough to cover these operating expenses.

Higher priced goods are also associated in the consumer's mind with higher quality goods. Fashion items that have and maintain high quality are usually higher cost goods. Higher quality for an apparel item can be more expensive fabric or fibers, for example, cashmere instead of acrylic. Higher quality for a bath towel could be deep pile and luxurious hand. Higher quality in an appliance might be more options, improved styling, and use of materials that are more expensive. (For example, the manufacturer might use pewter on a trim instead of plastic.) Improved quality can also be achieved with new designs, improved fit or size, and improved construction. All of these factors are achieved by the manufacturer with increased costs. Higher priced goods can also be associated with newness of fashion, licenses for new images, or use of established brands. In a competitive market, the manufacturer can insist on higher prices for these quality features.

In addition, high priced goods require a more expensive store image. Consumers equate high prices with evidence of luxury. Luxury in retail image can be achieved through new and exciting signs, fixtures, lights, and other store features. For example, the size and decor of the dressing room can convey an image to the consumer. A large dressing room with soft lighting and nice furniture tells the consumer that this is an upscale store with high quality merchandise. To achieve and maintain such a retail image, markups and other adjustments must be large enough to cover the inflated operating expenses and costs.

*S*ummary

Establishing the retail price of an item is a very important decision. The three price elements of retail price, cost, and markup must be examined. Retail price is the initial price of an item in the store. Cost of goods is the wholesale price of an item. Markup can vary from individual markup to gross margin and is used to cover the operating expenses and profits needed for a store. These three elements can be expressed in dollars and percentages and can be calculated based on their relationships. However, an appropriate retail price is more than just a mathematical calculation. The retail price affects the store image and the purchasing behavior of the consumer. A retail price that is too high can reduce overall revenues. A retail price that is too low can rob the store of markup dollars needed to pay the operating expenses and to supply a profit. Therefore, the right price must be determined to motivate a purchase from the consumer and make a profit for the store. Merchandising judgment, along with mathematical ability, is needed to establish the optimum retail price that will be at a level appropriate for the target consumer, the store, the merchandise, and the marketplace.

Key Terms

Activity-based accounting
Average markup
Component addition
Competitive markets
Cost
Cost of goods
Cumulative markup
Gross margin
Gross markup

Higher priced goods
Individual markup
Initial markup
Keystone markup
Loss leaders
Maintained markup
Market pricing
Markup
Net sales

Past records
Past records method
Periods of inflation
Price lines
Price points
Retail price elements
Retail price relationship
Sales volume
Spreadsheet

Discussion Questions

1. What are the three price elements?
2. Why does a store need markup?
3. Who determines the cost of an item?
4. Why is setting the retail price an important consideration for a store?
5. What are the methods for setting the retail price?
6. How can the retail price be set for an item that has been carried in the store for several seasons?
7. What is the best method for setting the retail price for a new fashion item?
8. What information is needed to determine the best retail price for an item?
9. If the cost of an item has an increase, what will happen to the retail price? Why?
10. Why do small stores have higher markups than large discount stores?

Exercises

Price Elements

1. A small briefcase has a cost of $25.00 and the markup is $21.00. What is the retail price of the briefcase?

2. A pair of pajamas has a markup of $22.00 and a cost of $18.00. What is the retail price?

3. A coat retails for $129.00, and the cost is $65.40. What are the markup dollars?

4. A suit has a markup percent of 43.30% and a retail price of $256.00. What is the cost percent?

5. A wallet item retails for $22.68. What is the cost of the item when the cost percent is 53.00%?

6. The newest vase in the store has a retail price of $56.98. The markup percent for the vase is 42.50%. What are the markup dollars?

7. An item has a retail price of $23.50 and a markup of 34.50%. What are the markup dollars?

8. A pair of gloves has a retail price of $34.50. The standard markup on gloves is 52.50%. What is the cost of the gloves?

9. A set of dishes costs $29.50, and the standard store markup is 45.50%. What will be the retail price of the dishes?

10. A pair of boots had a cost of $89.00 and cost percent of 42.50%. What is the retail price?

11. For a special sale, the buyer bought at the market 10 dozen pairs of socks for $224.50. The markup for the sale is 45.00%. What will be the retail price for one pair of socks?

Cost

12. The buyer finds a line of picture frames at the cost of $12.74 per frame. The buyer thinks that the frames can be retailed for $45.00. What should be the expected markup percent?

13. What is the markup percent for shorts that cost $255.00 a dozen and retail for $34.60 per pair of shorts?

14. The baby department received a shipment of stuffed toys that each costs $8.50 and retailed for $22.30. What is the markup percent?

15. The buyer found a line of children's stuffed toys for $40.00 a dozen. The retail price of one toy is set at $7.55. What is the markup percent?

Individual Markup to Gross Markup

$12 \times 10 = 120$ M

1. The buyer had a $12.00 markup on each book. Ten books were sold. What was the total markup?

$160 \times 25.50 = 4,080$ =M

2. A department contained 160 handbags. Each handbag had a $25.50 markup. What was the total potential markup (gross margin) for the department?

$160 \times 65 = 10,400$ =R

3. If each handbag in Problem 2 retailed for $65.00, what was the total retail sales potential for the department?

$MU\% = M\$ / R \times 100$

$120 / 10,400 \times 100$

$M\% = 1.15$

4. What is markup percent (gross markup percent) for the handbag department in Problem 2?

$484,878 / 6 = 80,813$ units

5. A retail store sells every item for $6.00. Last year, the store had retail sales for the year of $484,878.00. How many units were sold?

$4,000 / 12 = 333.3 / 12$ $27.7?$

6. A buyer found a source that has belts priced at $12.00 per dozen. If the buyer spends $4,000.00 with this vendor, how many belts will be purchased?

$1.5 / 680$

7. If the markup on one fur coat is $680.00, how many coats will the store have to sell for a gross markup of $1.5 million?

$200 \times 4 = 800$

8. If the markup for a solid color tie is $4.00, what is the potential gross markup for the department if 200 solid colored ties are bought?

160×4.90

9. If the markup for a striped tie is $4.90, what is the potential gross markup for the department if 160 striped ties are sold?

10. Which group of ties (the ties in Problem 8 or 9) has the potential for a greater gross markup for the store? Why?

Computer Exercises

General Directions

- Set up the following retail price spreadsheet using a computer spreadsheet program.
- Save your work on your disk.

- You should have one file for all problems. Just scroll down to the rows below the first problem to start the second problem. Number each problem.
- In the upper right corner of the spreadsheet, place your name, date, and file name.
- A single problem should be printed on one page. You may have multiple problems on one page, but you should not split a problem across two pages.

	$	%
Retail		100.00%
− Cost		
= Markup		

Price Elements

1. What are markup and cost percentages on a rug at $126.95 retail and $56.00 cost?

2. The cost of a blanket is $43.00, and the retail price is $82.00. What is the cost percent for the blanket? What are the markup dollars and the markup percentage for the blanket?

3. What are markup and cost percentages for shorts that cost $255.00 a dozen and retail for $34.60 each?

4. For a special sale, the buyer got 10 dozen pairs of socks for $224.50. Markup for the sale is 45.00%. What are the retail price and cost percentage for the socks?

5. The buyer wants to have a line of bags that sell for $79.00 per bag. The regular markup on a bag for the department is 43.50%. What is the maximum cost that the buyer may pay for one bag?

6. A set of sheets is found in the market at $45.00 a set. Using market pricing, the buyer thinks that these sheets may retail for $70.00. What is the maximum markup percentage that this pricing will achieve?

7. Gold jewelry is very popular with a store's customers. The buyer wants to get a higher markup than in the past. A ring is purchased in the market at cost for $150.00. The usual store markup is 76.00%. What would be the retail price with the usual markup? What is the price if the markup is 96.00%?

8. Place mats cost $1.50 in the market. The buyer finds some mats in a new color and wants to sell these at a higher price point than the mats in current colors. Use changes in markup percents to show how two separate price points can be used with one cost.

9. The standard retail price of dress boots is $250.00 for a shoe department. The buyer needs to get a markup percent of 43.50%. What is the cost the buyer can pay to achieve this markup?

10. The department markup on men's wing tip shoes is 68.00%. One group of shoes has a retail price point of $198.00. What should be the cost of shoes to use this markup? The buyer also wants shoes at the $250.00 and $380.00 retail price points. Keeping the same markup percent, what would happen to the potential costs of these two groups of shoes?

*P*rofit and Loss Statements

*O*bjectives

After completing this chapter, the student will be able to

- identify the structure of a Profit and Loss statement
- explain the reasons for using a Profit and Loss statement
- calculate components of a Profit and Loss statement
- discuss relationships between markup and other components of the Profit and Loss statement

The basic **Profit and Loss statement**, or the **P & L statement** as it is called in the trade, is a formal document that is used for a variety of functions within a retail business. In fact, much of the planning that is done in the store is based on this financial document. This statement provides a "big picture" look at and a succinct expression of the sales, markup, and profit for a business. A very simple Profit and Loss statement is often called a skeletal Profit and Loss statement. Development of a P & L statement includes (a) explaining the reasons for the P & L statement, (b) identifying the structure of the statement, (c) calculating the elements in the statement, (d) defining the components in the P & L statement, and (e) explaining ways to expand the statement.

The P & L statement is fundamentally based on the retail price elements and their relationships. The retail price elements of retail, cost, and markup parallel the statement components of net sales, cost of goods, and gross margin. The retail price relationship, as covered in Chapter 2, is useful when examining one item, several items, or groups of items. The P & L statement is used for examining these dollar values and percentages for an entire business or business unit; therefore, the concept of volume becomes an essential part of the P & L statement. **Sales volume** for many retailers is equated with net sales, indicating the amount of sales for the business. The retail price at which one item is sold is combined with the retail prices of all the items that are sold to become the **net sales** amount. Likewise, the cost of goods for one item is combined with the costs of goods for all of the items to become the **cost of goods** in the P & L statement. A master P & L statement is created for the entire business; however, separate stores or divisions of a business may have separate statements.

The P & L statement may be called a variety of names depending on the purpose for using the statement. The P & L statement may be called an **income statement**. Managers who are planning sales or accountants who are formulating analyses may use this term. The name income statement reflects the aspect of the statement using the expected dollar sales and is a positive approach to the statement. This name would be good when presenting information to stockholders or other persons who are interested in the financial health of the retail company, for example a loan officer. Some personnel may not like the term **profit and loss** because of the negative connotations of loss; therefore, the P & L statement is also called an **operating statement**. This name implies the function of the P & L statement that expresses all of the operating expenses and shows the dollars needed to pay the bills for the company.

Functions of the P & L Statement

The P & L statement is developed to cover a specific period. This time can be monthly, semiannually, or annually and coincides with the planning periods for the company. An annual P & L statement may be divided into smaller statements to show both the yearly figures and the figures according to smaller planning periods. Retailers generally have annual statements and semiannual statements; however, monthly or weekly statements are becoming more common as retailers must carefully plan how to operate their business. Shorter periods for statements also help retailers who carry fashion goods because these goods are received into the store quickly, or within a specifically defined season, and must be sold more quickly than basic merchandise. Monthly or weekly statements can be used to indicate statements of cash flow—that is, the dollars that are brought into the store as income and the expenses that are paid to vendors and other services to operate the company.

The P & L statement is used as a **planning tool** before the year or other period occurs. With the P & L statement, a retailer can plan the expected sales, cost of goods to be sold, and the margin needed on these goods to cover the operating expenses and profit. (See Chapter 2 for basic retail price relationships.) The statement can also be used as an **analysis tool** because, after the planned period passes, the actual amounts collected and paid can be compared to the planned amounts from the P & L statement. The retailer needs to know how close the actual sales and expenses for the company were in relation to the plan. When differences between planned and actual are noticed, the retailer must also try to understand the reasons for these differences and to consider what must be done to the operation of the retail store, or the plan, for the two statements to be more in line for the future. Using these monthly statements, a retailer can pinpoint problems or concerns and take immediate action because these problems will impact the next month, the next quarter, or the next season. For example, a reduction in actual sales, relative to planned sales; an unexpected increase in operating expenses; or an unexpected increase in cost of goods sold must be examined and adjustments made at once to ensure that the retailer's annual financial goals will be met.

Structure of the P & L Statement

The **skeletal Profit and Loss statement**, or skeletal P & L statement, is best written in a spreadsheet format, which allows the retailer to make adjustments easily during planning and to generate subtotals and totals with subtotals. A standard format is suggested for all

P & L statements. For learning the P & L statement, mathematical symbols of addition, subtraction, and equals are placed to the left of the line items and can be used to assist in remembering the relationship of the elements. These mathematical symbols are rarely shown on actual P & L statements. The spreadsheet in Figure 3.1 is a P & L statement.

	$	%
Net Sales		
− Cost of Goods		
= Gross Margin		
− Operating Expenses		
= Net Operating Profit		

As shown in Figure 3.1, the P & L statement contains the components of net sales, cost of goods, and gross margin. **Gross margin** contains two components (operating expenses and net operating profit) and is the difference between sales and cost of goods. **Net operating profit** is sometimes called **profit before taxes.** This term clarifies that although operating expenses have been subtracted from the gross margin, the taxes, which could vary greatly among retailers depending on retail structure and many other factors, have not been removed. In addition, net operating profit is also called simply **net profit**; terminology that can be confused with **profit after taxes.**

Net profit after taxes is what is commonly expressed as the **bottom line**; however, the terms profit and bottom line are used in a variety of formats in retail. Bottom line may be any one of the defined measures of profits. As shown in the sample statement, the net profit is the bottom line of this P & L statement. The origin of the expression, bottom line, becomes obvious when a P & L statement is viewed. The bottom line, especially if referencing profit after taxes, for many retailers, is most important because this money is available to pay stockholders, to reinvest into the company, or to disperse to those who control the company. A view of the bottom line only can provide a much-skewed view of a company and can create problems in its operation. Without good sales and lower costs, the profit line may not have any value or may become a loss.

P & L components may be expressed in both dollars and percentages. Dollars represent both dollars that the retailer plans to receive from customers and dollars that are paid in bills to vendors for merchandise supplies, equipment and services provided by such skilled individuals as plumbers, cleaners, sales staff, and other service personnel. The use of percentages allows the retailer to make comparisons between this year's profit and a previous year's profit and between a store's P & L statement and the statement from another store or an industry standard. The relationship between dollars and percentages in the P & L statement is very similar to that found in the retail price relationship formula.

An example of a completed, but skeletal, P & L statement is shown in Figure 3.2. In this example, a retail store has an annual sales figure of $100,000.00 and a cost of

	$	%
Net Sales	100,000.00	100.00
− Cost of Goods	60,000.00	60.00
= Gross Margin	40,000.00	40.00
− Operating Expenses	30,000.00	30.00
= Net Operating Profit	10,000.00	10.00

goods of $60,000.00. With the gross margin of $40,000.00 and operating expenses of $30,000.00, the net operating profit, or profit before taxes, is $10,000.00. When values are placed on appropriate lines and percentages are calculated, the skeletal P & L statement would appear as shown in the figure. Procedures for making these calculations and a sample problem are located in the next section of this chapter.

Calculations for the P & L Statement

When using the P & L statement, the retailer knows that the elements in the statement are related—as the elements in the simple retail price calculation are related. The simplest relationship in the P & L statement is the combination of net sales, cost of goods, and gross margin. For review of the retail price elements, their relationship is expressed in the **retail dollars** formula

$$\text{Retail \$} = \text{Cost \$} + \text{Markup \$}$$

A similar relationship is found among net sales, cost of goods, and gross margin (the first three lines of the P & L statement). This relationship is called the **net sales dollars** formula and is written

$$\text{Net Sales \$} = \text{Cost of Goods \$} + \text{Gross Margin \$}$$

Through algebraic changes, the net sales dollars formula can be rewritten to solve for cost dollars and for gross margin dollars. The formula for **cost of goods dollars** is

$$\text{Cost of Goods \$} = \text{Net Sales \$} - \text{Gross Margin \$}$$

and that for **gross margin dollars** is

$$\text{Gross Margin \$} = \text{Net Sales \$} - \text{Cost of Goods \$}$$

If any two of the first three elements of the P & L statement (i.e., net sales, cost of goods, or gross margin) are known, the other of the first three elements can be identified. This situation could occur when a retailer knows the desired gross margin for the business and the sales volume that were planned and wants to determine the dollars allocated for the cost of goods.

Sample Problems: P & L Statement

Problem 1

The retailer has planned the sales to be $120,000.00 for the month. The cost of goods during this period will be $60,000.00. What is the expected gross margin?

Step 1. Known values are entered into the P & L spreadsheet. Net sales dollars are $120,000.00 and cost of goods is $60,000.00.

	$	%
Net Sales	120,000.00	100%
− Cost of Goods	60,000.00	50%
= Gross Margin	60,000	50%
− Operating Expenses		
= Net Operating Profit		

Step 2. Using the gross margin formula, the value of the gross margin dollars can be calculated from the known values of net sales and cost of goods. Insert values into the following formula and calculate the result.

Gross Margin $ = Net Sales $ − Cost of Goods $

(Computer tip: This process can also be completed directly on the P & L spreadsheet, by subtracting cost of goods line from net sales line. The gross margin dollars formula can be inserted on the gross margin line of the spreadsheet.)

	$	%
Net Sales	120,000.00	
− Cost of Goods	60,000.00	
= Gross Margin	60,000.00	
− Operating Expenses		
= Net Operating Profit		

Problem 2

The retailer is told by the corporate planner that the business must have a gross margin of $45,000.00 to cover the expenses for the period. The net sales for the period are planned at $105,000.00. What are the dollars allocated for cost of goods?

Step 1. The known values are entered into the P & L spreadsheet. Net sales dollars are $105,000.00 and gross margin dollars are $45,000.00.

	$	%
Net Sales	105,000.00	
− Cost of Goods		
= Gross Margin	45,000.00	
− Operating Expenses		
= Net Operating Profit		

Step 2. The value of the cost of goods dollars can be calculated from the known values of net sales and gross margin with the formula

Cost of Goods $ = Net Sales $ − Gross Margin $

COG = 105,000 − 45,000

	$	%
Net Sales	105,000.00	
− Cost of Goods	60,000.00	
= Gross Margin	45,000.00	
− Operating Expenses		
= Net Operating Profit		

Problem 3

The retailer knows that a gross margin of $75,000.00 is needed to cover expenses, and cost of goods is planned at $85,000.00. What are the net sales needed to complete this P & L statement?

Step 1. The known values are entered into the P & L spreadsheet. Gross margin dollars are $75,000.00 and cost of goods are $85,000.00.

	$	%
Net Sales		
− Cost of Goods	85,000.00	
= Gross Margin	75,000.00	
− Operating Expenses		
= Net Operating Profit		

Step 2. Using the net sales formula, the value of the net sales dollars can be calculated from the known values of cost of goods and gross margin.

Net Sales $ = Cost of Goods $ + Gross Margin $

N.S = 85000 + 75000

(Computer tip: When using a computer spreadsheet, the net sales dollars formula can be inserted on the net sales line of the spreadsheet. Using cell addresses in spreadsheets for columns and rows, the formula would be Sum (B3 + B4). This action would add the values in cells B3 and B4.)

	$	%
Net Sales	160,000.00	
− Cost of Goods	85,000.00	
= Gross Margin	75,000.00	
− Operating Expenses		
= Net Operating Profit		

The P & L statement can also be viewed as percentages. As stated earlier, percentages are useful for making comparisons across stores or across periods. The net sales price is the base most commonly used by retailers for calculating the P & L statement. Other segments of the industry, especially apparel manufacturers and wholesalers, use cost as the basis for the statement. Retailers use the net sales price because it represents the retail price and is what the consumer sees when shopping. For this book, the base value for calculating percentage will always be retail, not cost. The net sales value or the sales volume is used as the base value when determining the percentages of any of the other P & L components. For this book, the percentage for net sales will always be 100%. For the P & L statement, retail is expressed as the net sales dollars.

The formula for **net sales percentage** is

Net Sales % = Cost of Goods % + Gross Margin %

This formula can be manipulated with algebra and be rewritten to be the **cost percentage** formula or the **gross margin percentage** formula, as follows:

Cost of Goods % = Net Sales % − Gross Margin %

or

Gross Margin % = Net Sales % − Cost of Goods %

As with retail price, the net sales percentage is always 100% when net sales is the base for the rest of the P & L statement.

Sample Problems: P & L Statement as Percentages

Problem 1

The cost of goods percentage is 60.00%. The gross margin percentage is 40.00%. What is the net sales percentage?

(Hint: At each step, unless otherwise noted, insert the values in the formula and calculate. This process can also be done directly on the P & L spreadsheet, by adding or subtracting the appropriate lines.)

Step 1. The known values are entered into the P & L spreadsheet.

	$	%
Net Sales		*100*
− Cost of Goods		60.00
= Gross Margin		40.00
− Operating Expenses		
= Net Operating Profit		

Step 2. Using the net sales percentage formula, the value of the net sales percentage can be calculated from the known values of cost of goods percentage and gross margin percentage.

Net Sales % = Cost of Goods % + Gross Margin %

(Computer tip: When using a computer spreadsheet, the net sales dollars formula can be inserted on the net sales line of the spreadsheet.)

	$	%
Net Sales		100.00
− Cost of Goods		60.00
= Gross Margin		40.00
− Operating Expenses		
= Net Operating Profit		

(Hint: This problem can actually be solved without calculations because the value of net sales percentage is always 100%. Knowing this information is a good way to check the mathematics calculations in more complex problems in the future.)

Problem 2

The cost of goods percentage is 55.00%. What is the percentage for gross margin?

Step 1. The known values are entered into the P & L spreadsheet.

    (Hint: Remember to enter the value of net sales. It is 100%.)   *100 −55 = 45*

	$	%
Net Sales		100.00
− Cost of Goods		55.00
= Gross Margin		*45*
− Operating Expenses		
= Net Operating Profit		

Step 2. Using the gross margin percentage formula, gross margin percentage can be calculated from known values of cost of goods percentage and net sales percentage.

Gross Margin % = Net Sales % − Cost of Goods %

	$	%
Net Sales		100.00
− Cost of Goods		55.00
= Gross Margin		45.00
− Operating Expenses		
= Net Operating Profit		

Interrelationship among the P & L Statement Elements

Each element in a P & L statement is interrelated. As shown by the formulas, net sales are related to cost of goods and gross margin. Cost of goods is related to net sales and the necessary gross margin. A directional change in one element will create a change in the other elements. This change may or may not be created in the same direction. In fact, often the change is in the reverse direction. For example, if the cost of goods rises and the net sales remain the same, the gross margin will have to be reduced. The same factors taken into account for the retail price relationship must be considered when making changes in the P & L elements.

This interrelationship can be considered mathematically using both the dollar formulas and the percentage formulas. The combination of dollars and percentages is similar to the relationships examined with the retail price elements. Knowing these relationships is extremely useful when planning for future sales, determining cost of goods, or adjusting gross margin. The basic formula for expressing this relationship in dollars and percentages is the same as for the retail price relationship. The formula for the **P & L relationship** is

Results $ = Base $ × Rate %

Base dollars are always net sales dollars, and results dollars are either cost of goods dollars or gross margin dollars depending on rate percentage. By inserting the appropriate elements, this formula, through algebraic manipulation, can be rewritten to solve for each P & L element. A net sales relationship with a cost of goods percentage is called **cost of goods dollars and percentage** formula. This formula is used to find cost of goods dollars when cost of goods percentage and net sales dollars are known. The formula is

Cost of Goods $ = Net Sales $ × Cost of Goods %

The net sales relationship with gross margin percentage is called the **gross margin dollars and percentage** formula. This formula, which is used to find gross margin dollars when gross margin percentage and net sales dollars are known, is

Gross Margin $ = Net Sales $ × Gross Margin %

This relationship can be best viewed in spreadsheet format because a column can be used for dollar values and a column can be used for percentage values. Using a computer and formulas in selected cells, values of the P & L statement can be calculated quickly and can be examined for the effects of a change in an element. This feature is very useful in planning.

Sample Problems: P & L Statement in Dollars and Percentages

Problem 1

What are the gross margin dollars if the gross margin percentage is 45.00% and net sales are $36,000.00?

Step 1. Set up the format for the P & L statement, and enter the known values.

	$	%
Net Sales	36,000.00	100.00
− Cost of Goods		
= Gross Margin		45.00
− Operating Expenses		
= Net Operating Profit		

(Hint: The value of net sales percentage is always 100%.)

Step 2. Using the following formula, calculate the dollar value of the gross margin, and enter this value in the cell for gross margin dollars.

Gross Margin $ = Retail $ × Gross Margin %

Gross Margin $ = $36,000.00 × 45.00%

> *(Note: The percentage can be reformatted to decimals for ease of calculation.)*

Gross Margin $ = $16,200.00

(Computer tip: The gross margin dollar formula would be entered in the gross margin cell, which on the following spreadsheet is B4. The formula would be B2 × C4. This formula would generate the dollar value of gross margin.)

	$	%
Net Sales	36,000.00	100.00
− Cost of Goods		
= Gross Margin	16,200.00	45.00
− Operating Expenses		
= Net Operating Profit		

(Hint: When viewing this formula on the spreadsheet, a triangle is formed between the elements in the formula and the answer.)

	$	%
Net Sales		
− Cost of Goods		
= Gross Margin		
− Operating Expenses		
= Net Operating Profit		

(Hint: The remainder of the values can be calculated with subtraction or the relationship formulas. As the spreadsheet increases in columns and rows, more ways to find the answers become available. One set of calculations may not be right or wrong, just dif-

ferent. The calculations can be made in several ways, and answers can be checked. If the same answers are found from different ways, the spreadsheet is said to square, or the answers are considered correct—if all calculations and formulas are accurate.)

Step 3. Find the cost of goods percentage. Use the cost of goods percentage formula to subtract the gross margin percentage from the net sales, and place this value in the spreadsheet.

Cost of Goods % = Net Sales % − Gross Margin %

Cost of Goods % = 100.00% − 45.00%

Cost of Goods % = 55.00%

	$	%
Net Sales	36,000.00	100.00
− Cost of Goods		55.00
= Gross Margin	16,200.00	45.00
− Operating Expenses		
= Net Operating Profit		

Step 4. The value of cost of goods dollars can now be calculated. Use the cost of goods dollars and percentage formula, and place this value in the spreadsheet in the cost of goods dollar cell.

Cost of Goods $ = Net Sales $ × Cost of Goods %

Cost of Goods $ = $36,000.00 × 55.00%

Cost of Goods $ = $19,800.00

	$	%
Net Sales	36,000.00	100.00
− Cost of Goods	19,800.00	55.00
= Gross Margin	16,200.00	45.00
− Operating Expenses		
= Net Operating Profit		

Each of these dollar and percentage relationship formulas must contain a matched pair of elements. For example, gross margin dollars must be used with gross margin percentage, and cost of goods dollars must be used with cost of goods percentage. If a combination of information is known, such as cost of goods dollars and gross margin percentage, then a combination of formulas must be used. In the retail world, this mismatch of information is common. The retailer may have a gross margin percentage that is dictated by a corporate plan, and the cost of goods may be developed by the buyer in terms of dollars. The retailer must have both dollars and percentages to complete the P & L statement. Another situation may exist where the gross margin is determined based on past bills. The amount of the gross margin in this situation is in dollars. The cost of goods may be determined from last season or from other stores. This value is best given in percentages because the volume or dollar amount of goods sold may not be the same from season to season but the percentage or ratio of cost of goods to sales dollars is expected to remain the same. In this second situation, the retailer knows the dollar amount of gross margin and the percentages expected for cost of goods. The net sales and the rest of the P & L statement must be calculated.

Sample Problems: P & L Statement when Pairs of Values Are Not Known

Problem 1

The retailer must operate with a gross margin percentage that is expected for every planning period. That value is 45.50%. The cost of goods as determined by the buyer is expected to be $68,900.00. What is the value of the net sales dollars?

Step 1. Enter the known values into the P & L spreadsheet.

	$	%
Net Sales		100.00
− Cost of Goods	68,900.00	
= Gross Margin		45.50
− Operating Expenses		
= Net Operating Profit		

(Hint: Remember that net sales percentage is always 100%.)

Step 2. Find a pair of values—either the cost of goods dollars and percentages or the gross margin dollars and percentages. Using the cost of goods percentage formula, calculate the cost of goods percentage, and enter the value into the spreadsheet.

Cost of Goods % = Net Sales % − Gross Margin %

Cost of Goods % = 100.00% − 45.50%

Cost of Goods % = 54.50%

	$	%
Net Sales		100.00
− Cost of Goods	68,900.00	54.50
= Gross Margin		45.50
− Operating Expenses		
= Net Operating Profit		

Step 3. Now that a pair of values is found, the percentage and dollars formula can be used to find the value of net sales. The pair of values is cost of goods dollars and percentages. This pair forms a triangle when the net sales dollars are considered. Use the following formula to calculate the net sales dollars, and enter the value into the spreadsheet.

Cost of Goods $ = Net Sales $ × Cost of Goods %

(Hint: Use algebra to solve for the net sales dollars.)

Net Sales $ = Cost of Goods $ / Cost of Goods %

Net Sales $ = $68,900/54.50%

Net Sales $ = $126,422.01

	$	%
Net Sales	126,422.01	100.00
− Cost of Goods	68,900.00	54.50
= Gross Margin		45.50
− Operating Expenses		
= Net Operating Profit		

Step 4. Find the value of the gross margin dollars. This value can be calculated by two different formulas. For the simplest formula, use the gross margin dollars formula, and enter the value into the spreadsheet.

Gross Margin $ = Net Sales $ − Cost of Goods $

Gross Margin $ = $126,422.01 − $68,900.00

Gross Margin $ = $57,522.01

(Hint: This process is equivalent to subtracting the line for cost of goods from net sales.)

	$	%
Net Sales	126,422.01	100.00
− Cost of Goods	68,900.00	54.50
= Gross Margin	57,522.01	45.50
− Operating Expenses		
= Net Operating Profit		

Gross Margin

The gross margin element in the P & L statement is usually divided into two elements: operating expenses and net operating profit. **Operating expenses** are the sum of the cost of doing business, except the cost of goods. These expenses include such items as sales persons' salaries, bags, paper and pencils, and cleaning of carpets. A more thorough examination of operating expenses will be made in the expanded profit and loss chapter. Net operating profit is the amount of money that remains from gross margin after the expenses are paid. Profit is noted as before taxes, and additional lines can be added to account for taxes and profit after taxes. (The decision on allocation of taxes is made relative to the organizational and legal structure of the business and is beyond the scope of this study.) Gross margin is occasionally stated as **gross profit**, but this terminology is confusing because operating expenses have not been subtracted from gross margin. Without paying for operating expenses, profit is not realized; therefore, the term gross profit is rarely used because the implication is that the entire difference between net sales and cost of goods is a take home profit. This situation is definitely not true, although consumers often mistakenly think that half of the retail price of the item is profit. In retail, the bills must be paid as for any business. For many retailers, the term **profit**, without any modifiers, is used interchangeably with the term, net operating profit, or the bottom line on the P & L statement.

The formula for calculating **gross margin dollars** from the operating expense dollars and profit dollars is

$$\text{Gross Margin \$} = \text{Operating Expense \$} + \text{Profit \$}$$

This formula may be manipulated with algebra to find **operating expense dollars** or **profit dollars**. The associated formulas are

$$\text{Operating Expense \$} = \text{Gross Margin \$} - \text{Profit \$}$$

and

$$\text{Profit \$} = \text{Gross Margin \$} - \text{Operating Expense \$}$$

This relationship can also be expressed in terms of percentages with the following formulas:

$$\text{Gross Margin \%} = \text{Operating Expense \%} + \text{Profit \%}$$
$$\text{Operating Expense \%} = \text{Gross Margin \%} - \text{Profit \%}$$

and

$$\text{Profit \%} = \text{Gross Margin \%} - \text{Operating Expense \%}$$

The elements of gross margin, operating expenses, and profit form the bottom three lines on the skeletal P & L statement. One should remember that the operating expenses and profit are subcategories of gross margin. These two elements are not added to the gross margin and cost of goods to create net sales. Only the gross margin needs to be added to the cost of goods to make net sales. When the gross margin is added, the operating expenses and profit are automatically included. Adding the operating expenses and profit ($30,000.00 + $10,000.00) gives the value of the gross margin ($40,000.00). (See Figure 3.3.)

Figure 3.3

Profit and Loss statement for $100,000.00 with Gross Margin, Operating Expenses, and Profit.

	$	%
Net Sales	100,000.00	100.00
− Cost of Goods	60,000.00	60.00
= Gross Margin	40,000.00	40.00
− Operating Expenses	30,000.00	30.00
= Profit	10,000.00	10.00

To complete the P & L statement, the gross margin and cost of goods ($40,000.00 + $60,000.00) are added to create the value of net sales ($100,000.00). The entire dollar column is not added as one column, but must be added in stages or parts to coincide with the meaning of the items on the lines. This fact is also true for calculating percentages. (See Figure 3.4.)

Figure 3.4

Profit and Loss statement for $100,000.00 with Percentages for Net Sales, Cost of Goods, and Gross Margin.

	$	%
Net Sales	100,000.00	100.00
− Cost of Goods	60,000.00	60.00
= Gross Margin	40,000.00	40.00
− Operating Expenses	30,000.00	30.00
= Profit	10,000.00	10.00

Sample Problems: Gross Margin as a Function of Operating Expense and Profit

Problem 1

The operating expenses for a retailer are determined to be $145,000.00, and the profit is planned as $45,000.00. What is the needed gross margin to cover these elements?

Step 1. Enter the known values.

	$	%
Net Sales		
− Cost of Goods		
= Gross Margin		
− Operating Expenses	145,000.00	
= Profit	45,000.00	

Step 2. Calculate the value of the gross margin dollars, and enter the value into the spreadsheet.

Gross Margin $ = Operating Expense $ + Profit $
Gross Margin $ = $145,000.00 + $45,000.00
Gross Margin $ = $190,000.00

	$	%
Net Sales		
− Cost of Goods		
= Gross Margin	190,000.00	
− Operating Expenses	145,000.00	
= Profit	45,000.00	

(Hint: The dollar value of net sales or cost of goods cannot be calculated without knowing the dollar value of at least one of those elements. With only operating expenses and profit, only the bottom three lines can be calculated.)

Problem 2

The gross margin for a retailer is $125,000.00, and the operating expenses are $50,000.00. What is the value of the profit dollars?

Step 1. Enter the known values.

	$	%
Net Sales		
− Cost of Goods		
= Gross Margin	125,000.00	
− Operating Expenses	50,000.00	
= Profit		

Step 2. Calculate the profit dollars. Enter the profit dollars into the spreadsheet.

$$\text{Profit \$} = \text{Gross Margin \$} - \text{Operating Expense \$}$$

$$\text{Profit \$} = \$125{,}000.00 - \$50{,}000.00$$

$$\text{Profit \$} = \$75{,}000.00$$

	$	%
Net Sales		
− Cost of Goods		
= Gross Margin	125,000.00	
− Operating Expenses	50,000.00	
= Profit	75,000.00	

With the profit and operating expense lines, the net sales, cost of goods, and gross margin lines combine to form the skeletal P & L statement. As previously stated, this statement can be calculated in both dollars and percentages and is represented in a spreadsheet format. These elements are all interrelated, and changes that occur in one line of the P & L statement will be reflected on the remaining lines in some manner—either by increases or decreases. As a retailer makes plans for the next year, the next month, or the next season, information may be known about some of the elements in the P & L statement without knowing all of the elements. The plan must be completed by calculating the unknown elements of the P & L statement to have a complete statement. For example, operating expenses may be established by looking at last month's bills. Profit may be determined by an established dollar value or percentage. Cost of goods may be determined by the buyer. The retailer must put this information together into one P & L statement.

An element may have to remain fixed in value or percentage because of corporate plans or management requirements. This fixed amount must be considered when calculating or estimating changes in the P & L statement. Further adjustments may be needed to handle changes that occur. Adjustments that may affect the P & L statement include unexpected price increases in the cost of goods, operating expenses that are larger than expected, and a decrease in anticipated sales. Inclement weather during a month, such as a major snowstorm that was not in the forecast, could reduce sales for the month. The reduction in sales would reduce the amount available for covering costs and expenses and could result in a lower than expected profit.

This combination of information requires that the retailer be able to use all of the formulas, possibly in conjunction with each other or in a stepwise manner. The combination formulas that contain both percentages and dollars can be helpful when using information from various sources. These formulas require matched pairs of information; therefore, the formulas for dollars or the formulas for percentages must also be used.

Sample Problem: P & L Statement Information in Multiple Formats

The retailer is planning the profit and loss information for next year. The cost of goods are planned to be $188,900.00. The value needed to cover all the operating expenses is $120,600.00, and the anticipated profit is $30,000.00. Complete the P & L statement to find the missing values.

Step 1. Enter the known values.

	$	%
Net Sales		100
− Cost of Goods	188,900.00	
= Gross Margin	150,600.00	
− Operating Expenses	+ 120,600.00	
= Profit	30,000.00	

Step 2. Examine the information that is given. The operating expense dollars and profit dollars are given, and the gross margin dollars and net sales dollars must be calculated. Calculate the value of the gross margin dollars with the following formula, and enter the value into the spreadsheet.

(Hint: The gross margin dollars formula that has operating expenses and profit is used because of the known values. The other gross margin dollars formula requires knowing net sales, which is not yet known.)

Gross Margin $ = Operating Expense $ + Profit $

Gross Margin $ = $120,600.00 + $30,000.00

Gross margin $ = $150,600.00

(Hint: This value can be found by adding the bottom two lines of the spreadsheet.)

	$	%
Net Sales		
− Cost of Goods	188,900.00	
= Gross Margin	150,600.00	
− Operating Expenses	120,600.00	
= Profit	30,000.00	

Step 3. Reexamine the current values, and determine what is the next value to be calculated. The cost of goods dollars and the gross margin dollars are now known and are combined in the net sales dollars formula. Calculate the net sales dollars. Enter the value into the spreadsheet.

Net Sales $ = Cost of Goods $ + Gross Margin $

Net Sales $ = $188,900.00 + $150,600.00

Net Sales $ = $339,500.00

	$	%
Net Sales	339,500.00	
− Cost of Goods	188,900.00	
= Gross Margin	150,600.00	
− Operating Expenses	120,600.00	
= Profit	30,000.00	

Step 4. The percentages can be found by using formulas that combine the percentages and the dollars. Enter the value obtained from the following formula into the spreadsheet.

Cost of Goods \$ = Net Sales \$ × Cost of Goods %

(Hint: Use algebra to solve for the cost of goods percentage. Net sales are always the base. Also, remember that the net sales percentage is always 100%.)

Cost of Goods % = Cost of Goods \$/Net Sales \$ × 100.00
Cost of Goods % = \$188,900.00/\$339,500.00 × 100.00
Cost of Goods % = 55.64%

	\$	%
Net Sales	339,500.00	100.00
− Cost of Goods	188,900.00	55.64
= Gross Margin	150,600.00	
− Operating Expenses	120,600.00	
= Profit	30,000.00	

Step 5. Find the gross margin percentage. The gross margin percentage value can be found either by the gross margin percentage formula (Gross Margin % = Net Sales % − Cost of Goods %) or by the gross margin dollars and percentage formula (Gross Margin \$ = Net Sales \$ × Gross Margin %). If the former is chosen,

Gross Margin % = Net Sales % − Cost of Goods %
Gross Margin % = 100.00% − 55.64%
Gross Margin % = 44.36%

Enter the value into the spreadsheet.

	\$	%
Net Sales	339,500.00	100.00
− Cost of Goods	188,900.00	55.64
= Gross Margin	150,600.00	44.36
− Operating Expenses	120,600.00	OP.%=OP\$/N\$ X100
= Profit	30,000.00	P%=P\$/N\$ X100

Step 6. Find the percentages for operating expenses and profit. These values can be found by using the **P & L relationship** formula. Net sales are still the base. The formulas are

Operating Expense \$ = Net Sales \$ × Operating Expense %
Profit \$ = Net Sales \$ × Profit %

Manipulate the formulas with algebra to solve for operating expense dollars or for profit dollars. Calculate the values, and enter them in the spreadsheet.

Op EX % = OpEx\$ / N.S. \$ X 100

Profit % = Profit \$ / N.S \$ X 100

OP Ex % = OE $/N$ x100
120600/ 339,500 x100
op Ex% = 35.52

Profit % = P$/N$ x100
30,000/339,500 x100
8.84

	$	%
Net Sales	339,500.00	100.00
− Cost of Goods	188,900.00	55.64
= Gross Margin	150,600.00	44.36
− Operating Expenses	120,600.00	35.52
= Profit	30,000.00	8.84

(Hint: The gross margin percentage formula can be used to determine whether the spreadsheet squares: Gross Margin % = Operating Expense % + Profit %.)

Every value in the P & L statement is related to all other values. When a P & L statement is used as a planning document, these values are guides for operating the business. When one value varies from the plan, the other values will be affected. Changes may not be desirable and may require swift action by the retailer to bring the values back to plan. An increase in sales could result in an increase in gross margin and an increase in profit; however, an increase in sales above planned sales could cause negative results. For example, if an increase in sales were realized due to additional advertising or costly special events, or if an increase in sales caused increased needs for sales persons for stocking or selling, the results would be, in all cases, higher operating expenses. For these reasons, an increase in sales could mean a reduced profit instead of an expected increase in profit. On the other hand, if expenses were reduced to such an extent as to cause a reduction in sales volume, the result would also be a reduced profit. For example, reducing the number of sales persons reduces operating expenses but may reduce sales because consumers who cannot find merchandise or cannot find a cashier may not buy. Therefore, a computerized spreadsheet would be helpful in visualizing what changes will have what effect on the total P & L statement. Regardless of the method chosen, accurate planning and adjusting for the retail operation, throughout the period, are very important.

Loss

The Profit and Loss statement is called both terms because a loss can and does occur in business. The profit line can also be the loss line. The loss, or the bottom line, is unfortunately a common occurrence in apparel retailing. Careful planning, merchandising, and listening to the customer are important aspects to creating a profit instead of a loss.

An examination of the P & L statement can provide information about a loss. If sales are smaller than expected and the cost of goods is fixed, then the gross margin may be too small to cover the operating expenses, and a **loss** is incurred. When the operating expenses are larger than the gross margin, a loss occurs. An unexpected bill for snow removal, a roof leak, the need to hire more sales staff, or a larger than average utility bill are items that can create an extra large value for operating expenses. If the unexpected is not part of the plan, or the operating expenses are not adequately watched, the loss can become a reality. On a spreadsheet, the value of the loss on the bottom line can be written in red; thus, the saying is created of being **in the red**. **In the black** would refer to having a profit. The loss may also be written inside of brackets or [ ], and a minus sign, −, is not commonly used.

Sample Problem: A Loss for a P & L Statement

The retailer is planning the profit and loss information for next year. The cost of goods is planned to be $188,900.00. The value needed to cover all the operating expenses is $120,600.00. The net sales are planned as $339,500.00. However, the value of the operating expenses rises to an unforeseen $160,000.00. Instead of the anticipated profit of $30,000.00, a loss is incurred. What is the size of the loss in both dollars and percentages?

Step 1. Enter the known values.

	$	%
Net Sales	339,500.00	
− Cost of Goods	188,900.00	
= Gross Margin		
− Operating Expenses	160,000.00	
= Loss		

Step 2. Calculate the value of gross margin dollars using the following formula. Enter the value into the spreadsheet.

Gross Margin $ = Net Sales $ − Cost of Goods $

	$	%
Net Sales	339,500.00	
− Cost of Goods	188,900.00	
= Gross Margin	150,600.00	
− Operating Expenses	160,000.00	
= Loss		

Step 3. Reexamine the current values and determine what is the next value to be calculated. Calculate the loss with the following formula, and enter the value into the spreadsheet.

(Hint: Loss replaces profit in the profit dollars formula.)

Loss $ = Gross Margin $ − Operating Expense $

	$	%
Net Sales	339,500.00	
− Cost of Goods	188,900.00	
= Gross Margin	150,600.00	
− Operating Expenses	160,000.00	
= Loss	[9,400.00]	

Step 4. The percentages can be found by using the formulas that combine the percentages and the dollars. For example, Cost of Goods $ = Net Sales $ × Cost of Goods %. Enter the values in the spreadsheet.

(Hint: Use algebra to solve for cost of goods percentage. The net sales are alw٠ the base, and the net sales percentage is always 100%.)

	$	%
Net Sales	339,500.00	100.00
− Cost of Goods	188,900.00	55.64
= Gross Margin	150,600.00	44.36
− Operating Expenses	160,000.00	
= Loss	[9,400.00]	

Step 5. Find the percentages for operating expenses and loss. These values can be found by using the base × rate formula. Loss will replace profit in the formula. Net sales are still the base. The resulting formulas are

Operating Expense $ = Net Sales $ × Operating Expense %

Loss $ = Net Sales $ × Loss %

Manipulate the formulas with algebra to solve for operating expense percentages or for loss percentages. Calculate the values. Enter the values in the spreadsheet.

	$	%
Net Sales	339,500.00	100.00
− Cost of Goods	188,900.00	55.64
= Gross Margin	150,600.00	44.36
− Operating Expenses	160,000.00	47.13
= Loss	[9,400.00]	[2.77]

(Hint: The loss percentage formula can be used to determine whether the spreadsheet squares: Loss % = Gross Margin % − Operating Expense %.)

The relationship between the elements of the P & L statement is a delicate balance and poses a complex relationship. Many diverse factors can affect the P & L statement—hiring of sales persons, damage to the carpet, adverse weather conditions, poor consumer confidence, or an unexpected best selling item. Running a retail business requires many skills to understand the financial picture and to merchandise the goods. In many ways, the P & L statement can appear deceptively simple. A few errors in planning or a few good days of selling can make the difference between a loss and a profit. However, the combination of formulas and the interrelationships among the line items are very complex.

*S*ummary

The Profit and Loss statement is a financial overview of the retail business. The P & L statement has a variety of names, but the elements are always the same: net sales, cost of goods, gross margin, operating expenses, and profit or loss. The P & L statement is used as a planning tool and an analysis tool for a year, a month, or any other planning period. The P & L statement can be expressed in dollars and in percentages and is often written in a spreadsheet format. The rows or lines on the spreadsheet represent each of the elements in the P & L statement.

... of goods	Loss	Profit
Gross margin	Net operating profit	Profit and loss
Gross profit	Net profit	Profit and Loss statement
In the black	Net sales	Profit after taxes
In the red	Operating expenses	Profit before taxes
Income statement	Operating statement	Sales volume
	P & L statement	Skeletal Profit and Loss statement
	Planning tool	

Discussion Questions

1. What are the elements of a Profit and Loss statement?
2. How can the Profit and Loss statement help a retailer to operate in the black?
3. What are the functions of a P & L statement?
4. When a planned P & L statement does not match the actual P & L statement, what should the retailer do?
5. Why is the P & L statement also called an income statement?

6. What is the relationship of operating expenses to gross margin?
7. Why is gross profit a misnomer for gross margin?
8. If cost of goods increases during the year, why is a loss possible?
9. Why might increased sales actually result in a drop in profit?
10. Why is the P & L statement written both in percentages and in dollars?

Exercises

Skeletal Profit and Loss Statements

General Directions

Set up and complete the skeletal Profit and Loss statements.

1. Cost of goods is $480,600.00, gross margin is 40.00%, and profit is $18,000.00.

2. Operating expenses are 33.00%, net sales are $330,000.00, and gross margin is 45.00%.

3. Gross margin is $5,000.00, net sales are $20,000.00, and anticipated operating expenses would be 35.00%.

4. Net sales are $15,000.00, cost of goods is $8,200.00, and expenses are $5,800.00.

5. Net sales are $250,000.00, cost of goods is $135,800.00, and expenses are 38.00%.

6. Net sales are $787,890.00, cost of goods is 48.50%, and expected profit is 6.50%.

7. Net sales are $88,800.00, gross margin is 45.00%, and operating expenses are $45,600.00.

8. Net Profit is $12,000.00, gross margin is $107,000.00, and gross margin percent is 44.50%.

9. Cost of goods is $7,000.00, net profit is $900.00, and cost of goods

10. Profit is $4,000.00 and 5.00%, and gross margin is $52,000.00.

11. A store has a cost of goods of $489,800.00, and the expected gross margin is 49.50%.
   a. What are the expected retail sales?
   b. Operating expenses are $225,000.00. What will be the profit percent?

12. A store has retail sales of $278,960.00 for the first six months. The cost of goods sold during that time was $130,000.00. What will be the gross margin percent?

13. For the last three months of the year, the expected profit is $128,000.00. Cost of goods runs $250,000.00 with a 35.00% gross margin. What are the maximum operating expenses that the store can incur? Is this reasonable? Why or why not?

14. If a store experiences a major loss, what strategies can the store undertake to change the loss into a profit? What is the possibility that these will work?

15. If a store wants to increase the profit income, what strategies might they try? Why?

Computer Exercises

General Directions

- Set up the skeletal Profit and Loss statements using the computer spreadsheet program.
- Use formulas to calculate missing values and to complete the statements.
- Save your work on your disk. You should have one worksheet for all problems. Just scroll down below the first problem to start the second problem. Save the spreadsheet as "P & L statement."
- In the upper right corner of the spreadsheet, place your name, date, and file name.
- Worksheets should be on one page. You may have multiple worksheets on one page, but you cannot split a worksheet across two pages.

Skeletal Profit and Loss

1. Net sales are $15,000.00, cost of goods is $8,200.00, and expenses are $5,800.00.

2. Cost of goods is $480,600.00, gross margin is 40.00%, and profit is $18,000.00.

3. Net sales are $250,000.00, cost of goods is $135,800.00, and expenses are 38.00%.

4. Net sales are $787,890.00, cost of goods is 48.50%, and expected profit is 6.50%.

5. Profit is $4,000.00 and 5.00%, and gross margin is $52,000.00.

6. A store has a cost of goods of $489,800.00. The expected gross margin is 49.50%. Operating expenses are $225,000.00. What will be the profit percent?

7. A store has retail sales of $278,960.00 for the first six months. The cost of goods sold during that time was $130,000.00. What will be the gross margin percent?

8. For the last three months of the year, the expected profit is $128,000.00. Cost of goods runs $250,000.00 with a 35.00% gross margin.

Profit and Loss with Change

Create a spreadsheet for the basic information in each problem. Once the spreadsheet is created for the planned situation, copy the spreadsheet, and adjust the information as given for comparison.

1. Net sales are $1,590,000.00. The cost of goods is expected to be 48.00% of the net sales. What is the gross margin? The cost of goods is actually 52.00% of net sales. What is the gross margin?

2. The gross margin is planned as 52.35% of net sales. Net sales are planned to be $489,990.00. What is the planned cost of goods? At the end of the month, net sales are less than expected, only $420,000.00. What is the gross margin percentage, if cost remains as planned?

3. The cost of goods is planned at $56,890.00. The gross margin must be $49,990.00 to cover expenses and profit. What are the needed net sales? If net sales are only $100,000.00 and cost remains as planned, what happens to gross margin?

4. Net sales are planned as $2,330,600.00. Cost is estimated to be 48.55% of net sales. What is the planned gross margin? Expenses are higher than expected, and gross margin actually needs to be $1,500,000.00 to cover all expenses and planned profit. If cost remains as planned, what is the volume of net sales that are needed to cover the cost of goods and the necessary gross margin?

*E*xpanded Profit and Loss Statements

*O*bjectives

After completing this chapter, the student will be able to

- identify the elements of the expanded Profit and Loss statement
- discuss the interrelationship of the elements
- define the types of markups found in the expanded Profit and Loss statement
- define initial markup
- explain how the Profit and Loss statement can be used for financial control

The skeletal P & L statement provides a financial overview of the status of the retail store. The skeletal form of the P & L statement is composed of five elements: net sales, cost of goods, gross margin, operating expenses, and profit. By reading the bottom line of a current P & L statement, the retailer can clearly see the profit status of the company. Although useful for a quick view of income, costs, and expenses, the skeletal P & L statement is limited in the information that it can impart. For a more detailed view of the company's financial situation, this basic P & L statement can be expanded. The **expanded Profit and Loss statement** is created by providing details for the elements, including net sales, cost of goods, and operating expenses. An expanded P & L statement can be considered similar to an outline. Major categories of the statement (outline) are the five elements, and details are added under each of the elements to provide information about their contents. To accommodate these details, additional lines are included with dollars and percentage columns for the incomes and expenditures that are incurred within each element.

Net Sales

Net Sales is the total value of sales after adjustments have been made for losses to the sales. During the daily operation of a retail business, sales made to customers and dollars in the form of cash, checks, or credit cards are placed into the register. However, not all transactions result in income. Some activities by customers take dollars out of the cash register instead of putting dollars in the cash register. For example, a customer uses a recently purchased item and decides that it does not meet expectations. The customer may return this item to the store and demand to have a refund. If a customer discovers, while shopping, that an item is damaged or soiled, that shopper may request a reduction in retail or purchase price. When refunds or retail price reductions are given to customers, these activities reduce the value of **gross sales** (also called **initial sales**). The P & L spreadsheet expands to express these reductions. (See Figure 4.1.)

Figure 4.1

Expanded Profit and Loss Statement for Reductions.

	$	%
Gross Sales	105,000.00	105.00
− Reductions	5,000.00	5.00
= Net Sales	100,000.00	100.00
− Cost of Goods	60,000.00	60.00
= Gross Margin	40,000.00	40.00
− Operating Expenses	30,000.00	30.00
= Profit	10,000.00	10.00

The equal (=) symbol and minus (−) symbol are shown on P & L statements in the figures for this book as reminders of formulas that are associated with elements in the statements. Actual P & L statements used by retailers do not have these algebraic signs in the left margin.

The formula for finding **gross sales dollars** is

Gross Sales $ = Net Sales $ + Reductions $

This formula can also be calculated in percentages. The **gross sales percentage** formula would be

Gross Sales % = Net Sales % + Reductions %

Sample Problems: Gross Sales

Problem 1

A retailer planned net sales of $567,890.00 and planned reductions to be $47,800.00. What is the value of the planned gross sales?

(Note: For this problem, only three lines (or rows) of the P & L statement will be used because of the limited amount of information given in the problem.)

Step 1. Enter the known values.

	$	%
Gross Sales		
− Reductions	47,800.00	
= Net Sales	567,890.00	

Step 2. Calculate the value of gross sales using the gross sales dollars formula.

Gross Sales $ = Net Sales $ + Reductions $

Gross Sales $ = $567,890.00 + $47,800.00

Gross Sales $ = $615,690.00

Enter the value into the spreadsheet.

	$	%
Gross Sales	615,690.00	
− Reductions	47,800.00	
= Net Sales	567,890.00	

(Computer Hint: Using cell addresses in the spreadsheet, the value of gross sales dollars can be found by entering the formula of B4 + B3 into cell B2. This adds the value of net sales to the value of reductions.)

Problem 2

A retailer plans for reductions to be 5.00% of the net sales. What is the percentage of gross sales?

Step 1. Enter the known values.

(Hint: Remember net sales percentage is always the base value or 100%.)

	$	%
Gross Sales		
− Reductions		5.00
= Net Sales		100.00

Step 2. Use the following formula to find the gross sales percentage.

Gross Sales % = Net Sales % + Reductions %

Gross Sales % = 100.00% + 5.00%

Gross Sales % = 105.00%

Enter the value into the spreadsheet.

	$	%
Gross Sales		105.00
− Reductions		5.00
= Net Sales		100.00

Gross sales, reductions, and net sales are related within the P & L statement. They are calculated in dollars and percentages. These relationships can be expressed in the **gross sales dollars and percentage** formula and in the **reductions dollars and percentage** formula as follows:

Gross Sales $ = Net Sales $ × Gross Sales %

Reductions $ = Net Sales $ × Reductions %

These combination formulas are useful when operating a retail business because dollars may be known for one value, but percentages are predicted on other values. Percentages are often used in planning and for comparison to a standard or to a previous planning period. When the percentages are known, the dollar values must then be calculated. For example, a retailer calculates planned sales in dollars and knows that the average reduction percentage for this retail store should be the same percentage as the other stores in this corporate chain. The specific reduction dollars for this store can then be calculated.

Sample Problems: Gross Sales in Dollars and Percentages

Problem 1

The retailer of a specialty shop has planned sales dollars of $2,468,000.00. Average reductions for this store type are predicted to be 7.50%. The retailer needs to know the dollar value of these reductions. What is the gross sales amount needed to cover reductions?

Step 1. Enter the known values. *(Hint: Net sales percentage is 100%.)*

	$	%
Gross Sales		*107.50*
− Reductions		7.50
= Net Sales	2,468,000.00	100.00

Step 2. Calculate the value of reduction dollars using the following formula.

Reduction $ = Net Sales $ × Reduction %

Reduction $ = $2,468,000.00 × 7.50%

Reduction $ = $185,100.00

Enter the reduction dollars into the spreadsheet.

	$	%
Gross Sales		
− Reductions	185,100.00	7.50
= Net Sales	2,468,000.00	100.00

Step 3. Calculate the value of gross sales dollars.

Gross Sales $ = Net Sales $ + Reductions $

Gross Sales $ = $2,468,000.00 + $185,100.00

Gross Sales $ = $2,653,100.00

Enter the value into the spreadsheet.

	$	%
Gross Sales	2,653,100.00	
− Reductions	185,100.00	7.50
= Net Sales	2,468,000.00	100.00

Step 4. Calculate the value of gross sales percentage.

Gross Sales % = Net Sales % + Reductions %

Gross Sales % = 100.00% + 7.50%

Gross Sales % = 107.50%

Enter the value into the spreadsheet.

	$	%
Gross Sales	2,653,100.00	107.50
− Reductions	185,100.00	7.50
= Net Sales	2,468,000.00	100.00

(Computer Hint: Value of gross sales percentage can be checked by using the gross sales dollars and percentage formula.)

Gross Sales $ = Net Sales $ × Gross Sales %

   (Hint: Use algebraic changes to obtain the formula to solve for gross sales percentage.)

Gross Sales % = Gross Sales $/Net Sales $ × 100.00

Gross Sales % = $2,653,100.00/$2,468,000.00 × 100.00

Gross Sales % = 107.50%

Problem 2

The retailer knows that gross sales are 107.30% of net sales. The net sales are $35,500,000.00. What is the dollar value of the reductions?

Step 1. Enter the known values.

	$	%
Gross Sales		107.30
− Reductions		7.3
= Net Sales	35,500,000.00	100.00

Step 2. Calculate the value of the reduction percentage.

Gross Sales % = Net Sales % + Reductions %

   (Hint: Use algebra to rearrange the formula to solve for reduction percentage.)

Reduction % = Gross Sales % − Net Sales %

Reduction % = 7.30%

Enter the value into the spreadsheet.

(Hint: Subtract values in net sales percentage line from gross sales percentage line.)

	$	%
Gross Sales		107.30
− Reductions		7.30
= Net Sales	35,500,000.00	100.00

Step 3. Find the value of reduction dollars using the combination dollars and percentage formulas.

Reduction $ = Net Sales $ × Reduction %

Reduction $ = $35,500,000.00 × 7.30%

Reduction $ = $2,591,500.00

Enter the value into the spreadsheet.

	$	%
Gross Sales		107.30
− Reductions	2,591,500.00	7.30
= Net Sales	35,500,000.00	100.00

Step 4. Complete the spreadsheet using either the gross sales dollars formula or the gross sales dollars and percentage formula. Either formula will give the value of gross sales dollars. Enter the resulting value into the spreadsheet.

	$	%
Gross Sales	38,091,500.00	107.30
− Reductions	2,591,500.00	7.30
= Net Sales	35,500,000.00	100.00

A change in reductions can affect the rest of the P & L statement. With the relationships among the elements in the P & L statement, a change in gross sales can become a change in the bottom line. Reductions from gross sales obviously affect net sales. Whether the reductions of gross sales become a reduction in profit depends on many factors and cannot be immediately determined, but the potential for the reduction to cascade down the P & L statement is obvious. These reductions are important elements to consider when planning a retail operation. Actual value and impact on business must be evaluated with care. At times, a retailer must have a short-term view of the business such as when a bill must be paid; however, a long-term view is necessary when understanding customer loyalty and employee happiness.

Sample Problem: Reductions and Effect on P & L Statement

The retailer has planned the following P & L statement for the month of July. However, by the end of July, reductions are $7,999.00. What will happen to the profit dollars?

	$	%
Gross Sales	105,000.00	105.00
− Reductions	5,000.00	5.00
= Net Sales	100,000.00	100.00
− Cost of Goods	60,000.00	60.00
= Gross Margin	40,000.00	40.00
− Operating Expenses	30,000.00	30.00
= Profit	10,000.00	10.00

Step 1. Replace the planned reductions value with the actual value, and remove dollar values for net sales, gross margin, and profit. All percentages, except for net sales percentage, which remains 100.00%, will change because the value of net sales dollars changes. All elements are dependent on preceding values because of the relationship among P & L elements.

(Computer Hint: If the P & L statement were established using formulas to calculate values, changing reductions would automatically recalculate the related values.)

	$	%
Gross Sales	105,000.00	
− Reductions	7,999.00	
= Net Sales		100.00
− Cost of Goods	60,000.00	
= Gross Margin		
− Operating Expenses	30,000.00	
= Profit		

Step 2. Calculate the value of net sales dollars.

Gross Sales $ = Net Sales $ + Reductions $
Net Sales $ = Gross Sales $ − Reductions $
Net Sales $ = $105,000.00 − $7,999.00
Net Sales $ = $97,001.00

Enter the value into the spreadsheet.

(Computer Hint: Subtract the reduction line from the gross sales line.)

	$	%
Gross Sales	105,000.00	
− Reductions	7,999.00	
= Net Sales	97,001.00	100.00
− Cost of Goods	60,000.00	
= Gross Margin		
− Operating Expenses	30,000.00	
= Profit		

Step 3. Calculate the remaining dollar values.

Gross Margin $ = Net Sales $ − Cost of Goods $
Profit $ = Gross Margin $ − Operating Expenses $
Enter the values into the spreadsheet.

	$	%	
Gross Sales	105,000.00	R% +N% = GS %	2
− Reductions	7,999.00	R%=R$/N$ X100	1
= Net Sales	97,001.00	100.00	
− Cost of Goods	60,000.00	COG%=COG$/N$ x100	3
= Gross Margin	37,001.00	GM%=N%−COG%	4
− Operating Expenses	30,000.00	OE%=OE$/N$ X100	5
= Profit	7,001.00	P%=GM%−OE%	6

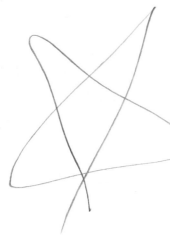

Step 4. Complete the spreadsheet by calculating the percentages, using the combination dollars and percentage formulas as needed. For example, use Reduction % = Reduction $/Net Sales $ × 100. Enter the values into the spreadsheet.

(Hint: Some of these values could be found with subtraction. Some variation in the hundredth decimal place may occur due to rounding and the formula for calculation.)

	$	%
Gross Sales	105,000.00	108.25
− Reductions	7,999.00	8.25
= Net Sales	97,001.00	100.00
− Cost of Goods	60,000.00	61.86
= Gross Margin	37,001.00	38.14
− Operating Expenses	30,000.00	30.92
= Profit	7,001.00	7.22

With no other changes, an increase in reductions will result in a decrease in net sales. The decrease in net sales will be represented in a decrease in gross margin, and the decrease in gross margin, without reductions in operating costs, will cause a decrease in profit. This situation is a very simple one. A year without adjustments to every element of the P & L statement would be most unusual for all retailers. The following example is provided to show interrelationships of elements.

Reductions are more than a simple lump-sum value and include the elements of customer returns, employee discounts, markdowns, and stock shortages. Each value can become a **line item** in the expanded P & L statement. In a computer spreadsheet, each line item is represented on a separate row of the spreadsheet. Some stores do not have each of these line items, but most stores have markdowns and stock shortages. Reduction dollars and the reduction percentage can be calculated from the values of the elements that combine to make reductions. The formula for **reduction dollars** is

$$\text{Reduction \$} = \text{Customer Returns \$} + \text{Employee Discounts \$} + \text{Markdowns \$} + \text{Stock Shortages \$}$$

In a P & L statement, these elements appear as shown in Figure 4.2.

Figure 4.2		$	%
Expanded View of Reductions.	Gross Sales	105,000.00	105.00
	− customer returns	1,000.00	1.00
	− employee discounts	500.00	0.50
	− markdowns	2,500.00	2.50
	− stock shortages	1,000.00	1.00
	= Net Sales	100,000.00	100.00
	− Cost of Goods	60,000.00	60.00
	= Gross Margin	40,000.00	40.00
	− Operating Expenses	30,000.00	30.00
	= Profit	10,000.00	10.00

The formula for calculating **net sales dollars** from these items is

$$\text{Net Sales \$} = \text{Gross Sales \$} - (\text{Customer Returns \$} + \text{Markdowns \$} + \text{Employee Discounts \$} + \text{Stock Shortages \$})$$

This formula, as with the other formulas in the P & L statement, can be used to calculate either dollars or percentages. A different formula is required for a mixture of dollars and percentages.

Customer Returns

Customer returns are the items that customers bring back to the store after the items have been purchased and taken out of the store. In every store, some customers buy items and then change their minds. When they bring these items back to the store, the items become customer returns. If the store has a **return policy**, the sales staff may accept the items and return money to the customer. The return policy may include a number of regulations governing the return of items. Stores may have a **no questions asked policy**. These stores will take any item that is returned, even if the item was used or not sold in the store. Such a policy is very liberal. Although some customers may take advantage of this liberal policy, many customers find this policy to be very appealing. Other stores may require a receipt or proof of purchase, have a time limit for refunds, provide only credit on future purchases, or allow only exchanges of merchandise that is at a same or higher price. A return policy is part of the store policies, affects the image of the store, and alters how customers view the store.

For a variety of reasons, customers return items to the store. Many items are often bought to match in size, style, or color with other items. Once the item is home, a customer may judge that the item is not a match. Apparel items must fit for most customers to enjoy wearing them. Many customers do not take time to try on the items in the store. When the items are home, the customer tries on the item and finds that the fit is not acceptable. Items for the home may need to fit a space within a room or must match other furnishings. Customers cannot bring a couch that they own into the store to find the right draperies or pillows to match. They must be able to take the items home on trial and return them if not satisfied.

Items are also bought for psychological reasons. When a customer has used an item for a period, it may be judged to be just not right. Often, customers cannot express the reason. They say "no real reason, just don't like it." A return policy also allows a customer to return an item if the item shrinks, breaks, or fails in other ways. The wise retailer will allow a dissatisfied customer to return an item because a satisfactory return will result in a happy customer who returns to purchase more items. Many customers never use the return policy but feel more confident in the purchase because the policy exists and the potential to return something unwanted is available. In the short term, a return may be a reduction in income, but if the customer is happy and makes another purchase, the long-term effect is an increase in income. Customer loyalty may be developed by a retailer's acceptance of a few short-term reductions.

Customer loyalty may also be improved by the use of allowances. **Allowances** are amounts that are used to reduce the retail price of the item, for the consumer, based on damage to the item or on some other problem the customer may have in association with buying the item. When a customer notices dirt on an item or other signs of damage, the customer may be more willing to buy the item if the price is reduced. This reduction pleases the customer, making the person feel positive about the business. A retailer will gain by moving damaged merchandise and by encouraging return of a buying customer. Allowances may also be made for purchase of a new and higher priced item when a customer returns something that is not satisfactory and needs a replacement. Allowances help a retailer with inventory flow and provide extra satisfaction for the customer. If a business allows sales associates to make allowances, the retailer must plan for these and have a suggested amount or maximum amount noted that the sales associates could make without prior approval. Having a set procedure will speed the sales transaction and further increase customer satisfaction and loyalty and will keep allowances within budgeted amounts.

Employee Discounts

Employee discounts are also short-term reductions that are designed to create long-term income. **Employee discounts** are special reductions in the retail price of items sold by the business to the employees of the business. This reduction functions to create goodwill among employees, increase sales in the store, reduce employee turnover, discourage employee theft, and ultimately sell more merchandise. When employees buy and use the merchandise, they have a better knowledge of products and their performance. Employees, who feel good about the business or who feel that the business cares about them, will remain in employment longer than employees will who feel disenfranchised. Employees who have retail discounts tend to purchase both for themselves and for their families. For apparel retailers, these purchases are particularly important when an employee is required to wear clothing sold by the business. Traditionally, retailers have required their sales staff to wear the current season's clothing while at work. This wearing insures that the employee is appropriately dressed for the store and the customers. By wearing the store's items, an employee is also advertising items and is providing customers with "live" displays of new merchandise.

As stated earlier, discounts on merchandise make purchase of the items more available to employees and discourage theft. If purchasing the items is encouraged, the employee is more likely to pay for the items, especially if the payments are payroll deducted. These financial benefits for the retailer may not be immediately shown in the bottom line because the discounts cause an immediate reduction in sales. However, with patience and foresight, the retailer will see an increase in income because satisfied employees will continue to work for the retailer, reducing sales associate turnover; family members of employees will shop in the store; and employee theft should be reduced. Additionally, the customer benefits because the sales personnel possess knowledge and experience with fit, care, quality, and other attributes of the merchandise.

Markdowns

The retailer is in the business of making sales to customers. Sales are made to customers at the original or initial retail price. The **initial retail price** is the first price that is placed on the item when it is put on the sales floor. However, some sales made in the retail store are made at a discounted or **markdown price**. The proportion of discounted sales to initial price sales is increasing for many retailers. The ratio of items sold at the initial price to those sold at a marked down price varies across store types. High fashion stores with new and innovative merchandise and stores with a high-quality image may sell few items at markdown. Other stores have most items marked down during the selling season.

The decision about number and size of markdowns affects the image of the store. Overall, volume of sales also enters into the decision about the number of marked down items because more items sold at a lower price may bring in more money than fewer items sold at a higher price. Regardless of the size of the mark-downs or the volume of the marked down items, markdowns reduce the original retail price and affect the sales dollars and ultimately the profit for the store. The size, number, and frequency of markdowns are decisions that are covered in Chapter 15. The function of the discussion at this point is to examine the relationship of markdowns to the remaining elements in the P & L statement. As with other elements in the P & L statement, an increase in the value of the mark-downs could have a negative effect on profit, unless other intervening circumstances occurred.

Sample Problem: Increased Markdowns and Profit Adjustment

The retailer has the following P & L statement planned for next season; however, larger than expected markdowns occur during the period. The retailer finds that mark-downs were actually $4,890.00. If no other changes occur, what will happen to the net sales, gross margin, and profit?

	$	%
Gross Sales	105,000.00	105.00
– customer returns	1,000.00	1.00
– employee discounts	500.00	0.50
– markdowns	2,500.00	2.50
– stock shortages	1,000.00	1.00
= Net Sales	100,000.00	100.00
– Cost of Goods	60,000.00	60.00
= Gross Margin	40,000.00	40.00
– Operating Expenses	30,000.00	30.00
= Profit	10,000.00	10.00

Step 1. Enter the value of markdowns, and remove related values. In other words, remove all percentages and remove the dollars for the net sales, gross margin, and profit.

	$	%
Gross Sales	105,000.00	
– customer returns	1,000.00	
– employee discounts	500.00	
– markdowns	4,890.00	
– stock shortages	1,000.00	
= Net Sales		
– Cost of Goods	60,000.00	
= Gross Margin		
– Operating Expenses	30,000.00	
= Profit		

(Computer Hint: If the spreadsheet is computerized, the retailer can replace planned markdown dollars with actual amounts, and changes in related elements will be revealed.)

Step 2. Find the net sales dollars.

Net Sales $ = Gross Sales $ − (Customer Return $ + Employee Discount $ + Markdown $ + Stock Shortages $)

Net Sales $ = $105,000.00 − $7,390.00

Net Sales $ = $97,610.00

Enter the value into the spreadsheet.

	$	%
Gross Sales	105,000.00	
− customer returns	1,000.00	
− employee discounts	500.00	
− markdowns	4,890.00	
− stock shortages	1,000.00	
= Net Sales	97,610.00	100.00
− Cost of Goods	60,000.00	
= Gross Margin		
− Operating Expenses	30,000.00	
= Profit		

Step 3. Calculate the dollar values of gross margin and profit. Use the dollar formulas.

Gross Margin $ = Net Sales $ − Cost of Goods $

Profit $ = Gross Margin $ − Operating Expense $

(Hint: Subtract the appropriate lines of the P & L statement.)

Enter the values into the spreadsheet.

	$	%
Gross Sales	105,000.00	
− customer returns	1,000.00	
− employee discounts	500.00	
− markdowns	4,890.00	
− stock shortages	1,000.00	
= Net Sales	97,610.00	100.00
− Cost of Goods	60,000.00	
= Gross Margin	37,610.00	
− Operating Expenses	30,000.00	
= Profit	7,610.00	

Step 4. Calculate the percentage values, using the combination dollars and percentage formulas as needed. For example, use

Reduction $ = Net Sales $ × Reduction %

(Hint: Formula is rearranged with algebra to solve for percentage.)

Reduction % = Reductions $/Net Sales $ × 100

Enter the values into the spreadsheet.

	$	%
Gross Sales	105,000.00	107.57
− customer returns	1,000.00	1.02
− employee discounts	500.00	0.52
− markdowns	4,890.00	5.01
− stock shortages	1,000.00	1.02
= Net Sales	97,610.00	100.00
− Cost of Goods	60,000.00	61.47
= Gross Margin	37,610.00	38.53
− Operating Expenses	30,000.00	30.73
= Profit	7,610.00	7.80

A negative effect on profit would occur because net sales dollars are dependent on gross sales dollars and total value of reductions—including markdowns. If gross sales remain constant and part of the reductions increases, then the net sales will be reduced. Reduced net sales will result in a reduced gross margin, if the cost of goods remains the same. A reduced gross margin, if operating costs remain the same, will result in a reduced profit because of their relationship. An increase in markdowns causes a decrease in net sales and cascades down the lines in the P & L statement to the bottom line.

Stock Shortage

Stock shortages are the inventory that is lost, stolen, or damaged. These shortages reduce the number of items that can be sold to the customer. If the items are lost or otherwise not available to be sold, then the amount of income that was predicted for the period will be reduced. Retail businesses are operated and shopped by people. People make errors in counting, stocking, and selling, resulting in losses. Inventory may be lost when items are physically misplaced. For example, a shirt of one brand is placed on a rack with another brand. Doing a physical count of the store may result in overlooking the shirt. Items are also lost between dressing room and display floor. For example, an item may be returned by a customer and the item is set aside and never returns to the proper rack. Sometimes items are lost by mathematics, or at least the value of the item is lost. The sales person who enters $14.00 instead of $41.00 actually "loses" $27.00 in income for the store, in addition to lost taxes on the value. Or, the sales person who fails to take a markdown or incorrectly calculates a markdown will also cause a mathematical or "paper" loss to the retailer. When doing physical inventory counts, people can lose their place in the count and record that 62 items are on the shelf when actually 72 items are on the shelf. The use of bar codes, electronic code readers, and inventory databases are helping retailers to reduce loss from human error. Forgetfulness and other human errors are best corrected by establishing policies and routines for processes and by training employees to follow these policies.

Stock shortages also occur because items are stolen by either employees or customers. Both types of theft are major problems for retailers. Employees must have access to the merchandise and to the cash drawers to facilitate sales; however, freedom on the sales floor, in stock rooms, and in break rooms creates situations that may encourage employee theft. Training procedures, adequate pay scales, established employee purchase procedures (as well as handling and securing of employee packages during the workday), and good supervision are ways to reduce employee theft. These actions may raise the cost of operating the business, but fewer reductions will raise the net sales value. Other more stringent polices of shredding the trash, removing personal items from the floor, designating an employee entrance/exit location and policy, and restricting access of employees to specific areas in the store are necessary in some businesses to control inside theft. Every action in the business has the potential to increase or decrease one or more lines in the P & L statement.

Customers who steal from the store can remove entire racks of items within seconds. Customer theft is called **shoplifting**. Some stores use tags, wires, or ink vials to restrain the merchandise or to deter the shoplifter. These antitheft devices cost money and raise operating expenses. They also reduce sales because customers may not be able to look at and feel the items without assistance. Antitheft strategies may also reduce customer interest in an item. An item that is behind glass may not be as appealing as an item that is on an open display. When antitheft devices are used, the number of items that a customer handles, tries on for fit, or looks at for size and features is reduced. A reduction in shopping will lead to a reduction in purchasing, and this restriction may increase the number of returns that occur and further reduce the value of net sales.

Cost of Goods

Cost of goods is the final cost of the goods. Cost of goods includes all goods available for sale, both on-hand and incoming inventory. The cost of goods value starts with the invoice costs and is adjusted for transportation and insurance to cover the merchandise when being shipped, cash discounts, and alterations or workroom costs. These charges are part of operating the business, but are included in cost of goods instead of operating expenses because they apply directly to the volume of goods that are brought into the store for selling. **Invoice costs** are also called the **wholesale price, billed gross wholesale costs**, or **list costs**. The invoice costs are shown on the bill that is sent by the vendor or manufacturer of the goods. The vendor's list price for the items is a base cost that is adjusted for transportation and other vendor services. Standard polices or negotiations between the retailer and the vendor determine who will pay for transportation. **Transportation**, the cost of moving the goods from the vendor's warehouse (loading dock) to the retail warehouse or store (loading dock), may also include insurance to cover the merchandise while in transit. This insurance is separate from the regular business insurance and may be billed with transportation or billed separately. **Cash discounts** are the reductions in the billed costs or list cost that retailers receive from vendors when the bill is paid by a preset date. Additional information, about how invoice costs of goods and other billable charges are determined, is covered in Chapter 13. Determination of cash discounts is also discussed in Chapter 13.

Alterations or **workroom costs** are those expenses that occur in preparing the merchandise to be placed on the floor or to be sold to a specific customer. Workroom costs can include steaming, tagging, and repairing items; however, when the business is a multiple store business, the checking in, ticketing, steaming, and other preparations of goods for the sales floor are charged to the receiving and marking room of each store and are considered as direct or controllable expenses. The condition of the goods as they are received from shipping varies with the vendor and the packaging techniques that are used. As with other costs, the cost of more expensive packaging, preticketing, or other vendor servicing may be offset by reduced workroom costs at the retail store and by a reduction in employee theft or error. Alterations are common costs in men's wear items. At upper level price points, men's trousers come from the manufacturer with no hem. The pants are hemmed in the store to the fit specifications of the customer. The cost of doing this alteration is often covered by the retailer and no direct charge is given to the customer. However, to cover this expense as with other expenses, profit will be reduced or net sales must be increased. Some stores use free alterations as a way to create a high price or quality image for the store. The alterations become a service that they offer to their customers. If alterations are done in the store, but the customer is charged a fee, the alterations costs are not an addition to the invoice cost of goods. The formula for calculating the **cost of goods dollars** is

$$\text{Cost of Goods \$} = \text{Invoice Cost \$} + \text{Transportation \$} + \text{Alterations \$} - \text{Cash Discount \$}$$

The value of cash discounts is subtracted because cash discounts are money credited to the retailer, thereby reducing the cost of goods. With the additional line items or rows, the P & L statement appears as shown in Figure 4.3.

Figure 4.3

P & L Statement with Expansion for Cost of Goods.

	$	%
Gross Sales	105,000.00	105.00
− customer returns	1,000.00	1.00
− employee discounts	500.00	0.50
− markdowns	2,500.00	2.50
− stock shortages	1,000.00	1.00
= Net Sales	100,000.00	100.00
− invoice for goods	50,000.00	50.00
− transportation	5,000.00	5.00
− alterations	1,000.00	1.00
+ cash discounts	4,000.00	4.00
= Gross Margin	40,000.00	40.00
− Operating Expenses	30,000.00	30.00
= Profit	10,000.00	10.00

C.O.G.

In the P & L statement shown in Figure 4.3, the cash discounts will also have a sign different from the other items because only the cash discounts are income and will add to the value of the sales. Some retailers consider cash discounts a profit cushion because the initial retail price is calculated based on the billed wholesale price, which is stated prior to the cash discount.

Calculations within the P & L statement for cost of goods are made similar to other elements in the P & L statement, which are designated with both dollars and percentages.

The percentages are based on net sales. For example, the $4,000.00 for alterations equals 4.00% of net sales, as determined from the **alterations dollars and percentage** formula

$$\text{Alterations \$} = \text{Net Sales \$} \times \text{Alterations \%}$$

Each element in the cost of goods can be calculated in a similar manner. Each line item is also interrelated with the other P & L elements. For example, an increase in invoice amount would reduce the value of the gross margin if no other adjustments were made, which would in turn reduce the value of profit. To calculate this effect, the value of the cost of goods would be replaced with the value of each line item in the following **gross margin dollars** formula:

$$\text{Gross Margin \$} = \text{Net Sales \$} - \text{Cost of Goods \$}$$

With the insertion of the items for cost of goods, the formula becomes

$$\text{Gross Margin \$} = \text{Net Sales \$} - (\text{Invoice Cost \$} + \text{Transportation \$} + \text{Alterations \$} - \text{Cash Discount \$})$$

Operating Expenses

Operating expenses are the expenses incurred by the retailer that cover the costs of the normal functions for buying and selling. These expenses are the costs of running a retail business. On a P & L statement, operating expenses are stated in terms of dollars and percentages. Operating expenses include a diverse and varied set of items: accounting fees, advertising, bags for purchases, bank charges, depreciation on equipment and furnishings, floor maintenance, legal fees, licenses, writing implements and other office supplies, rent, utilities, wages, and workman's compensation, plus many, many more necessities.

Two classification methods are used to examine or classify operating expenses: direct/indirect and variable/fixed. **Direct expenses** can be directly attributed to a department, a function, or a specific activity. For example, direct expenses are salaries for each department, and specialized hangers used in the suit department. Direct expenses may also be known as **controllable expenses** because the retailer has some control through choice and supervision to reduce or retain these expenses; however, in a competitive economic situation, all expenses must be controlled, evaluated, and reduced if possible to control retail prices. **Indirect expenses** are general expenses that are incurred from running the total business and are not directly caused by any one activity. Examples of indirect expenses are heating, carpet cleaning, rent, utilities, and building insurance. The direct/indirect method is useful for investigating what activities cause which expenses.

Variable expenses change with the volume of sales/stock or time of year. Examples of variable expenses are heating, snow removal, supplies for selling and wrapping such as bags and boxes, receiving and marking room costs, and suit hangers. More suit hangers are needed if more suits are sold. Volume can be estimated, but the number is not a constant. **Fixed expenses** remain the same for every period or inventory. Examples of these expenses are the manager's base salary and building insurance. Fixed expenses do not change regardless of the volume of business that the store has. A store that is busy with sales will have the same insurance as a store that has limited sales. To examine expenses by the direct/indirect method, this portion of the spreadsheet has the format that is shown in Figure 4.4. The **total operating expense** formula is

$$\text{Operating Expense } \$ = \text{Indirect Operating Expense } \$$$
$$+ \text{ Direct Operating Expense } \$$$

or

$$\text{Operating Expense } \$ = \text{Variable Operating Expense } \$$$
$$+ \text{ Fixed Operating Expense } \$$$

Figure 4.4			$	%	$	%
	Direct Operating Expenses					
		Clerk Salaries				
		Coat Ads				
	Indirect Operating Expenses					
		Manager Salary				
		Heating				
		Telephone				

Spreadsheet for Operating Expenses Detailed as Direct and Indirect Expenses.

Operating expenses are sorted to improve the retailer's ability to examine and control expenses. These breakdowns of operating expenses provide management with a tool for controlling costs and setting retail prices. In large stores, the expenses may be allocated to various departments. Each department may have to be an individual **profit center** using activity-based accounting. If individual profit centers are used, indirect expenses may be allocated according to some percentage or set ratios.

Sample Problem: Operating Expenses

A store has the following expenses for the month of November: newspaper ads for a dress sale—$79.56, weekly management salaries—$5,800.00, bags for suits—$34.55, cleaning—$232.50, telephone—$75.98, and miscellaneous—$165.99. Place the values in the appropriate cells and make calculations to determine the requested information,

What are the direct expenses?
What are the indirect expenses?
What is the total amount for all expenses?

			$	%	$	%
Direct Operating Expenses						
		Dress Ads	79.56			
		Suit Bags	34.55			
					114.11	
Indirect Operating Expenses						
		Manager Salary	5,800.00			
		Cleaning	232.50			
		Telephone	75.98			
		Misc.	165.99			
					6,274.47	
Total Operating Expenses					6,388.58	

An expanded view of operating expenses can be integrated into the P & L statement. Gross margin can be divided into operating expenses and profit; therefore, the following **gross margin dollars** formula is proposed:

$$\text{Gross Margin \$} = (\text{Direct Operating Expense \$} + \text{Indirect Operating Expense \$}) + \text{Profit \$}$$

Using the relationships of rate $\times$ base to relate dollars and percentages, the preceding formula can be used to find operating expenses relative to net sales. The following formula is used to find the **operating expense dollars and percentage:**

$$\text{Operating Expense \$} = \text{Net Sales \$} \times \text{Operating Expense \%}$$

The **operating expense percentage** formula is

$$\text{Operating Expense \%} = \text{Operating Expense \$/Net Sales \$} \times 100$$

For components of operating expenses, the same relationship can be used

$$\text{Direct Operating Expense \%} = \text{Direct Operating Expense \$/Net Sales \$} \times 100$$

These relationships can be expressed in a spreadsheet format. The format for the expanded P & L statement, which includes the expansion for operating expenses, is shown in Figure 4.5.

	$	%
Gross Sales	105,000.00	105.00
− customer returns	1,000.00	1.00
− employee discounts	500.00	0.50
− markdowns	2,500.00	2.50
− stock shortages	1,000.00	1.00
= Net Sales	100,000.00	100.00
− invoice for goods	50,000.00	50.00
− transportation	5,000.00	5.00
− alterations	1,000.00	1.00
+ cash discounts	4,000.00	4.00
= Gross Margin	40,000.00	40.00
− direct operating expenses	20,000.00	20.00
− indirect operating expenses	10,000.00	10.00
= Profit	10,000.00	10.00

Figure 4.5

P & L Statement with Expansions for Direct and Indirect Operating Expenses.

Sample Problem: Operating Expenses

A sweater department has net sales of $156,000.00. Indirect expenses are allocated as 10.00% of net sales. Direct expenses include wages of $24,000.00, replacement of bags at $500.00, new shelves for display at $1,230.00, advertising for this month's sale of $456.00 and miscellaneous expenses of $13,500.00. What are the values of the direct and the indirect expenses? What is the percentage for the direct operating expenses? If profit must be $16,800.00, what is the markup percent that must be made by this department?

Step 1. Set up a spreadsheet, and insert the known values into it.

	$	%
= Net Sales	156,000.00	100.00
− Cost of Goods	*100,714*	*13 5%*
= Gross Margin	*55,286*	*21.11*
− direct operating expenses	*39,686.0*	*25.11*
− indirect operating expenses	*156000*	10.00
= Profit	16,800.00	*10.77*

Step 2. Calculate the missing values for operating expenses.

Indirect Operating Expense $ = Net Sales $ × Indirect Operating Expense %
Indirect Operating Expense $ = $156,000.00 × 10.00%
Indirect Operating Expense $ = $15,600.00

Direct Operating Expense $ = Sum of Individual Direct Expenses
Direct Operating Expense $ = $24,000.00 + $500.00 + $1,230.00
                           + $456.00 + $13,500.00
Direct Operating Expense $ = $39,686.00

Direct Operating Expense $ = Net Sales $ × Direct Operating Expense %
Direct Operating Expense % = $39,686.00/$156,000.00 × 100.00
Direct Operating Expense % = 25.44%

Enter values into the spreadsheet.

	$	%
= Net Sales	156,000.00	100.00
− Cost of Goods		
= Gross Margin	*72,086*	*46.21*
− direct operating expenses	39,686.00	25.44
− indirect operating expenses	15,600.00	10.00
= Profit	16,800.00	

Step 3. Complete the following calculations to fill in the spreadsheet.

Gross Margin $ = Operating Expense $ + Net Profit $
Gross Margin $ = ($39,686.00 + $15,600.00) + $16,800.00
Gross Margin $ = $55,286.00 + $16,800.00
Gross Margin $ = $72,086.00

Gross Margin $ = Net Sales $ × Gross Margin %
Gross Margin % = Gross Margin $/Net Sales $ × 100
Gross Margin % = $72,086.00/$156,000.00 × 100
Gross Margin % = .4621 × 100.00
Gross Margin % = 46.21%

$$\text{Cost of Goods } \$ = \text{Net Sales } \$ - \text{Gross Margin } \$$$
$$\text{Cost of Goods } \$ = \$156{,}000.00 - \$72{,}086.00$$
$$\text{Cost of Goods } \$ = \$83{,}914.00$$

$$\text{Cost of Goods \%} = \text{Cost of Goods } \$/\text{Net Sales } \$ \times 100$$
$$\text{Cost of Goods \%} = \$83{,}914.00/\$156{,}000.00 \times 100$$
$$\text{Cost of Goods \%} = .5379 \times 100.00$$
$$\text{Cost of Goods \%} = 53.79\%$$

$$\text{Profit \%} = \text{Gross Margin \%} - \text{Operating Expense \%}$$
$$\text{Profit \%} = 46.21\% - (25.44\% + 10.00\%)$$
$$\text{Profit \%} = 10.77\%$$

Enter values into the spreadsheet.

	$	%
= Net Sales	156,000.00	100.00
− Cost of Goods	83,914.00	53.79
= Gross Margin	72,086.00	46.21
− direct operating expenses	39,686.00	25.44
− indirect operating expenses	15,600.00	10.00
= Profit	16,800.00	10.77

Markups and Other Controls in an Expanded P & L Statement

Among the retail price elements, markup is the difference in value between the retail price of the item and the wholesale cost of the item. In the P & L statement, gross margin is the difference in value between the net sales and the cost of goods. Gross margin is the amount that remains to cover the costs of doing business and the desired profit. Markups of all types become a balancing line between the cost of goods and the other costs of operating the business. The P & L statement was expanded in this chapter to provide details of several major elements in the statement. Additional markups or margins can be examined to help analyze the additional line items in the expanded P & L statement.

Cost of goods was revealed to contain the invoice cost of the goods, transportation, cash discounts, and alterations or workroom costs. The invoice cost of goods and the transportation are directly attributable to the vendor and the individual items that are purchased. Cash discounts are a more general part of operating the business, and alterations costs are definitely in-store expenses. For this reason, an additional markup can be added into the P & L statement to further sort these elements. **Maintained markup** is used to distinguish between the costs directly attributable to the vendor charges for merchandise and the more general costs or incomes associated with handling the goods. The expanded P & L statement with the maintained markup is shown in Figure 4.6. The **maintained markup dollars** formula is

$$\text{Maintained Markup \$} = \text{Net Sales \$} - \text{Invoice Costs \$} - \text{Transportation \$}$$

Alternatively, this formula can also be written as

$$\text{Maintained Markup \$} = \text{Alterations \$} - \text{Cash Discount \$} + \text{Gross Margin \$}$$

This formula is expanded to include elements within gross margin. The expanded formula is

$$\text{Maintained Markup \$} = \text{Alterations \$} - \text{Cash Discount \$} + \text{Direct Operating Expense \$} + \text{Indirect Operating Expense \$} + \text{Profit \$}$$

Calculations of percentages and other variations of the maintained markup formula proceed as with the other formulas related to the P & L statement. **Maintained markup dollars and percentage** is calculated with the formula

$$\text{Maintained Markup \$} = \text{Net Sales \$} \times \text{Maintained Markup \%}$$

The maintained markup dollars and percentage formula is manipulated with algebra to assume the form

$$\text{Maintained Markup \%} = \text{Maintained Markup \$}/\text{Net Sales \$} \times 100.00$$

Maintained markup, as with other line items in a P & L statement, can be calculated from several formulas, including

$$\text{Maintained Markup \$} = \text{Net Sales \$} - \text{Gross Cost of Goods \$}$$

Figure 4.6		$	%
	Gross Sales	105,000.00	105.00
Maintained Markup within a Spreadsheet for an Expanded P & L Statement.	− customer returns	1,000.00	1.00
	− employee discounts	500.00	0.50
	− markdowns	2,500.00	2.50
	− stock shortages	1,000.00	1.00
	= Net Sales	100,000.00	100.00
	− invoice for goods	50,000.00	50.00
	− transportation	5,000.00	5.00
	= Mantained Markup	45,000.00	45.00
	− alterations	1,000.00	1.00
	+ cash discounts	4,000.00	4.00
	= Gross Margin	40,000.00	40.00
	− direct operating expenses	20,000.00	20.00
	− indirect operating expenses	10,000.00	10.00
	= Profit	10,000.00	10.00

An examination of maintained markup can provide comparison to other markups in the business; for example, the individual markup on one item or the gross margin on the total store income. This comparison can also be made with P & L statements in previous years, months, or seasons and can be made with P & L statements from other stores or industry standards. These markups, especially when examined as percentages, provide a statement of the costs of operating the store. The balance between the cost of the merchandise and the expenses for operating the store can be examined. The rule of thumb that was explained in Chapter 2 is a keystone markup or 50.00%, but the balance will vary with the type of stores and with the exact markup that is being considered. When examining the expanded P & L statement and comparing it to the maintained markup formula, the omission of several lines in the P & L statement is noted. The maintained markup has no adjustments for reductions and no consideration for gross sales values. The **initial markup** is the markup used to relate markup to the gross sales value. The initial markup contains all of the costs of operating a business except invoice cost of goods; therefore, by definition, the **initial markup dollars** formula is

$$\text{Initial Markup \$} = \text{Operating Expenses \$} + \text{Profit \$} + \text{Reduction \$}$$
$$+ \text{Transportation \$} + \text{Alterations \$}$$
$$- \text{Cash Discounts \$}$$

Initial markup dollars can also be expressed in terms of the balance between costs and markup. The initial markup dollar formula is

$$\text{Initial Markup \$} = \text{Gross Sales \$} - \text{Invoice Cost of Goods \$}$$

Initial markup, as other elements of a P & L statement, can be calculated in dollars and in percentages. This formula is the only dollar, or percentage, formula related to the P & L statement that cannot be calculated simply by subtracting subsequent lines on the P & L statement. The formula must be created independently from the format for the P & L statement. The **initial markup percentage** formula, when all percentages are known, is

$$\text{Initial Markup \%} = \text{Operating Expenses \%} + \text{Profit \%} + \text{Reduction \%}$$
$$+ \text{Transportation \%} + \text{Alterations \%}$$
$$- \text{Cash Discounts \%}$$

To find the initial markup percentage when dollars are known, the **initial markup dollars and percentage** formula is

$$\text{Initial Markup \$} = \text{Gross Sales \$} \times \text{Initial Markup \%}$$

or

$$\text{Initial Markup \%} = \text{Initial Markup \$/Gross Sales \$} \times 100$$

The base of this formula is gross sales dollars, which is different from all other formulas related to the P & L statement. This base is necessary to consider the initial or original retail price of the merchandise including adjustments for reductions. Using this formula when the individual elements of the P & L statement are known requires a substitution in the formula for the components of the formula. Initial markup dollars contain the values of operating expenses, profit, reductions, transportation, alterations, and an adjustment for cash discounts. A gross sale is the value of net sales plus reductions. The initial markup dollars and percentage formula can be rewritten as follows to include all elements:

$$\text{Initial Markup \%} = (\text{Operating Expenses \$} + \text{Profit \$} + \text{Reduction \$}$$
$$+ \text{Transportation \$} + \text{Aterations \$}$$
$$- \text{Cash Discounts \$}) / (\text{Net Sales \$} + \text{Reductions \$})$$
$$\times 100$$

Initial markup is an additional markup to be used in evaluating costs of operating the business and values of merchandise sold. Income as described in a P & L statement becomes a balance between dollars expended for merchandise and dollars used to operate the business. For a profit, each markup following initial markup should be smaller. Maintained markup should be smaller than initial markup, gross margin should be smaller than maintained markup, and operating expenses should be smaller than gross margin. When practicing good merchandising skills, dollars will be available to pay bills and to flow into the bottom line for profit.

Summary

The basic P & L statement is a skeletal statement. Each line item, or component, in the statement can be detailed and expanded into several items. The details of the expanded P & L statement include gross sales, reductions, transportation, maintained markup, cash discounts, alterations, and direct and indirect operating expenses. The percentages are subdivided, and all parts of a major component must total the percentage of the component. Each line item can be calculated in dollars and percentages. Percentages continue to be based on net sales.

In addition to gross and maintained margins, an initial margin or markup can be calculated based on gross sales. This markup includes reductions and all costs associated with invoice cost of goods, details on operating expenses, and profit. With the use of solid merchandising plans, goods can be sold with a profit. However, if costs or reductions exceed related margins, a loss can occur. Markups can be used to examine relative costs associated with selling merchandise. When markups are calculated in percentages, they can be compared easily with other markups, including those of separate departments, other stores, or past and future years. Overall, P & L statements are planning tools and control tools used for determining operational costs and for achieving profit.

Key Terms

Allowances
Alterations
Billed gross wholesale costs
Cash discounts
Controllable expenses
Cost of goods
Customer returns
Direct expenses
Employee discounts
Expanded Profit and Loss
   statement

Fixed expenses
Gross sales
Indirect expenses
Initial markup
Initial retail price
Initial sales
Invoice costs
Line item
List costs
Maintained markup
Markdown price

No questions asked policy
Operating expenses
Profit center
Reductions
Return policy
Shoplifting
Stock shortages
Transportation
Variable expenses
Wholesale price
Workroom costs

Discussion Questions

1. What is the purpose of the expanded P & L statement?
2. What is the difference between net sales and gross sales?
3. Why must the retailer plan for reductions?
4. How can employee discounts save the retailer money?
5. What is the best way to reduce shoplifting? Why?
6. What costs are involved with buying goods besides the invoice charges?
7. Why would a retailer want to separate expenses into fixed and variable?
8. How can direct expenses be used to control costs?
9. Why should all departments carry a portion of the indirect expenses to form profit centers?
10. What is the function of the initial markup?

Exercises

Gross Sales

1. A retailer had net sales of $467,890.00 and reductions of $47,890.00. What was the value of the gross sales?

2. If a retailer had net sales of $546,890.00 and gross sales of $678,453.00, what were the dollars for reductions?

3. The reductions for a store totaled $45,687.00. The net sales were $356,600.00. What was the percentage of the reductions?

4. The net sales for a store were $1,556,500.00. The reduction percentage was 8.55%. What was the dollar amount for reductions?

5. For a store, the reduction percentage was 7.82%. What was the gross sales percentage?

6. Complete the sales portion of the spreadsheet for the following department information:

   Gross sales: $1,256,600.00
   Net sales: $1,000,000.00

7. Set up and complete the P & L statement to determine gross margin percent based on the following figures:

Gross sales:	$500,000.00	Operating expenses:	45.00%
Net sales:	$250,600.00	Profit:	5.00%

8. Set up and complete the P & L statement to determine gross margin percent based on the following figures:

Gross sales:	$400,000.00	Operating expenses:	$156,000.00
Net sales:	$300,600.00	Profit:	5.00%

Reductions

1. Set up and complete the P & L statement to determine gross margin percent based on the following figures:

Net sales:	$250,600.00	Operating expenses:	44.80%
Reductions:	7.80%	Profit:	6.50%

2. Determine the total reductions for the following amounts:

Stock shortages:	$1,450.00
Employee discounts:	$2,000.00
Markdowns:	$5,500.00
Customer returns:	$10,000.00

3. What is the percentage of employee discounts if net sales are $46,800.00 for the month and the employee discounts are $590.00 for the same month?

4. Set up and complete the profit and loss spreadsheet, using the following amounts:

Profit:	5.00%	Stock shortages:	$1,350.00
Operating expenses:	$82,500.00	Employee discounts:	$2,500.00
Markdowns:	3.00%	Net sales:	$187,000.00
No customer returns			

   (Hint: Be certain to calculate a cost of goods.)

5. Set up and complete the profit and loss spreadsheet, using the following amounts:

Customer returns:	$10,000.00	Stock shortages:	$1,350.00
Operating expenses:	$82,500.00	Employee discounts:	$2,500.00
Markdowns:	3.00%	Net sales:	$187,000.00
Cost of Goods:	$95,150.00		

(Hint: Be certain to calculate a cost of goods.)

How did the change in customer returns affect the profit percentage in this problem compared to the profit percentage in the previous problem?

Maintained Markup

1. Set up and complete a P & L statement, using the following amounts:

Gross sales:	$500,000.00	Alterations:	$4,000.00
Cash discounts:	$3,000.00	Transportation:	$800.00
Operating expenses:	45.00%	Invoice:	$250,600.00
Reductions:	$30,200.00		

2. Set up and complete a P & L statement for *The BedShop*. Insert the following dollar amounts: net sales $44,000.00, profit $500.00, operating expenses $22,000.00, markdowns $500.00, alterations $300.00, stock shortages $60.00, employee discounts $30.00, and cash discounts of $800.00. You will need individual rows for each category of reductions and for invoice. No transportation is charged.

3. Set up and complete a P & L statement for the *T-SHIRT STORE*. The following information should be used: Net sales are $501,500.00, invoice for goods is 52.00%, transportation was provided by the manufacturer, no alterations are allowed, cash discounts were received and amounted to $15,045.00, reductions are calculated at 5.00% of net sales, and operating expenses are $240,000.00.

4. Set up and complete the P & L statement, using the following amounts:

Gross sales:	$600,000.00	Alterations:	$3,000.00
Cash discounts:	$43,000.00	Transportation:	$1,000.00
Invoice:	$256,000.00	Operating expenses:	52.00%
Reductions:	$20,000.00		

5. Set up and complete a P & L statement for *The Shoe Shop*. Use the following amounts:

Net Sales:	$44,000.00
Profit:	$500.00
Customer Returns:	$1,000.00
Operating Expenses:	$22,000.00
Markdowns:	$2,500.00
Transportation:	$2,300.00
Alterations:	$300.00
Stock shortages:	$60.00
Employee discounts:	$30.00
Cash discounts:	$700.00

6. Set up and complete the P & L statement for the *SHIRT STORE*. The following information will be used: Net sales are $551,500.00, invoice cost of goods are 42.56%, transportation was provided by the manufacturer, no alterations are allowed, a cash discount is planned as 4.00%, reductions are calculated at 5.00%, and operating expenses are $340,000.00.

7. Set up and complete the P & L statement for *The Shoe Store*. Insert the following dollar amounts:

Net sales:	$444,000.00
Profit:	$2,500.00
Customer returns:	10.00%
Operating expenses:	$122,000.00
Markdowns:	$5,500.00
Transportation:	$1,300.00
Alterations:	none allowed
Stock shortages:	$610.00
Employee discounts:	none allowed
Cash discounts:	$1,700.00

Operating Expenses

1. Create a spreadsheet to show annual operating expenses for the *TECH T-SHIRT* store with two subcategories (direct and indirect expenses) and a total. Direct expenses are as follows: ads $10,000.00 and salaries $101,000.00. Indirect expenses include utilities $9,000.00, insurance $11,000.00, and rent $70,000.00. Create labels for the columns and rows. Format the spreadsheet for dollars. Use the sum function to get subtotals and formula for the final total. Use the following format:

	Subtotals	*Total*
Direct Expenses		
Advertising		
Salaries	_____	
Indirect Expenses		
Utilities		
..(continue to list).....	_____	
		_____

2. A suit department has net sales of $256,000.00. Indirect expenses are 10.00% of net sales. Direct expenses include wages of $28,000.00, replacement of bags at $500.00, new hangers for coats at $1,330.00, advertising of $560.00 for this month's sale, and miscellaneous expenses of $13,500.00. Set up and complete a worksheet as in the previous problem for the calculation of the expenses.

3. The suit department in the previous problem has profit of $12,000.00. Use this information and operating expense subtotals to set up and complete a P & L statement with the following format:

	$	*%*
Net Sales		
− Cost of Goods	_____	_____
= Gross Margin		
− Direct Operating Expenses		
− Indirect Operating Expenses	_____	_____
= Profit		

4. Set up a P & L statement for *Bob's Boots*. If net sales are $99,000.00, and cost of goods are $60,000.00, what is the value of the gross margin? The store experienced a loss this year of $1,500.00. What is the value of the operating expenses? What is the operating expenses percentage?

5. Of the operating expense dollars for *Bob's Boots* (previous problem), 48.00% of the expenses are direct expenses. The store has sales' salaries of $15,000.00. What is the value of the remaining direct expenses? What are the total indirect operating expenses? What is the percentage of operating expenses, based on net sales?

6. Use the P & L statement for *Bob's Boots* (previous problem) to determine the P & L changes for the following two situations:

   a. For the next year, net sales rise to $109,000.00. Cost of goods dollars and operating expense dollars remain the same. Find the operating expenses percent.

   b. If net sales drop to $80,000.00, what will be the operating expense percentage ?

   Show each situation with a new P & L statement. Percentages will have to be recalculated for each P & L statement.

Overview of Margins

1. Set up and complete a P & L statement, and determine maintained markup and gross margin percentages for the following:

Gross sales:	$480,000.00	Alterations:	$ 4,000.00
Profit:	6.00%	Reductions:	$14,750.00
Invoice (w/trans):	$292,000.00	Cash discounts:	1.00% (of invoice)

2. Set up and complete a P & L statement, and determine maintained markup and gross margin percentages based on the following:

Net sales:	$280,000.00	Alterations:	$4,000.00
Profit:	$7,000.00	Operating expenses:	$92,000.00
Cash discounts:	$3,000.00	Transportation:	$2,000.00
Reductions:	$12,000.00		

3. Set up and complete a P & L statement, and determine maintained markup and gross margin percentages for the following:

Net sales:	$370,000.00	Alterations:	$3,500.00
Profit:	5.00%	Stock shortages:	$1,550.00
Operating expenses:	$92,500.00	Employee discounts:	$2,100.00
Markdowns:	3.00%	Cash discounts:	$5,500.00

Initial Markup

1. Determine the initial markup percentage for the following:

Net sales:	$280,000.00	Alterations:	$4,000.00
Profit:	$7,000.00	Stock shortages:	$1,200.00
Operating expenses:	$92,000.00	Employee discounts:	$600.00
Markdowns:	$10,200.00	Cash discounts:	$3,000.00

2. Determine the initial markup dollars and percentages for the following:

   (Hint: Set up a Profit and Loss statement to determine the dollars and percents.)

Net sales:	$370,000.00	Alterations:	$3,500.00
Profit:	5.00%	Reductions:	$14,700.00
Operating expenses:	$92,500.00	Cash discounts:	$5,500.00

3. Determine the initial markup percent for the following:

   (Hint: Set up a Profit and Loss statement to determine the dollars and percents.)

Gross sales:	$480,000.00	Alterations:	$4,000.00
Profit:	6.00%	Stock shortages:	$1,200.00
Invoice (w/tran):	$292,000.00	Employee discounts:	$600.00
Markdowns:	$10,200.00	Cash discounts:	$2,920.00

4. Determine the initial markup percent for the following:

Gross sales:	$500,000.00	Alterations:	$4,000.00
Cash discounts:	$3,000.00	Transportation:	$800.00
Operating expenses:	45.00%	Invoice:	$250,600.00
Reductions:	$30,200.00		

5. For the *T-SHIRT STORE*, the following information will be used: Net sales are $501,500.00, invoice cost of goods are 52.00%, transportation was provided by the manufacturer, no alterations are allowed, cash discounts are $7,823.40, reductions are calculated at 5.00% of net sales, and operating expenses are $240,000.00. What is the initial markup percentage?

6. A department has the following figures planned for the month: 38.50% operating expenses, 3.10% profit, reductions of 12.60%, and alterations of 2.80%. No cash discount is given. What is the planned initial markup percentage?

7. *The Shoe Store* has a yearly plan of 42.30% operating expense with 18.00% reductions and 3.90% cash discounts. To achieve an 8.50% profit, what must the initial markup percentage be?

8. If the following figures are for the Coat Department, what is the maintained markup percentage?

Gross sales:	$258,500.00
Invoice:	$119,400.00
Gross margin:	$122,800.00
Transportation:	$8,900.00
Alterations:	$850.00
Operating expenses:	$60,000.00

   What is the profit percent? What is the initial markup percent?

Computer Exercises

General Directions

- Set up the Profit and Loss statements using a computer spreadsheet program.
- In the upper right corner of the spreadsheet, place the name, date, and problem number.
- Save your work. Place each problem below the first on one worksheet.

- Print the worksheet. Small problems may be printed with two or more on one page.
- Be certain that a problem does not "run on" to multiple pages. Do not print "run on" sheets.
- Print all formula sheets (if this is possible for your computer).
- Turn in your printed sheets and formula sheets.

Expanded Profit and Loss Statements

1. Set up a Proforma expanded P & L statement. Have rows for titles, headings, and the values of gross sales, reductions, net sales, invoice costs, transportation, maintained markup, alterations, cash discounts, gross margins, operating expenses, and profit. Use indents for reductions, invoice costs, transportation, alterations, cash discounts, and operating costs. Set up columns for dollars and percents.

2. Set up a P & L statement for *Bunnies Bathing Suit Shop*. Using the format in Problem 1 insert the following dollar amounts: net sales $144,000.00, profit $4,500.00, operating expenses $49,000.00, markdowns $5,100.00, alterations $2,300.00, stock shortages $600.00, employee discounts $300.00, and cash discounts of $1,800.00. No transportation is charged. Using formulas, complete the P & L statement.

3. Set up a P & L statement, and determine maintained markup and gross margin percents for the following:

Net sales:	$288,000.00	Alterations:	$4,600.00
Profit:	$9,000.00	Reductions:	$12,000.00
Operating expenses:	$98,000.00	Transportation:	$2,000.00
Cash discounts:	$3,600.00		

4. Set up a P & L statement, and determine maintained markup and gross margin percents based on the following:

Net sales:	$370,000.00	Alterations:	$3,500.00
Profit:	5.00%	Reductions:	$14,750.00
Operating expenses:	$92,500.00	Cash discounts:	$5,500.00

5. Set up an expanded P & L statement for the *SHIRT STORE*. Net sales are $581,500.00, invoice cost of goods are 52.00%, transportation is provided by the manufacturer, no alterations are allowed, no cash discounts are obtained, and reductions are calculated at 3.00% of net sales. The indirect operating expenses for the *SHIRT STORE* are advertising costs $10,000.00, management salaries $101,000.00, utilities $8,000.00, insurance $11,500.00, gift-wrap supplies $440.00, and cleaning/windows $1,600.00. The direct expenses are bags for suits $200.00, suit department sales commissions $3,000.00, and suit hangers $500.00.

   Sort the direct and indirect expenses with appropriate row labels. Have subtotals for direct and indirect expenses. *(Hint: You will have to add rows.)* Have a total for all expenses. Use the sum function to get subtotals and a formula for the total. Be sure to format the cells as needed.

6. Set up a P & L statement for *Brads Boots*. For Year 1, net sales are $99,000.00, cost of goods is $60,000.00, and operating expenses are $40,500.00. Create a column for Year 2. *(Hint: You will need to add one new column and add new label (dollars) for Year 2. Be certain that the column labels for the years are centered over the $.)* Show how Year 2 could have an increased profit even though the sales volume decreases to $98,000.00. What must be changed? How likely is this change? Explain. (Type the answers to the questions below your P & L statement.)

CHAPTER 5

*S*trategic Planning

*O*bjectives

After completing this chapter, the student will be able to

- identify the strategic planning process
- explain the importance of strategic planning
- discuss the steps in strategic planning
- describe the retail mix and store image
- explain the importance of customers

The retail business is very competitive. In many places in the world, including the United States, many retailers exist and compete for the same retail customers. The overstoring of the retail business has a serious impact on any retailer because every customer has many options for shopping and buying goods. Customers have two decisions to make—first, they must select what retail business to patronize, and second, they must select from a multitude of products that often offer the same features and are at the same price. Some customers become store loyal and constantly shop in one store; however, other customers are known as cross-shoppers because they may shop in an exclusive specialty store for one product and shop in a discount store for other products. Their shopping preferences change with products, time constraints, family demands, or other life events. Sometimes price, convenience, time, stress, or shopping experiences may be the force behind the selection of a specific store or product. At other times, the same customer may be motivated by brand, quality, occasion for use, or acceptance by a peer group. Traditional methods of examining the customer may not be accurate in today's highly competitive and overstored markets.

In a market with unlimited and intense competition, few businesses can find new ways to be unique or innovative because someone else has probably already thought of the idea; however, business owners must constantly strive to be well organized and targeted to meet the financial demands of the business and to meet the needs of customers. To be successful in a crowded and price-competitive market, each retailer must plan carefully, merchandise according to plan, and evaluate progress relative to the plan. Achieving the twin goals of profit and consumer satisfaction requires careful planning at all stages of merchandising—planning, buying, and selling. The strategic planning technique allows a retailer to analyze carefully goals of both the business and the customer to achieve the purpose of the business.

Strategic Planning

In a competitive environment, many managers of businesses pose the following questions: "What business should we pursue?" "Which customers should we attract to support this business and the products that we purchase?" and "How do we develop and sustain a competitive advantage to ensure profitability of the business?" **Strategic planning** is a series of steps or a process of operating a company according to a plan that has specific goals and can assist owners and managers to seek answers to these broad questions. In general, retailers are in business to provide merchandise and services for consumers, but what customers, what types of merchandise, what prices of merchandise, what assortments of merchandise, and what formats of retail are all individual matters that must be considered when determining how to develop and sustain a competitive advantage.

Strategic planning should be a methodical and organized process to ensure the inclusion of broad ideas and tiny details. Many companies may address some of these steps in sales meetings, in weekly management sessions, or in new initiative summits, but few owners and managers take the time to complete the entire process for a company. People often say they are too busy "running the store" to take time to plan, but that statement ignores the value of planning. Time spent in planning now will improve how well the business operates in the future. The nine steps of the strategic plan are as follows:

1. develop a vision statement for the company,
2. scan the internal and external environments,
3. determine issues critical to the company,
4. select the problem to be solved,
5. determine the specific strategy to achieve the solution,
6. identify a plan of action within the specific strategy,
7. implement the specific activities and monitor the process,
8. evaluate the outcome of the specific activities, and
9. make recommendations for the future.

The planning process should be formalized, but it may be limited to an afternoon meeting within a small company or be expanded to an extensive week-long retreat in a large corporation. The **planners** are those personnel who will work through the strategic planning process. Planners may be limited to upper management personnel or in some companies may include teams of employees who represent cross-functional areas and hierarchical integration. Each step is important to the entire process and is based on the merchandising philosophy that is framed and expressed in Steps 1–3, developed and refined in Steps 4–7, and executed and evaluated in Steps 7–9.

Vision Statement

The strategic plan starts with a broad vision of the company and the market and narrows to operational activities designed to fulfill the vision and to obtain the company's goals. To begin the process and to initiate Step 1, the retailer must be able to articulate a vision statement for the business. The **vision statement**, when formulated, provides direction to and expresses the core values and goals of the company. The vision statement for many retailers selling fashion goods is often called the merchandising philosophy. A **merchandising philosophy** explains the company's role in the selection and presentation of merchandise for the customer. The policy provides a foundation for merchandising policies including presentation techniques to attract and retain the desired customers. Vision statements are often broad business expressions of the merchandising philosophy.

Examples of a vision statement for a fashion retailer are as follows: "This company will be a leader in providing fashion goods to consumers who want to be stylish and innovative." "This company will provide the best quality goods at the lowest prices for all customers." "Our company will be a leader in trendy clothing for those customers who are young at heart." Fashion leadership, value pricing, and quality merchandise are often parts of a vision statement for retailers who sell fashion goods. Service is another merchandising aspect that may be part of a vision statement. Providing high levels of service may be a vision designed to draw customers who want to be treated to a salon type selling experience. This vision of superior customer service may be combined with the desire to provide fashion forward products or high quality products for a merchandising philosophy that is appropriate for attracting a certain segment of customers.

Environmental Scan

In Step 2, the planners must scan the internal and external environments for the business. Through this step of strategic planning, the retailer must do an **environmental scan** to consider the opportunities and barriers in the market and the strengths and weaknesses of the current business. Market opportunities include expansions of new businesses in local economies, influx of new population groups into a geographic area, growth of customer bases through Internet access, or closures of related businesses. Each of these events would provide an opportunity to increase sales through new customers. Any events that expand the economy and provide increased income for a market would provide the potential for expanded sales. External barriers to a company's success include a sluggish economy, a slowdown in consumer spending, and an increase in numbers and strength of competitive businesses. These events lead to reductions of employment, decreases in discretionary income, and an overall downturn in consumers' interests and abilities to purchase fashion goods. All of these market conditions may be impacted by changing demographics, unpredictable weather conditions, unsettled political situations, and seemingly unrelated technological and sociological events. Events anywhere on the globe could have a local impact. (Additional market scan information is provided in Chapter 6.)

Strengths of the business may be exhibited in positive characteristics such as a broad and loyal customer base, a newly renovated physical facility, location in an expanding mall, strong vendor relationships, a stable and positive image, the retention of well trained and long-term employees, and well established channels of distribution. These strengths are the assets of the company and may include a strong financial basis, with adequate capital for expansion or viable cash flow; however, assets are more than monetary factors. On the other hand, the retailer may have weaknesses and be challenged by such incidents as declining sales, high markdowns, heavy inventories, low margins, limited or lack of profits, escalating overhead expenses, or an eroding customer base. Assets can be enhanced or removed according to the vision and the opportunities that the retailer sees in the market. Without opportunities in the market, the assets have limited value and the weakness can become overwhelming.

Critical Issues

All aspects of the internal and external environments must be noted and considered when planning. Failure to identify every opportunity or threat can jeopardize the most extensive plan; however, not every environmental issue will be critical to each business for each situation. The environmental scan can result in numerous listings of opportunities and barriers. The list can be too large for any one company to address. In Step 3, the strategic planning process can assist the retailer in determining what opportunities, as identified in Step 2, can be best met with the current business strengths or assets. At this stage, the strategic planning process guides the planners to narrow the breadth of the plan and use assets to achieve a focused attack on the market.

To meet a market opportunity, issues critical to the business operation must be evaluated. **Critical issues**, both strengths and weaknesses, include the amount of capital that may be available for change, the volume of cash flow that is needed for daily operations, the number of employees that will be involved with the change, the amount and location of current inventory, and the commitments for merchandise, space and other obligations that the company must meet. Generalized market opportunities and barriers must be matched with assets and weaknesses of the company. For example, a market expansion must be fitted by planners with the business capital needed to provide increased inventory or space to address the growth. All areas of the business must be investigated: management, distribution, promotions, personnel, and buying.

Within a large corporation with multiple business units, planners must consider the impact of changes in one business upon the other business units. Many retailers today operate noncompeting businesses within the corporation. Cannibalization of other units within a company should not occur because of growth or reductions within a unit. For example, a company that owns both bricks and clicks must ensure that growth of the Internet aspect of the business does not draw customers from the store aspects of the business. As discussed in Chapter 1, Internet shopping can be compatible with store shopping, but Internet shopping and catalog shopping can siphon sales away from a store. To avoid this negative action, special merchandise may be offered on the Web that is not available in the store or special in-store services of gift wrapping or personal shoppers may be used to entice customers into the store.

Planners must revisit the vision often and continue to use the merchandising philosophy to guide the plan. For example, a retailer who is dedicated to quality products at a discounted price must be certain that expenses incurred in expansion will not alter profit margins that are designed to bring the expected lower prices to loyal customers.

Problem Selection

Keeping the vision as the guide for the plan, Step 4 directs the planners to select the problem to be solved. Most markets provide multiple opportunities to be investigated and multiple barriers to be avoided. Most companies have multiple strengths to leverage toward the opportunities and weaknesses that will provide additional barriers to change. Planners must use **problem selection** to determine which set of assets and weaknesses will be addressed at any given point. Using a comparative analysis of risks and benefits, planners can determine what is the best opportunity for change for the company. Change may be growth or reduction. For example, if the company is experiencing a negative financial environment, internally and externally, the change needed may not be growth, but downsizing or retrenchment of assets. Occasionally, a company expands without planning or does not note signs of a downturn in economy and must reengineer its organization to adapt to the environmental changes. On the other hand, an environmental scan could alert planners to the potential for growth in a niche market or in a new geographic area. With multiple opportunities to change, the planners must determine which opportunity or problem to address. Few companies have the financial or personnel resources to implement multiple strategic actions at one time.

Planners may select an opportunity or problem for various reasons. The opportunity that is most similar to the current business may be attractive because this opportunity may require few "start up" costs and few changes. This change may not provide the highest financial returns for the investments but would be a "safe" investment. On the other hand, the planners may be willing to assume more risk and enter new ventures that will attract new customers or that involve new products with different channels of distribution. These opportunities may provide a higher risk of failure than other changes but often have more long-term benefits. Planners may also find that they have limited choices in what new strategies to implement. Choice may be dictated by financial need. A business that is suffering from reductions in sales, restricted cash flow, or reduced customer base may have to take actions to increase margins by reducing operating costs or altering buying and inventory patterns.

Before refocusing or changing the merchandising strategy, the retailer needs to determine whether the present assortment of merchandise is providing the best mix for the majority of its customers or its major customer base. The retailer must also assess whether the vendors are providing the level of fashion forward styling that is desired and whether the quality is appropriate for the customers' interests. The retailer needs to consider that if major changes are made through the strategic planning process, new sources of products will have to be investigated and new vendors will need to be approached with new negotiations and distribution plans. The development of a private label or house brand with products made specifically for the retailer may be a consideration. Changes in vendors may result in changes in technology needed for inventory management. Computers and software may be needed or may need updating to deal with selected vendors. Willingness and ability to make these changes are considerations when selecting the problem.

Specific Strategy

With a problem selected, the planner must verbalize it into a strategy to achieve the desired solution. The **specific strategy** provides the employees of the company with a specialized vision and provides customers and vendors with an idea of the changes that will be taking place in the company. The strategy is often finalized with a slogan or statement similar to the vision statement. For example, a company, known for its discount prices, plans to increase the amount of fashion forward goods that are carried by the firm. The strategy, or refocused merchandise direction, is expressed by the following slogan: "We strive to provide more of the latest fashions at the same low prices." A company that wishes to include more apparel items in a firm that has traditionally had more housewares and hardware items may have a slogan that states the following: "Check us out for more new clothes." If a company that has traditionally had adult clothing plans to expand to children's wear, the new slogan might be "Now, you can bring the whole family for a one-stop shopping experience."

Downsizing is a possible strategy for companies that need to eliminate layers of management, close unproductive stores, or consolidate job roles and responsibilities into fewer positions. Such reductions in work force in a company are rarely announced as a negative slogan. Announcing a slogan of "We are closing stores to save us money" would not attract many new customers, but announcing "Our new look will tell you about our new products" would entice customers to come see the changes. Once inside the store, customers would see the results of changes such as less inventory and more focused buying because the store might have a fresh new open look, and, with less clutter, customers could more easily find the desired products.

Action Plan

The next step in the strategic planning process is to identify specific activities needed to support the implementation of the chosen and specific strategy. Once the vision, market opportunities, and business assets are identified and brought into focus, and the problem is selected and verbalized, the retailer must examine the day-to-day operations of the company. The way that the business is run must fit with the vision. This fit may affect the present business structure including the operation of management, sales, merchandising, and distribution. The specific and day-to-day interpretation of the strategy becomes the **action plan**. Careful interpretation of the strategy must be performed to ensure that the vision is maintained, that the financial basis is in place to support the plan, and that company personnel are well informed about the strategy. Support must be sought throughout the company to enable a successful implementation. For sustained success, a major strategy that involves change will be highly dependent upon all personnel.

For a successful action plan, detailed procedures for all aspects of the company must be created. A retail company is a very complex organization with many interdependent units. The hows and whys of the strategy must be developed for each functional area within the company. Geographically and organizationally, the distance between the planners and the sales associates may be very large, but within every retail organization, the sales associates are the personnel who will ultimately interpret or represent the strategy to the customer. For example, the new strategy may be "Improved customer service." This strategy must be specified to explain to the sales associates exactly what they must do that is different from what they had done previously. Action plans for this strategy could include weekly training sessions for sales associates, hiring of new sales associates, placement of personal shoppers within certain merchandise departments, improved telephone access for customers, and reduced reply time for email inquiries. Action plans can include very specific details about percentage of change, reductions of time, or increases in activities.

Specific functional activities or personnel groups can be designated within the action plans. A strategy that is destined to change aspects of the company may require promotional activities to inform the customers about the changes. For example, revised advertising slogans and increased media exposure will be needed to inform customers. The action plan will include not only suggestions for more advertising but also specific information about numbers of ads, outlets for promotions, and date and length of time for exposure of the new strategy. This level of detail is needed to ensure success of the new strategy.

Implementation

A timeline is needed to determine the **implementation** of the specific activities and to monitor the process. Most strategies are implemented over a series of months. Large, multi-unit companies will need to determine whether the capital is available for implementing the change in all units at one time and whether the impact of such a massive change is needed. Alternatively, the planners may determine that the changes should be implemented in stages. One store group or one set of business units at a time may be converted. When the strategy involves large amounts of capital expenditures, such as store renovation and new signage, the costs per unit may prohibit simultaneous, multi-store implementation. On the other hand, the need for downsizing or other restructuring may call for extreme action and immediate and complete implementation of the plan must be instituted.

Change does not occur unless the strategy is implemented. Personnel at all organizational levels within the company must be informed and empowered to make needed changes. Dates of implementation must be determined and followed to prevent confusion by company personnel and by customers. Companies may even advertise the implementation date as part of their action plan; however, many companies prefer to implement action plans and monitor progress to determine smooth flow of operations before announcing changes to the customers. A grand reopening traditionally occurs after the change has been fully implemented. With customers who desire high levels of change and excitement, a company may use the outward signs of implementation as an advertisement of the change. Construction work for renovation may be covered with signs that invite the customer to return by a certain date. Contests or other interactive activities may be used to increase customer interest and to reduce customer complaints about the inconveniences that the change causes. Promises of gifts, reduced prices, or other services can be used to make shopping more fun during and following implementation of action plans.

Evaluation

All good plans must include an evaluation of the outcome of the specific activities and their contributions to the vision. **Evaluation** requires good record keeping and adequate measures for comparison. For example, measures of employee productivity, sales volume, and inventory levels may be compared with previous values to determine the effect of the change. Adequate evaluation is also dependent upon the availability of previous data about the performance of the company. A company that has not previously participated in strategic planning may lack data from previous periods of operation. In the absence of such data, the planners can track the amount of change relative to the initial point of implementation or change relative to industry standards. The measures used in developing the P & L statement are important to consider when evaluating a plan. These measures are standards used in the industry and standards used when banks and other financial agencies evaluate the profitability of a company. Increases in sales volume, reductions in operating expenses, and increases in profits are simple measures that provide quick views of operational activities. As discussed in Chapters 3 and 4, these measures are actually not as simple as they seem but are often interrelated and not isolated measures. In addition, increases in operating costs are needed to achieve increases in sales or reductions in costs of merchandise.

Some companies choose to use outside evaluators at this stage in the strategic planning process. Auditors, accountants, or other specialists may be used to provide evaluations of the effectiveness of the strategy. Of course, effectiveness must be defined by the planners in order for any parties to make evaluations. If a lack of cash flow is part of the problem that promoted the new strategy, then cash flow should be one of the evaluation measures at this stage. Improvements in nonrelevant measures may improve the appeal of the strategy but may not improve the financial situation for the company. As the retailer plans for a business, the goal of consumer satisfaction and the reality of profit margins must not be ignored. Vision statements and all other outcomes of planning must constantly be evaluated for their contribution to the business's ability to attract customers and to make a profit.

Recommendations

After evaluation, **recommendations** are made for the future. The evaluations made in Step 8 may indicate that adjustments are needed in the action plan for the strategy. If actualization of the strategy is achieved, the recommendation may result in the selection of a new problem. Merchandising is not a static operation but is ever changing and constantly evolving. The market, the consumer, and fashions are in a constant state of flux. Planners for a company must constantly return to Steps 2 and 3 to determine the state of the environment and the critical issues for the company. Consumers have many places to spend or save their money. The retailer must be very careful to create a business that will appeal to consumers and encourage them to spend money buying merchandise and services.

Retail Mix

At an operational level, the retailer must develop a **retail mix**, by integrating several facets of the retail business. The retail mix is a series of stimulus **cues**, both visual and mental, that the consumer uses to identify the retailer. This set of cues in the minds of the consumers becomes the image. This **image** is the store image for a brick-and-mortar store. A catalog company or a company that exists only on the Internet also has an image. For companies with a presence in more than one area, the image becomes a conglomeration of all the sources of cues. The cues received from a catalog will blend in the consumer's mind with the clues received from the brick-and-mortar store. The image is the character, personality, or mental impression the company presents to the consumer. Image is how the customer identifies with and differentiates among companies.

Whatever cues are offered, they must blend to make a cohesive image. This image must be appealing to the target customer and must be different from the competition. Prior to patronizing a retail business, the consumer will have expectations based upon experiences with and promotional information from the retail business. Word-of-mouth from friends and family can also affect the image. Image should be a reflection of what the business represents in value, convenience, service, and citizenship in the community. The retailer tries to get the image to be a mirror of the merchandising philosophy or vision that is determined in strategic planning. An image must be distinct, clear, and consistent for the business to be differentiated from other retail establishments. The image of a business becomes a major tool in attracting and sustaining a particular consumer, for selecting a location or designing a Web site, and for hiring and training personnel. Image, or retail mix, is composed of levels of the following cues: history, retail type, environment, merchandise policy, fashion level, pricing strategy, services available, and promotional directive. This combination of cues is illustrated in Figure 5.1.

History

The **history** of a retail business includes the philosophy of the founders and the period of time in which the business originated. The original vision of the founders may permeate the policies and procedures of every function of the business. Decisions made during tough economic times or times of economic growth may remain with the company after the environment changes. In addition, the longevity of the business affects

Figure 5.1

Image Cues
in Relationship
to Retail Image.

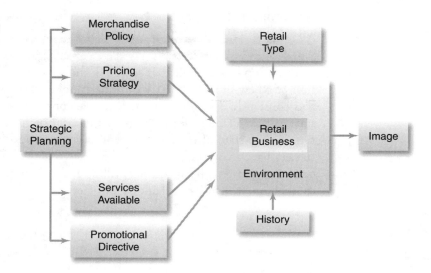

consumer perception. The adult consumer, who as a child accompanied a parent or grandparent to a specific regional retailer, may have developed a loyalty to that retailer. Current expectations are affected both positively and negatively by experiences. Viewing an extravagant Christmas display as a child may create pleasant memories and positive feelings about a retail business even though the company is no longer maintaining the promotional events. Businesses are also associated with certain geographic regions or cities and may be assumed by consumers to project the images of those places even though the retailer does not supply the products that fit the image. Loyalty of a customer can be very powerful and long lasting, which is an asset for a retailer; however, dislike of a business is also powerful, can be based on a fleeting experience or inexact memory, and can continue regardless of change or retribution by the retailer.

Images must be carefully crafted and formulated to make the business unique among other retail establishments. Ownerships of retail businesses often change, and images can remain intact even with organizational change. A retailer with a strong and positive image may keep the name, signage, and other image cues even when the business is purchased and owned by other management. Large corporations often own multiple, separate retail businesses. The corporate name may not be known to or acknowledged by the consumer at the local level. In fact, some corporations have multiple units within a region or within a mall, each unit with a unique image, differential customer base, and individual product assortment. If the images are maintained, even a retail business with a strong image can own other businesses with equally strong but unaltered images. If retail cues are allowed to change and no longer support the image, even the most loyal customers may question the new direction of their favorite retail establishment. This occurrence is definitely a negative process for the retailer. A retail image is more difficult to change than establishing the image initially.

Retail Type

The most common types of retail businesses, as noted in Chapter 1, are mass merchandisers, department stores, specialty or limited line retailers, mail order or catalog businesses, and discounters. These businesses exist as brick-and-mortar operations but may have catalogs or Web sites in addition to the stores. Catalog only retailers or Web only retailers are also selling apparel to consumers. Retail type refers to broad categories of retail businesses, each with a variety of subtypes within the categories. The consumer has preconceived ideas or images of each retail type and associates this image with the individual retail businesses that fall within a retail type. Based on their pre-formed images of businesses within a retail type, consumers think they know what is offered by a specialty or department store or a discount store in terms of product categories, quality, price, services, and promotional events. For example, the consumer expects the specialty department store to provide fashion forward merchandise with excellent service. To achieve this image, this retail type would have high quality merchandise that changes often and is displayed in an environment of elegance and luxury. The consumer may find the presence of a grand piano in a marble-floored atrium, combined with personal sales attention and fashion forward merchandise. The consumer would not be surprised to find high prices. The entire set of cues is very clearly related to the vision that a consumer would have of this retail type.

Another retail type that already has a distinct image in the consumer's mind is the large discounter. Its image is different from the specialty retailers but equally strong. The discounters combine a wide variety of merchandise, low prices, national brands, and easy inside-the-store access with limited numbers of sales personnel. These retail businesses appeal to a wide range of customers who are interested in obtaining value merchandise at a reasonable price with limited shopping efforts. The consumer expects convenience, savings, and one-stop shopping when entering a large discount store. Both of the previously described retail types have been very successful in developing and maintaining their associated images.

Retail types that have blurred images experience difficulty in maintaining their customer base. Cues offered to the consumer must make a cohesive image. When an individual retail business or a large corporate chain within a retail type has cues that vary from the set type image, the consumer is confused and often angered. For example, a consumer will be very disappointed when the knit shirt that was purchased at a specialty department store shrinks when washed for the first time. The image of the specialty department store is that the merchandise will be of excellent quality. A consumer will say, "For the price I paid for this shirt, I didn't expect it to shrink!" If these experiences happen too often, the consumer may readjust the image that is held not only for the individual store, but also for the entire retail type. In this manner, failure of a major retail business within a retail type may contaminate the image of all businesses within that retail type.

Environment

The **environment** cue for image refers to the physical attributes of the store, catalog, Web site, or other visual representation of the business. In the traditional brick-and-mortar store, the environment is the physical appearance of the store. For the physical store, many components can be controlled or manipulated to support the vision statement and the chosen strategy. Some of the subcues for environment include the following: geographic location, type of surrounding retail center, exterior environment near the center, and the store's exterior appearance and interior décor. Geographic location of the retail store can be explored with several questions. What major traffic arteries provide access to the area? Are the traffic patterns safe and easy to maneuver, or is the traffic heavy at peak shopping periods? Does the store have good visibility from major roads or main aisles within the center? Is the store or the center a **destination shopping** point, one to which consumers travel specifically for shopping? These subcues can be combined to determine the **convenience** or the time, place, and effort required for shopping at a store, with a catalog, or on a Web site. For store retailing, convenience also includes hours of operation, size of parking lots, width of aisles, and proximity to retailers. For nonstore retailing, convenience may include toll-free numbers, knowledgeable and ready sales associates, easy return policies, and free shipping.

The retail center in which the store-based business is located sets the first ambiance for the store. The appearance of a retail center is not only the physical look of the structure, but also the other retailers in the center. The **tenant mix** of the center is a description of the other retail stores within the center. These are the neighbors of the retail store and are comparable to the ads, link buttons, and pop-up menus that appear when opening a home page of an Internet retail site. When brick-and-mortar retail centers are developed, stores with complimentary product offerings are sought as tenants. These stores will provide consumers with a range of products for selection. In addition, several stores that offer products that are shopped through an extensive comparison process (e.g., shoes, automobiles, and tools) may be located together in one retail center, giving the consumer the opportunity to comparison shop in one location. Anchor stores may be situated first in mall development, and then small stores are filled between the anchors. As retail centers age and businesses close and are replaced, the tenant mix may become diverse and without focus. This arrangement lacks an attractive image and is not pleasing to most consumers. Without a focused image and a limited customer base, the businesses in this type of center will not be profitable.

The **exterior appearance** of a retail center or an individual store space is an important aspect of the environment and includes signage, façade color and building materials, awnings and banners, and landscaping. Exterior appearance for a store is similar to the look of the home page for a Web site or the front cover of a catalog for mail order retailing. The type of building materials, their color, and cleanliness provide cues to the consumer and create expectations as to the products, price, and services. For example, a stucco façade painted a muddy brown suggests to a consumer that the store would house product offerings from the U.S. southwest or from Mexico. Consumers use stereotypes to interpret what they see in store exteriors. Experience has shown many shoppers that stereotypes may be misleading, but few shoppers are willing to risk an unwelcome surprise. The exterior décor and entrance of the store, similar to that of a Web home page or front page of a catalog, should make a shopper feel welcome.

The signage is an important aspect of the exterior décor of the brick-and-mortar store. **Signage** includes the signs at the roadside or drive entrance; signs, lettering, or name plates on the store fronts; and the lettering or other written information on the windows and front doors. These items set the mood and imply the type of store including the products that the store will carry. Selecting the style, type, colors, and materials used in signage lettering is important and should be planned in conjunction with the strategy and action plans of the business.

The **entrance of the store** or the front door, entryway, or other places where the consumer first enters the individual store should be obvious immediately to the consumer and consistent with the store image. Retailers frequently use storefront banners and awnings to identify storewide events, to establish a theme for a special event, or to tie the store to the community. Banners are also used on catalog front pages and Web pages. In addition to adding eye appeal, awnings are functional coverings to protect the consumer from the weather elements and to prevent glare on store window displays. Exterior lighting should be attention getting or dramatic. These subcues at the entrance should provide immediate visual cues to denote the personality and character of the store interior. The customer should be instantly enticed to come into the store, browse, be engaged with the merchandise, and purchase.

Upon entering the store, the **interior décor** of the store should appeal to four of the five senses of the shopper: sight, smell, hearing, and touch. Interior décor includes lighting; smells and aromas; basic walls, floors, and fixtures; and merchandise displays. Interior lighting should accentuate the merchandise presentation by calling attention to both the color and styling details of the merchandise. The type and range of audibility of any music should also support the image of the store, help to establish the desired atmosphere or mood of the store, and be consistent with the listening habits of the target customer. The smell or aroma at the store entrance should be planned carefully because the olfactory sense is known to have a great impact on customers' emotions and buying habits. Scents such as potpourri or pine can be introduced into the store to create a certain illusion, or the scent of the product itself can create an atmosphere that is conducive to buying. For example, the smell of freshly baked bread in a bakery, the scent of popcorn in a movie theater, or the odor of new leather products in an accessories department may induce the consumer to linger longer than expected, to make a purchase, or to purchase more than initially planned. Various consumer groups react differently to scents. The retailer should research the scents that are proposed, investigate consumer reaction, and carefully moderate the level and type of scents within the store. Personal preference of a store manager is not a sufficient reason to select olfactory or auditory cues for a store.

In addition to sight, sound, and smell, the consumer reacts automatically to the tactile component of the interior décor, as well as to the merchandise itself. Wall coverings, carpet or flooring, furniture, and fixtures have textures as well as meaning to the consumer. The store interior should be themed to fit with the store's vision and strategic plan and be appealing to the target consumer. The interior décor becomes a subtle backdrop to the merchandise presentation and contributes to the atmosphere or ambience of the décor.

Merchandise presentation is the visual organization and storage of merchandise in a manner conducive to sustained and productive consumer shopping. The items that compose the interior décor should support a concise and clear store image. For example, fixtures that are pipe racks or other types of metal tubing symbolize a store that carries low priced and often, low quality merchandise. On the other hand, wooden shelves, stands with wooden bases, or ornately carved racks signify high quality merchandise and a high level of service to most consumers. Creating an effective merchandise presentation to attract the desired target consumer is crucial to a retailer's success. Fashion forward or trendy merchandise classifications require vibrant, innovative presentations. The retailer must balance decisions of cost and functionality with application to image. In addition, retailers, while creating an exciting and enticing image, must remember that merchandise must be safely housed and floor space must be maximized to build optimum sales. (Additional information on merchandise presentation is provided in Chapter 16.)

The retailer may or may not have control over the exterior or interior décor of the building. In large retail centers, landlords and major or anchor tenants may have control of the visual aspects of the building and the surrounding spaces. In addition, some decisions on environment are made at corporate offices to maintain a consistent and recognizable image across geographic differences. Some large corporations maintain a real estate department that functions to determine all sites, signage, and building specifications. Age of the building, trends in store or retail center planning, and local or regional ordinances may prohibit or restrict the retailer from executing the desired décor or signage. In historic districts, exclusive vacation areas, or other environmentally conscious neighborhoods, exterior décor may be highly regulated. Size and types of signs, colors of exterior walls or façade, and renovations within the interior could be restricted by local governments.

Merchandise Policy

From the entrance and general impressions of the interior décor, the consumer will move to the merchandise. **Merchandise policy** is a long-range plan to guide decisions about the retail or vendor matrix, the merchandise assortment, standards for quality, the use of brands, the fashion level of the products, and the merchandise presentation. The merchandising policy is so important to many functions of the retail organization that it is often part of the vision statement or strategy plan of the business. A clear and concise policy is needed and must be communicated to all personnel at all levels of the organization.

Merchandise assortment describes the total mix of merchandise that is carried by the retailer. Assortment descriptions or characteristics include the product classifications that are carried, the breadth and depth of the assortment, the quality standards, the array of brands, the fashion level of the merchandise, and the vendor matrix used to supply these products.

First, the retailer must determine which product classifications will be carried. **Product classifications** are broad categories or groupings of merchandise (e.g., sportswear, outerwear, and dresses). (Extensive explanation of product classifications is given in Chapter 10.) The retailer must select classifications of merchandise that fit with the vision and strategic plan and are preferred by the target consumer. Retailers select to specialize in some product classifications for a variety of reasons—personal preference, past experience, vendor relations, or history. Due to limited space, direction of merchandise policy, or lack of merchandise presentation tools, the retailer may omit certain product classifications in the assortment mix. For example, some specialty shops do not carry outerwear, even though their customers buy outerwear, because coats are bulky items and require much more square footage and length of racks for display space than is required by sportswear, tops, or dresses. Many department stores have stopped carrying furniture because of the space required to carry a wide enough assortment to make shopping interesting for consumers. Other retailers opt not to carry intimate apparel, shoes, or accessories due to the lack of expertise in selling the product. In addition, selection of product could be limited because vendors require the purchase of too many units in order to purchase the items relative to the retailer's need.

Merchandise breadth and depth explain the number of classifications of goods and the number of items that are carried by one retailer. In general, the retailer must decide whether the merchandise will be **broad and shallow** with a wide array of product classifications represented among the merchandise but few items within each class, or **narrow and deep** with few classifications but many items within each class. Every business, even a large business, has a finite amount of space for holding and displaying inventory. Catalog companies and Web-based firms have the advantage that they can display goods that they may not have in inventory because they will expect the manufacturer to ship directly to the customer. With the explosion of products available in the market and the almost infinite number of vendors from which to source, the retailer must pick and choose which items are to be displayed in the store or on the pages of a catalog or Web site.

Standards to evaluate the quality of the merchandise must be established relative to the expectations of the target consumer. A **quality product** is one that meets the expectations of the consumer, whether that is for ten years of wear and comfort in a pair of blue jeans or four hours of wear and fashion forward styling for a bridal dress. For the retailer, standards of quality may include construction details, selection of fabrication or other raw materials, and other physical evidence of the formation and durability of the product. The retailer must remember that quality is often perceived very differently by the consumer. For consumers, quality is evaluated by characteristics that they can observe such as price, brands, fiber content, designer labels, style, and other aesthetic cues. Characteristics such as price and brand are often not directly related to quality but are used as cues by consumers. For sustainability of repeat business, quality may also be associated with the dependability of the items. The retailer would need to understand the expected function of the item and its potential for durability. This characteristic might be especially important for some products. For example, mothers may purchase pants for small children and expect the items to last, without having the knees fray, until the child has outgrown the pants. The purchasers of tent equipment, backpacks, and other canvas items expect the items to continue to shed water and protect people and possessions for an extended time. When items have a high initial cost, the expectations of durability rise.

The choice of brand is another decision that the retailer must evaluate and control. **Brand** refers to a name of the product, which often is a company name that identifies the product in the mind of the consumer. A brand is developed and strengthened through advertising, labels, packaging, and other marketing techniques. A **brand policy** is needed that keeps the merchandise assortment in line with the vision and strategy. The choices for brand include national, international, or global brands; designer labels; private, house, or store brands; and unbranded merchandise. Merchandise carrying designer labels, or global, international, or national brands are often called **brand named goods**. The retailer must determine the mix ratio of known brands to brands that will be unfamiliar to the consumer. National, international, or global brands carry their own image due to extensive advertising generated by the manufacturer and their associated retailers. Consumers expect certain characteristics from these brands, including price, fit, and dependability. For example, when making a tool purchase, the consumer may select a national brand and assume that the tool will maintain the desired level of quality. Many national brands have money-back guarantees that help persuade the consumer to trust this brand. Many consumers base their purchase decisions on brand name alone and are willing to pay more money for these brands. The retailer may also pay a premium for the privilege of carrying these branded merchandise items in the merchandise assortment.

Retailers may develop a **private label** or brands that carry a name unique to the business to be competitive with the major brands. These brands are also called house brands or store brands, especially when they carry the name of the business as the brand name. These private brands can provide better quality merchandise at lower price points and can fill voids in a merchandise mix by offering style characteristics and fabric selections in specific merchandise categories not available from branded vendors. Retailers usually have more control over the manufacturing of this private label merchandise; therefore, the retailers have more control over markdowns and inventory levels and can adjust wholesale prices to take higher markups on the product. For these reasons, private label goods provide better margins, higher profits, and a higher return on investments than brand named goods. Private label merchandise typically comprises 10% to 18% of the total merchandise assortment for retailers who carry private label goods. In some merchandise categories, especially in basic goods, the retailer with a private label may carry as much as 25% of the mix in private label goods. Small-sized retail businesses may not have the financial or personnel resources needed to develop and secure private label merchandise; therefore, they will select merchandise with a vendor's name or names that the vendor created but did not nationally market.

Fashion Level

When establishing the merchandise policy, the fashion level of the merchandise is an important aspect to be considered. **Fashion level** is the degree of newness and differentiation that is intrinsic in a product. Fashion level when applied to the product becomes an explanation of the fashion product life cycle and when combined with the merchandising process is called the **buying–selling curve**. (See Figure 5.2.)

Fashion level varies along a continuum from high fashion and fashion forward items to basic goods. For example, high fashion items are trendy, new, and different

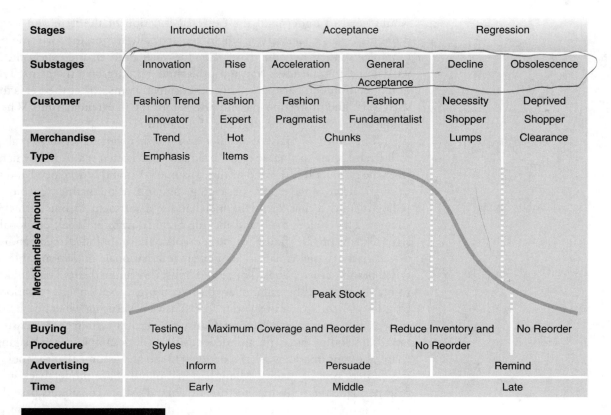

Stages	Introduction		Acceptance		Regression	
Substages	Innovation	Rise	Acceleration	General Acceptance	Decline	Obsolescence
Customer	Fashion Trend Innovator	Fashion Expert	Fashion Pragmatist	Fashion Fundamentalist	Necessity Shopper	Deprived Shopper
Merchandise Type	Trend Emphasis	Hot Items	Chunks		Lumps	Clearance
Merchandise Amount				Peak Stock		
Buying Procedure	Testing Styles	Maximum Coverage and Reorder		Reduce Inventory and No Reorder		No Reorder
Advertising	Inform		Persuade		Remind	
Time	Early		Middle		Late	

Figure 5.2	Characteristics of the Buying–Selling Curve.

from current or previous merchandise; are purchased by fashion trend innovators; and are bought by the retailer in very small amounts. Fashion forward items are in the acceptance stage, are bought by fashion pragmatists, are carried by the retailer in peak amounts, and are sold by persuasive advertising. In contrast to the fashion items that rise and fall in popularity and in inventory levels, basic items are constant in characteristics and are always desired at some standard level by the consumer. The retailer must know and understand the fashion level that is desired by the customers. The fashion level that is desirable to a customer will often change by the customer as well as the season and the time within the selling season. In addition, some customers always want fashion forward goods, and other customers are satisfied with fashion basics or fashion after it is tested and accepted by the fashion forward customers. The retailer can study fashion theory to know more about the characteristic of fashion level.

With the buying–selling curve information, the retailer can describe the direction and speed of fashion at various stages in the merchandise process and make decisions related to the fashion level and timing of the merchandise assortment. For example, in the early stages of the curve, or the introduction stage including innovation and rise phases of a product or season, the retailer will have consumers who are interested in purchasing innovative, designer, or trendy products that are offered in limited quantities. These consumers are willing to pay full price and expect to receive maximum service in the purchase of Product A. Other consumers will wait until Product A is still new but proven as a desirable product by peer acceptance of the product and compatibility of the product with their present clothing wardrobe. These consumers buy during the acceleration phase of the acceptance stage. These consumers expect to find **complete assortments**, in other words, the store fully stocked with these desirable products. Consumers who buy Product A in the general acceptance phase of the buying–selling curve make purchases based on product durability, practicality, and price. Meanwhile, the consumers who bought Product A are now interested in Product B, which is the next new, innovative, and trendy product.

In this manner, the fashion level of a retailer's merchandise assortment plays an important role in establishing the image of the retail business. The fashion level reflects the degree of fashion leadership that the retailer wishes to have the business project and the stage of the fashion product life cycle that its assortments should represent. A retailer who selects products to sell primarily in the rise phase will assist the business's image of being fashion forward. A retailer who carries a merchandise assortment that is primarily in general acceptance will not promote an image that is fashion forward. As with other aspects of image, the fashion level of the merchandise must be compatible with the remaining cues in the image. For example, fashion forward merchandise must be supported with a trendy environment and a history of carrying fashion goods for the image to be effective.

The **retail or vendor matrix** is a listing of vendors, manufacturers, or other suppliers who provide merchandise for the retail business. Retailers should evaluate their vendors, and develop partnerships with those vendors who supply the right product, in the right amount, at the right time, and at the right price. Using well-defined criteria, a retailer can evaluate the productivity of the vendor/retailer relationship. Some retailers choose to limit the number of vendors and do more business with fewer vendors. A new vendor is added only if an old one is removed or completely new product categories are needed and cannot be serviced through the existing vendors. Many retailers find that efficiencies, resulting in increased profit margins through better buying and lower operating expenses, can be developed by creating meaningful and proactive partnerships with a select number of vendors. Other retailers choose to use a wide variety and a changing matrix of vendors to ensure the change and interest level that they desire in the products. Regardless of the type of method utilized by a retailer for vendor selection, each vendor's product offering must be evaluated for the compatibility with the vision of the company and the planned image of the business unit.

Pricing Strategy

Another important cue when establishing a retail image is the **pricing strategy** or pricing policy of the business. Price must fit the image and can range from full price to everyday discounted prices. Pricing policies vary across retail businesses, as do the other image cues. The pricing strategy of a business is based on general strategies that are developed in the planning process. Price must be coordinated with the other cues of image and must fit the disposable income capabilities of the target consumer. For example, the mass merchandiser or discount retailer seeks a pricing strategy of low prices on average to better quality products with some name brands included in the merchandise assortment. The target customer for the mass merchandiser has come to expect better quality merchandise at the lowest price with minimal customer service. Mass merchandisers can provide this price strategy by achieving a rapid turnover of limited merchandise assortments with lower operating costs and larger sales volumes than found among department stores or specialty stores.

Any pricing strategy must cover the cost of goods sold, the overhead operating expenses, and reductions with an expected profit. The right price must attract the desired end customer, maintain customer loyalty, and provide a profit for the retailer or the shareholders. Markdowns and other retail price adjustments must also be considered when determining the pricing strategy. Markdowns become part of the image for a retail business. The size, timing, and promotion of markdowns have meaning to the consumer. Traditional modes of markdowns have conditioned the consumer to expect markdowns on certain merchandise and at certain times of the year. The type of products and the factor of fashion obsolescence can affect markdowns. For example, fashion forward items project a prestigious image and are positioned as new and trendy on the buying–selling curve. The consumer who desires this product will expect high initial prices and early and deep markdowns. In contrast, a basic product that is sold throughout the year will be expected by all consumers to have a reasonable price and rarely receive a markdown. The retailer who carries a large number of basic products would be expected to have this more conservative pricing strategy. Fashion conscious consumers would be shocked and suspicious if very trendy designer products were sold at the first of the season at very low prices. A retailer who previously had an image of being fashion forward would weaken this image if the pricing strategy did not fit with the merchandise assortment and the historical cue that consumers expect. The methods for establishing retail prices and associated pricing strategies were discussed in Chapter 2.

Services Available

Services include both the number and type of services that are available to the customers through a wide variety of activities. **Services** include the following: the assistance of sales associates and personal shoppers or wardrobing personnel; the availability of credit—both major credit cards and store credit; gift wrapping and return policies; the presence of personal amenities such as rest rooms, air-conditioning, valet parking, strollers, in-store restaurants, and shopping bags; and the convenience of toll-free numbers, customer complaint departments, email, Web sites, and package delivery. Services are expensive for the retailer but cannot be ignored when appropriate for the image.

The assistance of sales associates is directly related to the number, availability, and training of sales associates and other selling personnel. Their training can include selling techniques, positive and friendly attitudes, and product knowledge. Some selling personnel are specially trained for bridal consulting, personal shopping, and other specialty services. Selling services range from the full service of salon selling to self-service.

Salon selling is the ultimate in luxury and service for a customer. The retailer who provides salon selling has sales associates who present the merchandise to the customer while the customer relaxes on a comfortable chair in a homelike setting. Services can include drinks and hors d'oeuvres, alterations, assistance in selecting accessories, and soft lighting with multiple mirrors. With salon selling, the merchandise is often not on display; instead, a sales associate discusses the merchandise with the customer, makes suggestions for items, and brings appropriate items from the stock to show to the customer. The customer may try on the items, or a model of an appropriate size may first wear and display the items. Salon selling can include the services of a personal shopper, who becomes the customer's buyer in the market and selects new items that are known to be desired by the customer from the new merchandise available in the major markets such as from New York or Atlanta.

Self-service is at the other end of the service spectrum from salon selling. In self-service selling, all merchandise is displayed and accessible to all customers. The customer must walk along the aisles, find the needed items, and remove them from shelves before taking everything to a centralized checkout station. Self-service does promote add-on buying if the merchandise is properly displayed with compatible items placed together. The traffic patterns and shelf location can also promote additional purchases. These aspects of the self-service environment require that the promotions cues be well integrated with the services cues to evolve an effective and harmonious image. Convenience is often touted as a major aspect of self-service, but is actually a variable in all aspects of selling and includes the time, place, and effort required for a customer to complete the sale. For store retailing, convenience includes hours of operation, size of parking lots, width of aisles, and proximity to other retailers. For nonstore retailing, convenience may include toll-free numbers, easy return policies, and free shipping.

Liberal return policies and credit are designed to encourage consumers to buy more than they need with reduced risk. Consumers often want to try the merchandise and are unsure of how a spouse or friend will react. The assurance of an easy return reduces the worry about a product. Credit allows customers who may not be able to pay for items at one time to spread the payments across several months. Credit also encourages customers to buy now and pay later, which often encourages customers to buy more than they would if paying by cash or check. Air-conditioning, valet parking, strollers, and in-store restaurants encourage customers to stay longer inside the store. The longer customers stay in the store, the more likely they are to purchase merchandise. This theory also applies to Web sites. Sites that are interesting and easy to negotiate will keep a customer's attention and will increase the number of items purchased.

What is considered a desirable service for one customer may not be desired by a second customer. In addition, the services desired at one point in the buying–selling curve may not be needed or used in another point on the curve. For example, a retailer who sells fashion forward, high priced, and high quality merchandise may have a luxury interior of the store with many well-trained sales associates who spend large amounts of time attending to the customers' every need. However, twice a year, at the end of the winter and summer seasons, this retailer may place all season end merchandise on open racks, provide only a centralized checkout system, and reduce sales associate help to straightening and restocking merchandise. The customer who has enjoyed, and paid for, the luxury of salon selling may find this twice a year self-service sale a fun experience especially when the sale is accompanied with deep discounts in price. Again, the image must be developed through the coordination of cues that are appropriate for the retail business and are targeted into a focused view for the consumer.

Promotional Directive

The promotional directive for a retail business is another cue that receives direction from the strategic planning process and affects image. The **promotional directive** of the store determines the promotional mix and the marketing communications techniques used to carry the message of the mix to the consumers. The **promotional mix** encompasses advertising, sales promotions, special events, public relations, visual merchandising, and personal selling. The **marketing communications techniques** used to communicate this mix include the media utilized, the amount and type of communication, and the content and believability of the communications. In the past, retailers have advertised in local newspapers and on local radio or television stations to promote their businesses, but today's consumers use and peruse a wide variety of other media. Direct mail, catalogs, national and international magazines, cable television stations, and Web sites are used as media to promote a retail business. Advertising may consist of communications that promote the store or the merchandise.

In addition, advertising may cover sales promotions that highlight discounted prices. Sales promotions may also include gifts with purchases (GWP), purchase with a purchase (PWP), or point-of-sale or point-of purchase (POS/POP) rebates. All of the sales promotions are intended to highlight specific merchandise and to promote increased sales of this merchandise and associated merchandise. The PWP promotions of buy one item and get the second item at a reduced price encourages the customer to buy two items when one item was probably the intended purchase.

The GWP purchases are often used with items that have high markups such as cosmetics and promote the sale of expensive and new items. Requiring the customer to purchase a high minimum dollar amount to receive the gift promotes volume buying among customers.

Special events create excitement and change for a business to make that business unique in a competitive market. For fashion retailers, excitement can come from a constant flow of new merchandise. Each time the customer enters the store the merchandise that is viewed would be new and appealing. Many customers shop regularly in stores and examine catalogs or Web sites frequently. The appearance of new merchandise will quickly be noted by these customers. Both the fashion retailer and the nonfashion retailer may use entertainment for excitement. Entertainment within special events can be trunk shows, fashion shows, videos, and designer appearances. For the nonfashion retailer, entertainment may include lectures by noted personalities, music, and sports activities or rides. Celebrity endorsements and appearances are used to create excitement for consumers. The endorsements may be for specific products or for entire lines of merchandise. Malls and the surrounding retail environment for the retail business may also contribute to special events. The carousel is a ride that has often been placed in many malls to bring entertainment. Hockey rinks and swimming pools are used in some malls to bring excitement and to attract new customers. As consumers change in their preferences for merchandise and environments, retailers must constantly seek new events to be special or noteworthy.

Public relations or the store's community involvement also plays an important part in building an image. Involvement in charitable benefits, sporting events, artistic endeavors, or community self-help programs signifies to the consumer that the retail business is a good citizen in the community. The retailer must choose publicity and public relations events carefully. Community involvement must be matched to other cues in the image, and the retailer must support events or programs that target consumers deem worthy and important to their concerns within the community. Public relations money spent on events that are socially unacceptable for a specific consumer or are offensive in their presentation to the consumer can result in controversy and loss of sales.

Image pulls all the stimulus cues together under one label. This label must be clear and easy to define. Image for a retail business can often be summarized in one word or one phrase. For example, the image of a specialty department store is service. These stores have high quality merchandise with maximum service in luxurious surroundings. The presence of a grand piano and pianist in the store is combined with fashion forward merchandise and personal sales attention. The merchandise and service is offered at a high price point. The entire set of stimulus cues is very clearly related in the vision of this store type and is clearly identified by the consumer. The target customer for a specialty department store is a consumer who is interested in high fashion, expects good quality service, and has the income to afford the prices. On the other end of the service spectrum are the big discount stores. They too have developed a different and unique image. These discount stores combine a wide variety of merchandise, low prices, branded merchandise, and easy access to target any consumer who is interested in obtaining value merchandise at a reasonable price. The major discount store customer is looking for convenience, one-stop shopping, and savings. Both retailers have been very successful in developing and maintaining their image.

An image is an expensive component to develop and must be maintained diligently. The components of the image do have costs associated with them. The presence of trained sales staff, the constant movement of merchandise, a liberal return policy, and a wide breadth of merchandise would have associated costs much higher than self-service, static merchandise, no returns, and narrow merchandise selection.

The pricing of the merchandise and the allocation of operating expenses must be carefully planned to accommodate these costs. To ignore an image can be a disaster for a retailer. Consumers can be confused by changes or conflicts in image, and, if confused, they often seek other retail options. If the image is mixed, the retailer lacks strength and fails to maintain identity in the mind of the target customer.

All functions of a retail business must acknowledge and adhere to the image. For example, billing procedures seem to be a separate function that might be isolated from image, but the retailer must remember that when the charge card bill is received by the consumer in the mail that bill is an emissary of the retailer. The charge card bills for a specialty department store must maintain the same image of quality and service as the store.

In summary, an image must be a cohesive set of cues that are focused to create a picture in the minds of the target consumers. From the strategic plan, the retailer must create a merchandising policy, select a pricing strategy, and determine the services available and the promotional direction that are appropriate for the retail type and for the history and environment in which the retail business operates. These cues must be coordinated with the retailer's knowledge of the target consumer, competition, and the broad retail market. These cues must be consistent and viable to create an image that will differentiate the retail business from the competition and appeal to a broad base of target consumers. Creating profit and maintaining consumer satisfaction are the intended goals of a well-crafted image.

Target Consumer

Strategic planning emphasizes the need to understand both the company and the market and to make a match between the two environments; therefore, understanding the company's customer is an important support process to strategic planning. For a strategic plan to be successful, a match between company and customer is necessary. As explored in Chapter 1, marketing is getting the right product at the right market configuration for the right customer. That "right customer" is the **target customer** or, as known in retail, the **target consumer**. The target consumers are the customers of the retailer. They are the group to which the company image will appeal. Retailers, the media, and especially marketing groups utilize information about target consumers to understand how consumers think, what will appeal to the consumer, how they can motivate these consumers, and what will stimulate the buying behavior or purchase decisions of the consumers.

A set of customers may represent a large undifferentiated market to which is sold an undifferentiated product, or they may represent one narrowly focused segment or **niche market** to which a specialized product is offered. The undifferentiated market is also called a **mass market**. The same product is sold to all customers within the market. Major discount stores sell many products that are appealing to the mass market, meaning that most customers within a market area would be interested in shopping in that store and would be interested in purchasing those products. Basic goods such as white athletic socks or women's pantyhose are products that are appealing to and worn by many consumers. Specialty stores appeal to a narrower segment within the broader market. They sell items that have distinct features that may appeal to a select set of customers. Customers of a certain age group or activity group may find these items appealing. These items generally sell at higher price points than undifferentiated products, further restricting the market appeal of the product.

In between the two extremes of mass market and niche market is the segmented market approach. In the **segmented market**, the market is considered heterogeneous with multiple segments. The same product is sold within each segment, but the product must be differentiated for each segment. Differentiation can be achieved with actual change in product features, especially color. However, differentiation is often achieved through advertising and promotions with different appeals made to each market segment. With a competitive market, few goods can survive as undifferentiated products. Even mass merchandisers have adopted celebrity spokespersons and developed brands to compete with the niche products of specialty stores. With target marketing, the company targets the customer and aligns the product with that target customer. This technique of determining the right product and the right promotion for the right customer is called **product positioning**. The product is positioned to be right for the customer.

When trying to understand and quantify the characteristics of a population, the retailer should look for trends or long-term changes in the population's characteristics. The process of product positioning is costly in both time and money. The retailer will not want to change strategies for very short-term events but should focus more on long-term changes when doing strategic planning. Trends do exist within the U.S. population and across the world's population. For example, the population in the United States and in the world is aging. More people are living longer, and large generations of people are entering middle age. In turn, the birth rate has slowed or stagnated in many countries. Other trends, such as shifts in size and proportion of ethnic populations, are occurring. The retailer should take advantage of the many sources of information about consumers and populations such as the information provided by the U.S. Census Bureau. (Additional information about trends is presented in Chapter 9.)

Many ways exist to segment a market. Traditional segmentation methods use **demographics** or basic data about a population's personal characteristics. Demographics include data about age, income, gender, occupation, educational level, and place of residence. The merchandise categories of women's wear, men's wear, and children's wear indicate the use of gender as a market segmentation tool. Age is often used within children's wear to determine style, sizing, and product categories. Income has traditionally been used to segment customers into groups that are willing to pay higher prices for better quality goods; however, customers at all income levels are now demanding quality products at reasonable prices—the strategy of many large discount retailers.

Demographics may not be adequate for the modern consumer. For example, many consumers who are old by age are not "old" in their fashion interest. They may be traveling or active with many social events and desire new, updated apparel items. In addition, a market separation based on gender may be unreliable. Men and women are often interested in many similar activities, topics, and items. For example, both men and women can have an interest in sports whether as a spectator or participant. Also, income is not always an indicator of interest in spending on fashion forward items. Some population groups are more interested in fashion forward goods than other population groups and are willing to spend increased percentages of their income on these items.

To avoid some of these categorical inadequacies, today's marketers use a variety of additional segmentation tools. **Lifestyle** segmentation represents a combination of age, income, occupation, and leisure-time interests. This segmentation method is used by marketers and retailers who are trying to reach specialty markets with sports-related products or cruise wear. Lifestyle segmentation has been used successfully with a variety of products including sports drinks, automobiles, and health care products.

This segmentation method can be used to present a group of products that traditionally were considered as unrelated products. For example, a picnic basket, fine glassware, and sportswear with collegiate emblems can be grouped together for a display that shows items sold for football game tailgating parties. These products may be simultaneously displayed in a store display or on a Web site to stimulate further purchasing among the target consumer group.

Psychographics, the personal interests and attitudes about activities and issues within society, is a segmentation tool used when retailers are trying to define a narrow segment for a specialized product. This segmentation method may be used to identify and reach consumers who have high levels of interest in a variety of social or political issues. The issues of social conservancy, sustainable resources, and environmental consciousness are concerns that can be addressed through psychographic profiling of consumers. Companies that produce products that are environmentally friendly such as beauty products that are not tested on animals or shirts made of organically grown cotton may find that the traditional segments of age or income are not applicable as identifiers for potential consumers. Instead political awareness, concern for the environment, membership in specific organizations, and other measures of attitude and actions are more appropriate methods of segmenting the population.

Age and stage or **generational segmentation** is also used by marketers to identify market segments. This segmentation method combines the age with the life-cycle stage of the same consumer. For example, consumers who are first-time parents have more shopping needs in common with each other than with consumers of the same age who are single or have no children. Parents tend to spend money on products for their children before spending for products for themselves. Adults without children tend to buy products for themselves with the majority of their spending. Various segmentation sets are used for this method, which often result in segments with labels that represent the generation or the stage. For example, the GI generation is used for the elderly consumer who is old enough to have served in World War II or DINKS is the acronym used for two-income couples with no children.

Target Marketing

The process of understanding the company's abilities and the customers characteristics and wants is a continuous process. The strategic marketing process is a continuous loop of targeting, action, evaluation, and readjustment of the target or the product. **Target marketing** is a specialized form of strategic planning that includes the steps of (a) development of company objectives in line with the vision, (b) environmental scan of the market, (c) identification of market opportunities, (d) characterization of specific target markets, (e) selection of markets and market approach, (f) implementation with product positioning, and (g) evaluation with control and repositioning. Environmental scans, as described in the next chapter, and company audits are necessary to keep the company vision and operations and the needs and wants of the target customer aligned. To instigate a target marketing process for a company, the retailer needs information about the consumer and the markets. Communication between the trading partners in the pipeline becomes very important in a competitive market. Focus groups, surveys, merchandise returns, credit card purchases, and cash register sales are all important sources of information about the target customer, and the Internet poses a new and exciting way for companies to talk to their target customers.

Summary

Strategic planning can assist the company in analyzing both the company and product and the target customer. Positioning products to the target customer is a continuous process. The final stages of strategic planning direct the planners to evaluate the results of the implementation and to make adjustments for future directions of the company. A company can choose among several market approaches to target the customer, but with any approach, the efforts must be focused and well planned. The company must also consider its financial position and the costs associated with reaching the target customer.

Key Terms

Action plan	Image	Promotional mix
Age and stage	Implementation	Psychographics
Brand	Interior décor	Quality product
Brand named goods	Lifestyle	Recommendations
Brand policy	Marketing communications	Retail mix
Broad and shallow	techniques	Retail matrix
Buying–selling curve	Mass market	Retail type
Complete assortment	Merchandise assortment	Salon selling
Convenience	Merchandise breadth and depth	Segmented market
Critical issues	Merchandise policy	Self-service
Cues	Merchandise presentation	Services
Demographics	Merchandising philosophy	Signage
Destination shopping	Narrow and deep	Special events
Downsizing	Niche market	Specific strategy
Entrance of the store	Overstoring	Strategic planning
Environment	Planners	Target consumer
Environmental scan	Pricing strategy	Target customer
Evaluation	Private label	Target marketing
Exterior appearance	Problem selection	Tenant mix
Fashion level	Product classifications	Vendor matrix
Generational segmentation	Product positioning	Vision statement
History	Promotional directive	

Discussion Questions

1. What is strategic planning?
2. Why do companies in a competitive environment need strategic planning?
3. How does a company develop an image?
4. What cues would a company need to develop an image of value pricing?
5. What can a catalog company do to create an image?
6. What are the costs and benefits of creating excitement and change in a store?
7. What are the characteristics of a mass market?
8. Describe a product that might be differentiated and sold in several markets.
9. If a company is changing a product, how can target marketing be used to guide the product development decisions?
10. When a retailer tries to target two market segments with the same marketing messages or merchandise mix, what are the potential problems that may be encountered?

Exercises

1. Identify four major retail firms. Read financial statements or stock reports for each company, and state their vision statements. Identify their current strategy or slogan.

2. Select a general external market condition that is being discussed in current economic news, and determine what strategy a retailer might choose to address this environmental condition.

3. Identify a slogan used by a current retailer, and itemize an action plan that would be needed by the merchandise function to implement that strategy.

4. Observe the print ads of several major discount firms, and determine what strategies those ads support.

5. Select a retailer, who has announced a recent change in strategy, and determine what measures would be needed to evaluate the success of that strategy.

6. Using Figure 5.1, identify a successful current retail business, and define the cues for that business.

7. Using Figure 5.1, identify a current retail business that is experiencing loss of sales. Define the cues for that business. Identify the cues that are not cohesive for that business.

8. Identify a retail business that was successful in the past 100 years but is no longer in operation. Using Figure 5.1, determine which cues were not maintained or were not changed to meet changing consumer demands.

9. Select an international retail business, and determine how the image cues change for the business depending on the country of operation.

10. Select an established retail business, and determine what is the market segmentation for that business and how the target consumer is identified for that business.

*P*lanning Sales

*O*bjectives

After completing this chapter, the student will be able to

- perform an environmental scan
- plan sales for a continuing business
- calculate sales for a continuing business
- plan sales for a new business
- calculate sales for a new business

Planned sales are the basis for estimating many of the components in a Profit and Loss statement. Sales projections also become the foundation for planning stock needs for the store and are the beginning quantitative analysis for a buying plan. The sales plan must estimate at a macrolevel the number of customers and the purchases for each consumer. Throughout the year, planned sales also provide guidance for sales goals for staff and other benchmarks for the store's activities.

The document used to define planned sales is called a **sales plan**. Sales plans can be divided into planning periods: one year, six months, one quarter, or one season. The period for sales plans should correspond to periods used for other plans, such as strategic plans, buying schedules/plans, or planned promotions. A sales plan covering a six-month period would allow for the development of a six-month promotion plan.

The sales plan may be developed by a variety of people depending on the store structure. The small store may be owner operated with sales planned by the owner. In large stores and chain stores, the sales plan may be made by top-down planning, by a team, or by one person from the reports of many separate people. In top-down planning by upper administration, a sales goal would be provided to the buyer after the plan is developed. The buyer would then know how many sales are expected from the merchandise that he/she will plan to purchase. In the team planning method and in the compilation method, the buyer may be asked to participate in planning sales because he/she will have information about past sales, upcoming new merchandise, and consumer trends that can be used to help establish a sales plan. Store managers and department managers may also be asked to contribute information about their local situations. Many companies have recognized the importance of team planning and are using this method. Computer networks and real-time communication allow teams to operate even when team members are not geographically close.

An estimation of sales must be optimistic to provide incentive for growth and ample coverage of expenses; however, the plans must be realistic and, at times, conservative to ensure complete sell-through and appropriate turnover of inventory. If sales plans are overestimated, stock purchases can result in stockpiled inventory, which can result in an **overbought** situation for the buyer. An overbought situation exists when the buyer has too much inventory in relation to the planned levels. Unfortunately, for the buyer, excess inventory cannot be returned to the vendor, and this excess prevents the buyer from purchasing new inventory. This excess inventory as well as old inventory can result in a loss of fashion freshness for the merchandise and the store. Stores that sell fashion goods must constantly be aware of fashion trends and have new stock to reflect the consumer's interest. Increased stock caused by an overestimation of sales can also cause operating expenses to rise. If the sales plans are not met, cash may not be available to meet financial obligations, and money must be borrowed to pay the bills. Increased stock can also cause a need for more storage and a rise in taxes or insurance.

Underestimation of sales and decreased stock also has a negative impact on the store. Low sales estimates can result in too few sales associates being assigned to the store, an understocked store with an empty look and stock outs in some merchandise, and, finally, lost sales. An accurate sales projection is critical to the store's survival. The development of such a sales plan starts with a scan of the environment and can be calculated for either a continuing business or a new business.

Environmental Scanning

Appropriate and accurate information make an accurate sales plan possible. Regardless of who develops the sales plan, information must be collected to provide a realistic basis. Chapter 5 described the strategic planning process, and one of the first steps in this process is **environmental scanning**, observing characteristics and trends in the marketplace. Knowledge of what is happening in the world, the country, and the region must be known to aid in the competitive survival of a company. Companies do not exist in a vacuum but must operate within a marketplace that is constantly changing. That marketplace becomes the company's environment and may be as large as the globe or as small as the local community. Personnel at all levels of the company should be aware of events and conditions that can change the sales potential for a company.

As more large companies use team planning, personnel at the store level will be asked to supply information for the environmental scan. In large companies, team members located in the corporate headquarters will interact with personnel in stores throughout the region and, perhaps, the world to scan the economic environment, consider annual promotional events, and review weather forecasts for trends and events that may impact the store, the customers, and the potential sales.

The retail business operates in an **economic environment**, which occurs at the local, regional, state, national, and global levels. The economic environment may be positive or negative depending on business growth, employment levels, and other economic indicators within the realm of the business. Changes in the economic environment that should be considered in the sales plan include projected growths or reductions in employment rates; mergers, openings, or closings of competitors; rates for money lending; and general business trends.

General economic trends (e.g., employment, consumer price indexes, industrial price indexes, and interest rates) are also important items that should be considered. Industrial price indexes give information about available supply and costs of raw materials such as cotton, wool, and petroleum needed to produce the products that are ultimately purchased by the retailer.

Many sources can be used to obtain information on the variety of trends that can affect a sales plan. Sources of such information include federal agencies (e.g., U.S. Department of Labor), banks and financial institutions, business newspapers (e.g., *Wall Street Journal*), market research services, and news services. In addition, much of this information is now available on the Internet. Local economic conditions can be studied with newspapers for notification of building permits, rezoning, road construction, or other infrastructure that could impact the store; local news services for government policy changes and local activities; and chambers of commerce for incoming new businesses and competitive market information. Information about economic conditions in countries other than the United States can be found from governmental agencies within specific countries, on the Internet (e.g., National Trade Data Bank), in national newspapers, on cable network stations, and from market information services.

Positive **economic indexes**, building permits for new housing construction, and new building starts can signal increases in income for a market. A low unemployment rate is a positive sign when planning for sales. Low unemployment rates may indicate that many people have jobs, most people who have jobs are not worried about keeping a job, and finding a new job would be easy. This situation makes the consumer feel more comfortable about spending money, which is especially positive for selling fashion goods. A low unemployment rate could be construed as a reason to plan for a large increase in sales for a coming period. On a local level, changes in road patterns and new building permits for retail businesses can have positive or negative impacts on a store. A new road may bring more car traffic by the store and more potential consumers, or a change in road patterns may bypass the old route and reduce the number of potential consumers who pass the store every day. New commercial construction should be viewed for location and type. Some nearby competition may stimulate business or may siphon traffic from a store. Projecting changes in traffic flow is difficult but of primary importance when creating a sales plan.

When estimating sales, **promotional events** (i.e., activities that promote, advertise, or create notice for the store) must also be planned. They may or may not include price reductions. Promotional events should generate more consumer traffic within the store and an increase in sales. Some promotional events result in increased cash register sales without price reductions, so these events will increase the overall sales for the period. These promotional events include sales that highlight merchandise for Mother's Day, Father's Day, Christmas, Valentine's Day, and other holidays, some of which may be associated with religious events or federally mandated events. Special merchandise may be carried in the store during these holiday times.

Stores also have promotional events to celebrate store events such as store anniversaries, Founder's Day, and seasonal events such as Back-to-School and Spring or Harvest Sales. Planning sales for these events requires special care to ensure that ample merchandise is available to keep the store looking fresh and well stocked.

Although some promotional events include price reductions, the increases in consumer traffic may result in overall increases in sales. When sales dollars are set for each promotional event, corresponding plans can be made in other functional areas. Store managers can use the sales goals to set goals for sales associates, buyers can use the goals to plan for purchasing merchandise for the promotional event, and visual merchandising staff can plan windows, advertising, special events, merchandise presentations, and displays for achieving these sales goals. In a small store, the planning for promotions and adjustment of sales are also made, even if the decisions are done by the same person. For any size or type of store, sales do not just happen but are the result of careful planning.

Although **predicting the weather** is often difficult, weather is an important factor to consider when calculating sales for a fashion goods company. Predicting the weather involves the short-term and long-range forecasts for temperature and precipitation. A winter with plenty of cold weather will create increases in sales of coats, sweaters, gloves, bedding, and other warm items. Spring rains are the perfect days to promote raincoats, umbrellas, umbrella stands, and colorful doormats. Rain or snow may increase sales for some stores located in enclosed malls where consumers congregate to walk and socialize outside of their houses. In addition, a week of gray, rainy weather may send shoppers to local malls looking for entertainment and bright vistas. Periods of rainy days require visual displays that are exciting and often changing.

Excesses in weather can also be harmful to sales. If a spring has an abundance of rain, a winter has excessive snow, or any season has unseasonably high or low temperatures, sales may be reduced because consumers cannot get to the store to shop on days with bad weather. Telephone sales, catalog sales, or sales on the Internet, if used by the store, may rise on these days. Unfortunately, in some areas where ice, snow, or flooding occurs, stores may be closed resulting in lost sales that are never recovered.

If using past sales data to calculate future sales, past weather patterns may be used to enlighten explanations of the sales patterns. For example, if the sales of sweaters were up last year, the sales volume may have been the result of a change in weather from previous years or the increase in sales could be indicating a growth trend for the classification. Careful and detailed analysis of the data and the environmental scan information would be needed to determine the difference between the two impacting factors.

A **scan of the competition**, another important part of the environmental scan, involves the observation of the business activities of competitive businesses or those businesses that are marketing to the same target customers including in-store, Web site, and media. For a large or multi-unit company, the competition must be considered for the entire market area, which may be a global consideration, and at the local level for individual store units. Overall, a large company may have limited competition, but within specific geographic areas, the company may have competition from locally owned stores of one or several units. For a single-unit company, the competition aspect of the environmental scan will be concentrated at a local level, and all local, regional, national, and international companies that have local businesses will be scanned. Competition from nonregional or nondomestic companies that contact consumers through a catalog or Internet site must also be considered.

Business publications such as *Wall Street Journal, Daily News Record*, and *Stores* can provide general information about a competitor's store activities; however, specific information about the merchandise carried in a store, the fixturing, and the consumer activity within a store must be collected at the individual store level. Many companies, large and small, use **secret shoppers**. These shoppers are store employees or personnel for a specific service, who appear to be regular consumers but peruse the stores located within the same mall, street, or strip center. Secret shoppers can observe quantity of stock on shelves and fixtures, condition of the store such as cleanliness of carpets and color of walls, number of consumers in the store, and number and activities of sales associates. Several secret-shopping trips should be made at various times of the day and days of the week to capture a total picture of the competition. Mall management or local business associations could be approached for general information about a site and for a sales overview.

In summary, information from environmental scans is very important to the accuracy of a sales plan. Each member of a company can contribute to the environmental scan, which provides the background for the future of the company. A new scan must be framed from the signals in the current scan while taking into account information collected from company personnel, government documents, public media, and paid market research services. All of this information can paint the picture of the business environment, but judgment from the company's management is still needed to determine how these factors may affect the future of the company and the potential sales for the business.

Establishing a Sales Plan for Continuing Businesses

History about the company is useful in predicting future sales. **Sales history** is gathered from in-store sources. Traditionally, the buyer was responsible for keeping ledgers on the type and volume of merchandise that was purchased and to supervise inventory at the end of the season to determine what merchandise actually sold. Computerized cash registers and bar codes on individual items can now provide a wealth of information available at any time during the selling season. Merchandise characteristics, frequency of sales, total amounts of the sales, and other data are collected at the point of sale simply by entering the item's bar code. Software programs written to use this data can display inventory information by code, by date, by price, by style groups, or by color and provide information about what was sold, when it was sold, and to whom it was sold.

Computer inventory systems are generated databases containing all inventory information that is maintained with specialized software on computers with a large storage space and active search capabilities. Information can also be retrieved relative to the merchandise brands or vendors that are selling well and the amount and type of items that remain in inventory. From this information, the buyer can determine the number of customers who buy specific brands and the products that should be targeted for special promotions and specific product offerings. A potential sales increase can be pinpointed for products and customers, and more accurate sales forecasts can be formulated with just a few keystrokes. Without a computerized inventory system, a buyer needs to visit the store and walk through the department to determine what is selling. Some of the newer computer programs even report what items were sold in conjunction with other items. When planning for actual purchasing, such co-purchase information could be useful in building add-on sales and determining item groups. At this stage in sales planning, the volume by week, month, or other period will be the major focus.

Persons who use this data must remember a number of caveats. First, **point-of-sale data or POS** data are a record of past sales, not a projection of future sales. Second, POS data indicate what was sold. Few, if any, POS programs report what product was requested by the consumer that was not available in the store or on the Web and what items were not sold. Third, the data are accurate only if the sales staff is careful in encoding the information. For example, one red picture frame scanned and the number four key hit is not the same sale as scanning two red frames, one blue frame, and one white frame. While the consumer and the sales associate may think the first method is faster, the second method more accurately reports the sale. The proper scanning of merchandise is important in entering inventory, in selling inventory, and in returning inventory to stock because of customer returns. Sales associates must be trained to use the computerized cash registers properly and to communicate to impatient consumers the need for accuracy in checking their purchases.

Another part of past history includes the planning that was done for the preceding year. Last year's actual sales volume should be compared to the planned sales for that year. An examination of past projections and actual sales figures can provide information about the accuracy of previous sales plans. The following questions should be asked about the comparison: "Was the projection too high or too low?" "What internal or external factors were responsible for the difference?" The preceding year's environmental scan can provide clues to these questions such as changes in competition and bad weather. For example, an over-projection in sales of bathing suits might be explained by a cool and rainy summer when a hot dry summer was expected. Other factors such as over-representation of expectations, overly cautious risk-taking, or bad judgment could contribute to a mismatch between planned and actual sales.

Sales volume from the **previous planning period**, which may be the last six months, last year, or the comparable season from the previous year, is only part of the information needed to plan projected sales. No two years in retail sales are the same. For example, with predicted high unemployment, high bank loan rates, and other indices of economic downturn, the planned sales for the next year may need to be decreased from the current year. Positive economic signs include low unemployment and high levels of consumer confidence as exhibited by a rise in consumer spending and drop in consumer saving. During this type of economic situation, the projected sales for the next year could be raised relative to the current year. If the store has been in business for a number of years, the previous five-year sales history may be reviewed for trends in sales volume. A continual rise in sales can indicate the safe decision of a projected rise in sales for the next year.

Planning based on sales history has its limitations; therefore, specific planning for merchandise and for the store must also be performed. When a vendor is no longer used because the vendor's merchandise is not profitable or the merchandise is not suitable for the target customer, the retailer will need to make a **change in vendors**. Such changes in vendors, in vendor prices, or in vendor promotional support should be considered with care relative to the needs of the business. New lines of merchandise may be needed or wanted. The business may be choosing to reposition its image or to seek new target consumers.

Operating expenses should also be reviewed. Possible changes when planning for next year include cost increases in utilities or rent and planned pay raises and promotions for staff. In addition, stores need constant maintenance and upgrades to keep their image fresh and exciting for their target consumers. All of these expenses must be factored into a decision about sales.

Finally, if growth is desired, plans must be made for retail business expansion and sales growth. **Retail business expansion** or growth may include expanding an existing store, increasing the number of stores, or expanding a business to a new outlet such as starting a new catalog or creating a Web site on the Internet. Although sales for a new outlet or door may be based on existing businesses, sales for a new store, catalog, or Internet site are usually projected separately from the existing business.

Increases in sales must be planned. They do not just happen! Using the entire general environmental scan information, past sales history, and merchandise or store specific details, forecasts can be made for the future of the company. Increases in sales must be projected to create goals for growth. Once the increase is determined, short-term actions can be planned to work toward the projected sales figure using a realistic approach. For example, a decrease in planned sales should trigger a reexamination of stock, operating expenses, and profit levels to ensure a stable future for the company.

Calculating Planned Sales for a Continuing Business

After examining the external environment and the store records, the direction of change for planned sales can be determined and the amount of change can be projected. The **direction of change** can be to increase or decrease the sales for next year or to remain stable with no changes from last year. Stability of sales or no change does not require additional calculations but is rarely seen in a competitive market. The amount of change may be selected by various methods: a standard rule of thumb (i.e., 5–10% growth or 1% plus rate of inflation), a rate suggested by a trade association, or an arbitrary percentage based on merchandising instinct. Once the direction and percentage of change are selected, the planned sales can be determined from the previous year's sales figure. When calculating planned sales, the actual sales figure (not the planned figure) from the previous period (e.g., last year) is considered as the base.

Calculating planned sales is a two-step process: (1) determine the dollar amount of change and (2) determine the planned sales. The formulas for dollar amount of change are

$$\text{Amount of Increase } \$ = (\text{Base Year Sales } \$ \times \text{Increase }\%)$$
$$\text{Amount of Decrease } \$ = (\text{Base Year Sales } \$ \times \text{Decrease }\%)$$

Second, to determine the planned sales dollars, the dollar amount of change that was calculated is added to the base year. For an increase in planned sales dollars, the formula would be

$$\text{Planned Sales } \$ = \text{Base Year Sales } \$ + \$ \text{ Amount of Increase}$$

For a decrease in planned sales dollars, the formula would be

$$\text{Planned Sales } \$ = \text{Base Year Sales } \$ - \$ \text{ Amount of Decrease}$$

The two-step process can be combined into one formula. To calculate a planned sales figure using last year's sales dollars, last year would be the base year. The following formula would be used to calculate an **increase in planned sales dollars**:

$$\text{Planned Sales } \$ = \text{Base Year Sales } \$ + (\text{Base Year Sales } \$ \times \text{Increase }\%)$$

To calculate a **decrease in planned sales dollars**, the following formula would be used:

$$\text{Planned Sales } \$ = \text{Base Year Sales } \$ - (\text{Base Year Sales } \$ \times \text{Decrease }\%)$$

Sample Problem: Increase in Sales

In December, a store manager of a small specialty shop began to make plans for the next year. The store had sales of $246,000.00 for this year. The store manager made a thorough environmental scan including sending a secret shopper to observe the competition, talking to the sales staff, reading the Department of Labor report on unemployment, subscribing to an economic news service, and speaking to the mall manager. The store manager decided to plan for a 4.00% increase for next year. What is the value of the planned sales for next year?

Step 1. Select the appropriate formula, based on the given information.

$$\text{Planned Sales } \$ = \text{Base Year } \$ + (\text{Base Year } \$ \times \text{Increase }\%)$$

Step 2. Insert the information from the problem and calculate sales.

Planned Sales $ = $246,000.00 + ($246,000.00 × 4.00%)

Planned Sales $ = $246,000.00 + ($9,840.00)

Planned Sales $ = $255,840.00

Additional forecasting methods for estimating sales volume include statistical processes and calculations that are more extensive. Statistical projections from correlation analysis, multiple regression or econometric models in deterministic situations with no random elements, time-series analysis, and projection under uncertainty such as using frequency tables and conditional probability are other possible methods. These methods require a degree of mathematical sophistication and a large volume of past history data and other market related data. Multiple regression and time-series analyses are mathematical ways to incorporate many of the variables observed in the environmental scan. For example, the high temperature for every day and amount of precipitation are weather variables that could be used in a regression equation to explore relationships with sales volume over time. Use of these statistical methods is aided by appropriate computer software and a powerful computer processor.

Other complex mathematical techniques include exponential smoothing or decomposition. Exponential smoothing calculates a weighted moving average of past sales with additional calculations to account for seasonal factors and the component of irregularity. This method tries to capture some of the seasonal and fashion changes that are often found in fashion goods. Decomposition splits the total sales forecast into merchandise classifications and in some cases into SKU level according to an importance rating assigned to each classification or SKU. Although useable by any company with enough data to make the calculations viable, these techniques are normally used by large, multi-unit companies that have 5 to 10 years of past sales history and 100 or more stores from which to collect data. In addition, government agencies use many of these techniques in forecasting future economic conditions. As with other sales forecasting methods, the results are only as accurate as the information that is used to make the calculations.

Establishing a Sales Plan for New Businesses

Opening a new business holds many challenges even for the most experienced owners. Owners of small, independent boutiques and owners of large multi-unit companies face a similar challenge, the establishment of a sales plan. A sales plan is a detailed plan with dollars that indicates the volume of sales that the business wishes to achieve in the next period. The sales plan may include a percentage increase for growth. When a business has a sales record of accomplishment, determining planned sales is part calculation and part forecast. If the business has current stores in operation, the projection of sales for a new store can be made based on the history for similar stores in the company. Although forecasting for a new store with no history may be very difficult, this planning activity is still very important to the success of the business. In the competitive environment of the fashion goods business, few if any companies would share their sales history with a newcomer, "the competition." If a new business hired a seasoned merchandiser, the person may bring past history information; however, few personnel leaving a company are allowed to take specific records or computer programs with them. A seasoned merchandiser who can bring experience to a new business is highly valued.

A new business has no sales history; therefore, other sources of information must be used as a basis for predicting planned sales. General business plans, environmental scanning, planned promotional events, detailed merchandise and store plans, and weather forecasts become even more important when no sales history is available. Starting with the right inventory levels and keeping a strong flow of cash in the business is vital to the survival of a new store. An inflated planned sales estimate can cause an overage in inventory. As stated earlier, **too much inventory** can make a store look crowded and restrict availability of cash, which can be an unprofitable start for a new business. Dollars are expended for advertising and other promotional events to pull consumers into the new store. If these consumers are disappointed by the look of the store, they may never return. If cash is not available to pay for the new merchandise, access to future markets may be restricted. A bad credit rating from failure to pay bills could be the end of a new or any future business. Therefore, forecasting the right amount of sales can be as critical as the right selection of merchandise.

For a new store, three methods can be used to determine planned sales: (1) market studies of the population base, (2) predicted dollar amounts per square foot of selling space, and (3) cost plus or dollars needed to cover all planned expenses. Each one of these methods uses estimated dollar amounts to build a planned sales amount. The estimations become a proxy for the past sales dollars. The success of each method depends on the availability of the needed proxies or dollar amounts, the accuracy of these amounts for specific store and product classifications, and the adjustments made to fit local conditions. The importance of careful and accurate planning must be emphasized because vitality of the store, freshness of the merchandise, and availability of cash flow are contingent on an accurate sales plan.

Calculating Planned Sales for a New Business—Market Study Method

Market studies including expenditures, spending patterns, and other demographic information about populations may be available from trade associations, local business associations, private consulting or marketing firms, and the Census Bureau. Private consulting or marketing firms can provide information tailored specifically to a store or about a target market. **Surveys** by mail, phone, or store/mall intercept may be used to gather information about potential customers and their shopping habits. **Primary sources** of data, such as a variety of surveys, can provide excellent, focused, and directly collected information about a market and the consumers in the market, but these market tools are time consuming and require skilled personnel to perform accurate and dependable work. Surveys would require extensive work by the hired firm or by an in-house market division. On the other hand, basing market decisions on government or other **secondary sources** would cost less but would also be less accurate for the specific local market. Firms that are skilled in market studies can provide quick, reliable information, but this service does cost. Purchasing market information can be a desirable method; however, the skills and time savings of an outside firm must be evaluated versus the skill levels and available time of store personnel.

For some product classifications or unique niche markets, dollar information about markets and sales may not be available. A business that wants information about new merchandise or a very narrow selection of merchandise may not find this information available except from a market research service. Target markets focusing on consumers who have not been previously addressed such as specific ethnic groups or consumers competing in a new sports activity may be covered by generally available information. Estimations could be made based on similar products or markets if such similarities exist. In addition, market information and projected sales per square foot are often derived from regional or national information and may not be accurate for local conditions. Therefore, market information must be used with caution.

Market studies can provide information about the expenditure patterns of the population. This information would appear as dollars spent **per capita**, meaning the dollar amount one person spent on an item in a period. Expenditure information is available for U.S. consumers from the Department of Commerce; however, expenditures for apparel and other textile products are often aggregated in data from the U.S. government. This aggregate information would be useful for general planning and for planning sales for a large store with broad categories of merchandise. To be useful for fashion goods planning, expenditure information must be provided according to specific merchandise classifications. This specific information may be purchased from trade associations or from market research services.

Per capita information refers to the information about a person, who would be a potential target customer. When per capita information is known, the number of persons in the market area must be identified. The total population in a geographic region is the beginning figure, but one store or one business will rarely capture all the consumers within a market. Other stores will be in competition for the consumers' purchasing dollars.

The number of consumers within a market who will shop in one store is the **market share** for that store. The percentage of market gathered by the retailer, or the market share, will depend on the competition in the market, the appeal of the new store, the marketing ability of the new manager, and the willingness of shoppers to change stores. The market share is also reduced by consumers who shop on the Internet or from catalogs.

The **market study method** combines two areas of information: the dollars per capita for the item and the number of consumers in the market share. To calculate planned sales by this method, a two-step calculation is made. First, the dollar amount per capita would be multiplied by the number of people in the market. This figure would provide the total projected sales for the market. Second, the total projected sales would be adjusted for the anticipated market share for the store.

The formulas and steps for the market study method are as follows:

Step 1. Total Projected Sales $ = Expenditure $ per Capita × Population #
Step 2. Planned Sales $ = Total Projected Sales $ × Market Share %

This two-step process can be rewritten into one formula for planned sales by the **market study method**:

$$\text{Planned Sales \$} = (\text{Expenditure \$ per Capita} \times \text{Population \#}) \times \text{Market Share \%}$$

Sample Problem: Market Study Method

A manager of a new shoe store has started to make plans for the store's opening. The manager has contacted a local business organization and several trade associations and has collected information for calculated planned sales. The U.S. government has estimated that average annual expenditure for shoes is $120.00 per capita. The total market area for the store includes 35,000 people.

The market contains four other places to buy shoes. Store One is a large shoe store and has been at its current location for 20 years. Store Two has just renovated and is about eight years old. The other two locations are shoe departments within midsize department stores. The manager estimates that the new store should capture about 10.00% of the market in its first year. What is the value of the planned sales for this store?

Step 1. Identify the known information for the formula.

Total Projected Sales $ = Expenditure $ per Capita × Population #

Expenditure $ per Capita = $120.00

Population # = 35,000

Step 2. Enter the information and calculate the value of sales.

Total Projected Market $ = $120.00 × 35,000

Total Projected Market $ = $4,200,000.00

Step 3. Calculate the planned sales.

Planned Sales $ = Total Projected Market $ × Market Share %

Market Share % = 10.00%

Planned Sales $ = $4,200,000.00 × 10.00%

Planned Sales $ = $420,000.00

Calculating Planned Sales for a New Business—Square Foot Method

Trade associations and other business references can provide information about expected sales relative to the size of the store. This measurement is common in business. In fact, several operating expenses can be predicted based on the square foot size of a store; for example, sales, rent, and overhead. The square foot dimension or **square foot size of a store** refers to the overall size of the selling floor. Back room space, inventory space, and other workrooms are not included in the selling floor size. With experience from a previous business, sales per square foot estimates may be highly accurate for the merchandise classification but should be adjusted for the local conditions. In addition, sales for a new store may not be equivalent to the sales of an established business. Sales for a new store could be high because of the excitement and interest generated by the new store, or sales for a new store could be low because consumers have not changed their shopping patterns to include shopping in the new store. An established business may have a loyal following that is not automatically generated by a new store. A rule of thumb or estimate often used in the retail business is that a new business will take three to five years to become established and to show a substantial profit.

The sales estimates based on square foot size vary greatly across merchandise classifications. Some items such as household linens require a large selling space, while some items such as jewelry require very small selling space. An inexpensive comforter may need three square feet of selling space and may have a retail price of $55.00. Fine quality jewelry can occupy very small spaces and can have very high price values. A diamond ring takes less than six square inches of selling space but can have a retail price of $3,500.00. Therefore, the expected sales per square foot for a jewelry department will be much higher than the sales per square foot prediction for a household linens department. The planned sales will also vary with the pricing strategy of the store, overall merchandise quality of the store, store image variables, and other environmental variables. **Sales per square foot** values from trade and other sources are averages and must not be treated as accurate estimates for a specific merchandise classification or for a specific store.

The calculations to develop a planned sales figure by the **square foot method** are relatively simple. The size of the selling floor is measured, and the square footage is multiplied by an estimate of dollars per square foot, yielding the **square foot method** formula

$$\text{Planned Sales } \$ = \# \text{ Square Feet} \times \$ \text{ per Square Foot}$$

Sample Problem: Sales per Square Foot Method

A manager of a new shoe store has started to make plans for the store's opening. The manager has contacted a local business organization and several trade associations and has collected information for calculating planned sales. For shoes sold in a small shop, the average annual sales per square foot are $525.00. The manager uses a tape measure and finds that the size of the selling floor is 20′ by 40′. What is the value of the planned sales for this store?

Step 1. Determine the appropriate formula, based on the given values.

Planned Sales $ = # Square Feet × $ per Square Foot

$\# \text{ Square Feet} = 20' \times 40' = 800 \text{ sq ft}$

$\$ \text{ per Square Foot} = \$525.00$

Step 2. Insert the values, and determine the result.

Planned Sales $ = 800 sq ft × $525.00

Planned Sales $ = $420,000.00

Calculating Planned Sales for a New Business—Cost Plus Method

When making a business plan for a new store, operating expenses as well as sales must be planned. As shown in Chapter 3, the Profit and Loss statement is used to represent planned sales, planned cost of goods, and planned markup. In the **cost plus method**, the markup is established by the component addition method. An estimation is made of the operating expenses and profit. A "rule of thumb" is used to determine the cost of goods. Previous experience can be used to determine cost of goods relative to markup, or with no additional point of reference, a keystone markup can be used. The markup can be doubled to determine the related cost of goods. The value of planned sales is a result of the combination of planned markup and planned cost of goods.

Using this method, a sales plan is estimated with a sales volume large enough to cover operating expenses, but the potential for achieving this level of sales is uncertain. At all times, the volume of sales must be double checked to ensure that it will provide enough income to purchase new merchandise and to cover costs. Often this method is good as a control or check for other sales planning methods, rather than as the sole method of calculating planned sales.

The formula for estimating planned sales by the **cost plus method** is

$$\text{Planned Sales \$} = \text{Planned Cost \$} + \text{Planned Markup \$}$$

Sample Problem: Cost Plus Method

A manager of a new shoe store has started to make plans for the store's opening. The manager has estimated the operating expenses for the store. The operating expense estimate includes salaries, rent, advertising, telephone, cleaning, bags, electricity, insurance, and other miscellaneous expenses. The markup or total value of operating expenses and profit is $210,000.00. Planned markup is expected to be equal to planned cost. What is the value of the planned sales for this store?

Step 1. Use the cost plus method formula.

$$\text{Planned Sales \$} = \text{Planned Cost \$} + \text{Planned Markup \$}$$

Step 2. Insert the given values, and calculate the result.

$$\text{Planned Sales \$} = \$210,000.00 + \$210,000.00$$
$$\text{Planned Sales \$} = \$420,000.00$$

To gain confidence in the planned sales figure, sometimes two mathematical estimates of sales may be calculated or other less structured and more subjective methods could be used. **Subjective methods** usually depend on the opinions of some experts such as the company owner, other top managers or executives, or the buyers. Team planning based solely on the opinions of the team members is called **jury of executive opinion** or obtaining consensus. If the buyer is allowed to make the sales estimates and uses only opinion, then the method would be called **user's expectation**. Subjective opinion alone is rare in a business that uses computers and electronic cash registers to track sales and inventory; however, this method might be used by businesses that are managed very autocratically or by businesses without access to computers. In most instances, subjective and objective methods are used in conjunction with each other. The risk of incorrect sales estimates is very high, and most decision makers think that the more information applied to the decision, the better satisfied one could be with the outcome. Therefore, use of multiple methods is common in many stores, with executive opinion being the last method applied to the sales estimate.

*S*ummary

Planned sales are the foundation of the Profit and Loss statement and are the basis for determining stock levels. Accurate planned sales are needed to ensure the right level of inventory within a store. Proper inventory levels affect the image of the store, the availability of fresh merchandise, and the release of cash for payment of bills. An environmental scan will provide knowledge of general economic climate, demographics of the surrounding population, and store-specific information that is important for accurate planning. Information is available from a variety of government, trade, and store sources. This environmental information may be collected by a wide array of store personnel. For example, information about consumer shopping habits may be collected from sales associates, and general information about economic trends, from analysis done by top management. Some stores use team planning to ensure that all aspects of the marketplace are included in the development of a sales plan.

The method for calculation of planned sales is dependent on the availability of previous sales information. If a store has a past sales history, this information can be used as a basis for calculating planned sales. When planning for a new business, trade information or market research studies provide some generic basis for building a sales plan. In addition to sales information, a sales plan must be adjusted for future changes, promotional events, and other store specific activities. Regardless of who makes the plan and how the plan is made, it will influence many aspects of the company's operation for the coming year. The accuracy of the plan is essential to the survival of a business in a competitive marketplace.

Key Terms

Changes in vendors	Overbought	Scan of the competition
Computer inventory systems	Per capita	Secondary sources
Cost plus method	Point-of-sale (POS)	Secret shopper
Direction of change	Predicting the weather	Square foot method
Economic environment	Previous planning period	Square foot size of a store
Economic indexes	Primary sources	Subjective method
Environmental scanning	Promotional events	Surveys
Jury of executive opinion	Retail business expansion	Too much inventory
Market share	Sales history	User's expectation
Market studies	Sales per square foot	
Market study method	Sales plan	

Discussion Questions

1. What is a sales plan?
2. Why are sales plans so critical to the success of a store?
3. What other plans are made relative to the sales plan?
4. What is the role of a buyer when sales plans are made by team planning?
5. How can planned sales be affected by promotional events?
6. If the buyer wants to add new merchandise classifications to the store, what would be the best method of planning sales?
7. Why are sales per square foot different for shoes than for men's ties?
8. What is the advantage of calculating planned sales by several methods?
9. Explain the differences between planning sales for a new business and planning for a business that is five years old.
10. How could the Internet be used to assist with an environmental scan?

Exercises

Planned Sales for Continuing Businesses

1. *The Bountiful Boutique* had sales of $889,000.00 for last year. They plan to increase sales by 4.00%. What are the planned sales for this year?

2. Economic indicators are identified as negative, and a decrease in sales is planned. Last year the store had $4,000,000.00 in sales. A 10.00% decrease is planned. What are the planned sales for this year?

3. If sales for this year are $4,500,000.00 and next year is expected to increase by 2.50%, what is the planned sales figure for next year?

   (Hint: This year becomes the base year.)

4. Sales for last year were $1,500,000.00. Sales for this year are planned to be $1,650,000.00. What is the dollar amount of increase? What is the percentage of increase?

5. Sales for last year were $100,000.00. Sales for this year are planned to be $160,000.00. What is the percentage of increase?

6. In the Baby and Infant Department, the sales for the first six months were $58,000.00. The sales for the last six months were $79,000.00. What was the percentage of increase?

   (Hint: Use the first six months as the base year.)

7. The projection for the local economy is a downward turn because of closings and layoffs at a regional industrial plant. The Chamber of Commerce is advising retailers to expect a drop in sales. To plan for next year, the store manager is predicting a 3.00% drop in sales. Last year's sales were $995,800.00. What will be the amount of sales for next year? If the manager wants to maintain the same profit level, what will he or she have to do? Explain.

   (Hint: Think about the interrelation of items in the P & L.)

8. A store had sales of $4,689,000.00 last year. A 5.70% loss has occurred this year. What is the value of this year's sales?

9. A store had sales of $480,000.00 this year. This year's sales were 12.00% more than last year. What was last year's sales figure?

10. A department had sales of $52,000.00 in Month 6. This amount was $2,000.00 more than Month 5. What was the total for sales in Month 5?

    (Hint: Yr1 $ − (+) (Change % × Yr1 $) = Yr2 $.)

Planned Sales for New Businesses

1. Determine the total projected market dollars for the following market. The population for a small town is 26,600. Expenditure dollars per capita for ladies' dresses are $122.00.

2. The market share for a new store is predicted at 33.30% of the total projected market. Total projected market dollars are $1.5 million. What are planned sales for the new store?

3. A store wants to expand with a new addition that is 40' by 20'. The new merchandise will be lamps and small home fashion accessories. Sales per square foot for this merchandise are expected to be $280.00. What are the planned sales for the addition?

4. A manager brags that the projected sales for the store will be $2,000,000.00. You know that the store is an average size store of 60' by 80'. What are the expected dollars per square foot for the merchandise in this store?

5. A market study reveals that the potential for growth in the area would support an additional $241,000.00 in sales for costume jewelry. Sales per square foot for jewelry are $200.00. How many square feet would be necessary for the costume jewelry sales to reach the increased amount?

6. You own a luggage shop on the southwest side of a major city. Within your market area, you have a population of 35,000 people. Per capita expenditure for luggage is $56.00. In the past year, business has been poor. You wonder if there is too much competition, and go out to survey. You find 4,800 square feet of selling floor space in the market. Sales per square foot for luggage are $120.00. Are there any potential sales dollars left for you?

7. For shoes, your sales market has been determined to contain 15,000 consumers. The average person spends $75.00 per year on shoes (annual per capita expenditure). What is the total potential in sales for this market?

8. The average per capita expenditure for leisurewear is $180.00, but only 0.20% of that is spent on specialty items such as bicycle shorts. You own a bike shop and want to decide what you could expect if you added bike clothing to your merchandise assortment. You are in a large town with 350,000 people. With very little competition in the area, you expect to have 55.00% of the market share. What are the potential sales for your store? If the clothing section of your store were 10' by 15', what would be the sales per square feet of this new department?

9. The manager of a new store has estimated the operating expenses to be $158,800.00 and the expected profit for the store is $1,800.00. What is the markup for the store? If this were a keystone markup, what would be the costs of goods for the store? What are the planned sales for the store?

10. A department store manager wants to expand into the store space next door in the mall. The markup on the new merchandise is expected to total $256,890.00. The store uses a keystone markup. What are the planned sales for this new space? If the sales per capita for this merchandise are $56.00, how many consumers must purchase in the new addition to meet this sales projection?

Computer Exercises

General Directions

- Save your work on your disk.
- You should have one worksheet for all problems. Just scroll down below the first problem to start the second problem. Number each problem.
- In the upper right corner of the spreadsheet, place your name, date, and file name.

- A problem spreadsheet should be printed on one page. You may have multiple spreadsheets on one page, but you cannot split a spreadsheet across two pages.
- Work the following problems on the computer. Use the spreadsheet format as shown. Enter values from the information provided by the problem. Use formulas to find all additional values.

Planned Sales for Continuing Businesses

For problems 1–3, use the following spreadsheet format.

	$	%
Retail		100%
− Cost		
= Markup		

1. The manager of a new store has estimated the operating expenses to be $158,800.00 and the expected profit for the store is $1,800.00. What is the markup for the store? If this were a keystone markup, what would the cost of merchandise be for the store? What are the planned sales for the store?

2. A new store has total markup expectations of $567,450.00. The markup will be 45.00% of the new total potential sales. What are the planned sales for the store?

3. The manager of a new store calculates operating expenses to be $629,890.00 and wants a profit of $30,000.00. With a keystone markup, what are planned sales for the store? The manager wonders what planned sales will be if profit were raised to $40,000.00.

For problems 4–8, use the following spreadsheet format.

	$	%
Last Year's Sales		
+ Increase in Sales		
= Planned Sales		

4. Sales for last year were $100,000.00. Sales for this year are estimated to be $160,000.00. What is the percentage of increase?

5. Last year's sales for the Bedding Department were $56,890.00. The predicted increase in sales is 4.50%. What are the planned sales for this year?

6. In the Baby and Infant Department, the sales for the first six months were $58,000.00. The sales for the last six months were $79,000.00. What was the percentage of increase?

   (Hint: Use the first six months as the base year.)

7. Last year's sales for the Shoe Department were $16,940.00. The predicted increase in sales is 3.50%. What are the planned sales for this year?

8. What will be the percentage increase needed to have planned sales of $18,000.00? of $20,000.00?

9. Sales for last year were $1.5 million. This year a decrease of 2.80% is predicted. What are the sales planned for this year? If this decrease is 3.00%, what will be the planned sales?

10. How much is the decrease if planned sales are estimated at $1.0 million?

11. For Year 1 for *Brad's Boots*, net sales were $99,000.00, cost of goods were $60,000.00, operating expenses were $40,500.00. For Year 2, Brad hopes to increase sales by 10.00%. He plans to decrease total operating expenses by 4.00%. Cost of goods will remain the same. Use formulas and copy commands to complete the spreadsheet. What happens to the profit dollars? Why?

    (Hint: Year 1 + (Year 1 × %).)

12. For Year 1 in the Shoe Department, sales are $250,000.00, cost of goods is $135,800.00, and expenses are 38.00%. For Year 2, the expenses become $125,000.00. Net sales and cost of goods remain at the same dollar amounts. What happens to profit?

13. For Year 1 in the Linen Department, cost of goods are $480,600.00, gross margin is 40.00%, and profit is $18,000.00. In Year 2, the cost of goods rose to $520,000.00. If the sales held to the Year 1 amount, what must be done to expenses to keep the profit equal to the Year 1 amount?

14. For *The Big Store*, complete the following exercises:

    a. Using the pro forma spreadsheet, insert the following information for *The Big Store*. For Year 1, the following figures were: net sales, $25,000.00; costs, $10,000.00; operating expenses, $8,000.00.

    b. For Year 2, the manager projects an 11.00% increase in net sales and plans to use cost-cutting methods to decrease operating expenses by 4.00%. The cost of goods remains the same. Using this data and formulas, show a P & L statement with columns for Year 1 and Year 2.

    (Hint: New net sales (NS) with increase would be NS + [NS × .11].)

15. For a Bed and Bath Department, adjust the sales and other retail components of the Profit and Loss statement for increased profit.

    For Year 1, start with net sales of $35,000.00, costs of $20,000.00, and operating expenses of $18,000.00.

    For Year 2, increase the cost of goods by 15.00%. Net sales and operating expenses remain the same. Show the P & L including Year 1 and the adjusted Year 2. What is the effect on Profit?

    (Note: Type your reply to the problem's question below the P & L before printing.)

16. For the same Bed and Bath Department, make the following adjustments for the estimations for next year's Profit and Loss statement:

    For Year 1, use Year 1 of the P & L in the previous problem. For Year 2, increase the cost of goods by 10.00%, and keep the net sales at the same level. For Year 2, what must be done to the operating expenses to keep the profit at or around 25.00%?

    Show the Year 2 figures with the final adjustment. Comment on the adjustments that must be made to the operating expenses.

17. For a P & L for *Merchant Plus*, make the following adjustments in the fourth quarter:

    a. Use a format similar to previous problems, but have three column pairs (i.e., Jan–Sept, Oct–Dec, Total).

    b. *Merchant Plus* has the following figures for the first nine months: net sales are $568,000.00, cost of goods are $380,000.00, and operating expenses are $200,000.00. The total plan was for net sales of $800,000.00, cost of goods of $450,000.00, and operating expenses of $250,000.00. Using this data, set up a P & L statement that shows to-date, remaining, and total figures.

P*lanning Stock*

O*bjectives*

After completing this chapter, the student will be able to

- discuss types of stock
- explain the importance of stock and stock flow
- define average stock
- discuss the importance of turn
- explain methods for increasing turn
- identify stock methods

For most customers, shopping is an important part of buying any item because they want to look at, feel, and compare the items. For this reason, items that must be viewed, tried on, or handled are called **shopping goods**. Shopping, as a precursor to buying, varies by costumer and product. Apparel items are often tried on by the customer prior to purchase. Retailers who sell through catalogs or Web sites must provide convenient return policies for customers who want to try on items and return them because they were "just shopping." When buying audio products, customers want to listen to CDs and other audio recordings prior to buying the item. Home furnishing items are often taken home for approval to determine if they coordinate with interior furnishings. For many products, customers also want to have additional information about the merchandise that they are buying and will watch videos, read pamphlets, and ask sales associates questions.

Catalog companies and Internet companies often have sales associates who are available by telephone or email to provide customers with information beyond what is viewed on the page. Customers will view magazines and Web sites to gather ideas about lifestyle assortments of merchandise. Some customers will try to duplicate the visions they see in magazines or displays, while other customers shop for ideas and inspirations about product choice.

Consumers shop for a variety of reasons. Some customers like to shop for entertainment. They stay in the store, peruse a catalog, or surf a Web site because they find them fun and entertaining. These customers want to see what is new and may come to the store at least once a week, flip through a catalog every evening, or view Web sites every day. Seeing the merchandise gives them ideas about what they need and want, how to combine the items with their existing possessions, and how and where to use the merchandise. While some customers shop for ideas or entertainment purposes, other customers shop for comparison purposes. They want to view similar items to compare for fit, price, feel, and other characteristics. Other customers want to spend very little time in the store. They want to enter, look, find, and buy. They need to see a complete stock selection so that they can find the color, brand, or size they want.

Each one of these customer types shops and needs to see stock before buying. All three types of customers need to feel satisfied when they enter and leave the store, and more importantly, they should find an item that they "must" buy before leaving the store. A completely stocked, freshly stocked, and neatly stocked store is important to selling merchandise. In fact, a selection of merchandise or stock is needed to generate sales; therefore, stock levels become related to sales goals. Once sales goals are established for a store, the retailer must then decide how much stock is needed to generate the desired sales goal.

Stock

Stock, in a retail store, is found in three places. **Floor stock** is merchandise that is currently on the selling floor. This merchandise is available for customers to handle and examine. Most of this stock is on display fixtures, shelves, or mannequins. A very limited amount of stock may be kept under counters, above shelves, or behind curtains or wall panels if the store has these features. **Backroom stock** is merchandise that has been received into the store and is ready to go to the floor when space is available or the time is appropriate. This stock can be used readily to replenish or refresh the floor stock. The backroom stock is available to allow the store staff to restock shelves and to provide a continuous flow of stock onto the floor. Floor stock and backroom stock combined are called **stock on hand**. Stock on hand for a catalog retailer or an Internet retailer has a different meaning. These retailers may have warehouses to hold stock ready for shipment to customers; however, many of these retailers may not actually keep stock on hand but depend on vendors to ship the stock directly from manufacturing plants.

Stock on order is stock that has been ordered from the manufacturer or vendor but has not yet been received by the retailer. This stock may be in any stage of the pipeline or distribution channel from an order form and raw goods at the manufacturer to finished items sitting in a warehouse or on a truck. Nonstore retailers may have agreements with vendors for a projected volume of sales and, thereby, a set amount of stock on order with their vendors. Although this stock is not actually in the hands or warehouse of the retailer, the retailer must consider stock on order as purchased stock and plan for payment because the commitment has been made to receive and pay for this stock. Part of the buying negotiations results in an agreement between the vendor and retailer for terms of the sale. (Additional information about terms of sale is found in Chapter 13.) These terms include the due date for payment of the invoice and other payment agreements for the stock. If an order has been placed, payment will be expected.

Management of stock is an important aspect of merchandising. Stock is vital to sales in the store and must be maintained for the customer to shop; however, stock also costs the retailer money. The invoices or bills for new stock must be paid, often before the stock is actually viewed by or sold to the customer. When money is tied in stock, cash is not available to pay other expenses for the store such as employees' salaries or utility bills. Stock must be sold to release the money and facilitate cash flow. Stock represents an investment for the retailer. As with many investments, purchase of stock is risky for the retailer. Selection of most stock is made on speculation, as the retailer, who is the buyer for the customer, predicts months ahead of time what the consumer will want. (Forecasting and buying are the subjects of Chapters 9 and 12.) Before merchandise is purchased for stock, the retailer must know **stock levels** or how much stock is needed.

Average Stock

Before levels of stock can be considered, the retailer must know some additional stock information. Stock is reported as **beginning of the month (BOM)** or **end of the month (EOM)**. BOM is the level of stock at the beginning of the month or on the first working day of the month. EOM is the level of stock at the end of the month or on the last working day of the month. With a computerized cash register, computer databased inventory, and the use of bar codes, a weekly, daily, or hourly report of stock levels is possible. For some retailers with these systems, a daily level is reported. With this reporting, the store would have a beginning of the day (BOD) and an end of the day (EOD) report.

The EOM or end of the reporting period becomes the BOM or beginning of the next reporting period. For example, the retailer takes a stock level before closing the store on June 30. At 11:30 pm on June 30, the level is $54,890.00. The cash registers are closed, the customers are gone, and the retailer locks the store. The next morning, when the retailer comes to open the store, the level is still $54,890.00. This level is the BOM for July 1. This fact, although trivial sounding, is useful for doing additional calculations and plans concerning stock levels.

The BOM values and EOM values are needed for the calculation of average stock. **Average stock** is the amount of stock that is generally carried in the store during a select period. This value provides the retailer with an estimation of the amount of stock that is in the store at any one time. This information is particularly useful to retailers who do not have complete cash register and inventory systems and is informative to all retailers in planning and controlling the margins in the store. Average stock can be found for a day, a week, a month, a quarter, or any other period used in planning by the retailers.

The formula for finding **average stock for one month** is

$$\text{Average Stock \$} = (\text{BOM \$} + \text{EOM \$})/(1 + 1)$$

This formula would provide the retailer with the average value of the stock during one month.

Sample Problem: Average Stock for One Month

The retailer had a BOM for June of $489,900.00 and an EOM in June of $532,880.00. What was the average stock in the store during the month of June?

Step 1. Insert the known values into the average stock formula.

$$\text{Average Stock \$} = (\text{BOM \$} + \text{EOM \$})/(1 + 1)$$
$$\text{Average Stock \$} = (\$489,900.00 + \$532,880.00)/2$$

Step 2. Calculate the value of average stock.

Average Stock \$ = \$1,022,780.00/2
Average Stock \$ = \$511,390.00

The average stock formula can be generalized to cover multiple periods. If the retailer knows the BOMs and EOMs for several months, an average for the quarter, six-month period, or year can be calculated. This information is helpful when comparing this year's activities with last year or comparing this store with another store in the company. If a retailer were planning to increase sales and needed to know past sales information, this formula would be needed. The **average stock** formula that can be applied to any number of months is

$$\text{Average Stock \$} = (\text{BOM } 1 \text{\$} + \text{BOM } 2 \text{\$} + \cdots$$
$$+ \text{BOM}_i \text{\$} + \text{EOM}_i \text{\$})/(\text{\# of BOM} + 1)$$

or

$$\text{Average Stock \$} = (\Sigma \text{BOM \$} + \text{EOM \$})/(\text{\# BOM} + 1)$$

The formula is read as the sum of the values of the BOM in the average period plus the value of the final EOM is divided by the number of BOMs in the average period plus 1 for the final EOM. This formula covers all the stock from the beginning of the first month through the following BOMs to the final stock count at the end of the last month. Each BOM represents the EOM of the previous month; therefore, no EOMs are needed except the last EOM of the period. If the average stock were calculated for four months, then the formula would have four BOM values and one EOM value. The number in the denominator of the formula would be 4 + 1 or 5. Regardless of how many months are in the period of calculation, only one EOM value, the last EOM, is used.

Sample Problem: Average Stock for a Period

A store has the following BOM figures for the Hat Department: January \$2,600.00, February \$4,200.00, March \$3,300.00, and April \$2,800.00. What is the average stock figure for the first quarter of the year?

Step 1. Set up a BOM and EOM chart for the store.

	Jan	Feb	Mar	April
BOM				
EOM				

Step 2. Enter the known values.

	Jan	Feb	Mar	April
BOM	\$2,600.00	\$4,200.00	\$3,300.00	\$2,800.00
EOM				

Step 3. Determine the values for the EOMs.

(Hint: Remember that the BOM of a period is the same as the previous EOM. For example, the BOM on the morning of February 1 was the EOM on the night of January 31.)

$\sum$ = the sum of.

	Jan	Feb	Mar	April
BOM	$2,600.00	$4,200.00	$3,300.00	$2,800.00
EOM	$4,200.00	$3,300.00	$2,800.00	

(Computer Hint: If this chart is developed in a spreadsheet the values for the BOM can be copied into the appropriate EOM.)

Step 4. Use the average stock formula to find the average stock for the first quarter (or first three months) of the year.

Average Stock $ = (ΣBOM $ + EOM $)/(# BOM + 1)

Average Stock $ = ([$2,600.00 + $4,200.00 + $3,300.00]
              + $2,800.00)/(3 + 1)

Average Stock $ = ($10,100.00 + $2,800.00)/4

Average Stock $ = $12,900.00/4

Average Stock $ = $3,225.00

Stock Turn

Stock turn is a value or an expression of how fast merchandise moves through the store. Stock turn is typically called **turn** with no modifiers because turn is primarily a concern of stock. The merchandise activity of moving through the store describes the process of an item arriving at the store's loading dock, being placed on the shelves or fixtures, and exiting the store by being sold to a customer. So, an item that moves through the store can be described as entering the back door (identified by the arrival on the loading dock) and exiting the front door (identified by the sale of the item to the customer). The amount of time between those two events (arrival and exit) is the time that the stock sits or hangs on the store floor. The longer the item is on the floor, the more the item ages by losing fashion newness through time passing and by handling, which results in soiling and other damage.

If turn is high or fast, the merchandise moves quickly through the store. If the turn is low or slow, the merchandise is moving slowly through the store. For example, a turn of one for a month indicates that within the month the entire set of stock entered the store, sat in display, and was sold. At the end of the month, none of the original stock remained in the store. If the turn is four, this indicates that four sets of stock entered the store and were sold during the period. A turn of eight is faster than a turn of four. A turn of eight has eight sets of merchandise moving through the store during a period. For a turn of eight, twice as much stock would be bought and sold in the store than when the store had a turn of four. Evaluation of turn is, as with other measures in retail, important when compared to other stores or periods.

This concept of turn is demonstrated in Figure 7.1. For item Style 1, the turn is slower than for item Style 2. For Style 1, four units were purchased by the buyer and arrived at the store loading dock at the same time. Over a period of four weeks, one item was sold per week. The last item was in the store for almost four weeks before it was sold. For Style 2, four units were purchased by the buyer, but only one item arrived at the beginning of the first week. The second unit arrived at the beginning of the second week and so forth for the remaining weeks. For Style 2, as with Style 1, one item was purchased by a customer per week. So, as one unit of Style 2 was sold, the second unit of Style 2 was received by the store. At any one time during the four weeks, a maximum of two units of Style 2 were in the store.

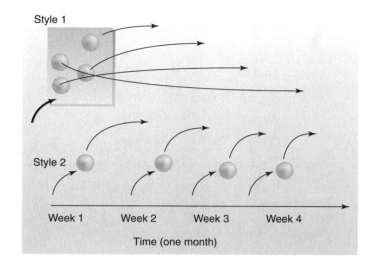

Figure 7.1

Stock Turn for Style 1 and Style 2.

A faster turn creates more sales for less investment. A unit of Style 1 or Style 2 has a cost of $1.00 per unit. The retailer has $4.00 and buys four of Style 1 at $1.00 per unit. These items are sold in the store. The retailer sold four units of Style 1 and the investment was $4.00. The turn for Style 1 was one. Four units entered the store at the same time and remained until sold. For Style 2, the retailer has $1.00, buys one unit, and sells that unit. With the profits, the retailer buys another unit of Style 2 for $1.00 and sells that unit. This continues until four units of Style 2 have been bought and sold. For this style, the retailer has bought four items but has only invested $1.00.

The formula for calculating turn is a comparison of sales to stock. The value of turn is in units without qualifiers. Turn is a number, not a dollar amount and not a percentage. The formula for **turn** is

Turn = Net Sales $/Average Stock $

This formula compares the average amount of stock that is kept in the store relative to the sales for the same period. Therefore, if net sales represented one month, then the average stock figure would also be for the same one month.

Sample Problem: Stock Turn

For Style 1 and for Style 2 in Figure 7.1, the units sold for $2.00 at retail. At the end of five weeks, the net sales for each style was $8.00. What was the turn for each style?

Style 1

Step 1. Find the value of the average stock.

Average Stock $ = (BOM $ + EOM $)/(1 + 1)
Average Stock $ = ($8.00 + $0)/2
Average Stock $ = $4.00

Step 2. Insert the known values into the turn formula.

Turn = Net Sales $/Average Stock $
Turn = $8.00/ $4.00

Step 3. Calculate the value of turn.

Turn = 2

(Note: Turn is a number. It has no qualifying descriptors; it is not a dollar amount and not a percentage.)

Style 2

Step 1. Find the value of the average stock.

Average Stock $ = (BOM $ + EOM $)/(1 + 1)

Average Stock $ = ($2.00 + $0)/2

Average Stock $ = $1.00

Step 2. Insert the known values into the turn formula.

Turn = Net Sales $/Average Stock $

Turn = $8.00/$1.00

Step 3. Calculate the value of turn.

Turn = 8

Although the same amount of merchandise was sold in the example, Style 2 had a faster turn. More merchandise was kept in the store for Style 1; therefore, with fewer dollars invested in the merchandise, the same amount of net sales was made. In addition, the merchandise in Style 2 was on the floor a shorter time and should be fresher than the merchandise for Style 1.

Sample Problems: Stock Turn

Problem 1

Store #123 sold eight wooden chests, which were to be used as night stands and were $100.00 per chest at retail. The eight chests sold for $800.00 in net sales. The value of the average stock of those chests was $200.00. What was the turn?

Step 1. Insert the known values into the turn formula.

Turn = Net Sales $/Average Stock $

Turn = $800.00/$200.00

Step 2. Calculate the value of turn.

Turn = 4

Problem 2

Store #124 also carried chests that retailed for $100.00. The store sold eight chests for a net sale of $800.00. The average stock value of those chests was $400. (More chests were kept in stock in Store #124 than in Store #123.) What was the turn for this store?

Step 1. Insert the known values into the turn formula.

Turn = Net Sales $/Average Stock $

Turn = $800.00/$400.00

Step 2. Calculate the value of turn.

Turn = 2

In this situation, the same amount of merchandise was sold. Both stores sold eight chests; however, the second store had a slower turn. More merchandise was kept in the second store during the selling period. At the end of the period, the store with the slower turn would have merchandise that had been in the store since the beginning of the period. The store with the faster turn would have new merchandise in the store throughout the selling period.

Higher or faster turns have several advantages for retailers. Faster turn enables stores to carry more variety in merchandise without high stock levels. If stock levels are high, then cash is invested in the stock and is not available for purchasing other items or for paying bills. Faster turn then keeps cash flowing into the registers and makes cash available. Faster turns also move more merchandise through the store within the same period relative to slower turns. Moving merchandise in and out of the store quickly allows the retailer the opportunity to change the merchandise frequently. This frequent change is good because the merchandise stays fresh and keeps customers coming into the store to see what is new. Even basic items such as white socks or pantyhose can be dirty, wrinkled, or damaged if the items sit on the shelves for long periods.

The traditional department store has five seasons: spring, summer, early fall/transitional, fall, and holiday. As stock was purchased and sold for each season, one turn occurred. The turn for this type of store was typically five. Basic goods that are stocked so that they are never out may have turns as low as one or two; however, these rates are changing through new vendor/retailer partnerships with automatic replenishment systems. With electronic exchange between vendor and retailer, basic goods that have a constant steady rate of sales may have turns as high as 20. Fashion specialists typically have higher turns than the traditional department store. Small specialty stores that are part of a chain or local boutiques often have turns of 8, 10, or 12. A retailer selling fashion oriented merchandise would want high turns to keep new items in the store. A turn of 12 would indicate all the merchandise in the store changed within one month.

When the merchandise is fashion merchandise, fast changes and freshness of items are extremely important. Part of the fashion appeal to the customer is that the merchandise is new. The more new merchandise that enters and leaves the store, the more changes the retailer can make in the stock. This situation is particularly useful when the retailer is unsure of the salability of the stock. For stock that is very new or very trendy, the retailer with fast turns can purchase small amounts of stock and replenish with the same or similar stock if sales are good. If sales are poor, the retailer will have little invested in the small amounts of stock and will have the money and opportunity to purchase different stock quickly.

For basic items, a fast turn is also beneficial. Small but steady levels of basic stock can be kept in the store. The fast turn means that, with every sale or with some periodic standard, the stock will be replenished. The retailer will never be out of the item and will never have to carry high levels of the stock. Again, the fast turn allows the retailer to carry more merchandise with less investment. Lower levels of stock also require less insurance to cover the stock in the store. The store will also have a more open appearance that encourages shopping by customers; crowded stores discourage and confuse customers. Customers tend to stay in a store longer and take more opportunity to select items for purchase when the store is not crowded.

Turn can be increased by several activities. Some of them are easy to control for the retailer and some take more careful planning. The simple act of reducing inventory can increase turn. Retailers often think of stock as potential sales. This thinking can lead retailers into believing that more stock makes more sales. This philosophy can cause retailers to become **overstocked**. Overstocked stores are crowded, have old merchandise, and frequently have lower turns. A point is reached at which more stock does not mean more sales; in fact, at some point more stock means fewer sales.

Careful buying with correct pricing will also increase turn. The buyer must purchase merchandise to provide a pleasing shopping experience for the customer. So a level of stock must be maintained that fills the store but does not cause overcrowding. Planning is very important for the careful buying needed to generate the desirable turn. Pricing the items was discussed in Chapter 2 and is further emphasized here because correct pricing will help the merchandise move through the store. If the merchandise is overpriced, the items will not be bought. If the items are underpriced, they may appear cheap or of lesser quality than similar or comparable merchandise. This negative comparison may reduce the sales potential of the incorrectly priced merchandise. Alternatively, the items may sell too quickly and the retailer will not receive enough money for the items to cover the desired markups. The buyer really receives only one opportunity to determine the correct price. After the items are priced, put on the floor, and viewed by the customer, no second chance is available for initial pricing.

Effective sales promotion is also important for increasing turn. Promoting items can draw attention to the items and move them from the store shelves to the customer's hands to become a customer's purchase. Special events sales, such as Father's Day, Valentine's Day, and Founder's Day, are designed to draw customers into the store and to increase sales of certain items. For example, ties, shirts, tools, and other gifts for men are promoted for Father's Day. The sales levels of these items should rise during the period before Father's Day. These increased sales will improve the turn for the men's department. Increasing the sales volume of regular price merchandise (i.e., merchandise that is not marked down for a sale) is one of the most effective activities to increase turn. However, without careful planning these sales could actually reduce turn. If extra merchandise is ordered for display during the sale and if sales volume does not increase beyond the level of the new stock, then extra stock will be added to the store.

Sales promotions must be carefully planned with buying. Another sales promotion that can be used to increase turn is a clearance sale. When the store is overstocked with end-of-the-season merchandise, a clearance sale can reduce prices to stimulate sales. The reduction in price must be low enough to encourage the customers to buy additional merchandise. To be effective, the sale must increase the volume of overall sales. This type of sale will increase turn but could reduce markups if the reduction in price was greater than the planned markdowns. Increasing turn will only improve the financial situation for the store if the gross margin and profits can remain as planned.

Turn can be too high. Turn must be made in balance with the replenishment rate. **Replenishment rate** is the speed of the stock coming into the store. If the turn of stock is higher than the replenishment rate, the store can become empty looking. **Stock outs** or broken assortments will occur. Stock outs will lead to lost sales and will offset the benefits of the higher turn. In this manner, inadequate stock levels can be damaging to the store just as overcrowding can damage the store's image and sales. A retailer who is planning to adjust turn and change the stock levels kept by the store must know the delivery capabilities of the vendor. If the vendor is an overseas manufacturer or if shipping is a problem, then the stock levels must be adjusted to allow for delays in delivery. Vendor/retailer **partnerships** are working relationships that are developed between a vendor, who may be a middleman or a manufacturer, and a retail buyer. The retailer will need a reliable partnership to have good control over the turn for the store.

Higher turns require more stock handling within the store than lower turns. If the turn for a store is over 12, the sales staff will be constantly replenishing stock to keep the store from looking empty and to prevent stock outs. In addition, high turns require more management of orders and receipt of goods. The buyer or whoever is placing the orders will spend more time placing orders for a store with a turn of 8 than for a store with a turn of 4. The cost of transportation also increases as the turn increases. Some stores with automatic replenishment systems have transportation of one new item at a time, usually by an airfreight system. The per-item transportation cost is much greater than shipping a bulk of items by rail or truck. The increased cost of a high turn must be offset by other changes in the store as observed in the P & L statement. For example, a system that keeps stock in place so that stock outs never occur will prevent lost sales from the stock outs or the lack of the right stock. A lost sale is rarely recovered, so the increase in sales may be balancing the increase in transportation. Moreover, the store looks fresher and has a successful image; therefore, the customer may stay longer, buy more, and return more often, which will also result in increased sales.

Rate of turn depends on merchandise classification, depth and breadth of merchandise assortments, and price ranges of merchandise. Before making changes to increase turn, the retailer should review what reciprocal changes and corresponding costs will occur. Careful planning and use of an expanded P & L statement are important tools for successful financial management.

Planning Stock

The amount or level of stock for a store is not a fixed number but is dependent on a number of variables. As previously discussed, stock is related to the desired sales volume and the rate of turn. Within these two broad concepts are many details that must be considered when determining stock. In general, more stock is needed than sales to allow for customer shopping. With apparel, many customers shop to obtain ideas about what items they want. They also need stock for comparison purposes. The same item in a selection of sizes is also needed for the customer to determine the appropriate size to obtain the desired fit for the item. In addition, stock is needed because customers expect a full store. An understocked store looks empty and may suggest to the consumer that the retailer is unsuccessful in buying and selling appealing merchandise. This image or impression can discourage a customer from making purchases or from making a repeat visit.

The rate of turn is related to the retailer's partnership with the vendor. Amount of stock depends on the frequency of reorders, the time needed to prepare and transmit orders, and the delivery time from the vendor. If reorders are placed frequently and merchandise is shipped in a timely manner, then stock levels can be lower than if orders are placed infrequently. When placing an order is a lengthy or time-consuming job, the buyer will be less willing to place frequent orders and will postpone ordering. Under these conditions, more stock is needed in the store and a lower turn will prevail. The use of computers for transmitting orders and for receiving shipping notices and invoices can shorten the time for preparing, transmitting, and processing orders. Delivery time from the vendor that is short and dependable can be a reason to keep less stock on hand and will encourage a faster turn of the merchandise. When a vendor is overseas and the merchandise must travel by boat and clear customs, the delivery times are often long and frequently undependable. The retailer will need to keep higher stock levels under these conditions, just in case something goes wrong and a quick delivery is not possible. Use of bar coding for invoice lists and for inventory management can shorten the time the stock stays in the backroom and can hasten its progress to floor stock. These small savings all contribute to faster delivery time and the potential to reduce levels of stock on hand.

Stock Planning Methods

Actual values of stock levels can be planned with a number of different formulas. These methods determine the value of stock that needs to be in the store. Before the buyer can shop for new stock, the amount of money that can be spent, or the value of the needed stock, must be known. These methods do not determine the size, style, or other variations of the items to be purchased. A retailer or buyer will make these style decisions after the value of the stock is determined. Two methods for planning the value of the stock are the basic stock method and the stock–sales ratio method.

The **basic stock method** uses a constant level of stock and adds an amount for sales. This method is also called the **average plus variation stock method**. Stability in the stock is emphasized with this method. This feature is very necessary for items that should never be missing from the store's inventory. In fact, some stores have a **never out list**—items that should always be in stock if the store is open. Certain sizes and colors in pantyhose, men's black dress socks, and other staple goods are examples of never out items.

The formula for the basic stock method starts with a base amount of stock that is always kept on hand and then adds an adjustment for the planned sales for the period. The **basic stock method** formula provides the retailer with a suggested BOM or the planned stock level for the beginning of the month and can be stated as

$$\text{BOM \$} = \text{Basic Stock \$} + \text{Planned Monthly Sales \$}$$

Sample Problem: Planned Stock—Basic Stock Method

A store keeps a basic stock of $4,500.00 per month in computer paper. The planned sales value for the month is $3,000.00. What is the planned stock for the merchandise?

Step 1. Enter the known information into the basic stock method formula.

   $\text{BOM \$} = \text{Basic Stock \$} + \text{Planned Monthly Sales \$}$
   $\text{BOM \$} = \$4,500.00 + \$3,000.00$

Step 2. Calculate the planned stock needed for the month.

   $\text{BOM \$} = \$7,500.00$

The **basic stock amount** provides a constant supply of merchandise or back-up inventory. This constant stock prevents stock outs, keeps the store filled with merchandise, and provides a backup stock in case deliveries are late. The amount of basic stock is determined by the type of goods, response time of vendors, store policy, season for the selling period, and planned promotions. The basic stock amount can be calculated by the retailer, or the amount may be determined by an industry or company standard. The accuracy and functionality of the basic stock method is very dependent on the appropriateness of the basic stock amount for the store and the merchandise. To calculate the basic stock amount, the retailer uses averages from previous selling periods. These previous periods may be years, quarters, seasons, or other accounting periods. The **basic stock** formula is

$$\text{Basic Stock \$} = \text{Average Stock \$} - \text{Average Monthly Sales \$}$$

This formula will provide the retailer with an estimation of the amount of stock that is constantly in the store and is not sold at that point. Average stock is calculated from an average of the BOMs in a period. For example, during one day in the store, 10 shirts of Brand X are on racks hanging on a fixture. Nine of the shirts are basic stock and one shirt is stock for sale. One shirt is sold during the day, and no shirts are restocked. If this pattern were charted over several days, the retailer could determine what was the average stock for the period and what were the average sales for the period. The retailer could use this information for determining the average stock needs for the store and add that to the planned sales to determine BOM stock as illustrated in the next sample problem.

Sample Problems: Basic Stock

Problem 1

The retailer has the following figures from the Shoe Department for the first four months. Average monthly sales for this department over the first quarter were $89,000.00. Using the first quarter figures, what is the value of the basic stock carried by this department?

	Jan	Feb	Mar	April
BOM	$120,000.00	$140,500.00	$110,000.00	$90,000.00
EOM	$140,500.00	$110,000.00	$90,000.00	$112,500.00

Step 1. Determine the average stock for the first quarter.

$$\text{Average Stock } \$ = (\Sigma\text{BOM } \$ + \text{EOM } \$)/(\#\text{ BOM} + 1)$$

$$\text{Average Stock } \$ = ([\$120,000.00 + \$140,500.00 + \$110,000.00]$$
$$+ \$90,000.00)/(3 + 1)$$

$$\text{Average Stock } \$ = (\$370,500.00 + \$90,000.00)/4$$

$$\text{Average Stock } \$ = \$460,500.00/4$$

$$\text{Average Stock } \$ = \$115,125.00$$

Step 2. Enter the known values into the basic stock formula and calculate the basic stock value.

$$\text{Basic Stock } \$ = \text{Average Stock } \$ - \text{Average Sales } \$$$

$$\text{Basic Stock } \$ = \$115,125.00 - \$89,000.00$$

$$\text{Basic Stock } \$ = \$26,125.00$$

Problem 2

If the planned sales for August for this Shoe Department are $75,000.00, what is the planned BOM for August?

Step 1. Enter the known values into the basic stock method formula.

$$\text{BOM } \$ = \text{Basic Stock } \$ + \text{Planned Sales } \$$$

$$\text{BOM } \$ = \$26,125.00 + \$75,000.00$$

Step 2. Calculate the value of BOM for August.

$$\text{BOM } \$ = \$101,125.00$$

This method is most appropriate for use with basic goods and for establishing model stock for never out items; however, the method is often used by retailers for all types of merchandise because of the ease of calculation. The retailer should realize that good judgment, a walk through the store, and conversations with buyers and sales associates are necessary to establish reliable basic stock figures. When basic stock is calculated, the retailer must evaluate the store situation to determine whether the basic stock is typical for the store and whether the stock levels are beneficial to the store. The basic stock method is a reliable and sound method for estimating stock needs. Previous records can give estimates of the stock and sales averages, but past performance is not always a measure of past success and is not an insurance for future success.

For fashion goods, the volume of stock would not stay consistent throughout the selling period. For this reason, a yearly, quarterly, or other long-term average might not provide an accurate estimate of the stock needs. The basic stock method tends to encourage the stability of stock instead of the rapid movement of stock. Using this method, a retailer would have to be very careful that the basic stock value does not encourage stagnant stock. With seasonal goods, the retailer must use judicious promotions and markdowns to remove old stock. In addition, procedures for moving stock forward from the backroom must be in place to keep stock moving in the store and to continue to offer fresh stock. Moving stock once it is on the floor is also important to create new displays and to encourage customers to stop and look.

A second method of calculating stock needs is the stock–sales ratio method. The **stock–sales ratio method** uses predetermined ratios for estimating stock relative to sales. This method focuses on the concept that sales are dependent upon the availability of floor stock for customer shopping. A specific amount of stock is required to achieve the planned sales. **Stock–sales ratios** relate stock requirements to planned sales and are an indication of the dollars of inventory needed to sell one dollar of merchandise. The formula for this method shows the relationship of stock at the beginning of the period, usually the month, to the sales planned for the month. The **stock–sales ratio method** formula is

BOM $ = Stock–Sales Ratio × Planned Monthly Sales $

Sample Problem: Stock–Sales Ratio Method

The Sporting Goods Department has stock–sales ratios of 3.4 for June and 5.6 for July. Planned sales for July are $56,000.00. What should be the planned stock level for BOM in July?

Step 1. Identify the correct stock–sales ratio.

July = 5.6

Step 2. Enter the known information into the stock–sales ratio method formula.

BOM $ = Stock–Sales Ratio × Planned Monthly Sales $
BOM $ = 5.6 × $56,000.00

Step 3. Calculate the correct BOM.

BOM $ = $313,600.00

The stock–sales ratios vary depending on the merchandise, the season, and other characteristics of the retail business; therefore, ratios vary from month-to-month, department-to-department, and retail type-to-retail type. Averages are used to create ratios for plans and comparisons. Ratios can be calculated from previous years or other selling periods, or they may be determined from industry or company standards. The National Retail Federation, other trade associations, or consultants to the industry could provide the retailer with ratios that are calculated for the merchandise or the season. The retailer who has careful accounting could make calculations based on the store records. With computerized inventory systems that are linked to computerized cash registers, the information would be easily available for any selected merchandise or time. Again, as with basic stock methods, the accuracy of the stock value will be dependent on the accuracy of the stock–sales ratios. When using past store data for calculations, the retailer must determine how well the stock situation functioned in the store. Questions to ask would include the following: "Did these past ratios provide adequate stock turn?" "Was new stock introduced at a timely rate?" "Did the stock level remain constant?" The formula for determining a **stock–sales ratio** from past records is

$$\text{Stock–Sales Ratio} = \text{BOM Stock \$/Monthly Net Sales \$}$$

(Note: Stock–sales ratios are not dollars and they are not percentages. They have no units. They are reported in decimals.)

Sample Problems: Stock–Sales Ratios

Problem 1

The retailer looks at last month's figures for a brand of luggage and finds the following information: net sales were $78,000.00 and the BOM was $199,800.00. What was the stock–sales ratio last month?

Step 1. Enter the known information into the stock–sales ratio formula.

$$\text{Stock–Sales Ratio} = \text{BOM \$/Net Sales \$}$$
$$\text{Stock–Sales Ratio} = \$199,800.00/\$78,000.00$$

Step 2. Calculate the stock–sales ratio.
$$\text{Stock–Sales Ratio} = 2.56$$

Problem 2

The net sales and BOM figures for the past six months for the store are shown in the following table:

	Jan	Feb	March	April	May	June	Total
Net Sales	$30,000.00	$40,000.00	$18,000.00	$20,000.00	$23,000.00	$20,000.00	
BOM	$56,000.00	$60,000.00	$43,000.00	$56,000.00	$67,000.00	$49,000.00	

The retailer wishes to use this information to determine a stock–sales ratio for the first half of the year. What is this ratio?

Step 1. Consider the stock–sales ratio formula and adjust for multiple months.

$$\text{Stock–Sales Ratio} = \text{BOM \$/Net Sales \$}$$
$$\text{Stock–Sales Ratio} = \Sigma \text{BOM \$/} \Sigma \text{Net Sales \$}$$

Step 2. Enter the known values into the formula.

$$\text{Stock–Sales Ratio} = (\$56,000.00 + \$60,000.00 + \$43,000.00$$
$$+ \$56,000.00 + \$67,000.00 + \$49,000.00)$$
$$/(\$30,000.00 + \$40,000.00 + \$18,000.00$$
$$+ \$20,000.00 + \$23,000.00 + \$20,000.00)$$

Step 3. Calculate the stock–sales ratio.

$$\text{Stock–Sales Ratio} = \$331,000.00/\$151,000.00$$

$$\text{Stock–Sales Ratio} = 2.19$$

(Computer Hint: If the net sales and BOM values are provided in a spreadsheet, formulas could be used for summing the rows and a simple division between the two sum cells would produce the stock–sales ratio.)

Methods for planning stock provide estimates of the stock value that would be needed for the beginning of a month or for other planning periods. These methods are based on values that are estimates or industry standards. The retailer must be a good merchandiser and realize that these values are guides, not absolute values. The store, the customer, the merchandise, and other characteristics of the retail situation may change the stock that is needed in a store. Competition from a newly opened store may lower sales, and stock levels would need to be adjusted. A sudden popularity of a fashion item may increase sales beyond the plan, and stock will need to be replenished more quickly. A severe snowstorm, a change in roads, or a sudden change in the economy are all factors that could affect the sales and thereby, affect stock levels. A retailer must be vigilant about stock to ensure that the stock remains fresh, is frequently changed, and is appealing to the customer.

Summary

Stock planning is important to maintain the correct level of inventory, and stock is needed to provide merchandise to sell. Stock and sales are closely related. New stock is needed to provide interest and excitement for the store and will encourage consumers to shop and to purchase. Too much stock makes a store appear crowded and discourages shoppers. Low levels of stock can result in stock outs of inventory and walk outs of unhappy consumers.

The amount of stock is also related to the turnover, or turn, of that stock. Turn is calculated as the average amount of stock in a set period. Turn is often calculated as turn per year, but the period could vary from one day to an extended period. If a store has a high rate of turn (e.g., 8 or 10 turns), the amount of stock needed at any one time to create a level of sales is lower than when the store has a lower rate of turn. The average rate of turn for a traditional department store is 4 or 5 turns per year. This number of turns corresponds to the traditional number of seasons in women's wear, indicating that new stock arrives for each season. As fashion changes have increased, turn needed to increase, and stock should move through the store at a faster rate or higher turn. Some specialty stores that carry fad goods and very fashion-oriented goods have stock turns as high as 15 or 18 turns per year.

Stock needs are calculated for the beginning of each month (BOM). Stock can also be examined on an annual or yearly basis relative to annual sales. When planning for a period, such as a season or six months, stock can be calculated for the total period and for each month within the period. When examining stock needs over time, the measures of average stock, basic stock, and turn are also used. Stock needs can be determined by a variety of methods including basic stock and stock–sales ratio. Basic stock depends on the existence of a basic amount of stock available for sale at all times. The basic stock should turn, but the level of that basic stock would remain the same. Stock–sales ratios can be obtained from trade organizations such as the National Retail Federation or can be calculated from history of the business. Ratios and basic stock levels are not the same for each classification of merchandise. The levels also must be adjusted for the shopping habits of the consumer, the levels and turn of the competition, and other business environment factors.

Key Terms

Average plus variation stock method	Floor stock	Stock on hand
Average stock	Never out list	Stock on order
Backroom stock	Overstocked	Stock outs
Basic stock amount	Partnerships	Stock–sales ratio
Basic stock method	Replenishment rate	Stock–sales ratio method
Beginning of the month (BOM)	Shopping goods	Stock turn
End of the month (EOM)	Stock levels	Turn

Discussion Questions

1. Why do retailers need to carry more stock than the amount of sales?
2. Why do customers shop before buying?
3. What is the reason for the buyer to monitor stock levels? For the department manager?
4. When average stock levels are known, what information is available?
5. How much stock is kept as basic stock? How should this vary by the fashion level of the merchandise?
6. How can basic stock contribute to low sales?
7. How fast should the turn be to keep stock fresh? How does this vary by fashion level of the merchandise?
8. What is wrong with too fast of a turn?
9. Why are stock outs bad for sales?
10. What is the best stock method for a retailer? How is this affected by the fashion level of the merchandise?

Exercises

Average Stock

1. The BOM for July was $40,000.00. The EOM for July was $35,000.00. What was the average stock for the month?

2. For the third quarter, the BOM for each month was $42,000.00; $36,600.00; and $29,900.00, respectively. What was the average stock for August?

3. If the average stock for a month was $66,000.00 and the BOM was $100,000.00, what was the EOM for that month?

4. Average stock was $489,000.00 for Month 1. The BOM for Month 2 was $560,000.00. What was the BOM for Month 1?

5. You are the new assistant buyer in Department #12. Your boss gives you the following BOM figures and asks you to find the average stock for the six-month period and for the first quarter. The six-month BOMs are January $100,000.00; February $80,000.00; March $70,000.00; April $110,000.00; May $120,000.00; June $120,000.00; July $100,000.00.

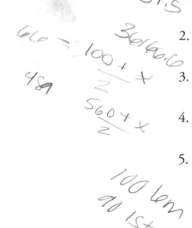

Turn

1. What is the stock turn if the annual sales of a department are $966,900.00 and the average stock is $161,150.00?

2. The average stock of a department is $248,000.00. The sales for that period are $345,000.00. What is the stock turn for the department?

3. The BOM for May is $1,100,000.00. The BOM for June is $950,000.00. The net sales for May are $4,000,000.00. What is the stock turn for May? Did this buyer replenish often or infrequently? How do you know?

4. What is the average stock in a department with annual sales of $1,750,000.00 and an annual stock turn of 4.50?

5. For July, a store had a BOM stock of $600,000.00 at retail. For August, the BOM was $560,000.00. July's net sales were $750,000.00. What was the stock turnover for the month of July?

Basic Stock Method   BS+MS = BOM

1. If planned sales for the period are $49,000.00 and basic stock is $39,990.00, what is the BOM inventory that is needed for the period?

2. Planned sales for the month of January are predicted to be $150,000.00. The Shoe Department always keeps a basic stock of $80,000.00. What is needed for the January BOM?

3. The BOM stock for curtains is planned to be $68,900.00. The planned sales for the month are $20,660.00. What is the basic stock that is kept for this merchandise?

4. The BOM for a department is $165,780.00. The basic stock kept by the department is $76,900.00. What are the planned sales?

5. The BOM for March was recorded as $17,980.00. Sales for that period were recorded as $9,999.00. What was the basic stock carried during that month? If average monthly sales for the store are $8,880.00, what is the average monthly inventory?

(Note: Basic Stock = Average Monthly Inventory $ − Average Monthly Sales)

6. In January, last year's planned sales were $489,500.00. This year, a 3.00% increase is expected. If the basic stock is projected to be $399,900.00, what is the BOM inventory need for January?

7. The average monthly sales for May are $6,600.00 for the past five years. The average monthly inventory for May is $22,800.00. If planned sales for this May are projected to be $7,000.00, what is the needed EOM for April?

8. Last year the department had $6,600.00 in net sales for the month of December. Sales in October were $5,000.00 and in November were $6,900.00. This year, the planned sales for December are $6,800.00. Last year, the BOM inventory was as follows: October $9,600.00; November $13,000.00; December $13,500.00; January $10,000.00. What should the stock level be for the beginning of this December?

Stock–Sales Ratio Method

1. The department has a stock–sales ratio of 3.30 for January. The planned sales for January are $100,000.00. What is the needed stock level for January?

2. A store has an average stock–sales ratio of 6.50. The annual net sales for the store are $2,600,000.00. What is the stock need for that store?

3. The department has stock–sales ratios of 3.40 for June and 5.60 for July. The planned sales for July are $56,000.00. What should the planned stock level be for July?

4. If the planned sales for the quarter are $54,680.00 and the stock levels are $454,000.00, what is the stock–sales ratio?

5. The stock–sales ratio for the Linen Department in December is 3.30. The BOM stock value in the department is $120,000.00. What are the sales for that department?

Stock and Turn Combined

The following figures are planned for the jewelry department:

	Jan	Feb	Mar	Qtr	April	May	June	July	Total	Avg
Pl Net Sales	$10,000.00	$6,000.00	$11,000.00		$9,900.00	$8,400.00	$12,600.00			
BOM	$33,000.00	$18,000.00	$28,000.00		$40,000.00	$30,000.00	$38,000.00			
EOM										
Avg Stock										
Turn										
S–S Ratio										
Basic Stock										

1. For the first six months of Department #28, these are the planned BOM stock figures. If the BOM for July needs to be $18,000, what was the average stock for the six months?

2. Using BOM as an indication of stock held in the department, what is the turnover planned by this department for the six months?

3. What is the turnover planned for February?

4. What are the stock–sales ratios for January and for June?

5. What is the stock–sales ratio for the first quarter?

6. Use these figures to calculate an average or historical basic stock value for the department.

Computer Exercises

General Directions

- Print and save all problems. (See directions for the Computer Lab–Profit and Loss Problems.)
- Add comments as requested at the bottom of each spreadsheet.

- Set up a Pro forma P & L with a Year 1 to Year 2 by creating the headings, columns, and rows of a Profit and Loss statement (with two sets of columns for dollars and percentages), last year's activities (Year 1), and this year (Year 2).

Planning Stock

1. *Six-Month Sales & Stock Plan for Buyers Unlimited–Stock–Sales Ratio Method*

   a. Set up a new P & L form. You will need a column to identify the factors in each row, six additional columns (one for each Month), and a total column. You will need headings for each column (factors, numbers for months, and total). You will also need rows for four factors: sales percentage, net sales, stock–sales ratios, and BOM stock.

   b. *Buyers Unlimited* has a total six-month sales plan for net sales of $440,000. The net sales percentage for Months 1 and 2 are to be 20%, net sales for Months 3–5 are to be 12% each, and Month 6 is to be 24%. The stock–sales ratios are 6.5, 5.2, 4.8, 3.3, 2.8, and 7.6 for each month, respectively.

   c. Use formulas to calculate the monthly sales.

   d. Calculate the BOM stock needed to reach the sales goal for each month and the total stock handled by the store. Use the stock–sales ratio formula to calculate the BOM stock needs.

2. *Average stock and average sales*

   a. Use the spreadsheet in the previous problem; and add another column for average, a row for EOM, and a row for turn and a row for average stock.

   b. The EOM for Month 6 is $700,000. The EOM for other months is the next month's BOM.

   c. Using formulas, find the average sales for the six-month period and the average stock and turn for each month and the six-month period.

3. *Six-Month Sales & Stock Plan for Buyers Unlimited–Stock–Sales Ratio Method*

   a. Set up a new P & L form. You will need a column to identify the factors in each row, six additional columns (one for each Month), and a total column. You will need headings for each column (factors, numbers for months, and total). You will also need rows for four factors: sales percentage, net sales, stock–sales ratios, and BOM stock.

   b. *Buyers Unlimited* has a total six-month sales plan for net sales of $580,000. The net sales percentage for Months 1 and 2 are to be 20%, net sales for Months 3–4 are to be 15% each, Month 5 is 10% and Month 6 is to be 20%. The stock–sales ratios are 6.6, 5.6, 4.2, 3.5, 2.6, and 7.8 for each month, respectively.

   c. Use formulas to calculate the monthly sales.

   d. Calculate the BOM stock needed to reach the sales goal for each month and the total stock handled by the store. Use the stock–sales ratio formula to calculate the BOM stock needs.

4. *Average stock and average sales*

   a. Use the spreadsheet in the previous problem, and add another column for average, a row for EOM, and a row for turn and a row for average stock.

   b. The EOM for Month 6 is $_____. The EOM for other months is the next month's BOM.

   c. Using formulas, find the average sales for the six-month period and the average stock and turn for each month and the six-month period.

CHAPTER 8

Six-Month Plans

Objectives

After completing this chapter, the student will be able to

- explain why a buyer needs a six-month plan
- identify the components of the six-month plan
- explain the stages of development for a six-month plan
- calculate component values for the six-month plan
- explain how the plan is not a static document
- discuss the buyers controls and skills used to formulate the plan

The **six-month plan** is a working document that the retailer uses to transition from the expanded P & L statement to the assortment plan for shopping in the market. The expanded P & L contains information on the value of sales planned, goods purchased, and reductions allocated. This information is in a summary format and provides financial guidance for all the operations in the retail store. The six-month plan operationalizes this information for the buyer and contains a monthly breakdown of sales, reductions, stock by BOM and EOM, and purchases for the entire business, for a department, or for a merchandise classification. The assortment coverage of the six-month plan is determined by the scope of responsibility for the buyer. This document becomes the financial foundation for the purchase of merchandise, containing predictions about future sales, money available for making purchases and reductions, and standards for EOM stock levels.

All the buying plans will evolve from this master plan and, at the end of the planning period, are evaluated against this plan. Plans are based on the bi-annual periods of spring (February–July) and fall (August–January). During each of the two six-month periods in a year and at the end of each period, the buyer will evaluate sales, purchases, stock levels, and reductions relative to this plan. The six-month plan becomes the control for the buyer. It provides projections for stock purchases and goals for sales quotas. The relationship between sales and stock is clearly visible in the six-month plan. Success in sales or failure in sales is clearly recorded in the plan, and the associated impact of these successes or failures on stock levels is readily visible. Changes in one month affect the success or failure in the next month. The plan becomes a rolling record of the store's merchandise activities and, therefore, provides guidance and control for the retailer and the buyer. Many buyers are evaluated on their ability to "**meet plan**." To meet plan implies that the actual values that are transcribed through the store activities are comparable to the values created in the plan. Thus, the ability to plan well and to execute the plan becomes an important part of the buyer's job.

A typical six-month plan is composed of rows representing sales, stock for BOM and EOM, reductions, and purchases at retail. A sample six-month plan is provided in Figure 8.1. A plan in the calculation stage will have one row for each component for the allocation method (e.g., percentage and stock–sales ratio) and one row for each component for the planned value. The columns of the six-month plan represent each month of the plan and a total. The plan also has an additional row for each component's actual values. These rows are completed as the months are completed in the store. Actual values can be compared with plan values.

The interrelationship among the retail functions is evident in the six-month plan. The sales are the direct responsibility of store managers, department managers, and sales associates. The reductions are handled by merchandisers, sales associates, and promotions managers. The purchase of stock for BOM is the responsibility of the buyers. The three functions of selling, buying, and promoting must interact smoothly and seamlessly for

Six-Month Plan for the Company—Spring Period

Last Year's Sales for Spring:				This Year's Sales for Spring:			
				Reduction %:		Reduction $:	
				Initial Markup %:			

Spring	Feb	Mar	Apr	May	June	July	Total
Mnthly % Plan							
Mnthly % Actual							
Sales $ Plan							
Sales $ Actual							
Red % Plan							
Red % Actual							
Red $ Plan							
Red $ Actual							
EOM $ Plan							
EOM $ Actual							
S–S Ratio Plan							
S–S Ratio Actual							
BOM $ Plan							
BOM $ Actual							
Pl Purch $							
Actual Purch $							
OTB cost							

Figure 8.1   Six-Month Plan Format.

the customer's best shopping experience. The success of each function, as interrelated with the other functions, is very clearly documented in this plan, and much of the information in the previous chapters is utilized in the development of the six-month plan. Decisions about sales, reductions, and stock are reflected in the decisions made in forming the six-month plan. The buyer needs extensive information to construct a viable six-month plan.

Development of the plan consists of three stages: **preplan stage**, **specific information stage**, and **calculation stage**. Each buyer and each retailer may have different approaches to the development of the plan. The buyer may be working for a retailer that maintains extensive records and previous data are readily available. In contrast, the buyer may be working for a new retail business or within a new merchandise classification, in which extensive data are not readily available. The existence or lack of previous data does impact some steps within the specific information stage and the calculation stage of the six-month plan development; however, the basic components, relationships of those components, and calculations for a six-month plan are generic to the retail situation.

Preplan Stage in Development of a Six-Month Plan

The preplan stage is the first stage in the development of a six-month plan. This stage of the six-month plan may be completed in conjunction with other generalized planning for the retail business (e.g., P & L statement development, strategic planning, and environmental scan for sales planning), or it may be a separate planning process completed by the buyer, assistant buyers, or a planning team. The preplan stage involves the gathering of generalized background information and provides guides, checks, and parameters for plan development. Four key issues covered by information from the preplan stage include the following: (a) identification of macrotrends or cultural barometers, (b) comprehension of the buying–selling process as related to the product life cycle of the merchandise assortment, (c) insight in the buying patterns of the target consumer, and (d) establishment of a clear, consistent image to attract the desired target consumer.

To address these key issues, the buyer in the preplan stage often draws upon the same information that is derived in the more general planning of strategic planning and image control that was covered in Chapter 5. In addition, the buyer uses information gathered in sales planning, which includes environmental scanning, as covered in Chapter 6, and in stock planning, which was covered in Chapter 7. Some retailers, and their buyers, conduct exhaustive research in the preplan stage both in conjunction with strategic planning and separate from that type of planning. The research establishes a substantial background for an accurate, workable plan in the calculation stage. As with strategic planning, many large retailers have resources and personnel to collect vast amounts of information about their retail organization, the target consumer, current competition, fashion trends, cultural barometers, and other external and internal factors that may affect the retail business. Smaller retailers may have these resources or may need to rely on major vendors, bankers, forecasting services, news forecasts, and stock reports to compile information in the preplan stage.

In addition to obtaining general information, buyers during preplanning should also shop both retail and other market competition, evaluate the market advantages of the competition, and conduct comparative product analyses for their targeted merchandise classifications. Buyers should analyze past, current, and future fashion trends specific to their store type and merchandise classifications and should identify what is currently being sold at retail among the competition. They should study market research findings from focus groups, surveys, and consumer boards or panels. They should read trade journals and consumer publications in addition to reading information about product testing and POS data. After integrating information from these sources, the buyer must determine how the six-month plan must reflect this general information and the specific information to satisfy the wants and needs of the target consumer.

The relationship of the preplan and specific information stages to the calculation of the plan is noted in the following examples. A retail business that has an image of frequent reductions and multiple promotions will have emphasis on reductions. This information is determined in strategic planning and preplanning processes. The buyer for this business will need to plan carefully stock levels to keep adequate supplies in the store. In another example, a business with a fashion forward image will want to consider high initial markups and fast turns because the merchandise will be very new and should change frequently. Other factors determined in preplanning are the size of the store, the projected inventory levels, and the overall desired look of the store, and will be important in making a six-month plan. A store that is expected to look sparse or a store that is expected to have a crowded feel will have very different stock allocations.

In summary, general background issues determined during other planning processes are used in making plans for many aspects of a retail business and are also relevant for review when developing the six-month plan. When making any plans, the buyer wants always to remember the store image and the customer characteristics. Customer satisfaction is a primary goal in retailing so the desires and characteristics of the customer should always be kept in mind when planning. During the next stage—specific information, the buyer will study, if available, actual figures from the six-month plan for the same season of the previous year or will obtain trade and other merchandising information to assist in calculations during the third and final stage of plan development.

Specific Information Stage in Development of a Six-Month Plan

During the specific information stage of plan development, the buyer gathers and analyzes merchandising and numeric data that will be used in the calculation stage of the plan development. If available, the buyer will study last year's sales figures, reductions, purchases, stock–sales ratios, and turnover. These provide the buyer with realistic information and actual occurrences in the business. Without actual previous data, general industry data and the buyer's merchandise knowledge must be used to assist the buyer in the calculation stage. The buyer will need information to determine the following parts of the six-month plan: (a) total planned sales and total planned reductions for the period, (b) guide for monthly distribution for sales, (c) guide for monthly distribution for reduction amounts, (d) method for planning stock, (e) planned BOM for the first month, and (f) target EOM for the last month. Specific information data may come from the strategic plan, the P & L statement, the preplan stage, other retailers or trade organizations, stockholders and board members, and historical data from the company.

Total planned sales and the related *total planned reductions* are often decided as part of the overall planning for the coming year and are, therefore, determined independently of the six-month plan development. In a business that conducts strategic planning, actions or decisions on goals for future sales and percentages for other aspects of the operation will be part of the planning process for both new and continuing businesses. Financial information, about sales and other line items available from the P & L statement, can also be used in determining sales volume and in selecting percentages needed for the six-month plan. These figures may be given to the buyer, or the buyer may have sole responsibility to determine sales and reductions based on various sources of information.

To determine *total planned sales*, buyers with or without previous sales information use information about national retail sales averages, average sales from similar retail outlets, and changing patterns of sales volumes for their stores or similar stores. The amount for total planned sales is the initial point of planning for the calculations of the six-month plan. All other calculations are based on this figure; therefore, great care should be exercised when making the decisions about total planned sales.

For a continuing business or a continuing merchandise classification, the actual figures for the same season in the previous year are analyzed and utilized as a basis for this year's plan. The buyer will compare planned sales with actual sales for the same period last year and decide what would have been a realistic figure for that period and reasons for the differences between last year's plan and actual figures. When the buyer has a realistic total sales figure for the same period from last year, the buyer will then determine the adjustments needed to last year's amount to set a figure for this year's planning period. An adjustment, or a percentage of increase or decrease for sales, is based on both external and internal factors relative to the retail business including general fashion trends. Information to determine the adjustment percentage may include economic conditions and other factors discussed in the planning processes from Chapter 5, the environmental scan described in Chapter 6, and the additional information gathered in the preplan stage. An increase may be necessary if the cost of goods for replacement merchandise will show an increase in price, or operating expenses may rise because of increases by suppliers or wage increases. A decrease could occur because of internal factors such as decisions to reduce sales staff or promotions. In some cases, the adjustments will be dictated by upper management, but many buyers will be given the latitude and freedom to predict the size of the change. The limits for change or adjustment must be realistic for the current market condition, and such limits are usually delimited by management.

With a new business, the P & L statement, the strategic plan, the preplan information, and a realistic view of the business prospects for the buyer's merchandise classifications are used to set a sales goal for the six-month period. For many businesses, a team approach to this part of the planning process is recommended and is followed by retailers, as competition requires increasingly careful planning. Detailed information about methods of determining sales figures without previous information was covered in Chapter 6. At the end of this step in the specific information stage, the buyer will have either a percentage to use for adjusting a previous period's sales total to the current total planned sales, when previous data are available, or a fixed dollar amount for total planned sales from one of the planning documents.

Total planned reductions are established and controlled to prevent erosion of the gross margin and a resulting loss of profit. The amount of reductions is viewed in the expanded P & L statement as an adjustment to total sales and, as noted in Chapter 4, can include the items of markdowns, returns, employee discounts, and shrinkage. Reduction planning is conducted to provide a guide, not a goal, to the buyer, to stimulate sales, and to increase turnover of merchandise assortment. Although reductions may be viewed in a comprehensive or summative format for the P & L statement, some businesses include only the markdown portion of reductions in the six-month plan. Using only the markdown portion of the reductions reflects the fact that markdowns are the major bane for many buyers and retailers, and if markdowns are not controlled, they result in the eventual demise of the retailer. In addition, markdowns are the one factor within reductions with the largest impact on sales, both as a reduction to the expected initial price and as a leverage or promotion to stimulate customers' purchases.

Although markdowns for many retailers are most important among the reduction items, some businesses also place shrinkage as a separate line item in the six-month plan. The size of the shrinkage amount may be established by corporate policy or determined from previous periods. Industry averages for shrinkage are between two and five percent of total sales when calculated separately from markdowns. Additional discussions of shrinkage can be found in Chapter 4. When markdowns or shrinkage are presented in a six-month plan as separate line items, the remaining reductions (e.g., employee discounts) are made as adjustments to sales or are placed as a separate line item labeled additional reductions. The exact mix of reductions that are included in the six-month plan may vary from business to business depending on corporate policies and accounting or taxation procedures. For the explanations of the six-month plan in this chapter, the generic term of reductions is used without qualifications of the content or breakdown within the area of reductions.

For a continuing business, the buyer considers the amounts used for reductions in the same period for the previous year and makes adjustments. Many buyers, merchandisers, or planners compare both reduction and sales figures for the last five years to reveal any common or useful patterns that may be applied to the current plan development. When analyzing the previous actual figures in a continuing business, buyers also note atypical events that may impact reductions. A special promotion with markdowns because of a new vendor, a unique community event, unusual weather conditions, or dramatic changes in economic or political conditions may occur only once for a buyer. For example, if a summer is unusually cool, the buyer may have to take extra markdowns to promote and sell the merchandise that is purchased specifically for hot weather. Reductions for that period may be larger than expected. The buyer must consider whether these once-in-a-lifetime events are actually periodic or annual events. A one-time sale may have been so popular that it should be repeated; however, the buyer must avoid consumer deceit and questionable legalities when planning one-time only events that occur annually. The buyer will also need to examine the amounts of old stock or inventory on hand at the beginning of the new season to make adjustments. With a firm figure for actual reductions noted from the previous period in last year, the buyer will need to determine the percentage for reductions. To determine a percentage for previous total actual reductions, the buyer will relate total actual reductions from the base period (or same period last year) to total actual sales from the same base period. The formula for calculating this percentage is the same as that used in the P & L statement. The formula for **total actual reductions percentage** is

$$\text{Total Actual Reductions \%} = \text{Base Period Total Actual Reductions \$} \\ / \text{ Base Period Total Actual Sales \$}$$

For example, the buyer determines, after analysis, that the appropriate reductions dollars for the spring period of last year were $22,000.00 and the total actual sales were $92,000.00, with an actual reductions percentage of 23.91%. As in the expanded P & L statement, any component of the reductions such as markdowns can be calculated with a similar formula. When the actual reductions percentage for the period in last year is determined, the buyer will use information from the preplan stage to determine adjustments that should be made to the percentage for this period. As a final check to the accuracy of the percentage, all buyers should study the general business outlook because a negative business outlook can translate into more reductions needed to motivate customers. Because of this process in the specific information stage, the buyer now has a percentage for total planned reductions. The percentage will be used in the calculation stage of plan development to determine the total planned reduction dollars.

Buyers that lack previous data will need to plan reductions based on trade information, environmental scanning, preplan information, and a cautious approach to markdowns. These buyers will develop an estimated reductions percentage to use in calculating the total planned reductions.

With a plan for total sales and reductions, the buyer will need a guide or method for determining the *monthly distribution of total planned sales*. The guide to distribution may be developed from guidelines given by upper level management, may be based on merchandising information, or may be adjustments from data of previous periods. In addition, seasons and geographic locations have a correlation to monthly sales. Buyers with both continuing stock and buyers with new merchandise classifications must consider the number of selling seasons within the six-month period and how much volume each season produces. For example, in the first six-month period, buyers may purchase merchandise for the spring and summer. Some early fall or transitional merchandise may also be included in this period, especially if Back-to-School promotions are planned. The second six-month period begins with a continuation of the early fall season and covers the winter or holiday seasons, including the famous after-Christmas sales and returns. Too much carry-over merchandise from the end of the planning period to the beginning of the next period can delay the influx of new merchandise. The buyer must be careful to coordinate seasonal openings with specific months so that appropriate new merchandise can be ordered. Every retailer or buyer in a continuing business or a new business must constantly evaluate what holidays and other events stimulate their consumers to purchase greater amounts of merchandise and to evaluate how important each event is to increasing overall sales volume for the six-month planning period.

For a continuing business, predicted future monthly sales are based on the past sales history of the business with adjustments for current and predicted business factors. Using the preplan information gathered in the analysis of total sales volume from previous periods, the buyer must consider sales on a monthly basis. When reviewing past sales history, specific months for major holidays should be pinpointed, and promotional events that created larger sales volumes should be noted. Holidays that have changing dates according to the calendar must be identified. Easter and Memorial Day are holidays that mark the beginning of new seasons for many retailers; however, the exact date of these events can vary for several weeks as in the case of Easter or several days as with Memorial Day. For many retailers, the specific month and the position of the week within the month in which the Easter holiday occurs become very important when planning both sales and delivery periods. For example, when Easter is observed in March, 20 percent of the sales for the period would be in March; however, when the holiday is observed in April, the sales for March should be revised downward and the sales for April should be adjusted upwards. The buyer with any continuing merchandise must consider the age of the in-stock merchandise at the beginning of the season, and how much new and full-priced merchandise versus older and reduced merchandise is in inventory.

A guide for distribution of sales values across the months for the buyer without previous data is to spread percentages evenly across the period; however, this method will quickly result in error because sales in most merchandise classifications of retailing are not evenly acquired throughout the year. Customers buy more electronic equipment in the month just before Christmas than any other month, and they buy more home repair items during the summer months in comparison to the winter months.

This fact of variance about stock and inventory was discussed in Chapter 7. For this reason, the buyer must examine the factors that influence sales on a bi-annual period and on a monthly basis. Sales volumes vary from month to month, season to season, and year to year. Many retailers actualize 40 to 45 percent of their total sales volume in the first six-month period (February–July) and 55 to 60 percent during the second six-month period (August–January). For other retailers, the majority of the sales may occur during the last three months of the year, and some stores find that 40 percent or more of their sales occur between Thanksgiving Day and Christmas Day.

Without previous data, a buyer can use merchandising knowledge to fine-tune the estimated monthly percentages as appropriate for their customers and products. Calendar-related items, merchandise classifications, and geographic locations are known to affect the volume of monthly sales. When viewing the calendar, the buyer should know that some months are slow or have low levels of sales while other months have higher amounts of sales. Months with major promotional events that are designed to generate sales without markdowns will have higher sales levels than more quiet months of March or June. These events may be related to holidays, cultural or social events, or store promotions. Examples of these events are Mother's Day, Back-to-School, and Valentine's Day. Months with religious holidays of Easter, Hanukkah, and Christmas have higher sales volumes. For some retailers, Memorial Day, Labor Day, or Halloween generate promotional events that impact the sales volume for the period preceding and including that day.

Some merchandise classifications are very seasonal, which is reflected in their monthly sales volume. Retailers who carry mostly warm-weather attire, pool or summer sports equipment, or other outdoor furnishings will find that most of their sales are during the warm-weather months and will have very few sales in the winter months. Many of these retailers seek alternative merchandise to carry during the cold-weather, six-month period. For example, a retailer who carried pool and deck furnishings in the summer may carry fireplace furnishings and ski equipment in the winter. For merchandise with a fashion emphasis, February is usually the smallest sales volume month, even with the inclusion of Valentine's Day, and December is the month with the largest sales volume. For many retailers, the August sales volume is larger than that of September. For some merchandise classifications, August sales are dependent upon Back-to-School business. Geographic locations may also affect sales volumes and distributions according to the month. For example, retailers located in ski resort areas, which may be found primarily in mountainous or northern locales, find that their sales are primarily in the winter months and may be forced to close during set periods of the retail year.

Regardless of previous data, merchandise classification, location, or season, retailers should keep very concise and accurate records of sales volumes and reductions throughout the year to use in planning future periods. After one year in business or with a new merchandise classification, the buyer should no longer be without data to aid in the development of a new plan. At the end of this step in the specific information stage, the buyer will have established a percentage of total planned sales to be assigned to each month within the six-month period.

In addition to a monthly spread of sales, the buyer will also need a guide for *monthly distribution of total planned reductions*. Reductions, similar to, but different from sales, also vary across periods, across months, and across seasons. The amount of reductions for each month is dependent on many factors, but primarily on the promotions plan because of the large portion that markdowns contribute to total reductions. Buyers should determine the dates throughout the six-month period when customers will expect markdowns and will require money for returns. For example, in the month prior to Christmas, the sales volume rises in most retail business; however, in contrast for reductions, the end of December and the month of January contain the famous after-

Christmas returns. As customer returns are often included as part of reductions, these post-Christmas months will have a higher volume of reductions than months where most customers are purchasing items for their own use and possibly at full price. The post-Christmas period is also noted for the after-Christmas sales, which may be expected by customers shopping for specific merchandise. Pre-Christmas weeks, Mother's Day, and other times that employees may purchase items for themselves may include more employee discounts, another aspect of reductions. Promotional events that include markdowns will also have to be considered because markdowns are part of reductions. The buyer should work closely with the promotions or events planning department to allocate the reductions budget properly and to consider stock needs to support the promotions. These markdowns and promotional considerations are different from the promotional events that will promote merchandise that is at a full price.

If the merchandise is seasonal in nature, the buyer should also recognize months or weeks that mark the end of the season. Some retailers have big end-of-the-season sales at the end of every season or a twice-annual sale at the end of every six-month period, when they reduce the price on the current season's merchandise to clear out the old inventory. These events make room for new inventory, generate interest and enthusiasm among customers, and release money needed to pay for the incoming new merchandise. These end-of-the-season reductions or clearances should be controlled and planned, which is good advice for any reductions, as noted in Chapter 4 in the discussion on reductions and in Chapter 16 on promotions. Reductions are never an excuse or a solution to poor planning, inadequate advertising, or bad buying. In addition, reductions, specifically markdowns, must be planned carefully to place them early enough in the season to insure that time remains for additional markdowns if needed within the same season. Occasionally, merchandise does not sell at the first markdown and additional markdowns are needed. On the other hand, the buyer must also be careful not to plan markdowns too soon in the season or to take markdown cuts that are too deep in the retail price. The timing and size of markdowns is detailed in Chapter 15.

When the previous season's data are available, the buyer will review planned reductions, actual reductions, and typical and atypical promotions that required markdowns within those months. The buyer will then determine the dollar value of each month's reductions. These actual monthly reductions dollars will be compared to the same period's total actual sales to develop a percentage for each month. The formula to determine the **actual monthly reductions percentage** from a previous or base period is similar to the formula used to find total reductions percentage and is stated as

Monthly Actual Reductions % = Base Period Monthly Actual Reductions $ / Base Period Total Actual Sales $

Additional methods for finding a monthly reduction percentage are used by some buyers with previous data, but these methods rely on formulas with different denominators than this formula. Using merchandising knowledge and information from the preplan stage, adjustments will be made from last year's data to arrive at this period's monthly percentages. These monthly percentages based on total sales should equal the total planned reductions percentage that was calculated in the previous step of the specific information stage. The six-month plan with its columns of total and monthly entries provides a check-and-balance system for the buyer.

Without previous data, the buyer must set a guide for monthly distributions based on the preplan and specific information stages. If no previous data are available, the percentages can be evenly spread across the period; however, this method will quickly result in error because reductions are not evenly made throughout the year. Without other guidance, the buyer should place at least 70 percent of the annual reductions into the last six months of the year, and over 60 percent of that amount should be placed in the last month of the last period. Additional fine adjustments could be made as noted in the preplan stage to coincide with periods of markdowns, clearances, and returns.

With or without previous information, reduction percentage targets may be given to the buyer by upper management or determined by the buyer based on information from the preplan stage. Whatever the method of determining the percentage, the buyer will find that large downward adjustments in reductions from previous periods is difficult. Although planning reductions is difficult, the buyer should attempt to plan realistic reduction figures because incorrect amounts of reductions will affect other portions of the P & L statement and the financial health of the business. Inventory levels, sales volumes, and the potential to purchase new merchandise are directly affected by the successful targeting of reductions.

The buyer will need to determine *levels of inventory* or *BOM* required to produce the planned sales for each month. When inventory is discussed relative to sales in the six-month plan, the buyer is usually discussing the BOM levels of stock. Several methods of determining stock relative to sales were discussed in Chapter 7. Both the desired stock levels and the methods to determine exact amounts of stock vary according to merchandise classification, store type, and other retail factors. For example, many merchandise classifications require floor stock for customers to view while shopping. Methods of calculating inventory or stock values relative to sales values must be determined prior to the development of the plan. The buyer needs to know the retailer's preferred method or the method that is most workable for that merchandise classification. The availability of previous stock and sales information may be the determining factor in selecting a stock method. The other determining factor may be the complexity of the computing equipment and the mathematical skills of the buyer. Some of the stock methods require more extensive calculations than other stock methods. The speed of turn, the delivery restrictions, and other stock-specific information are needed when determining the BOM for the plan. Final decision on the stock method may include input from the divisional merchandise manager, the general merchandise manager, and the store or unit manager.

The buyer who has previous information about similar planning periods will have data about actual sales volumes and stock levels. Buyers with this information can use the stock–sales ratio method of inventory calculation. These ratios can be standardized over time in a continuing business and should be available for the buyer's use. If standardized or corporate ratios are not available, but previous six-month plans are available, the buyer can use the stock–sales ratio formula and data from a previous period or for several periods to determine the exact stock–sales ratios for each month. The buyer can use these ratios in the calculation stage for identifying the BOM for each month. When the buyer is working in a continuing buying situation, the buyer will also need information about the final EOM of the previous planning period. The EOM from the last month of the previous plan must coincide with the BOM for the first month of the new plan.

When the previous monthly inventory levels are known, the buyer, utilizing the sales and stock dollars, can find the ratios by using the **stock–sales ratio** formula, which is

$$\text{Stock–Sales Ratio} = \text{BOM Stock \$/Monthly Net Sales \$}$$

For example, a buyer finds that a previous February had stock of $140,000.00 and sales of $52,000.00. Using the stock–sales ratio formula, the ratio for February is 2.69.

A buyer without previous data must use industry averages for the stock–sales ratios. This method has problems because various merchandise classifications, types of consumers, and store types require different levels of stock. A stock ratio of at least two times the sales should be planned if no other guidance is available. Again, the buyer should begin collecting data immediately during the first six-month period to provide background for future plan development. Without a computerized planning system and with limited previous data, the buyer may keep the stock calculations simple and use a basic stock or an estimated stock–sales ratio plan. These methods are simple to calculate, but may quickly result in overstocking or inadequate stock situations if sales have major fluctuations. The buyer should also remember that unplanned increases or decreases in sales or reductions will affect the stock situation.

The final information that the buyer needs is the *EOM for each month*. These figures are a simple rewrite of the BOMs found in the calculation stage, except the final EOM. For the first five EOMs in the six-month period, the value of one month's EOM is the BOM for the next month. The final EOM will depend on the BOM desired for the next plan period. For example, the final EOM in the spring period is the BOM of the fall period. In other words, the EOM for July is the BOM for August. Because August or February, depending on the period, is not yet in the planning cycle, the buyer will have to estimate the EOM for the final month. This figure has to be available to proceed to the calculation of planned purchases. For some buyers, the retailer or other manager will provide the final EOM figure. Many buyers, especially those working with continuing business and previous plans, wish to establish the EOM based either on previous data or on their estimates. Utilizing past experiences and information from the preplan stage, the experienced buyer will be able to adjust the estimated final EOM for a more accurate six-month plan. The final EOM becomes critical to the success of the next six-month plan. Planning is a constant and ongoing process and must continue even when a six-month plan is developed for the current operating period.

The conclusion of the specific information stage is the analysis of *planned purchases*. The term **planned purchases at retail** indicates the amount of merchandise that can be brought into stock during a given period. This merchandise amount is estimated in dollars and is used to indicate how much money the buyer will have to shop in the market and to buy new merchandise. These purchases are allocated to the individual months of the six-month plan to support the planned sales. By controlling the BOM inventory, the buyer can plan a steady flow of merchandise through the month and throughout the period. This flow of allocation permits the buyer to add excitement and newness to the merchandise assortments that will support the image desired by the retailer. To meet the plan, the buyer must be sure that an adequate supply of merchandise is on hand for each month until replenishment shipments are received into the floor stock to replace goods that sell. The buyer must plan for purchases to be received before the bulk of the merchandise will be sold. This imperative statement is especially true when major promotions are planned. Determining appropriate delivery and cancellation dates for planned purchases is very critical to maintaining adequate merchandise for customers. Most buyers find that allocating planned purchases and maintaining stock levels to meet plan is difficult because buyers have little control over late deliveries, cancelled goods, or predetermined start dates that vendors do not honor. The seasonality of the goods and the need for continuous replacement of basic stock complicates this difficult process.

The buyer with a continuing process and previous information will analyze past planned purchases, compare them to actual purchases for the same period, and compare those figures to the planned purchases for the new plan. Buyers without previous data must rely on the calculations using the other information developed in the six-month plan. For the plan to be successful, the buyer, with or without previous data, must make sure that receipts of merchandise are not too heavy for a particular month, quarter, or season. An imbalance in stock–sales ratios will affect future purchases, future reductions, the image of the retail business, and the overall viability of the business. **Planned purchases at cost** are used to indicate the wholesale value of the merchandise and are called **open-to-buy** or **OTB**. This value will correspond to the invoice value that was discussed in the expanded P & L statement in Chapter 4. To determine OTB, the buyer will need to know the initial markup percentage. Most buyers will be given this information, based on previous data or on the retailer's policy.

Calculation Stage in Development of a Six-Month Plan

The calculation stage of the plan requires a seven-step procedure. This process begins with the calculation of sales and concludes with the calculations providing the buyer with money to purchase new merchandise.

Step One—Total Planned Sales and Total Planned Reductions

This first step is the process of calculating total planned sales and total planned reductions. The figures for total sales dollars and total reductions percentage and dollars are written on the six-month plan, usually in a heading for the plan as a reference for the calculating and working aspects of the plan. When the previous period's or year's information about total sales is available, this data may also be written on the plan in the heading for reference.

With a continuing business, the total sales amount is determined as an adjustment from last year's sales. With information from previous seasons, the buyer would use an adjusted format of the planned sales formula from Chapter 6, and the **total planned sales** formula is

$$\text{Total Planned Sales \$} = \text{Base Period Sales \$}$$
$$+ (\text{Base Period Sales \$} \times \text{Increase \%})$$

With a new business, the total planned sales figure would be determined in the planning stages and simply incorporated into the plan.

The formula for calculating total reductions would be similar to the reductions formula used in calculating reductions for the P & L statement, or for any portion of the reductions as determined by the buyer or retailer (e.g., markdowns and shrinkage). The amount of the reduction percentage would be determined relative to the size of the percentage from the previous same period, or with a new business would be estimated from preplan information. In application to the six-month plan, the **total planned reductions** formula from Chapter 4 is

$$\text{Total Planned Reduction \$} = \text{Total Planned Sales \$}$$
$$\times \text{Total Planned Reduction \%}$$

For this six-month plan example and in the work problems at the end of the chapter, the total reductions are considered as a summed figure including all types of reductions for ease of calculations.

Sample Problems: Six-Month Plan—Step One: Total Planned Sales and Reductions

---

Problem 1

The buyer determines after reviewing information in the preplan and specific information stages that $195,600.00 is last spring period's total sales. Through research and discussion with managers, the buyer determines that a 15.00% increase for sales for the spring period for this year would be an appropriate increase. Find the amount of sales for this period.

Step 1. Determine the needed amounts from the problem.

Base Year Sales $ = $195,600.00

Increase % = 15.00% or 0.15 for calculations

Step 2. Insert the given values, and calculate the result.

Total Planned Sales $ = Base Year Sales $ + (Base Year Sales $ × Increase %)

Total Planned Sales $ = $195,600.00 + ($195,600.00 × 0.15)

Total Planned Sales $ = $195,600.00 + ($29,340.00)

Total Planned Sales $ = $224,940.00

(Note: This amount is adjusted to $225,000.00 for simplification of the sample problem and the remaining steps of the calculation of this six-month plan.)

Step 3. Place the information into the six-month plan.

(Note: The plan is written in thousands to save space and avoid confusion with too many zeros; therefore, $225,000.00 is written as $225.00 and the base year or last year sales amount is written as $195.60.)

Six-Month Plan for the Company—Spring Period

Last Year's Sales for Spring: $195.60		This Year's Sales for Spring: $225.00	
		Reduction %: 22.00%	Reductions $: $49.50
		Initial Markup %: 52.00%	

Spring	Feb	Mar	Apr	May	June	July	Total
Mnthly % Plan							
Mnthly % Actual							
Sales $ Plan							
Sale $ Actual							
Red % Plan							
Red % Actual							
Red $ Plan							
Red $ Actual							
EOM $ Plan							
EOM $ Actual							
S–S Ratio Plan							
S–S Ratio Actual							
BOM $ Plan							
BOM $ Actual							
PI Purch $							
Actual Purch $							
OTB cost							

Problem 2

Total planned reduction dollars for the business are estimated to be 22.00% of planned sales. The buyer needs to find total reduction dollars.

Step 1. Determine the needed amounts from the problem.

Total Planned Sales $ = $225,000.00

Total Planned Reduction % = 22.00% or 0.22 for calculations

Step 2. Insert the given values, and calculate the result.

Total Planned Reduction $ = Total Planned Sales $

$\times$ Total Planned Reduction %

Total Planned Reduction $ = $225,000.00 $\times$ 0.22

Total Planned Reduction $ = $49,500.00

Step 3. Place the information into the six-month plan.

Step Two—Monthly Distribution of Total Planned Sales

This second step involves the process of distributing total sales volume into monthly increments and allocating these units across months within the six-month period. In this step, the buyer will use percentages determined in the specific information stage of plan development. These percentages may be based on previous information or created from merchandising knowledge by the buyer. To calculate the **monthly planned sales dollars**, percentages for each month are assigned and calculations made for sales dollars for each month, using the formula

Monthly Planned Sales $ = Total Planned Sales $ $\times$ Monthly Sales %

Sample Problem: Six-Month Plan—Step Two: Monthly Distribution of Total Planned Sales

The buyer determines after reviewing information in the preplan and specific information stages that the monthly planned sales percentages for February through July should be 15.00%, 20.00%, 19.00%, 13.00%, 14.00%, and 19.00%, respectively. Place percentages in the appropriate cells for the months, and calculate the dollar values of each month.

For example, to calculate the dollar values for February, complete the following three steps:

Step 1. Determine the needed amounts from the problem.

Total Planned Sales $ = $225,000.00

Monthly Sales % for February = 15.00% or 0.15 for calculations

Step 2. Insert the given values, and calculate the result.

$$\text{Monthly Planned Sales } \$ = \text{Total Planned Sales } \$ \times \text{Monthly Sales } \%$$

$$\text{Monthly Planned Sales } \$ = \$225{,}000.00 \times 0.15$$

$$\text{Monthly Planned Sales } \$ = \$33{,}750.00$$

Step 3. Place February's information in the six-month plan.

(Note: The plan is written in thousands to save space and to avoid confusion caused by too many zeros; therefore, $33,750.00 is written as $33.75.)

Six-Month Plan for the Company—Spring Period

Last Year's Sales for Spring: $195.60		This Year's Sales for Spring: $225.00		
		Reduction %: 22.00%	Reductions $: $49.50	
		Initial Markup %: 52.00%		

Spring	Feb	Mar	Apr	May	June	July	Total
Mnthly % Plan	15.00%						
Mnthly % Actual							
Sales $ Plan	$33.75						
Sale $ Actual							
Red % Plan							
Red % Actual							
Red $ Plan							
Red $ Actual							
EOM $ Plan							
EOM $ Actual							
S–S Ratio Plan							
S–S Ratio Actual							
BOM $ Plan							
BOM $ Actual							
PI Purch $							
Actual Purch $							
OTB cost							

Step 4. Continue to calculate the monthly dollar values for sales, and place them in the plan.

Six-Month Plan for the Company—Spring Period

Last Year's Sales for Spring: $195.60		This Year's Sales for Spring: $225.00	
		Reduction %: 22.00%	Reductions $: $49.50
		Initial Markup %: 52.00%	

Spring	Feb	Mar	Apr	May	June	July	Total
Mnthly % Plan	15.00%	20.00%	19.00%	13.00%	14.00%	19.00%	100.00%
Mnthly % Actual							
Sales $ Plan	$33.75	$45.00	$42.75	$29.25	$31.50	$42.75	$225.00
Sale $ Actual							
Red % Plan							
Red % Actual							
Red $ Plan							
Red $ Actual							
EOM $ Plan							
EOM $ Actual							
S–S Ratio Plan							
S–S Ratio Actual							
BOM $ Plan							
BOM $ Actual							
PI Purch $							
Actual Purch $							
OTB cost							

During the working or actual period, the six-month plan must be closely watched for correspondence between plan and actual sales so that careful adjustments can be made. In addition, the buyer should keep careful records to provide data for the next planning period.

Step Three—Monthly Distribution of Total Planned Reductions

This third step is the process of distributing the total reductions volume into monthly increments. A reduction dollar amount is allocated for each month. The percentages, whether determined from previous sales or estimated from merchandising knowledge, can be assigned for each month, and the calculations can be made to determine the planned reductions dollars for each month, using the **monthly planned reduction dollars** formula

$$\text{Monthly Planned Reduction \$} = \text{Total Planned Sales \$} \times \text{Monthly Reduction \%}$$

Sample Problem: Six-Month Plan—Step Three: Monthly Distribution of Reductions

The buyer determines after reviewing information in the preplan and specific information stages that the monthly reductions percentages for February through July should be 2.64%, 3.08%, 2.64%, 3.96%, 4.40%, and 5.28%, respectively. Place the percentages in the appropriate row and columns for the months, and calculate the dollar values of each month.

(Note: The total of the monthly reduction percentages is equal to the total reduction percentage or 22.00%.)

For example, to calculate the reduction dollar values for February, complete the following steps:

Step 1. Determine the needed amounts from the problem.

Total Planned Sales $ = $225,000.00

Monthly Reductions % for February = 2.64% or 0.0264 for calculations

Step 2. Insert the given values, and calculate the result.

Monthly Planned Reductions $ = Total Planned Sales $
× Monthly Reductions %

Monthly Planned Reductions $ = $225,000.00 × 2.64%

Monthly Planned Reductions $ = $5,940.00

Step 3. Place February's information in the six-month plan.

Step 4. Continue to calculate the monthly planned dollar values for reductions. Place the monthly percentages and dollars into the plan.

Six-Month Plan for the Company—Spring Period

Last Year's Sales for Spring: $195.60		This Year's Sales for Spring: $225.00	
		Reduction %: 22.00%	Reductions $: $49.50
		Initial Markup %: 52.00%	

Spring	Feb	Mar	Apr	May	June	July	Total
Mnthly % Plan	15.00%	20.00%	19.00%	13.00%	14.00%	19.00%	100.00%
Mnthly % Actual							
Sales $ Plan	$33.75	$45.00	$42.75	$29.25	$31.50	$42.75	$225.00
Sale $ Actual							
Red % Plan	2.64%	3.08%	2.64%	3.96%	4.40%	5.28%	22.00%
Red % Actual							
Red $ Plan	$5.94	$6.93	$5.94	$8.91	$9.90	$11.88	$49.50
Red $ Actual							
EOM $ Plan							
EOM $ Actual							
S–S Ratio Plan							
S–S Ratio Actual							
BOM $ Plan							
BOM $ Actual							
PI Purch $							
Actual Purch $							
OTB cost							

In an alternative method for calculating monthly reductions, reduction percentages can be determined by comparing monthly reduction dollars to monthly sales dollars from a previous year. These percentages result in a percentage for each month. The dollar amounts for each monthly reductions percentage will be the same as those determined by the percentage of reductions relative to total sales method, but the percentage amounts will vary because the base value used in the two formulas is different. Some buyers use this form of monthly percentage because they have previous data to use in the calculations. Other buyers who have previous data use the percentage of total sales formula because this relates all values to total sales and to the P & L statement and other planning documents.

Step Four—BOM for Each Month

Step 4 is needed to further the plan and to prepare for the planned purchases calculations. Using the stock method selected in the specific information stage, the buyer will calculate the BOM for each month. A common method used by many buyers is the stock–sales ratio method. When using this method, the buyer will have determined ratios for each month and will apply the formula

$$\text{BOM Stock \$} = \text{Planned Monthly Sales \$} \times \text{Stock–Sales Ratio}$$

Sample Problem: Six-Month Plan—Step Four: BOM for Each Month

The buyer determines in the specific information stage that the monthly stock–sales ratios for February through July should be 4.44, 3.65, 3.94, 5.23, 4.37, and 3.15, respectively. Place the ratios in the appropriate row and columns for the months, and calculate the dollar values of the BOM for each month.

Step 1. Determine the needed amounts from the problem.

Planned Monthly Sales for February $ = \$33,750.00$

Monthly Ratio for February $= 4.44$

Step 2. Insert the given values, and calculate the result.

BOM Stock $ = Planned Monthly Sales $ $\times$ Stock–Sales Ratio

BOM Stock $ = \$33,750.00 \times 4.44$

BOM Stock $ = \$149,850.00$

Step 3. Place February's information in the six-month plan.

Step 4. Continue to calculate the monthly BOM, and place the monthly ratio and the monthly dollar amounts into the plan.

Six-Month Plan for the Company—Spring Period

Last Year's Sales for Spring: $195.60				This Year's Sales for Spring: $225.00			
				Reduction %: 22.00%		Reductions $: $49.50	
				Initial Markup %: 52.00%			

Spring	Feb	Mar	Apr	May	June	July	Total
Mnthly % Plan	15.00%	20.00%	19.00%	13.00%	14.00%	19.00%	100.00%
Mnthly % Actual							
Sales $ Plan	$33.75	$45.00	$42.75	$29.25	$31.50	$42.75	$225.00
Sale $ Actual							
Red % Plan	2.64%	3.08%	2.64%	3.96%	4.40%	5.28%	22.00%
Red % Actual							
Red $ Plan	$5.94	$6.93	$5.94	$8.91	$9.90	$11.88	$49.50
Red $ Actual							
EOM $ Plan							
EOM $ Actual							
S–S Ratio Plan	4.44	3.65	3.94	5.23	4.37	3.15	
S–S Ratio Actual							
BOM $ Plan	$149.85	$164.25	$168.44	$152.98	$137.66	$134.66	
BOM $ Actual							
PI Purch $							
Actual Purch $							
OTB cost							

Step Five—EOM for Each Month

This step determines the EOM. For five of the six months, this calculation is quite easy. The buyer knows that the BOM of one month is the EOM of the previous month. These figures can be copied from each month back to the previous month. The final EOM will depend on the BOM desired for the next planning period. Planning is a constant and ongoing process and must continue even after a six-month plan is developed for the current operating period. No actual calculation is needed to find BOM from EOM, so the **EOM** formula is

EOM for Month A = BOM for Month B

The buyer can use the BOM formula to estimate an EOM for the final month. This figure will be a rough estimate, which will be adjusted as actual figures are noted during the working aspect of the plan. The **estimated final EOM** formula is

Estimated Final EOM Stock $ = Planned Monthly Sales $

× Stock–Sales Ratio

Sample Problem: Six-Month Plan—Step Five: EOM for Each Month

The EOM for each month is the BOM for the next month.

Step 1. For the first five months, the buyer needs only to copy the BOM figures into the previous months' EOM cells.

Step 2. Find the EOM for the final month.

Estimated Final EOM Stock $ = Planned Monthly Sales $ × Stock–Sales Ratio

Estimated Final EOM Stock $ = $42,750.00 × 3.15

Estimated Final EOM Stock $ = $134,660.00

(Note: With data from sales history, EOM for July can be estimated from last year's BOM.)

Six-Month Plan for the Company—Spring Period

Last Year's Sales for Spring: $195.60		This Year's Sales for Spring: $225.00	
		Reduction %: 22.00%	Reductions $: 49.50%
		Initial Markup %: 52.00%	

Spring	Feb	Mar	Apr	May	June	July	Total
Mnthly % Plan	15.00%	20.00%	19.00%	13.00%	14.00%	19.00%	100.00%
Mnthly % Actual							
Sales $ Plan	$33.75	$45.00	$42.75	$29.25	$31.50	$42.75	$225.00
Sale $ Actual							
Red % Plan	2.64%	3.08%	2.64%	3.96%	4.40%	5.28%	22.00%
Red % Actual							
Red $ Plan	$5.94	$6.93	$5.94	$8.91	$9.90	$11.88	$49.50
Red $ Actual							
EOM $ Plan	$164.25	$168.44	$152.98	$137.66	$134.66	$134.66	
EOM $ Actual							
S–S Ratio Plan	4.44	3.65	3.94	5.23	4.37	3.15	
S–S Ratio Actual							
BOM $ Plan	$149.85	$164.25	$168.44	$152.98	$137.66	$134.66	
BOM $ Actual							
PI Purch $							
Actual Purch $							
OTB cost							

Step Six—Planned Purchases at Retail for Each Month

In the sixth step, the planned purchases at retail are calculated to provide the dollar amount available to purchase new merchandise each month. This amount is calculated by considering the value of the needed merchandise minus the value of the available merchandise or the merchandise on hand. Needed merchandise is the amount of merchandise needed for sales, reductions, and the EOM. Merchandise is needed to be sold, merchandise value is needed to cover the amount of reductions, and merchandise is needed to remain in the store at the end of the month. The merchandise available is the merchandise that the retailer currently owns. This includes the merchandise that is on hand at the BOM. If merchandise is on order, but has not been received, this should also be considered with available merchandise because money has been committed for the merchandise. The bills must be paid. The formula for **planned purchases at retail** is

Planned Purchases $ = Need $ − Available $

Written to correspond to the lines of the six-month plan, the formula is

$$\text{Planned Purchases } \$ = (\text{Sales } \$ + \text{Reduction } \$ + \text{EOM } \$) - \text{BOM } \$$$

Sample Problem: Six-Month Plan—Step Six: Planned Purchases for Each Month

The buyer needs to calculate the planned purchases for each month. The buyer will use the information that is in the six-month plan at the end of Step 5 to calculate the planned purchases for each month.

Step 1. Calculate the planned purchases for February, using the following formula and the values given:

$$\text{Planned Purchases } \$ = (\text{Sales } \$ + \text{Reduction } \$ + \text{EOM } \$) - \text{BOM } \$$$
$$\text{Planned Purchases } \$ = (\$33,750.00 + \$5,940.00 + \$164,250.00)$$
$$ - \$149,850.00$$
$$\text{Planned Purchases } \$ = (\$203,940.00) - \$149,850.00$$
$$\text{Planned Purchases } \$ = \$54,090.00$$

Step 2. Find the planned purchases for the remaining months. Enter the planned purchases values into the six-month plan.

Six-Month Plan for the Company—Spring Period

Last Year's Sales for Spring: $195.60			This Year's Sales for Spring: $225.00				
			Reduction %: 22.00%		Reductions $: 49.50%		
			Initial Markup %: 52.00%				

Spring	Feb	Mar	Apr	May	June	July	Total
Mnthly % Plan	15.00%	20.00%	19.00%	13.00%	14.00%	19.00%	100.00%
Mnthly % Actual							
Sales $ Plan	$33.75	$45.00	$42.75	$29.25	$31.50	$42.75	$225.00
Sale $ Actual							
Red % Plan	2.64%	3.08%	2.64%	3.96%	4.40%	5.28%	22.00%
Red % Actual							
Red $ Plan	$5.94	$6.93	$5.94	$8.91	$9.90	$11.88	$49.50
Red $ Actual							
EOM $ Plan	$164.25	$168.44	$152.98	$137.66	$134.66	$134.66	
EOM $ Actual							
S–S Ratio Plan	4.44	3.65	3.94	5.23	4.37	3.15	
S–S Ratio Actual							
BOM $ Plan	$149.85	$164.25	$168.44	$152.98	$137.66	$134.66	
BOM $ Actual							
PI Purch $	$54.09	$56.12	$33.23	$22.84	$38.40	$54.63	
Actual Purch $							
OTB cost							

If merchandise is ordered but not in the store and is expected within the month, the value of the merchandise on order should be considered and the planned purchase formula would be adapted; therefore, the **planned purchases when merchandise is on order** formula is

$$\text{Planned Purchases \$} = (\text{Sales \$} + \text{Reduction \$} + \text{EOM \$})$$
$$- (\text{BOM \$} + \text{On-Order \$})$$

This calculation will be needed for portions of the period that transition across seasons. For example, the buyer may order merchandise for early fall during the spring period. Part of this merchandise may arrive for retail sale during July and part of the merchandise may not arrive until August or September. The planned purchase calculations for August and September should be made with an inquiry about on-order merchandise.

Step Seven—OTB at Cost

The money available for planned purchases when calculated at cost is the open-to-buy (OTB) that is available for spending in the market. To calculate the OTB in terms of cost, the buyer would need to know the markup that is anticipated for the merchandise. The merchandise at cost would be the difference between the merchandise at retail and the markup. The **OTB dollars** formula would be similar to that for finding the cost of goods for the P & L statement and is

$$\text{OTB \$} = \text{Planned Purchases \$} \times \text{Cost of Goods \%}$$

Sample Problem: Six-Month Plan—Step Seven: Open-to-Buy at Cost

The buyer needs to calculate the cost or wholesale value of planned purchases for each month. Initial markup percent is 52.00%; therefore, the cost of goods estimated for the merchandise is 48.00%. Calculate the OTB for the months in the plan.

(Hint: Cost of Goods % = 100.00% − Initial Markup %.)

Step 1. Place the initial markup percentage in the header for reference.

Step 2. Calculate the OTB for February, using the following formula:

$$\text{OTB \$} = \text{Planned Purchases \$} \times \text{Cost of Goods \%}$$
$$\text{OTB \$} = \$54{,}090.00 \times 48.00\%$$
$$\text{OTB \$} = \$25{,}963.20$$

Step 3. Find the planned purchases for the remaining months. Enter the planned purchases values into the six-month plan.

Six-Month Plan for the Company—Spring Period

Last Year's Sales for Spring: $195.60		This Year's Sales for Spring: $225.00	
		Reduction %: 22.00%	Reductions $: 49.50%
		Initial Markup %: 52.00%	

Spring	Feb	Mar	Apr	May	June	July	Total
Mnthly % Plan	15.00%	20.00%	19.00%	13.00%	14.00%	19.00%	100.00%
Mnthly % Actual							
Sales $ Plan	$33.75	$45.00	$42.75	$29.25	$31.50	$42.75	$225.00
Sale $ Actual							
Red % Plan	2.64%	3.08%	2.64%	3.96%	4.40%	5.28%	22.00%
Red % Actual							
Red $ Plan	$5.94	$6.93	$5.94	$8.91	$9.90	$11.88	$49.50
Red $ Actual							

(continues on next page)

Six-Month Plan for the Company—Spring Period   (continued)

Spring	Feb	Mar	Apr	May	June	July	Total
EOM $ Plan	$164.25	$168.44	$152.98	$137.66	$134.66	$134.66	
EOM $ Actual							
S–S Ratio Plan	4.44	3.65	3.94	5.23	4.37	3.15	
S–S Ratio Actual							
BOM $ Plan	$149.85	$164.25	$168.44	$152.98	$137.66	$134.66	
BOM $ Actual							
PI Purch $	$54.09	$56.12	$33.23	$22.84	$38.40	$54.63	
Actual Purch $							
OTB cost	$25.96	$26.94	$15.95	$10.96	$18.43	$26.22	

Working Plan

When the period begins, the developed plan is used as a **working plan**. The complete six-month plan format has rows for both plan and actual figures. The success of the business is very dependent upon the success of sales, reductions, and purchases; therefore, the success of the plan is vital. A buyer will use the plan throughout the period as a system of checks and balances with the actual business activities. Throughout each month, the buyer will write the actual amount of sales, reductions, and purchases on the plan. When the buyer is using a working plan, the EOMs can then be calculated based on actual figures. The formula for finding the **actual EOM** is

$$\text{Actual EOM \$} = \text{BOM \$} - \text{Monthly Sales \$}$$
$$- \text{Reductions \$} + \text{Purchases \$}$$

The final EOM from the previous period becomes the BOM for the first month in the next period, and the values are subsequently calculated. This calculation proceeds from month to month and shows how changes in any of the components of one month in a six-month plan can affect stock levels and other values in the next and subsequent months. This process is called the **continuous plan method** because it uses current data and can be continually adjusted. This method is also used by some buyers with previous data to determine stock levels for a plan development.

When merchandise needs to be purchased, the buyer will check the amount allocated for planned purchases for that month. The buyer will also determine the most accurate planned purchase figure by using the actual figures. The buyer can use the planned purchase amount to make adjustments to meet plan. If too much inventory remains during that month, the buyer could reduce the amount of planned purchases for the next month. If a merchandise classification needs more reductions or needs to have new merchandise, the buyer would make these notations on the six-month working plan and make appropriate adjustments in ordering and promoting merchandise.

The buyer will need to keep all notations and explanations of changes to the plan. These items of information will be useful in making the six-month plan for the corresponding period in the next year. Throughout the working period, adjustments should be made to keep stock and reductions close to the plan, or determination should be made for why the plan should be altered. The working plan with its multiple rows allows the buyer to review quickly the status of sales, reductions, and stock.

An overstocked situation can be identified and adjustments can be made in sales quotas, reductions, or other measures can be taken to rectify the overstocked situation. Therefore, as stated previously, successful retailing is very dependent upon successful planning including the six-month plan. Planning is a continuous and on-going process, and paperwork with mathematics is a very real and everyday part of the job for a buyer.

Skills in Plan Development

Most buyers develop the six-month plan as a part of their job. In a few very large companies, a planning department may have the job of developing the six-month plans and other plans for the stores. For these companies, financial plans of many types will be developed by members of the planning department. A planning department is found most often in companies that are multichain firms with many buyers and many store managers. The coordination of overall P & L statements and specific statements for each store and perhaps each department or merchandise classification are developed. From these P & L statements, six-month plans are developed that allocate dollars to specific functions and months. When a company has a planning department, these firms will have accountants, strategic planners, and computer specialists to develop the plans. For a smaller company where a buyer does the planning, the buyer must have all of the skills of a team of planners.

To develop the six-month plan, the buyer must have excellent mathematical skills. The plan requires the use of percentages, ratios, and formulas. In addition to specific mathematical skills, the buyer needs a mathematical aptitude to be able to understand the numbers, see their relationships, and perceive appropriate adjustments. The buyer must also have abilities to see beyond the numbers. These numbers represent stock to be purchased, stored, and displayed. The stock movement must create an exciting, enticing store for the customer; therefore, the buyer must visualize that the numbers represent functions, activities, and merchandise all designed to sell merchandise and create customer satisfaction.

*S*ummary

A six-month plan is used by the buyer to convert the sales plan into a working document for determining the BOM and EOM stock levels on a monthly basis. The outcome of the six-month plan is the planned purchases needed for each month and the money that is available for shopping the market. The six-month plan also helps the buyer to control merchandise expenditures through the planning period. Planned versus actual values can be evaluated to determine the rate of sales and the movement of the merchandise. The six-month plan also links the promotion plan to the buying of merchandise. Many of the roles of the buyer are involved in the development of the plan.

Key Terms

Calculation stage
Continuous plan method
Meet plan
Open-to-buy (OTB)

Planned purchases at cost
Planned purchases at retail
Preplan stage

Six-month plan
Specific information stage
Working plan

Discussion Questions

1. Why does a buyer need a six-month plan?
2. What does the buyer need to know before creating a six-month plan?
3. What information can the buyer use from other planning processes?
4. Why does the buyer need to keep accurate records when using the six-month plan?
5. What issues affect or control how much merchandise a buyer can buy?
6. How does the plan change throughout the operating period?
7. If, by Month 3, the plan EOM is much smaller than the actual EOM, what must the buyer do?
8. How does the six-month plan relate to the reductions from the P & L statement?
9. Why does the buyer need to work with the promotions manager when developing a six-month plan?
10. What skills does the buyer need to be able to complete a six-month plan?

Exercises

Pro forma or sample six-month-plan worksheet:

Six-Month Plan for the Company—Spring Period

Last Year's Sales for Spring:		This Year's Sales for Spring:		
		Reduction %:		Reductions $:
		Initial Markup %:		

Spring	Feb	Mar	Apr	May	June	July	Total
Mnthly % Plan							
Mnthly % Actual							
Sales $ Plan							
Sale $ Actual							
Red % Plan							
Red % Actual							
Red $ Plan							
Red $ Actual							
EOM $ Plan							
EOM $ Actual							
S–S Ratio Plan							
S–S Ratio Actual							
BOM $ Plan							
BOM $ Actual							
PI Purch $							
Actual Purch $							
OTB cost							

1. Set up a six-month plan using the following data:

   Sales plan: Total $240,000
   Monthly percentages: 14.00%, 16.00%, 15.00%, 17.00%, 23.00%, 15.00%
   Reduction percentages: 2.63%, 2.48%, 2.19%, 1.90%, 1.75%, 3.65%
   Stock–sales ratios: 4.27, 3.86, 4.06, 3.70, 3.00, 4.06
   July EOM: $149,433
   Initial Markup Percentage: 52.00%

2. Set up a six-month plan using the following data:

   Sales plan: Total $336,000
   Monthly percentages: 11.00%, 19.00%, 15.00%, 19.00%, 21.00%, 15.00%
   Reduction percentages: 2.33%, 1.81%, 2.19%, 1.98%, 1.75%, 3.55%
   Stock–sales ratios: 4.05, 3.36, 3.06, 3.78, 3.00, 4.05
   July EOM: $124,400
   Initial Markup Percentage: 52.00%

3. Set up a six-month plan using the following data:

   Sales plan: Total $330,000
   Monthly percentages: 15.00%, 15.00%, 18.00%, 19.00%, 18.00%, 15.00%
   Reduction percentages: 2.3%, 2.1%, 2.9%, 1.8%, 1.5%, 3.5%
   Stock–sales ratios: 4.0, 3.6, 3.6, 3.8, 3.0, 4.0
   July EOM: $159,660
   Initial Markup Percentage: 52.00%

4. Set up a six-month plan using the following data:

   Sales plan: Total $638,000
   Monthly percentages: 14.00%, 14.00%, 20.00%, 19.00%, 18.00%, 15.00%
   Reduction percentages: 2.3%, 2.1%, 2.7%, 3.8%, 1.6%, 3.5%
   Stock–sales ratios: 4.0, 3.6, 3.6, 3.8, 3.0, 4.0
   July EOM: $359,660
   Initial Markup Percentage: 52.00%

   Change the Stock–Sales ratio for May to 4.7. What does the change do to planned purchases? How does this affect store operations? What must be done to get planned purchases to have a positive value? How can this be accomplished?

5. Set up a six-month plan using the following data:

   Sales plan: Total $300,000
   Monthly percentages: 10.00%, 20.00%, 18.00%, 19.00%, 18.00%, 15.00%
   Reduction percentages: 2.3%, 3.1%, 2.9%, 2.5%, 1.5%, 3.5%
   Stock–sales ratios: 4.0, 3.6, 3.6, 3.8, 3.0, 4.0
   July EOM: $289,660
   Initial Markup Percentage: 52.00%

   Change the reductions in February to 3.5% and in June to 4.5%. What does that do to planned purchases?

Computer Exercises

Six-Month Plans

General Directions

- Print and save as previously directed.
- Set up a Pro forma for a six-month plan on the computer. You will need eight columns (Spring, Feb, Mar, . . . July, Total)

- Right align labels. You will need eight rows (Mthly %, Sales Plan, EOM Plan, Reductions %, Reductions Plan, S–S Ratio, BOM Plan, and Planned Purchases).
- Format the appropriate rows for currency or percents (2 decimals).
- Add rows, columns, or lines for spacing and looks.
- The formulas that you will use are as follows:

  Sales plan: Each monthly sales plan is Total Sales $ × Monthly Sales %. Remember total sales will be an absolute cell (e.g., C4). Put the formula in one cell, and use the copy feature for the remaining cells.

  BOM Plan: BOM is Stock–Sales Ratio × Monthly Sales $. Copy into appropriate cells, and use the @ sum for the total.

  EOM Plan: The EOM of one month is the same as the BOM from the next month. Copy cell contents of a BOM to the appropriate EOM. (Check cell address.) Leave July EOM blank. It will be a given amount or found by formula in later problems. Use @ sum for the total (including final EOM).

  Red Plan: Monthly reductions are calculated as Monthly Reduction % × Total Sales $. (Use absolute reference for total sales.) Copy formula to remaining months. You will need an @ sum for total reduction dollars and a formula for total reduction percent (Total Reduction $/Total Sales $)—this will appear as ERR until numbers are added in later problems.

  Planned Purchases: Insert the formula for the first month: Planned Purchases = Monthly Sales $ + EOM $ + RED $ − BOM $, and copy the formula to the necessary cell for each month. Put in @ sum for total.

- The total sum for the planned purchases line should equal the amount found with Total Sales + Total EOM + Total Red − Total BOM (i.e., two ways will get to the same number.)

1. Use the following figures to set up a six-month plan:

   Total sales: $440,000
   Monthly sales percentage: 12.00%, 14.00%, 16.00%, 19.00%, 23.00%, 16.00%
   July EOM: $399,583
   Monthly reduction percentages: 2.63%, 2.48%, 2.19%, 1.90%, 1.75%, 3.65%
   Stock–sales ratios: 4.27, 3.86, 4.06, 3.70, 3.00, 4.06
   Initial Markup Percentage: 52.00%

   (Hint: Use formulas to calculate remaining values.)

   What is the value of planned purchases for July?

2. Copy the spreadsheet for Problem 1 to determine the effect of a change in stock–sales ratios.

   a. Change the stock–sales ratios for May to 4.7.
      How does this affect planned purchases?
   b. Comment on sheet below the planned purchases row.

3. Copy the spreadsheet from Problem 1 to determine the effect in a change in reductions.

   a. Change the reduction percentage in Feb to 3.5% and 4.5% in June.
      How does this affect the planned purchases?
   b. Comment on the sheet.

4. Copy spreadsheet in Problem 1, and add values for the actual expenditures to make comparisons. (This spreadsheet will be the type of sheet seen at a midpoint in the selling period.)

   a. Insert the following additional rows for actual values:
      Sales, RED, BOM, EOM, and Purchases
   b. In May, the buyer realizes that sales have been high and decides to check the actual numbers against the plan. These figures have been recorded so far this period:

      Actual Sales: Feb 60,300; Mar 54,000; April 62,000
      Actual RED: Feb 9,000; Mar 6,000; April 6,500
      Actual BOM: Feb 283,472
      Actual Purchase: Feb 64,664; Mar 52,300; April 56,100

5. Complete the calculations, and compare the outcome to plan, remembering the following:

   a. EOM for Feb will be a calculation:

      Actual BOM + Actual Purchases − Actual Sales − Actual RED.

   b. Mar BOM is Feb EOM.
   c. Calculate Mar EOM.
   d. Repeat the process for actual figures for April.
   e. Enter May BOM (from April EOM).
   f. How does May BOM actual compare with plan?
   g. What adjustments would be reasonable to correct the problem? Comment on the spreadsheet.

Comparing Actual with Plan

General Directions

- Set up a Pro forma for a six-month plan on the computer.
- Title eight columns (Spring, Feb, Mar, . . . July, Total).
- Right align labels.
- Title 13 rows (Mthly %, Sales Plan, Sales Actual, EOM Plan, EOM Actual, Red %, Red Plan, Reduction Actual, S–S Ratio, BOM Plan, BOM Actual, Planned Purchases, Actual Purchases).
- Format the appropriate rows for currency or percents (2 decimals).
- Add rows, columns, or lines for spacing and appearance.

1. Use the following figures to set up a six-month plan:

   Total sales: $354,600
   Monthly sales percentages: 13.00%, 15.00%, 15.00%, 16.00%, 24.00%, 17.00%
   EOM for July: $152,600
   Monthly reduction percentages: 2.54%, 2.48%, 2.19%, 1.80%, 1.65%, 3.22%
   Stock–Sales ratios: 3.68, 4.20, 3.84, 2.80, 3.00, 3.96

   (Hint: Use formulas to calculate remaining values.)

   What is the value of planned purchases for July?

2. In May, the buyer realizes that sales have been slow and decides to check the plan. These figures have been recorded so far this period:

   Actual Sales: Feb $40,000.00, March $48,000.00, April $50,000.00
   Actual Reductions: Feb $10,000.00, March $9,200.00, April $7,500.00
   Actual BOM: Feb $173,000.00
   Actual Purchases: Feb $110,000.00, March $45,000.00, April $16,000.00

   a. Complete the calculations for the remaining actual figures.
   b. Compare the actual situation to the plan.
   c. How does the May BOM compare with the plan? Place your comments on the spreadsheet.
   d. What adjustments are reasonable to correct the problems? Place your comments on the spreadsheet.

3. In May, the buyer realizes that sales have been aggressive and decides to check the plan. These figures have been recorded so far this period:

   Actual Sales: Feb $60,000.00, March $58,000.00, April $70,000.00
   Actual Reductions: Feb $10,000.00, March $8,100.00, April $7,000.00
   Actual BOM: Feb $173,000.00
   Actual Purchases: Feb $80,000.00, March $95,000.00, April $56,000.00

   a. Complete the calculations for the remaining actual figures.
   b. Compare the actual situation to the plan.
   c. How does the May BOM compare with the plan? Place your comments on the spreadsheet.
   d. What adjustments may be needed? Are there any problems? Place your comments on the spreadsheet.

*F*ashion Forecasting

*O*bjectives

After completing this chapter, the student will be able to

- describe the forecasting process
- explain why forecasting is essential to merchandising
- use observational information to develop a forecast plan

Depending on the approach the buyer takes, forecasting may be any combination of scientific calculations or wizardry and instinct. Forecasting requires that the buyer determine with as much accuracy as possible what the business's consumer will want in future purchases. Most apparel products are bought by customers who shop and then purchase. These customers depend on an assortment of available products to stimulate their interest and entice them to buy. This process necessitates that the buyer forecast an assortment of products to be housed and promoted to the customer. Although housing the product is reduced in nonstore retailing, the buyer or merchandise manager must still predict what products will appeal to the customer and provide an attractive display of these products for the shopping pleasure of the consumer. For many buyers, forecasting is done one year to six months ahead of the selling season. This traditional six-month schedule is especially true for apparel merchandisers' planning. This method corresponds with the traditional two seasons of fashion: fall and spring. As the fashion cycles have become shorter for many consumer products, the planning periods have shortened and the forecast is made for a shorter period. In fact, some buyers have reduced total time in the pipeline and are buying closer to the selling season.

Most buyers shop the market with some level of forecasting as part of the planning process. A buyer who is developing a private label program with an offshore contractor may need at least one year for making plans and completing production of the new products. For buyers working with vendor-managed products or autoreplenishment products, forecasting may be a simple adjustment of the color or size assortments. Even these simple adjustments require an accurate approximation of the purchasing requests of consumers. (A few buyers shop the market for customized orders. Usually, these orders are placed by a customer who is waiting to receive the requested merchandise. This merchandise is not part of forecasting.)

Overview of Forecasting

Forecasting is the systematic method of looking for pattern, trend, and change in the product preferences of consumers. The buyer must predict not only the product preferences of current customers, but also when changes will occur in these style preferences. Two aspects of forecasting are needed: qualitative and quantitative. The **qualitative aspect** is often called fashion forecasting or **qualitative forecasting**. The buyer must determine the styles, colors, fabrications, and brands that the consumer will desire. These features are often associated with the design preferences, lifestyle characteristics, psychographics, and other factors in consumer choice. This type of forecasting is needed for products as diverse as a silk scarf and a faux pewter faucet. Change and excitement in product assortment is desired in many product lines by many consumers. For many types of merchandise, a retailer's competitive positioning is dependent upon the ability to forecast and to assemble an exciting and enticing assortment of merchandise.

The **quantitative aspect** of forecasting is often called sales forecasting, determining order quantity, or **quantitative forecasting**. This type of forecasting includes calculating the numbers of items per style, per vendor, and per color. To start the sales forecast, the buyer must determine an overall sales goal, and the margins and stock values needed to meet this goal for a specific period. This information was discussed in Chapters 3, 6, and 7. The buyer decides how many items to buy, with each item classified by style, color, vendor, and size. Some retailers would consider additional categories such as price point or fashion level. A categorization with pricing of all items would result in the assortment plan by the buyer. (See Chapter 10.) The total value of the sales forecast in the assortment plan must match the dollars allocated for sales by the P & L statement and the amount of planned purchases allocation in the six-month plan.

Qualitative forecasting or **fashion forecasting** is the focus of this chapter. The process is more difficult when forecasting apparel because often the consumer does not know what will be purchased before seeing the merchandise. Large stores with high volumes of merchandise may have very sophisticated computer systems that use complex mathematical calculations to create forecasts. These forecasts depend on large databases of information. However, even the most complex software still requires input from humans and the insight of a successful merchandiser to make an accurate prediction.

Buyers of fashion goods including apparel, home fashions, and other consumer products are more concerned with the styling, fashionability, color, and distinctiveness of the merchandise than are many buyers of other types of products. Fashionability is of primary importance to apparel buyers; however, the fashion features of many products, including fashion colors for automobiles, paint, and appliances, are becoming important to other retailers. For example, style features and color are important in office furniture, home fashions, and computers. **Style features** are characteristics that affect the look, shape, or size of a product; can make a product more distinctive; and may position the product against the competition and more appropriately for the target consumer. Some computer companies use style features of nontraditional shapes and colors for their monitors, which make their brands visually distinctive from other brands. This difference appeals to some computer users. Style features have both negative and positive impacts on the product. The gain in marketability through increased style and color variety is a loss in the potential accuracy of the forecast. The more style features and color variations that are offered by vendors, the more difficult the job of forecasting becomes for buyers as they attempt to select the exact preference of a future customer. Products that change frequently, such as apparel, accessories, and home fashions, with millions of style and color variants are very difficult to forecast.

Successful forecasting is critical to the success of a retailer who sells fashion related merchandise. The right merchandise must be available when the consumer perceives a need for the merchandise. If the merchandise offered by the retailer motivates the consumer to buy, then a sale is made. If the margins are set to cover expenses and the price includes dollars to cover the cost of the merchandise, the sale will contribute to the profit of the business. If the merchandise is not wanted nor needed by the consumer and does not motivate the consumer to purchase, the merchandise will continue to remain unsold. No dollars contribute to the profit, and, within a short time, the retailer will be without cash to buy new merchandise or to pay bills. Sale of the merchandise is vital to the existence of the business. Cash flow is important to maintain fresh stock and to pay employees. In this way, fashion forecasting, because of its impact on the financial activities of the business, is critical to the success of the business.

Process of Fashion Forecasting

Fashion forecasting can be as simple as placing a repeat order for a group of merchandise items or it can be as complex as a six-month process made by a team of dedicated professional marketers. For most buyers, fashion forecasting involves the gathering of information in a myriad of ways from a plethora of sources. Most buyers forecast style, color, and fabrication for merchandise classifications. When the information is gathered, a series of choice sets result. **Choice sets** are the merchandise alternatives available to the buyer, from which the buyer must select the items for the store. In today's business world, more buyers suffer from too much information or the wrong information than the number of buyers that suffer from not enough information.

The **fashion forecasting process** varies for every buyer and for every business. Forecasting various products also differs, but some commonalities in the process exist for all buyers. The fashion forecasting process includes the basic steps of (a) understanding the vision of the business and profile of target customers (see Chapter 5), (b) collecting information about available merchandise, (c) preparing information, (d) determining trends, and (e) choosing merchandise appropriate for the business and target customers. Most buyers forecast both style and color for merchandise. This dual forecasting process may proceed simultaneously for both style and color, or the buyer may keep two sets of records—one for style and one for color.

Understanding the Vision of the Business and the Profile of Target Customers

Understanding the vision of the business and the target customer is discussed in Chapters 1, 3, and 5. This basic information is the foundation for all business activities; however, details about the retailer's business plan and the target customer are needed to direct the fashion forecast. Order processes, payment plans, computer capacities, and distribution methods are all business systems that can affect the selection of the merchandise and direct the forecast. For example, selection of style is constrained by the processes of the retailer's business systems. These constraints include limits on merchandise quantities from vendors, time requirements for processing orders, and preselection of vendors by management. Some small retailers may find that they are restricted from ordering merchandise because vendors have minimum requirements for order volume that exceeds the retailer's budget.

When forecasting merchandise to purchase for a retail business, the buyer must know the product specific criteria both for the business and for the target customer. For example, the business may have policies about color (e.g., everything must be white), sizes (e.g., everything must be a size 5, 7, or 9), or price point (e.g., everything must sell for $6.00). These policies will limit or control the forecast. **Product specific criteria** for the target customer include quality, color, fashion level, style, distinctiveness, brand name, and price. Brand becomes a qualitative criterion because of the image associated with branding and the fashion levels imagined by the consumer when considering brands. Many aesthetic aspects of the product are part of the qualitative features. Fashion criteria are often elusive features and interpreted differently by every person. This multi-interpretational characteristic further increases the difficulty of forecasting. In addition, the preference of the consumer can change depending on situational usage, prior performance of the product, and other extrinsic criteria. Most buyers will have target consumer information as part of the strategic planning process. Although the information should be up-dated regularly, the buyer will not necessarily collect additional consumer information simultaneously with product style and color information.

Collecting Information

Style and color information searches start with understanding the target market and the sales data from previous styles. When this consumer and business information is clarified, the buyer begins the search for new product information. To collect product information, the buyer completes a variety of activities. New style information comes from television, high price point and more fashion forward markets, street observations, vendors, market trips, fashion shows, and observation of competitors. Street observations are examples of **fashion counts** and can provide information about trend, which are used to observe a broad range of customers and determine current popular styles. The results of a fashion count are a tally of all observed wearing, carrying, or using products within a merchandise classification. Observations are recorded according to subclassifications within the major classification. Most buyers who are forecasting gather information from more than one source. These activities include (a) reviewing the general media (i.e., reading newspapers, watching television, and using other current events sources), (b) scanning fashion publications and literature from trade organizations, (c) using a fashion forecasting service, (d) attending trade shows and markets, (e) reviewing store information, (f) reviewing literature and information from vendors, (g) attending major social or sports events, (h) traveling to other areas within the United States and to other areas in the world, and (i) observing and pinpointing trends in other product categories that coordinate with or influence the product classifications being forecasted. Many of these activities are daily habits among most buyers. Good buyers learn to constantly scan the environment for information to help with their forecasts and to store that information in readily accessible formats.

Reviewing the General Media

To understand the future, the buyer must be continuously aware of major world events and minor local events. The inauguration of a new president or the installation of a new city mayor may have an impact on fashion. When the wife of a new president wears a hat to the national inauguration, the world waits and wonders if this will affect the millinery desires of future consumers. A new wallpaper pattern or lamp used on the set of the local television news broadcast could have a fashion influence on a local market. Many people see these television personalities and their environments every night and use them as role models for their own selection of products. When observing people who are in the media, the buyer should be scanning for new ideas, the continuation of a previous best seller, or a change in appearance. The buyer may want to focus on people who are considered leaders by the target customer so that the buyer is documenting new ideas and not following the current trends. For this reason, most consumer magazines would not be a good source of information; if the image is already in the average consumer magazine, then it is too late to incorporate it into a new forecast. Buyers must think about future seasons when making forecasts.

With the increase in Internet services, collecting and sorting information from the news has become easier for anyone with the basic Internet hookups. Many Internet providers allow the user to customize the user profile to filter and sort information from a myriad of news sources. By putting key words into the profile, a buyer can scan the update and learn about world and local events in a few minutes. This service is similar to previous services that provided news clippings to its customers.

Although the Internet is a time saver, the buyer should be aware that an idea for a fashion trend can come from anywhere in this fast-paced, news-laden world and should not limit the scan to preset profiles. Inspiration and insight can come from the simple act of reading the newspaper or watching the local weather. Fashion information is everywhere.

Scanning Fashion Publications

Reading and reviewing fashion information in the **trade publications** should be daily habits for the buyer of any fashion goods. For apparel merchandise, the most fundamental publication in this scan is *Women's Wear Daily*. The *Daily New Record* is vital for buyers who deal with men's wear. These newspapers are the equivalent of the *Wall Street Journal* for the fashion apparel business. Numerous other publications for more specific segments of the fashion industry are also important. For example, *Earnshaws* is important reading for buyers in the children's wear market. *Footwear News* is a must read for those who buy shoes. *Home Furnishings Today* covers the current activities in the home furnishings area, which includes information about small accessories and other fashion goods for the home. The gift market, plumbing supplies, and other products also have dedicated trade journals.

In addition to these specific product sources, trade organizations promoting fiber and other industry products and services offer fashion presentations, publications, and services to the retail buyer. For example, some fiber associations offer a seasonal or twice yearly trend forecast that provides color, silhouette, and fabric predictions for the apparel and home furnishings industries. Some fiber organizations publish fashion bulletins, reports, and market reviews. Fabric libraries and other research materials may be available from these trade organizations.

Many of these trade publications and information sources about the industry are now available over the Internet. Some of the sources have free access for limited versions of the publications, but require payment for more extensive versions. Other sources are available only on a payment basis. Additional new sources of trade information are being added at a rapid rate to the Internet. A buyer should scan the Internet to determine a selection of favorite Web sites for trade information. The advantage of this electronic format is the speed of access. The buyer can have today's news today instead of waiting for the newspaper to arrive in the mail. Another advantage is the ability of the provider to customize the information and for the reader to customize the receipt of the information. For example, a buyer could establish a user profile that highlighted all available information about the color red and the Scottish weave or any other target customer preference. A disadvantage of the Internet continues to be the lack of consistency in color representation. Other complaints about Internet scanning are the inability of a buyer to touch the fabrics and feel the textures and the lack of dependability of the source. Buyers should be aware that any person (young, old, experienced, or inexperienced) could develop a Web site without any training or knowledge of the industry.

Using a Fashion Forecasting Service

Fashion forecasting services scan the fashion world for the buyer. These services, for a fee, provide the buyer with information about new colors, styles, and other features. Services include identification of trends and information tailored to a target market. Some services provide only color information, others specialize in fabrics, and still others provide style information with sketches, photographs, or computer-generated images. Other forecasting services provide a comprehensive review of fashion information.

Specific color forecasting services may also be used. The oldest color association in the United States is the Color Association of the United States (CAUS). Other color services include The Color Box, and The Color Marketing Group, which is composed of personnel from a variety of industry segments with diverse product classifications. Color services may offer pictures of the color; fiber, fabric, or other raw materials samples in the color; and examples of merchandise using the color. Color services also name the color and may suggest color trends. Use of color samples is dependent on the quality of the color reproduction, and names of colors may create images that are not accurate. Exact reproduction of colors continues to be a challenge for all consumer product industries. Color analysis from previous sales data may not be available from sales and inventory systems and is something that a buyer should request if new computer systems are being installed.

The fashion forecasting service can provide the buyer with an assortment of sketches, color swatches, videos, photographs, and other visual aids that represent new ideas and repeating images. The presentations are often professionally developed and collected into booklets or boxes of materials. These services are now available on the Web with a password access for the buyer. For forecasts sent by mail or courier service to the buyer, fabric swatches, actual photographs, or yarn buttons may be included in the presentations. Prototypes or samples in full size or miniature may be available for some product classifications.

Forecasts from fashion forecasting services are often on a twice-annual basis or may be according to a preset number of seasons. The period of coverage varies with the service and may be a fixed time and the same for all customers, or changed to accommodate the individual buyer. Buyers should choose a service that will have forecasts timed to coincide with the buying cycle for their business. For buyers with traditional buying cycles of four or five seasons, many services may readily accommodate their needs. Buyers with more frequent buying times and shorter planning cycles may need to request specialized services.

A fashion forecasting service provides a number of advantages to a buyer. Time saving is one of the most obvious advantages. The staff from the service spends their time scanning the news media, the trade papers, and other sources. The staff also culls the information, sorts and organizes the information, and prepares the forecast from their research. Using a forecasting service also has disadvantages. The service may have its own "style" or way of viewing the future. This view is only useful to the buyer if the view coincides with the vision of the buyer's business and would be acceptable for the buyer's target customer. The information from a service can become repetitive and single focused, which may limit the newness of the forecast and may contribute to stale merchandise assortments for a buyer. The buyer may find that time is better spent doing personal research rather than reading the information from the services.

Forecasting services charge for their work. Fees for forecasting services range from a few hundred dollars to thousands of dollars depending on the assortment of services that are purchased. The cost of the service may be prohibitive for many buyers, and depending on the extensiveness of the information search needed by the buyer, the fee may not be justified. (Some products are more stable and have less change. This buyer may find that, with a minimum of record review, an accurate forecast may be made without outside information.)

Attending Fashion Shows and Markets

Attending fashion or trade shows appears to be a highlight of any fashion career. The image of jetting to a foreign country or a major domestic city to view the latest creations by famous fashion designers is an image that many people have about buyers. This image is only partially correct. Attendance at a major international fashion show is hard work for a buyer. The buyer must prepare for the show—reviewing business information, determining what shows will be seen, and pre-evaluating the designers whose shows will be visited. While at the markets, the buyer will want to see as many shows or product presentations as possible, which may require sprinting on foot from one tent or showroom to the next. Seating will be crowded, food will be limited and expensive, and accommodations will be overbooked. The buyer must work very hard to take notes and sketches and to gather as much information as possible in an impossibly short time. Yet, attending a major fashion or trade show is the best way to see the newest products and to sense the heartbeat of the fashion industry.

For apparel, major fashion shows take place twice a year in Paris. Other international shows for apparel are held in Milan and New York City. These shows are particularly important for buyers of women's fashions. Other shows with more regional coverage are held in major cities in the United States such as Atlanta, Chicago, Dallas, Los Angles, and Miami. The major fashion show for men's wear, MAGIC, is held twice a year in Las Vegas. Buyers who are primarily interested in children's wear, sportswear, accessories, or gifts may find that certain regional shows have more offerings for their clients than some of the major shows. Observing the shows for new ideas is not the same as attending the show for buying. When the buyer goes to market, the forecast should already be complete. When a buyer attends a major international show, but shops in more regional markets, the show might be viewed for ideas for next season. While at the market, buyers may also attend shows to buy a select group of merchandise for a few new trend concepts to complete the forecast and buying orders that have already been written. Shows for other products are centered in other cities at a variety of intervals.

The Internet has affected the buyer's attendance at fashion and trade shows as well as other areas of forecasting. Some designers of new products are doing simulcasts of their shows and making the live show available on the Internet as well as on the runway or in a series of kiosks. For a fee, a buyer can log on and view one of these live Web shows. Some product designers also have clips or portions of the show available for later viewing, again for a fee. Some e-commerce businesses provide the designers with a show service and make an assortment of shows and other information available to customers of the Web site. These sites allow buyers to view the shows from their office computers without the hassle and expenses of attending the shows. Of course, these buyers also miss the excitement of being in the crowd and the opportunity to observe the audience and the local retailers. Again, everywhere and everything should be scanned to provide information for the forecast. A popular new product could be emerging from the people on the streets as well as from the runways of Paris.

Reviewing Store Information

Store information can be collected from a variety of sources: store employees, want slips, style outs, and POS data. Gathering opinions from store employees is an important aspect of reviewing store information, but must be done with extreme care. Sales associates will have information that is directly sourced from customers, but often only a select few customers will voice opinions about current merchandise and even fewer customers express opinions about future wants in merchandise. Some businesses use a formal system of collecting information from consumers. This system involves the use of slips of paper called **want slips**. Blank want slips are kept at the cash registers and are completed by sales associates. When a sales associate rings merchandise for a customer, the associate should ask if the customer found everything and if the customer was looking for anything that was not found. This activity at the cash register can promote additional sales and will identify potential new merchandise for the business.

The collection of want slips can be beneficial for goodwill between the business and the customer. If the salesperson inquires about unmet wants and attends to them, the customer will feel that the sales associate is truly interested in the customer's needs and wants. The customer will feel that the business is really trying to achieve customer satisfaction. Want slips can also alert a buyer to merchandise that is out of stock and could be reordered if time permits a reorder. With some electronic cash registers, the information that would belong on a want slip can be entered directly at the cash register into an appropriate database. If paper want slips are used, the buyer will need to develop a routine for collecting and saving the want slips to ensure that no slips are lost. Buyers should acknowledge that this is not a statistically random method of determining consumer wants and should be used with caution because of biases that are inherent in this type of data collection method; however, in conjunction with other information collection methods, sales associates' information can be very insightful for the buyer.

Style outs examine current merchandise to determine trends, slow-selling items, and items that are hard to keep because they are so popular. Style outs are another method of collecting data from the store. This data collection method is a good activity for the buyer to complete while in a store in a merchandise department where sales associates or other company personnel can be involved. During a style out, the buyer will pull from the shelves and racks all merchandise from a group, category, or vendor that remains in stock. The buyer uses the purchase orders as a comparison of what was originally in the department and can observe the remaining merchandise. By noting what has been sold and what remains in the store, the buyer can determine visually what style features are selling and what features characterize the merchandise that continues to remain in the store. This data collection method is not a review of what items (e.g., skirt, blouse, or shower curtain) were sold, but a review of the style features (e.g., scoop neck, pink stripes, or clear plastic fabric) that were chosen by the customer. To do a style out, the buyer must have detailed knowledge of the merchandise that was purchased for the business. The purchases that are now being sold to consumers may have been made six to eight months earlier and may have included hundreds or thousands of units; therefore, the buyer must have a good memory for details and keep good notes in order to do an effective style out.

Reviewing Literature and Information from Vendors

For the buyer, many vendors will provide information and opinions about new products and fashion trends. Vendors who are apparel manufacturers have been working to develop the new product for several months prior to presenting the merchandise to the buyer. The vendor will have been to fabric tradeshows and may have marketing and product development staff in the business. Most vendors are very knowledgeable about their merchandise and about market activities; however, the buyer should be wary of this source and remember that the vendor's primary goal is to sell the merchandise. On the other hand, trustworthy relationships between buyers and vendors are extremely valuable, and a retailer–vendor partnership that is a long-term relationship is built on more than a profit motive. A vendor who wishes to have a long-term relationship with the retailer will be interested in the satisfaction of the retailer and the retailer's customer and will be judicious with advice and interested in the sell-through of the merchandise.

For buyers who are repeat customers, vendors can preselect merchandise that they think would satisfy the buyer's customers. The vendor becomes another scanning device for the buyer. Some vendors use their own databases and computer software to generate purchase orders for buyers that are completed prior to the buyer ever seeing any stock. These vendors will forecast the merchandise assortment with size, color, and quantities and may even place the stock in the business's distribution centers and floor space. The vendor may also warehouse the stock for the retailer. In a reverse direction of sharing for the partnership, vendors may consult the retailers in product forecasting. In order to obtain input from their major retail accounts, many manufacturers or vendors present their seasonal lines far in advance of the traditional vendor selling season to their best partners. This method, called **prelining**, not only helps the vendor solidify the seasonal offerings, but also provides advanced trend insight for the buyer. This level of partnership takes a long-time investment to develop and is very beneficial to both buyer and vendor, but is rare. (Vendor-managed stock is discussed in Chapters 7 and 14.)

To display or advertise new merchandise, the vendor may provide catalogs, videotapes, or password access to Web sites. With the flexibility and graphics capabilities of computers, the vendor may even use photographs and sketches to custom tailor a Web site for a buyer. The buyer can add these graphic sources to the collection of information from the general scanning activity, information gathered from a forecasting service, business information, and other sources of information. Buyers review these materials to gather ideas, find new sources of merchandise, and identify specific products to order.

Attending Major Social and Sports Events

By attending major social happenings and sports events, the buyer can observe products that are being worn, carried, or used by consumers in all fashion levels of the product life cycle. In a large group, fashion forward consumers and fashion followers will be represented. The buyer will also see consumers who are creating their own new fashion look. For the retailer who has limited access to other new information, these events are useful in providing insight into current activities of consumers. Fashion forward trends can be pinpointed and purchased for immediate delivery, or the trends that are observed can be adapted to fit the merchandise assortment of the individual retailer. Identifying new merchandise or new combinations of items will assist the retailer who is trying to provide fashion leadership, fresh assortments, and additional sales.

Traveling to Other Areas within the United States or to Other Areas of the World

Many large retail companies and some small retail businesses arrange for their fashion buyers to attend worldwide events in various areas of the world, or to power shop in major foreign retail markets. Additionally, many astute buyers plan vacations or travel to foreign countries on their own to observe other cultures and to gain insight into their potential influence on the apparel, home furnishings, home appliances, automobile, and other product trends in their home country.

Observing and Pinpointing Trends in Other Product Categories

Many times trends develop in one product category that will affect the design, color, or fabrication of another product category. Traditionally, intimate apparel garments are developed to support the sale of ready-to-wear garments; or hosiery and shoes are designed to coordinate with skirt lengths, pant styles, or particular trendy fabrications. A new color that becomes popular in apparel may influence the adoption of that color in home furnishings, gift items, and automobiles. The exchange of fashion ideas across products is often swift and multidirectional. When classifications are produced primarily in one country, that country can become a fashion leader in the classification, which means that those fashion forward items may trigger new fashion trends and earlier customer acceptance and demand for another product category in a specific style.

Preparing Information

The accuracy of information fed into the forecasting process has a direct effect on the accuracy of the forecast. Improved information about possible trends, style changes, and new vendors will assist the buyer in making a well-targeted forecast. Recording, storing, and organizing this information are as important as collecting the information. Some buyers keep files for cataloging information relative to fashion forecasting. Sales history is the most common file and often includes pictures. Some buyers keep a journal to record ideas, images, sketches, or other scraps of information. A bound book with blank pages can be used as a journal because the blank pages are more appropriate for sketches. Some buyers call this journal their report book. Other buyers prefer to keep a three-ring binder-style notebook and use plain pages, lined pages, and plastic sleeve pages. The plastic sleeves are a great way to keep samples of yarns, fabrics and other raw materials, swipes, and pictures and computer graphics. **Swipes** include any pictures that can convey a color, a style, or other features that may be important to the forecast.

Standard file cabinets and file folders may be used to store notes, photographs, sketches, and other sources of information. Some companies keep walls of corkboard in the buyer's offices or merchandising offices to keep style pictures and swipes available in a more visible way. These boards are particularly useful for moving and reconnecting information to develop themes and to identify trends. **Concept boards** that contain swipes, words, photographs, and other images may be developed to share ideas with a team or other members of the retail staff. These boards are often foam core boards of varying size (e.g., 2′ by 3′; 1.5′ by 2′). (Size may be dictated by company policy, the preference of the buyer, or the size of one's portfolio or office table.)

Keeping good notes about the source of fabrics, colors, or photographs is as important as keeping the visual evidence. The buyer would be very disappointed to choose a fabric sample as the central item in a season's purchases and discover that no one knows the source of the fabric and that it is untraceable. File labels with the name of the company, dates, addresses, and other pertinent information should always be affixed to samples. Note cards or other forms of labeling could be slipped in the plastic sleeve where a sample is kept, but this method allows the sample and the label to be separated. (When a buying team has many samples spread over a conference table, the labels and samples could easily become mixed.) A coding system could be used for vendors that are frequently used and that have current information in other files.

The use of a computer for data keeping is an option that may sound attractive, but could be very time consuming. Samples of all varieties could be scanned and collected into computer files. Scanning requires considerable time and the quality of the texture and color of the sample may be altered in the process. For a buyer who wishes to share information with a team member such as a department manager who is geographically distant, computer files might be a solution because of the time and expense saved in shipping the items. Computer files can also become a backup for the actual items. Computer-scanned images could be used as archival storage for information from previous seasons. If the information is in electronic format, some software solutions may be used to help sort and select merchandise. Use of electronically shared information can reduce the time between forecasting and sales. Quick Response systems that gather consumer data and share this data with manufacturers can reduce planning time and increase forecasting accuracy.

Determining Trends

The buyer must determine an overall trend for the coming planning period as well as specific items of merchandise. To achieve this balance, some companies keep two separate schedules for forecasting: long term and short term. **Long-term forecasts** provide an overall view of the marketplace as well as the changes in merchandise styles and cover a period of six months or longer. For a long-term forecast, general trends are noted and merchandise that is recognized as very popular or continuations from previous seasons are included. **Short-term forecasts** are for shorter time periods than long-term forecasts; for example, less than six months. They include specific information about style and color and are used to develop the assortment plan. Long-term forecasts provide direction for the buying (i.e., identification of trends), but the short-term forecast identifies specific merchandise items and also allows for changes in the specific selections to be made in response to early purchases. If the company is small and can place small orders or if the company is large, but has an established partnership with a manufacturer with flexible production, short-term forecasts are more workable with the vendors than long-term forecasts.

A trend may be a revision of a current trend or a change from the previous trend. A **trend** is the general increase in acceptance of a style or certain style features. The trend may be as specific as one item of merchandise, for example, the tank top. More often, the trend is a style feature or a general look, which can include color, fabric, shape, or parts of the item (i.e., collar, closures, edging, or trim). When the trend is identified, merchandise can be evaluated relative to this trend and selection of actual items can be made.

Identifying a trend may be as simple as counting the number of swipes in a file or as complicated as calculating a mathematical formula. Several methods of identifying trends may be used by buyers. A good buyer will always have a personal opinion or intuition about a trend as well as documentation for the trend. Collecting information is important to identifying the trend. Basic to an accurate forecast is adequate and accurate information. To identify possible trends as needed to complete the forecast, the buyer will review the swipes, brochures, notes, and other documentation that have been collected during the planning period. Some buyers, especially someone who buys for a small business, will use very simple and rather qualitative analysis when identifying trends. The buyer for a small business may have limited time or resources to do extensive quantitative analysis; however, with small but powerful computers anyone can do some sophisticated quantitative data analysis.

Qualitative trend analysis consists of reviewing the data collected during a period. The data will consist of the buyer's notes and all graphic information that has been collected about new merchandise and new media events. The buyer will also need the information about previous styles and trends that were selling well for the business. Some buyers use corkboards in their offices or file folders or simple stacks on a conference table to sort the data pieces and identify style features. The buyer is looking for an increased occurrence of something new. (In a recent season, the appearance of a lilac bridesmaid's dress in a popular movie signaled the start of a trend for pastel colors in the bridal wear market.) The buyer must be very open to new ideas, new sources, new information, and subtle changes in the world. A buyer can identify something new because of an in-depth knowledge of merchandise in previous seasons. An understanding of fashion theory, including the cyclical nature of fashion and the evolution of change, is also an important tool for the buyer. With qualitative trend analysis, the buyer depends on visual analysis of the collected data and on the buyer's own sense of what is new, exciting, or different.

Quantitative trend analysis depends on the mathematical analysis of data. To perform this type of analysis, the buyer or someone for the buyer would quantify the graphic information that has been collected. For example, the exact shades and hues of color in any swipes, photographs, or videos would be quantified. The number of times that these exact colors were viewed would also be noted. In addition, the person encoding the data may also quantify the situation in which the color was noted or the adjacent colors and style features that were seen. Style features and actual items of merchandise, including shapes and dimensions of the item, could be cataloged in this process. Some quantitative trend analyses include additional information about general economy, political events, and other world issues. The quantitative analysis process is time consuming and is best done by buyers who have many financial resources at their disposal. In addition, a decision about the investment of time and money versus the return in accuracy of forecast would need to be conducted before beginning a quantitative trend analysis.

The result of trend analysis is that the buyer has a guide for selecting merchandise. For example, the buyer would state that the trend for the next six months is for dark, jewel-tone colors and heavy, rough fabrics. Once the trend is identified, the buyer will need to be certain that this trend will appeal to and be purchased by the retailer's customers. For example, the buyer identifies that the trend is for dark rich colors. The buyer knows from history of the business that dark colors do not sell-through. The buyer must decide whether the trend is strong enough that the customer will change previous buying habits and accept the new trend or the trend must be adjusted to fit the customer. Perhaps the buyer will purchase the dark colors only for a limited amount of items, or the buyer will purchase only dark accessories.

Knowledge of the business and the target consumer is very important in focusing the trend to fit the business. A decision at this point in the forecast could greatly affect the salability of the retailer's merchandise and the future for the buyer. If a buyer discards a trend because the trend seems too extreme for the target consumer and the buyer is incorrect, the target consumer will be shopping the retailer's stores, catalogs, or Web sites and not see the desired new merchandise. If the desire for the new merchandise is strong, the customer will seek other sources for the merchandise. Also, if the buyer selects the trend and the target consumer chooses not to follow this trend, the retailer will hold excess merchandise that is not sold and again the customer who visits the retail sites will view merchandise that is not appealing to them. A customer who leaves because the merchandise is not appealing may shop elsewhere, be satisfied at the new location, and never return to the first location. For these reasons, forecasting the right merchandise is critical to the retailer's success.

Selecting Merchandise

Final merchandise selection is a major part of forecasting. Decisions for this step involve a number of activities and include style, color, fabrication, and brand. Activities may vary with the size of the company, the number of stores for which the forecast is made, and the budget that is allocated for the forecasting process. Small companies may have limited budget for travel, but will have more flexibility in the placement of small orders that are closer to the market. Preliminary to the final selection of merchandise, the following activities may occur: (a) buying samples from Europe or better markets and gauging colleagues and salespersons response and (b) buying a small amount of the merchandise and putting it in the store for a test run.

Test runs are small amounts of merchandise that are put into test markets to test or evaluate the salability of the merchandise. Some large, multistore retailers who develop their own merchandise actually place test runs or **floorsets** of the newly developed merchandise in selected stores located in specific geographic regions. These retailers use this **fastrack** method to identify best-selling styles, colors, and fabrications for specific consumers in specific geographic areas. In addition, these retailers utilize the information from the sale of these floorsets to develop new products for customers in other regions, especially when the weather differential between the geographic regions allows for a later entry of seasonal merchandise. For example, a new style of snow shovel can be **pretested** or placed into stores in a very northern region and later introduced into a mid-climate region that has a later snowfall. Using fastrack methods of merchandise entry, the retailer has a pulse on the items that will be accepted by most consumers before the peak selling season has arrived.

The test run must be completed early in or prior to the main opening of a season so that additional merchandise can be ordered if the test run proves that the merchandise is a strong-selling item. A test market can be a single store in a multi-store company, in catalogs for selected customers for retailers with catalogs, or on a Web site. For the retailer, an advantage to the virtual forms of selling (i.e., catalog or Web site) is the ability to show the items to the customer without having to stock them.

The merchandise selection aspect of forecasting is a series of choice sets for the buyer. A choice set contains alternative selections of merchandise. The choice set may be a set of individual items (e.g., six different blouses) or a set of multiple items (e.g., three sets of lamps, which represent all the lamps shown by three different vendors). The buyer must select which blouses or which dresses are to be purchased for the store. Although most buyers rarely think about how they decide on merchandise, decision rules are present when the buyer makes these choices. Most buyers use the conjunctive rule when buying apparel. The **conjunctive rule** is used by people as a means of eliminating a number of alternatives quickly. The person making the decision must set a minimum standard for each attribute (e.g., color or style feature) that is considered important. The product is then compared to the standards. If a product fails to match or exceed any one of the many standards set by the decision maker, the product is dropped from further consideration. The standard is set by the buyer's judgment, previous experience, and trend analysis. Using this information, the buyer must understand in specific detail the preferences of the target consumer and be able to develop a standard from those known preferences.

When selecting merchandise, the buyer must constantly remember that a **taste gap** may exist between the vendors, other fashion information sources, and the target consumers. The gap may be due to geographic, age, or economic differences. Previous information about style trends and actual merchandise sold can assist the buyer in determining a potential taste gap. Again, the buyer must depend on qualitative measures, previous information, and an understanding of the consumer to generate a well-targeted forecast, for success in forecasting.

The final forecast must be coordinated with all merchandise categories and with the strategic plans for the company. Final decisions about style and color are based on the factors of observation of samples, personal experience and opinion, opinions of other personnel in the company, price of the merchandise, and brand or vendor reputation. Small companies may actually have the opportunity to sample customers and use their opinions to influence the forecast. Larger companies may depend on generalized themes, vendor recommendations, and samples. Personnel within the company who may be polled include sales associates, department and store managers, associate or assistant buyers, and other colleagues. The final decision usually remains the task of the buyer. A successful forecast is usually rewarded by bonuses for the buyer. On the other hand, an unsuccessful forecast and unsold merchandise result in the loss of sales for the company and the potential loss of job for the buyer.

*S*ummary

Fashion forecasting is both the thrill and the curse of fashion merchandising. In an air of excitement, buyers may conduct a number of activities such as shop the markets, interview customers, and travel to see foreign fashion shows in the development of a forecast. However, the forecast process also contains the collection and processing of volumes of information, critical and careful decision making, and large amounts of paperwork. The forecast is the beginning of the merchandise assortment and as such determines the merchandise that will enter the store. Behind this forecast is careful understanding of store image and target customer.

Key Terms

Choice sets	Long-term forecasts	Style features
Concept boards	Prelining	Style outs
Conjunctive rule	Pretested	Swipes
Fashion counts	Product specific criteria	Taste gap
Fashion forecasting	Qualitative aspect	Test runs
Fashion forecasting process	Qualitative forecasting	Trade publications
Fashion forecasting services	Quantitative aspect	Trend
Fastrack	Quantitative forecasting	Want slips
Floorsets	Short-term forecasts	

Discussion Questions

1. Why is forecasting important in apparel merchandising?
2. What information is used in forecasting?
3. Why is vendor opinion good and bad in forecasting?
4. How can the buyer use a forecasting service and remain focused on the target customer?
5. How is the P & L statement related to forecasting?
6. Why must forecasts be long term?
7. What must be done in strategic planning to prepare for forecasting?
8. How can a buyer on a limited budget prepare an accurate forecast?
9. How can a style out assist the buyer in making a forecast?
10. What is the outcome of a successful forecast?

Exercises

Fashion Count

1. Perform a fashion count from observations of a situation. Prepare a tally spreadsheet with subclassifications and observations. Use a team to plan and complete the project.

   a. Meet with team to prepare tally sheet and plan.

      i.   Select a classification.
      ii. Determine subclassifications.
           The number of subclassifications will vary, but 8–10 is manageable. The subclassifications should first be by signification characteristics (e.g., for bathing suits—two-piece suits, mallots, racing-tank suits, and boy-leg sunsuits).
      iii. Use a second level of subclassifications as needed.
           This level usually contains fabrication, brands, or colors if these are major determinations in consumer selection.
      iv. Set up tally sheets.
           These sheets should contain all subclassifications, places for recording observations, and headings for time, date, and observer.
      v.   Divide territory.
           Select areas where the target consumer is likely to frequent. Each observer will need 75–100 observations. Observers should be spaced apart so that they are collecting information on a wide scope of the target population. A broad scope of coverage is most important.
      vi. Determine collection points.
           The observer should be able to easily observe the target consumers without interaction. The observer should also pick a location that is safe and that the observer can remain for an extended period.
      vii. Agree on collection day and time.
           All observations should be collected within a very short period, preferably within one day and within one 6-hour period. Fashion is an ever-changing phenomenon and is affected by many, many extraneous events. Control is important to data collection.

   b. Test the tally sheet.
      Do a test run of observing. This test run can be on a small and select population. The test population information should not be added to the final count. The test will assist the observer in observation skills and in subclassification identification. If subclasses are added or deleted, this information MUST be shared with the team.

    c. Perform the count.

      Each observer should have an IDENTICAL copy of the tally sheet. As the target consumers pass, the observer should record (usually with stick marks and bundles of five) the observation of the wearing of the classification. Every target consumer should be recorded. If a consumer is not wearing the classification item, a none (or no occurrence) should be recorded. If new subclassifications are noted, details should be recorded.

    d. Meet with the group to consolidate the tallies.

      A final tally sheet with totals for the subclasses should be made. The group can meet and consolidate the tally as a group, or one member can be responsible. A final tally sheet with count numbers and percentages should be created. Each subclassification must be expressed both in numbers and in percentages of total observations.

    e. Prepare a typed copy of the final worksheet.

      A final copy should be typed/printed with title, headings, rows, numbers and percentages, and team names.

2. Perform a fashion count using a magazine or trade newspaper. This is an individual project. If completed as a team project, each member of the team would select a different magazine and the results could be pooled.

    a. Select a fashion magazine, product, or classification.

    b. Complete the fashion count as itemized for the above count.

Concept Boards

1. Make a concept board to portray a general fashion trend.

    a. Collect graphic images from magazines, Web sites, fabric samples, newspapers, bags, or any other source of graphics images and color.

    b. Observe the collection of information.

    c. Determine a theme for the information.

    d. You may have to omit some of the data pieces that do not fit the theme.

    e. Arrange on a $2' \times 3'$ board the items that you have collected that support your theme. Remember rules of design when arranging the items. Glue the items that you have selected.

    f. Determine a title for your theme. You may create with paper, computer, or graphic labels this title and glue it to your concept board.

2. Make a concept board to portray the projected fashion forecast for a specific product classification. Use the steps outlined in the preceding project.

Computer Exercises

Databases for Forecasting

1. Use the tallies from one of the fashion counts in the Exercise section. Create a database with the subclassifications and tallies. The rows of the spreadsheet would contain the subclassifications found in the count. The column would contain the counts for each subclass.

a. Using the graphing features of the spreadsheet, create a bar graph of the totals for the subclasses.

b. Using the sort features of the spreadsheet, reorganize the list by ranking the subclasses from the one with the highest count to the one with the lowest count.

2. Repeat Exercise 1 with an additional fashion count. Make a prediction of the subclass most likely to sell based on the information.

3. Create a database using swipes and other fashion information.

a. Collect swipes, print outs of Web pages, notes about fashion issues, and other graphic material as suggested in information collection.

b. Review the information that you have collected.

c. Select one style feature that you see among your information (e.g., a new color or collar types).

d. Identify everything that you can about your style feature from the information that you have collected.

e. Group all the information from Step 3.d. into categories.

f. List the categories in a spreadsheet on the computer.

Style Feature: Collar Types		
Characteristics		
Long points		
....		
....		

g. Create columns for the number of occurrences and other relevant information.

Style Feature: Collar Types		
Characteristics	*Number of Occurrences*	*Other Information*
Long points		
Used with solid ties		
Round overall shape		

h. Using the information from the data collection process, complete the following table:

Style Feature: Collar Types		
Characteristics	*Number of Occurrences*	*Other Information*
Long points	5	Seen on movie stars
Used with solid ties	3	Solid tie and collar
Round overall shape	6	Ends of points are round, edges of collar are scalloped

i. You may sort the table according to the first column of the spreadsheet for an alphabetical listing of the style features.

j. To determine the style features that are most commonly cited, you would sort the table according to the column labeled "Number of Occurrences."

k. Write a general trend summary of the information in the table. Support your reasons for selecting this trend.

*A*ssortment Planning

*O*bjectives

After completing this chapter, the student will be able to

- identify standard methods of merchandise classification
- classify merchandise according to customer attracting features
- create an assortment plan

An array of merchandise contains a wide variety of features. These features can be grouped into various styles. For example, case goods can be grouped into styles. A large rectangular cabinet with doors that has shelves for audio and video equipment is an entertainment center. The same size cabinet that has drawers, hanging space, and some shelves is an armoire. Each style has a different function or purpose for the customer.

Another example is a grouping of jackets. A tuxedo jacket may have satin lapels, with a shawl collar, a fitted waist with one button, and a back that ends in a long hem that is described as two tails divided by a single center vent. The tuxedo jacket is a style, and the style is composed of a set of product features. Other product features in different combination or with different fabrications might create a riding jacket, a bomber jacket, or any one of numerous other jacket styles. Within the tuxedo jacket style are a set of product features including lapels, hem, bodice, fabric, sleeves, and pockets. Each item that is selected by the buyer can be described in a set of product features.

A buyer may select hundreds or thousands of styles when preparing a forecast that will include information about the style features of the new merchandise. Organizing this multitude of products is necessary to facilitate planning. For example, a buyer may encounter any number of upper garments for women. These items may have long and short sleeves. They may be of heavy fabric and be designed for wearing out of doors. The items may be made of lightweight silk and shaped to fit closely to the body for wearing under a jacket. The openings may be in the front, the back, on the shoulder, or completely lacking. The items may be black, white, green, blue, or any shade of the rainbow. In order to forecast assortments, plan for buying, analyze sales, or determine inventory levels, the merchandise must be classified. Small retailers may have hundreds of different items in inventory, and large retailers may have thousands or hundreds of thousands of items in inventory. Each classification of an item will receive an identifying number and each item will be a **stockkeeping unit** (SKU). To process any information about the entire inventory or about segments of the inventory, a classification system is needed.

Classification Systems

Before 1900, many consumers bought their merchandise in general stores. General stores carried a wide assortment of merchandise for the times, but compared to today's mega-stores, these general stores were small and had limited inventory. The owner of the general store kept inventory lists in a ledger as a list. By 1920, general stores grew in size and in inventory variety. Many general stores were replaced with the new retailing format of the department store. Managers of department stores kept track of inventory by departments. Again, they used ledgers with lists. Department stores continued to grow in number and size. After 1950, department stores carried a wide array of merchandise, still organized by departments. By 1970, inventory assortments in departments were too large and not well defined. Store managers and marketers devised a variety of methods of organizing merchandise assortments within the store. Lifestyle merchandising that grouped or organized merchandise by a theme or activity was conducted by many department stores. This marketing method provided customers with groupings of merchandise that would appeal to a target consumer. As companies grew and increased their holdings of merchandise, managers and buyers sought methods to organize merchandise that would allow for analysis, plans, and control.

Types of Systems

Merchandise classifications sort products by distinctive features and provide structure and organization for a collection of items. The traditional and primary classification method for the apparel product sorts the products by gender. Additional methods to categorize the apparel product include end use, fashionability, and seasonality. The **gender classification** has three main classes or categories: **men's wear**, **women's wear**, and **children's wear**. These categories are the basis for the U.S. **Standard Industrial Classification** codes (SIC codes) and for the newer **North American Industry Classification System (NAICS)**. Many manufacturers produce products in only one of the three categories. Although some products are unisex or are very similar across categories, the products are generally categorized by a primary gender category. For example, t-shirts are primarily men's wear items, but with little or no changes, they may be sold as women's wear or children's wear. According to this U.S. system, all types of apparel are numbered as SIC 23 with secondary classifications that reflect the three gender categories. For example, SIC 2311–2329 (or NAICS 315211) are men's wear, SIC 2331–2359 (or NAICS 315212) are women's wear, and SIC 2361–2369 are children's wear. (NAICS codes for children's wear are part of men's or women's wear codes.) Further classification divisions identify specific products within each of the three classes. The number SIC 2321 identifies men's shirts, and the number 2331 identifies women's blouses. This system has remained unchanged since the 1960s. However, the newer international system is being developed and is first being used with products on the Internet.

   End use refers to the occasion or purpose for which the apparel item will be worn. For example, clothing for women can be divided into multiple uses: career wear, eveningwear, sportswear, bridal, and maternity. Each of these events or uses has a specific need that must be met by the clothing that is worn. Career wear must be appropriate for use in the office and generally includes suits, tailored blouses, and some accessories. Sportswear is worn on weekends and after work. These items are worn for comfort and for their informal styling. Sportswear includes shorts, t-shirts, skorts, Capri pants, and many other items. Bridal wear is worn by a woman for a wedding. This primarily includes dresses of white and ivory for the bride and dresses of various colors for the bridesmaids. Bridal wear may also include formal, but subdued dresses for mother of the bride and versions of children's clothing for the flower girl. Tuxedos and formal suits for men may also be sold under this category. Accessories can be divided into items for the bath, the bedroom, or for the consumer. A "bed and bath shop" is found in many multiple-use stores.

For end use classifications, a detailed coding system is described by the National Retail Federation (NRF), the principal trade organization for retailers. Department stores are often organized according to some variation of the NRF end use system. In a large department store, sales areas may be labeled as sportswear, bridal, career wear, and other end uses. This method is used primarily by retailers because it relates closely to consumer usage and fits with the market and promotion activities of retailers. This system works well in organizing a department store because many consumers enter the store knowing for what type of item they are searching. For example, a consumer goes shopping and is looking for a dress for the mother of the bride; therefore, the consumer would look for the bridal department. In multiple-level stores, this order has been applied not only to departments, but also to floors. Fashion accessories and men's furnishings are often located on the first floor. Women's sportswear is located on the second floor. Bridal and evening wear are located on upper floors. Home accessories and bed and bath items are often located in the basement or on the top floor. This planning helps the consumer know where to look when entering a large store.

Fashionability and **seasonality** are classifications that are more elusive, but are extremely important to the operation of the apparel industry. Fashionability is evaluated on a continuum from highly basic to highly fashionable. Highly basic goods are products that change very slowly over time. Examples of these products are men's black socks, white t-shirts, a white oxford-cloth dress shirt, and a pair of blue jeans. Month after month and year after year, these products retain their original design and are produced and bought in quantity. At the other end of the continuum, highly fashionable goods are original designs that are produced once in limited quantities. These designs are used for one season of production; therefore, manufacturers who make highly fashionable products are constantly designing new products. Many famous designers and most new designers make products that can be grouped among the highly fashionable products; however, some designers or design houses, such as Chanel, make items that are considered classics and can be worn for many seasons and many years. For example, a Chanel jacket is "always in fashion," which makes it a highly basic product when classified by this method.

Seasonality refers to the length of time that a product remains in the sales arena and varies from highly staple products to highly seasonal products. Turnover is often used as a measurement of seasonality. A product line that turns two or fewer times per year would be considered highly staple. This type of product would retain the original design without change, including no change in color, for four to six months. The average turnover for the industry is four to six times. Highly seasonal product lines turn as often as 18 times in a year, and some apparel manufacturers are moving to a seasonless year with a continuous supply of new apparel products. These manufacturers must have a constant supply of new design ideas.

Customer Attracting Features

Systems provide an organized method of examining an assortment or set of merchandise. Each system is composed of a series of levels, which are hierarchically arranged. The first level in the system is called a class, and subsequent levels are subclasses. The exact hierarchical order of the levels is dependent on the system, the product, and the buyer. Products, when examined, are composed of a number of style features, color, and fabrications. The list in Figure 10.1 shows the components or classes and subclasses that may be part of a woman's knit shirt. The list is in alphabetical order for product analysis, but will be reordered to create an organized system. The process of creating order to a set of levels or product characteristics is a **sort**.

From the analysis of this knit shirt, the buyer identifies three possible levels for the classification: collar style, neck style, and sleeve length. An assortment of possible colors is also noted. The decision of what level to place first when doing a sort is a decision that the buyer or whoever establishes the system must decide. Typically, the sort begins with the style features and ends with color or brand. The fine tuning of a system and the decision to sort shirts, for example, first by the style of the neck rather than by the sleeve length is dependent on several factors. The style features with the broadest applications are often listed first. Other considerations for order of the style features are consumer preference, store policies, store strategies (e.g., brand importance and color emphasis), and type of merchandise. Color is often the last feature that is put into the system. The order of the style features is often set by the importance of **customer attracting features (CAF)**. In other words, the features for which the customer looks first would be the higher levels in the classification system or the trunk and main branches of the classification tree. For example, in bridal gowns, color may not be as important as waistlines, trains, and amount of beading or lace.

Organization of levels and the exact sort of product components will be dependent upon many factors. In shirts for career wear, fabrication or color may be very important because the shirt must match the suit with which it is worn. On the other hand, the exact neck style or sleeve closure is not important. Again, the buyer must consider what is important to the consumer who will be purchasing the item. Being able to use CAF requires that the buyer have an in-depth knowledge of the target customer. Each retail business will have its own, specialized, classification system. The system may be based on one of the traditional industry systems, may be a hybrid of several systems, or may have been created exclusively for the business. Most classification systems have a numbering system for identifying the items within the system. The numbering system is a multidigit system that provides a unique number for each item and identifies the placement of the item within the system.

Figure 10.1

Possible Levels of
Woman's Knit Shirt
from Product Analysis.

1. Collar Style
    a. Crew Neck
    b. Turtleneck
2. Neck Style
    a. High Neck
    b. Low Neck
    c. Scoop Neck
    d. V-Neck
3. Sleeve Length
    a. Long
    b. Short

Visual Format for a Classification System

The product classification systems are often displayed in a visual format for further analysis of product assortments and inventory control and evaluation. Two formats are commonly used: the tree format and the outline format. The **tree format** for displaying classification systems is shown as a tree with spreading branches to diagram the interrelationship across all parts. (See Figure 10.2.)

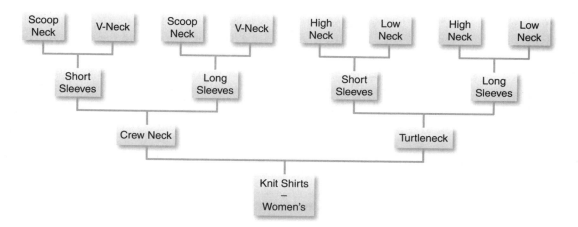

Figure 10.2	Tree Format of Classification System for Women's Knit Shirts.

Within the major class of women's wear, the term "knit shirts" is the base or trunk of the tree. The neck styles are the first level available within the knit shirts and are the main **branches**. The sleeve lengths are the second level or first subclass and are called minor branches. Additional smaller branches or **twigs** are used for the third level, the collar styles.

If the buyer traces a path from the trunk to one outer branch, a complete product with name, neck, and sleeves would be identified. The example shown in Figure 10.3 is a knit shirt that has a basic scoop-shaped, crew-style neck and long

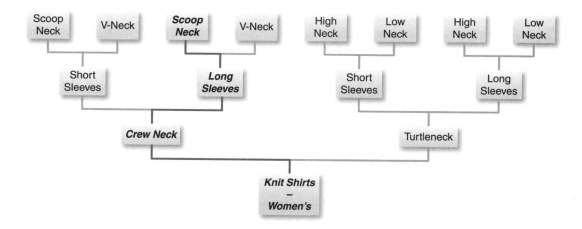

Figure 10.3	Tree Format of Classification System: Identifying One Item.

sleeves. This item may also have a common use name if it represents a basic style. For example, the shirt that is described in Figure 10.3 is often called a long-sleeve t-shirt. Additional smaller branches or twigs could be added to the tree to identify color, size, or other product features. This scoop neck, long sleeve, knit shirt may be red, blue, green, or print. For most classifications, the color and size are one of the last features to be identified. This general rule would not be true if color was a very important style feature for the season or if color was a major aspect of the business plan (e.g., everything in the store is black).

The classification system that is more commonly used is shown in an **outline format**. (See Figure 10.4.) The outline format in Figure 10.4 contains the same information as the tree format in Figure 10.2. The features on the same level of the outline are comparable. For example, crew neck and turtleneck are both basic neck styles of knit shirts. The next level describes sleeves and the next level gives more detail about the necks. Each level can have multiple descriptions of the style feature that is cited at that level, but only one class of style feature can appear on any level. Many levels are possible within this system. Additional levels could be added to accommodate color, fabric, and brands. Fewer levels with more details per level might be used by a buyer who buys for a retailer with a limited number of SKUs. Although the listing of each style feature seems to be excessive, this method provides a wealth of information when used with a computer program for inventory or with a simple spreadsheet. When each style feature is individually listed (i.e., the placement of a single style feature on one line) within a spreadsheet, the information can be sorted, searched, and used to prepare reports and establish trends.

Figure 10.4
 	
Outline Format of Classification System for Women's Knit Shirts.
	Knit shirts
	   Crew neck shirts
	      short sleeves
	         scoop neck
	         v-neck
	      long sleeves
	         scoop neck
	         v-neck
	   Turtleneck shirts
	      short sleeves
	         high neck
	         low neck
	      long sleeves
	         high neck
	         low neck

Again, to identify all of the style features of an item, the buyer would follow from the main levels or classes to the lower levels or subclasses and identify one style feature on each level. The sum of those features is the style of the item. The sum of the features that are identified in bold in Figure 10.5 indicate a woman's scoop, crew neck knit shirt with long sleeves. (Only one style feature per level is selected in Figure 10.5, for example only one sleeve type is selected—long sleeves. The short sleeve line is not selected.) Overall, a total of five style features are selected, and each one is mutually exclusive, but adds to the buyer's knowledge of the item.

When classification systems are organized in the outline format, they can be easily used in computer spreadsheets. Buyers can sort the database for the exact style feature desired, be that neck, sleeve, color, or other feature such as price or brand. Any feature that is keyed into the database and is held as a separate style feature can be

Figure 10.5	**Woman's wear**
	Knit shirts
Sample Classification	**Crew neck shirts**
System for Knit Shirts,	short sleeves
Identifying One Item.	scoop neck
	v-neck
	long sleeves
	scoop neck
	v-neck
	Turtleneck shirts
	short sleeves
	high neck
	low neck
	long sleeves
	high neck
	low neck

found in a search or a sort in a spreadsheet. The exact choice of the numbering system and the specific number of levels and classes that are in a system can vary from retail business to retail business. These factors do not affect the system's function. The important factors in developing a system are to identify single style features that are key to the customer, to sort each style feature into mutually exclusive classes, and to organize a hierarchical system that has the most important features listed first. A system must function to organize the merchandise and allow the buyer or other retail personnel quickly to group and review hundreds of SKUs. This organizational system provides structure for items selected in forecasting. The outline format is compatible with computer spreadsheets.

Sample Problem: Establish a Classification System for Formal Bridal Gowns

The buyer for bridal gowns uses past history, vendor information, and interviews with consumers to determine the sort process for a formal bridal gown. The buyer first determines that three components are most important to the bride: waists, trains, and color. The buyer must make a list of these components and the possible styles within each component.

Step 1. Make a list of the components and possible style features.

1. Color
   a. Ivory
   b. White
2. Style of Train
   a. Cathedral Train
   b. Chapel Train
   c. No Train
3. Style of Waist
   a. Empire Waist
   b. Long Waist
   c. Natural Waist

The buyer has also determined the order of the levels in the sort. The bride to be is first attracted to the dress because of the waistline. The waistline provides an overall definition of the dress and controls the effect that the dress will have on the bride's figure. The bride is next concerned about the length of the train because that style feature is related to the formality of the dress and the appropriate use of the dress for different settings. The buyer's research shows that the bride is least concerned with the exact shade of white or ivory for the dress color.

Step 1. The first sort is by waists (e.g., empire, natural, or long).
Step 2. The second sort is by trains (e.g., no train, chapel train, or cathedral train).
Step 3. The final sort is by color (e.g., white or ivory).

Formal Bridal Gowns
    Empire waist
        No train
            white
            ivory
        Chapel Train
            white
            ivory
        Cathedral Train
            white
            ivory
    Natural waist
        No train
            white
            ivory
        Chapel Train
            white
            ivory
        Cathedral Train
            white
            ivory
    Long Waist
        No train
            white
            ivory
        Chapel Train
            white
            ivory
        Cathedral Train
            white
            ivory

Assortment Planning

An **assortment plan** is an organized collection of related merchandise, which includes specifications for brands, colors, sizes, and material. The assortment plan is built or organized according to the classification system used by the retailer. The system should be made with customer attracting features in mind because the system will be used to plan the merchandise that will be bought by the buyer. An example of an assortment plan with classes and subclasses is provided in Figure 10.6. The process of developing

Figure 10.6	Sample Assortment Plan for Fall Planning.

Assortment Plan for Fall — Women's Wear			Total Fall Dollars: $100,000.00	
	Percentage of Stock	Total Dollars for the Class and Subclasses	Unit Cost for the Item	Number of Units
Knit Shirts				
Crew neck Shirts	50.00%	$50,000.00		
short sleeves				
scoop neck	5.00%	$5,000.00	$5.00	1,000
v-neck	5.00%	$5,000.00	$5.00	1,000
long sleeves				
scoop neck	20.00%	$20,000.00	$10.00	2,000
v-neck	20.00%	$20,000.00	$10.00	2,000
Turtleneck shirts	50.00%	$50,000.00		
short sleeves				
high neck	0%			
low neck	0%			
long sleeves				
high neck	25.00%	$25,000.00	$10.00	2,500
low neck	25.00%	$25,000.00	$10.00	2,500

this plan is the assortment planning process. The buyer must develop this plan to use as a shopping guide before ordering merchandise. The assortment plan is created by a merger between the forecast and the sales plan. The forecast provides the products that are to be purchased, organized by the classification system, and the general sales plan provides the dollars that are to be used to buy the merchandise. From this information, the buyer will predict the exact number of items of each type that will be purchased. Merchandise that is reordered each season can be determined with a revision of the previous season's assortment plan; however, in the fashion business limited amounts of merchandise are ordered by straight reorder. More and more of items in the stock for a fashion retailer are ordered as a new order without previous purchases.

The assortment plan can also be used to determine specific quantities of merchandise within each class or subclass. The more diverse the product assortment is for the retailer, the more need is present for a detailed assortment plan, which should be prepared prior to the buying trip.

The assortment plan may have several versions. The version that is most closely related to the forecast will be one that is organized as the customer might shop. The style features that would be considered first in the shopping process by the consumer would be the major classes within the merchandise classification and subclasses would be categories of additional features, and finally color, size, and vendor. With the addition of sales dollars and quantities, the assortment plan becomes the **quantitative** or **detailed sales forecast**. This quantitative forecast with both styles and volume is based on the quantitative information from the sales plan and the six-month plan and is used to make the buying lists for market trips. The detailed forecast combines the style information from fashion forecasting with the dollar information from sales planning.

An assortment plan is developed in both rows and columns. The rows are estab-lished with the following steps: (a) select general classifications of products, (b) divide the general classes into subclasses, (c) identify additional characteristics of the sub-classes that will be needed (e.g., colors, fabrics, and sizes), and (d) set up a spreadsheet with rows for classes, subclasses, and sub-subclasses. Next, the columns must be creat-ed for the percentage for each level, the dollar amounts for the levels, unit costs, and the number of units. The steps to complete the columns are (a) establish a total dollar amount, (b) determine the proportion or percentage for each class and subclass, (c) disperse the dollars according to percentages, (d) determine the unit costs for each item, and (e) calculate the units for each class or subclass. The percentage or propor-tion of each class within the total plan is part of the forecasting that the buyer must do. The buyer must plan how much of each type of merchandise is wanted. An exam-ple of this process is shown in the following sample problem, which provides a step-by-step development of a section of the assortment plan.

Sample Problem: Assortment Plan for Fall Planning

The buyer is planning for fall purchases of women's handbags. The buyer checks the forecast and determines that the bags for fall are to be in two major groups: clutch and hobo. Leather and fabric bags are predicted to be popular. The buyer decides from the forecast to get clutch bags made of leather and fabric. For colors, the predictions are for brown, blue, gray, and black. The buyer decides that the leather bags are to be brown and blue. The fabric bags are to be gray and black. Looking at the pictures in the forecast report the buyer decides that the most attractive hobo bags are brown and gray leather.

Step 1. Set up the format for the assortment plan, including the classification levels.

Assortment Plan for Fall—Women's Handbags			Total Fall Dollars:	
	Percentage of Stock	Total Dollars for the Class and Subclasses	Unit Cost for the Item	Number of Units
Clutch				
Leather				
Brown				
Blue				
Fabric				
Gray				
Black				
Hobo				
Leather				
Brown				
Gray				

Step 2. Determine the total number of dollars to be spent on the items.
The total dollars for the fall purchase of women's handbags will be $10,000.00. Place this amount into the appropriate cell in the spreadsheet.

Assortment Plan for Fall—Women's Handbags			Total Fall Dollars: $10,000.00	
	Percentage of Stock	*Total Dollars for the Class and Subclasses*	*Unit Cost for the Item*	*Number of Units*
Clutch				
Leather				
Brown				
Blue				
Fabric				
Gray				
Black				
Hobo				
Leather				
Brown				
Gray				

Step 3. Determine the percentage that will be allocated to each product.

Based on the information in the prediction report, the buyer decides that the clutch style will represent 70.00% of the bags, and the remaining 30.00% of the bags will be the hobo style. Among the clutch bags, part of the bags will be leather and part will be fabric. All of the hobo bags will be leather. The color is also determined by the buyer based on forecast information and previous sales as analyzed by color, and percentages are estimated for these levels. No brand or size is needed for these purchases.

Enter the percentages into the spreadsheet.

Assortment Plan for Fall—Women's Handbags			Total Fall Dollars: $10,000.00	
	Percentage of Stock	*Total Dollars for the Class and Subclasses*	*Unit Cost for the Item*	*Number of Units*
Clutch	70.00%			
Leather	30.00%			
Brown	15.00%			
Blue	15.00%			
Fabric	40.00%			
Gray	10.00%			
Black	30.00%			
Hobo	30.00%			
Leather	30.00%			
Brown	20.00%			
Gray	10.00%			

Step 4. Calculate the dollar amounts for the major classes.

The dollars for the major classes are determined by the **class dollars and percentage** formula

Class $ = Total $ × Class %

Clutch $ = $10,000.00 × 70.00%

= $7,000.00

Hobo $ = $10,000.00 × 30.00%

= $3,000.00

Enter results into the spreadsheet.

Assortment Plan for Fall—Women's Handbags			Total Fall Dollars: $10,000.00	
	Percentage of Stock	Total Dollars for the Class and Subclasses	Unit Cost for the Item	Number of Units
Clutch	70.00%	$7,000.00		
Leather	30.00%			
Brown	15.00%			
Blue	15.00%			
Fabric	40.00%			
Gray	10.00%			
Black	30.00%			
Hobo	30.00%	$3,000.00		
Leather	30.00%			
Brown	20.00%			
Gray	10.00%			

Step 5. Calculate the dollar amounts for the lowest subclass. This level is the level that deals with the actual product and will be the SKU level for purchases and inventory.

The dollars for the subclasses are determined by the **subclass dollars and percentage** formula

Subclass $ = Total $ × Subclass %

Brown Leather Clutch $ = $10,000.00 × 15.00%

= $1,500.00

Gray Leather Hobo $ = $10,000.00 × 10.00%

= $1,000.00

Assortment Plan for Fall—Women's Handbags			Total Fall Dollars: $10,000.00	
	Percentage of Stock	Total Dollars for the Class and Subclasses	Unit Cost for the Item	Number of Units
Clutch	70.00%	$7,000.00		
Leather	30.00%			
Brown	15.00%	$1,500.00		
Blue	15.00%			
Fabric	40.00%			
Gray	10.00%			
Black	30.00%			
Hobo	30.00%	$3,000.00		
Leather	30.00%			
Brown	20.00%			
Gray	10.00%	$1,000.00		

Step 6. Complete the subclass amounts using the **subclass dollars and percentage** formula.

Subclass $ = Total $ × Subclass %

Place the calculated values into appropriate cells in the spreadsheet.

Assortment Plan for Fall—Women's Handbags			Total Fall Dollars: $10,000.00	
	Percentage of Stock	Total Dollars for the Class and Subclasses	Unit Cost for the Item	Number of Units
Clutch	70.00%	$7,000.00		
Leather	30.00%			
Brown	15.00%	$1,500.00		
Blue	15.00%	$1,500.00		
Fabric	40.00%			
Gray	10.00%	$1,000.00		
Black	30.00%	$3,000.00		
Hobo	30.00%	$3,000.00		
Leather	30.00%			
Brown	20.00%	$2,000.00		
Gray	10.00%	$1,000.00		

Step 7. Identify unit costs for each item.

For example, the buyer determines that the unit cost for a blue, leather clutch will be $30.00. With the usual 50.00% markup, the buyer knows that this unit cost will yield a bag at $60.00, which will be in the right price point for the retailer. Unit costs for all final level subclasses will be determined. Costs are determined by the forecast information and store policy for markups and price points.

Complete the unit cost column for all subclasses.

Place unit costs into the spreadsheet.

Assortment Plan for Fall—Women's Handbags			Total Fall Dollars: $10,000.00	
	Percentage of Stock	Total Dollars for the Class and Subclasses	Unit Cost for the Item	Number of Units
Clutch	70.00%	$7,000.00		
Leather	30.00%			
Brown	15.00%	$1,500.00	$30.00	
Blue	15.00%	$1,500.00	$30.00	
Fabric	40.00%			
Gray	10.00%	$1,000.00	$10.00	
Black	30.00%	$3,000.00	$10.00	
Hobo	30.00%	$3,000.00		
Leather	30.00%			
Brown	20.00%	$2,000.00	$20.00	
Gray	10.00%	$1,000.00	$20.00	

Step 8. Calculate the number of units that can be purchased with the dollars allocated for the subclass, using the **dollars per unit cost** formula.

Unit # = Subclass $/Unit $

For example, the blue, leather clutch has a unit cost of $30.00. The dollars allocated to this item are $1,500.00. How many blue, leather clutches can the buyer order?

Unit # = Subclass $/Unit $

Unit # = $1,500.00/$30.00

Unit # = 50

Place the calculated values into appropriate cells in the spreadsheet.

Assortment Plan for Fall—Women's Handbags			Total Fall Dollars: $10,000.00	
	Percentage of Stock	Total Dollars for the Class and Subclasses	Unit Cost for the Item	Number of Units
Clutch	70.00%	$7,000.00		
Leather	30.00%			
Brown	15.00%	$1,500.00	$30.00	
Blue	15.00%	$1,500.00	$30.00	50
Fabric	40.00%			
Gray	10.00%	$1,000.00	$10.00	
Black	30.00%	$3,000.00	$10.00	
Hobo	30.00%	$3,000.00		
Leather	30.00%			
Brown	20.00%	$2,000.00	$20.00	
Gray	10.00%	$1,000.00	$20.00	

Step 9. Complete the calculations for unit numbers.

Assortment Plan for Fall—Women's Handbags			Total Fall Dollars: $10,000.00	
	Percentage of Stock	Total Dollars for the Class and Subclasses	Unit Cost for the Item	Number of Units
Clutch	70.00%	$7,000.00		
Leather	30.00%			
Brown	15.00%	$1,500.00	$30.00	50
Blue	15.00%	$1,500.00	$30.00	50
Fabric	40.00%			
Gray	10.00%	$1,000.00	$10.00	100
Black	30.00%	$3,000.00	$10.00	300
Hobo	30.00%	$3,000.00		
Leather	30.00%			
Brown	20.00%	$2,000.00	$20.00	100
Gray	10.00%	$1,000.00	$20.00	50

The percentages for the proportion of merchandise to be ordered for each class and subclass are dependent on two factors: previous sales records and assumptions about the salability of new products. From previous sales records, the buyer can determine the volume of sales for items with similar CAF and adjust these volumes relative to the success of the sales, the trend for increasing or decreasing sales, and buyer judgment. Assumptions about the sales of new products are formulated during the forecast. Store observations, observations of competition, position on acceptance curve, and past experience are predictors of average unit price. In other words, determination of the percentage of product classes and subclasses is based in part on mathematical calculations from previous sales and from estimation by the buyer.

When performing the assortment planning calculations, the numbers from the units per dollars formula, invariably, create decimal parts for the units of merchandise. The number of units cannot be expressed in decimals. For example, if the buyer had $2,550.00 total sales for coats and each coat cost $100, the number of coats that the buyer should purchase would be 25.5 coats (i.e., $2,550/$10 = 25.5). The buyer can buy 25 coats, but cannot buy one-half of a coat. The buyer must have some system of rounding for determining the number of units. Many buyers round down for all parts of units. In other words, the buyer would purchase 25 coats. Rounding up for numbers 5 and over and down for numbers 0 to 5, as is normally done in mathematical calculations, can contribute to overspending.

The final step is to review the plan and use the final plan for unit control. The assortment plan provides the buyer with a detailed shopping list. Using an assortment plan allows the buyer to select and purchase merchandise that was forecast, in amounts that are predicted to be accurate for the business and best for the target customer. If the buyer keeps within the plan, the incoming stock will be based on previous sales and the forecast. The forecast is made in conjunction with store and customer information. With this background, the assortment plan is designed to work in harmony with the inventory that is already in the store. Buying merchandise that is planned with emphasis on future sales and in keeping with present stock helps keep balanced stock within the business. With the assortment plan, the buyer can keep the new stock in balance with the sales plan. The buyer can spend time in the market looking at merchandise, selecting vendors, and finding new ideas instead of wondering how much of what items should be bought.

*S*ummary

Assortment planning is based on a merchandise classification system. The merchandise classification system allows the buyer to organize the thousands or hundreds of thousands of items that might be bought and inventoried in the business. With apparel and related items, the style features can come in an increasingly complex assortment. The combination of style features for a jacket can change with the seasons and throughout time. This unending complexity of style features must be organized to plan for purchases and to inventory stock. In addition to providing organization, the merchandise classification system used by a retailer must provide insight into the customer attracting features (CAF) that are desired by the target customers.

The assortment plan, with the merchandise classification system as the basis, provides the buyer with a detailed dollar plan for purchasing new merchandise. The addition of the sales projections or plans to the merchandise classification provides dollar amounts for purchasing. The dollar amounts are calculated at the subclass level to provide information about specific items. The projected unit costs are used to determine the number of units of each subclass of merchandise that should be purchased. Assortment plans are master plans that assist the buyer with determining what items to buy and how much of each item to purchase, based on the forecast information.

Key Terms

Assortment plan
Branches
Children's wear
Customer attracting features (CAF)
Detailed sales forecast
End use
Fashionability

Gender classification
Men's wear
Merchandise classifications
North American Industry Classification System (NAICS)
Outline format
Quantitative forecast
Seasonality

Sort
Standard Industrial Classification (SIC)
Stockkeeping unit (SKU)
Tree format
Twigs
Women's wear

Discussion Questions

1. Why does a buyer need a merchandise classification system instead of an alphabetized list of items?
2. Why do buyers at various businesses use different types of merchandise classification systems?
3. What are the two formats of merchandise classifications and what are their advantages?
4. How are branches and twigs related within the tree format?
5. What is the basic information that the buyer needs to begin the assortment plan?
6. How can an assortment plan help a buyer meet the goals of a balanced assortment?
7. How can an assortment plan help the buyer satisfy the customer?
8. Explain how store policies can affect the assortment plan.
9. What criteria can be used to evaluate an assortment plan?
10. How are percentages of classes determined for an assortment plan?

Exercises

Merchandising Classifications

1. Complete the merchandise classification system for shoes by answering the questions and placing the answers in the appropriate spaces.

   a. What are the three types of toes that could be found under flats?
   b. List another color besides blue under 1″ heels with open toes.
   c. What other type of toes could be found under 1″ heels?
   d. Describe a third type of heels found in dress shoes.
   e. Describe two types of toes that are found in the heel that was just selected.
   f. What other type of shoes could be sold besides dress shoes?

Classification System for Shoes *(Problem 1 continued)*

Dress shoes
    Flats
        a.1_____
        a.2_____
        a.3_____
    1″ heels
        Open toes
            Blue
            b._____
      c._____ toes
            Tan
            Black Patent
    d._____ heels
        e.1_____
        e.2_____
f._____ shoes

2. Complete the two-stage process to develop a classification system for suits.

Step 1. Identify the parts of a suit by listing the required style features.

    1. List five types of collars or necklines found on a suit.
        i.   _____
        ii. _____
        iii. _____
        iv. _____
        v.   _____
    2. List three types of closures found on suits.
        vi. _____
        vii. _____
        viii. _____
    3. List four jacket lengths
        ix. _____
        x.   _____
        xi. _____
        xii. _____

Step 2. Using the style features create the classification system with all possible SKUs.

    a. Use the neck line to create the first class sort.
    b. Use the closure types as the subclassification or second level. (Remember to add closure types of all five collars/necklines.)
    c. Use the jacket length as the final or sub-subclassification level. (Remember to add a jacket length for each subclassification.)

3. Observe the following classification system, and determine what is wrong with the system.

Step 1. Circle the things that are wrong with the system.

Step 2. Beside each error that was circled, explain the problem.

Step 3. Rewrite the system and fix the errors.

Classification Systems for Upholstered Furniture *(Problem 3 continued)*

Sofas
> Three-cushion
> > Tufted
> > Two-cushion
> > No tufts
> Pleated skirt

Chairs
> High Back
> > Low Back
> Wooden Arms
> > Self-covered Arms

4. Classify the following items in tree format to make a classification for socks. Classification systems are subdivided into classes and subclasses. Consider customer attracting features (CAF) when establishing the order for branches and twigs.

Happy allwear crew socks in 3 colors
StoreBrand crew socks with reinforced toes
Barbar knee socks in fashion colors
StoreBrand athletic tube socks with stay-up tops
Dayton knee socks with smell-guard
StoreBrand crew socks with slouch tops
All pro sneaker socks with cushion soles, stay-up tops, and reinforced toes
Fashion forever knee socks with reinforced toes
StoreBrand dress socks, sheer with reinforced toes
Tough guys athletic socks with double-thick toes and heels
StoreBrand anklets with lace trim
All pro tube socks with stay-in-place ribbing
Dayton athletic tube socks with reinforced toes
My Desire Sneaker socks with stay-up ribbing
L'amode tailored dress socks with ribbing and patterns
Barbar socks with crew tops and terry lining
Dayton athletic crew socks with smell-guard
Happy everyday knee socks with rib-stay-up top
StoreBrand knee socks with reinforced toes
Happy anklets, sheer weight, stretch top, and lace
Dayton crew socks with terry lining
All pro athletic tube socks with sweat-guard inside

(Note: You may have to add to the outline to complete the classification even if the details are not given from this group. Derive an entire classification from this list plus other possibilities. Do not sort by brand.)

5. Develop a classification system for hosiery: Classify the following items in outline form to class and subclasses, and consider CAF when selecting the order.

DN pantyhose, back seam, flocked bow on heel, reinforced top/toe, nude heel
Dayton pantyhose, tummy and hip control top, reinforced toe, nude heel
Designer All Sheer Support pantyhose, sandalfoot

PB support knee-highs, wide comfort top, reinforced toe and heel

Round the World support pantyhose, reinforced top, toe, and heel

Bershire pantyhose, reinforced top, ultra sheer legs, sandalfoot

Designer sheer-to-waist pantyhose, floral stripe, sandalfoot

PB sheer knee-highs, with comfort top, sandalfoot

PB all sheer pantyhose, sandalfoot

Dayton pantyhose, tummy and hip control top, reinforced toe and heel

Slender-most pantyhose and control top in one, sandalfoot

Round the World pantyhose, control top, ultrasheer legs, sandalfoot

Round the World sheer-to-waist pantyhose, striped, sandalfoot

Happy sheer support stockings, reinforced heel and toe

Happy sheer pantyhose, reinforced brief panty, nude heel, reinforced toe

Designer support pantyhose, reinforced top, demi-toe, nude heel

Round the World pantyhose, reinforced top and toe, nude heel

PB stockings, reinforced toe, nude heel

Under-things panty & hose in one, brief reinforced panty, reinforced toe, nude heel

Dayton support panty & hose in one, control top, reinforced toe, nude heel

Abby Party pantyhose, Swiss dot, sheer-to-waist, sandalfoot

PB pantyhose, control top, sheer legs, sandalfoot

Round the World pantyhose, sheer-to-waist, sandalfoot

Slender-most panty & hose in one, support legs, control top, reinforced toe, nude heel

PB sheer pantyhose, reinforced top and toe, nude heel

Designer ultra sheer bronze pantyhose, control top, sandalfoot

Dayton pantyhose, tummy and hip control top, sandalfoot

Dayton panty and hose in one, control top, sandalfoot

Happy support pantyhose, sheer-to-waist, sandalfoot

Round the World opaque pantyhose, sheer-to-waist, sandalfoot

Happy pantyhose, brief reinforced panty, nude heel and toe

Designer signature pantyhose, sheer-to-waist, sandalfoot

(Note: You may have to add to the outline to complete the classification even if not given from this group. Derive an entire classification from this list plus other possibilities. Do not sort by brand.)

Assortment Plan

1. Complete the following steps and use this information to answer the question:

   a. You have $250,000.00 to spend for the next three months.

   b. Your merchandise classification is listed in the chart.

   c. Flats are 50.00% of your stock, 1″ heels are 30%, and stiletto heels are 20% of stock.

   d. Within flats, the breakdown across toe style is 1/3, 1/3, and 1/3.

   e. A pair of flat shoes with a square toe cost $23.00.

   How many pairs of these shoes can you buy?

Season			Total Dollars	
	%	$	Unit Cost	# of Units
Flats				
Square toes				
Round toes				
Open toes				
1″ Heels				
Pointed toes				
Open toes				
Stiletto heels				
Open toes				

2. Complete the following assortment plan for socks:

    a. The total budget for socks is $20,000.00 for the summer season.

    b. Knee highs are 10.00% of the stock, crew are 30.00% of the stock, tube are 5.00% of the stock, anklets are 35.00% of the stock, and dress and sneakers each are 10.00% of the stock.

    c. Within knee and crew, each color is half of the class percentage.

    d. Brands within the color A for crew are split in half each for the subclass.

    e. Additional subclassifications can be added for tube, anklets, and dress socks.

    f. Unit cost of all socks is $3.00.

Season			Total Dollars	
	%	$	Unit Cost	# of Units
Knee				
color A				
color B				
Crew				
color A				
Brand A				
Brand B				
color B				
Tube				
Anklets				
Dress				
Sneaker				

3. The buyer is given a total budget of $51,550.00 for the fall season. Complete the following assortment plan for pants:

Pants—Fall Assortment Plan			Total $	
	%	$	Unit $	# of Units
Jeans				
5 Pocket				
☒ Basic Blue				
☒ Distressed				
Pegged				
☒ Basic Blue				
☒ Overdyed				
Loose Fit				
☒ White				
☒ Stone Washed				
Dress Trousers				
Pleated Fronts				
Cuffs				
Black				
Blue				
No Cuffs				
Black				
Blue				
Plain Fronts				
Cuffs				
No Cuffs				
Casual Pants				
Full Cut				
Twill				
Tan				
Blue				
Brown				
Slim Cut				
Total	100%	$	xxxxxxx	

4. The buyer is given a total budget of $32,580.00 for the fall season. Complete the following assortment plan for pants:

Throw Pillows—Fall Assortment Plan				Total $	
		%	$	Unit $	# of Units
Square					
	Corded				
		☒ Silk			
		☒ Tapestry			
	Plain				
		☒ Twill			
		☒ Chambray			
	With Tassels				
		☒ Silk			
		☒ Tapestry			
Round					
	Corded				
		Silk			
		Red			
		Blue			
		Tapestry			
		Yellow			
		Blue			
	Plain				
		Silk			
		Tapestry			
Specialty					
	Oblong				
		Tapestry			
		Red			
		Blue			
		White			
	Oversize				
Total		100%	$	xxxxxxx	

Computer Exercises

1. Develop a spreadsheet for an assortment plan using the merchandise classification provided and using the following store data for the percentages. Create a heading or title area by arranging the following information in readable format:

   a. Your Name and Date, Store Name
   b. Total Sales for Fall—$1,488,600.00
   c. Title for the spreadsheet: Assortment Plan for Spring
   d. Labels for Columns: Classification, Fall Percentages, Fall Dollars, Planned Spring Sales, Projected Spring Percentages, Unit $, Total Units
   e. Provide lines and spacing as needed within the Chart Area:
      Classification Labels (for rows): Dresses, Suits, Sweaters, Blouses [Basic, Fashion, Other], Sportswear [coordinated groups, separates].

Pro forma for Chart (sample)

Store:	The Store					Date:	
Buyer:	KINCADE					Fall $:	
Class	*Fall %*	*Fall $*		*Plan Spring $*	*Plan Spring %*	*Unit $*	*Total Units*
Dresses							
Suits							
Sweaters							
Blouses							
Basic		—		—	—	—	—
Fashion		—		—	—	—	—
Other		—		—	—	—	—
Sportswear		—		—	—	—	
C. group				—	—		
Separate				—	—		
Totals	100%	—		—	—	—	—

Data for the chart:

1. Percentages for Fall were as follows: Dresses were 5%, sweaters and blouses were 10%, suits were 25%, and sportswear was 50% (with 1/3 in coordinated groups and 2/3 in separates). Use formulas to calculate $ spent for the Fall. (% × Total F$.)

2. Dollars for Spring: Use these percentages to adjust the Fall dollars to determine the dollars for Spring. Dresses will increase 12%. Sweaters will decrease 5%. Blouses will increase 20%. Coordinated groups will decrease 11%. Separates will increase 18%. Use formulas to calculate $. The formula for $ is Spring $ = F$ × (1 +/− change %).

3. Percentages for Spring: Calculate the new ratios of items: this will be different from Fall. Use the formula for %: Spring % = S\$/Total S\$.

4. For the Spring Unit \$, the average unit cost is dresses \$53, suits \$120, sweaters \$23, blouses \$18, and sportswear—coordinated groups \$23 and separates \$17.

5. To find the Total Units per Classification, use formulas to find the number of units that can be purchased. The formula for number of units is # Units = Spring \$/Unit \$. (Units are in whole numbers only.)

(Note: Totals are needed at the bottoms of some columns.)

*U*nit Control

*O*bjectives

After completing this chapter, the student will be able to

- define unit control
- explain the need for unit control
- calculate average markup
- calculate cumulative markup
- calculate Open-to-Buy
- relate Open-to-Buy in six-month plan to unit control
- explain the importance of markup in benchmarking

Planning is important for a retailer to actualize the goals of the company. Among the final steps of the strategic control process are the steps of evaluation and adjustment. Unit control provides a structure and a process for evaluation and adjustment for the retailer. A buyer needs to constantly survey the merchandise to determine stock levels, needs for new merchandise, and opportunities for increasing sales. Every day, merchandise is sold and new merchandise arrives. The retail price of goods changes with reductions. Sales were predicted while planning for an upcoming period, but the actual sales are rarely identical to plan. Unexpected changes in the weather, the opening of a competing store, and the unpredicted appeal of new merchandise may alter the sales of merchandise. Changes in sales, reductions, and operating expenses can cause changes in the bottom line of the Profit and Loss statement, and can directly impact the level of stock in the store.

Each day in retail is different from the previous day. Controls are needed in retail to maintain expected profit levels, to carry merchandise desired by the consumer, and to keep the stock fresh and exciting. To maintain profit and to keep stock in balance with the plan, buyers, managers, and other personnel in retail use financial controls, which are calculated on all the dollar functions in the business. When these controls are related to the merchandise that is sold, they are often called **unit control**. Unit control is a technique where the buyer examines the cost, retail sale, and markup of the items that are sold by the retailer. Unit control is based on the concept that the control or the examination is completed at the unit level. The unit level could be the SKU, a class of merchandise, a department, a store, a division, or the entire retail business. The unit can be examined in a variety of periods. The time span for the unit control examination could be one day, one month, a season, one year, or any other planning period that is used or desired by the retailer. Unit control can also be used to examine past, current, or future actions within the business or to compare the activities of one business to an industry standard.

Markup

Markups are one form of unit control. Markups are the difference between sales and cost of goods and must be large enough to cover operating expenses and profit, but small enough to keep the retail price at a desirable level for the consumer. Markup includes an assortment of types: individual, gross (markup and margin), maintained, initial, and average. Individual markup refers to the markup on one item, and gross markup is the markup planned for several items, departments, stores, or divisions. Individual and gross markups were covered in Chapters 2 and 3, respectively.

The formulas for calculating individual markup in dollars and percentages are

$$\text{Retail \$} - \text{Cost \$} = \text{Markup \$}$$

and

$$\text{Retail \$} \times \text{Markup \%} = \text{Markup \$}$$

The latter formula, involving both dollars and percentages, can be rewritten as

$$\text{Markup \$/Retail \$} = \text{Markup \%}$$

Gross margin and maintained markups are used when examining the profit and loss structures for an entire retail business. (See Chapters 3 and 4). These markups are used to examine different components of the business. Maintained markup is used when cash discounts or alterations and workroom costs are broken out from cost of goods and operating expenses. The maintained markup can be used by a buyer to demonstrate the success in negotiating terms when purchasing goods, especially when the cash discounts are large. The overall markup used when reviewing the entire Profit and Loss statement is the initial markup. This markup is used to examine the influences of all expenses in operating the business except the invoice cost of goods.

Even with the best of planning, changes in cost of goods and changes in reductions can affect the markup that is achieved on the merchandise. In addition, returns and loss can affect the amount of merchandise that is available for sale. Initial markup is the target or goal of the business, but knowing the variability in operating a retail business the wise retailer periodically checks the plan and compares the plan to the original. The "real markups" must be calculated at each point in time. This comparison is part of the unit control activities. Markups used in the calculations for unit control include average markup and cumulative markup.

Average markup calculates markup over items of merchandise, over groups of merchandise items, or across departments or stores. The technique of averaging markup is used across a series of departments, products, or periods. Average markup is used to provide an overview of a situation. For example, the store may have two areas that sell clothing for boys. The manager knows the markup in Area 1 and the markup in Area 2, and then wants to know the average markup on the sale of all items for boys. The average markup technique can be used to calculate retail and cost dollar amounts for planning purchases.

The basic formulas for average markup are as follows:

$$\text{Total Retail } \$ - \text{Total Cost } \$ = \text{Total Markup } \$$$

$$\text{Total Retail } \$ \times \text{Total Markup \%} = \text{Total Markup } \$$$

When this formula is rewritten to form the markup percentage, it is considered the **average markup percentage** formula

$$\text{Average Markup \%} = \text{Total Markup } \$/\text{Total Retail } \$$$

This relationship can be shown in a spreadsheet format. (See Figure 11.1.) Two groups and a total are shown in this figure. The two groups can represent a wide variety of groups: two major classes of jewelry (e.g., costume jewelry and fine jewelry), two departments (e.g., women's sportswear and women's career wear), two managers, or two divisions of the business (e.g., North East region, South East region).

The spreadsheet used for average markup can be used to calculate values for more than two products or more than two departments. Any number of products can be averaged. The spreadsheet in Figure 11.2 shows the average markup for three products. Each product or other grouping requires its own two-column set of a dollar column and a percentage column. For example, Group A is felt hats, Group B is straw hats, and Group C is twill hats. The total represents the total for all hats. An example of another average markup with multiple groups might be Store 123, Store 124, and Store 125 in a multi-chain retail business. If three stores are the sum of the retail business, then the total represents the retail, cost, and markup for all of the retail business.

When viewing the spreadsheet for average markup, each column set should be viewed as an individual spreadsheet. The formulas of

$$\text{Retail } \$ - \text{Cost } \$ = \text{Markup } \$$$

$$\text{Retail } \$ \times \text{Markup \%} = \text{Markup } \$$$

and

$$\text{Retail } \$ \times \text{Cost \%} = \text{Cost } \$$$

are operational within each two-column set. These formulas also are true for the total column. As shown in Figure 11.3, the two columns under the Group A heading

Figure 11.1

Average Markup over Two Products or Departments.

	Group A		Group B		Total	
	$	%	$	%	$	%
R						
− C						
= MU						

Figure 11.2

Average Markup over Three Products or Departments.

	Group A		Group B		Group C		Total	
	$	%	$	%	$	%	$	%
R								
− C								
= MU								

Figure 11.3

Spreadsheet for
Average Markup with
One Group Highlighted.

	Group A		Group B		Total	
	$	%	$	%	$	%
R						
− C						
= MU						

would be considered as one markup problem with the dollars and percentages being calculated as is done for the individual markup problems.

The spreadsheet for average markup has a unique feature that allows the buyer to add and subtract dollars across the $ columns. The formulas for **total retail, total cost and average markup** include the following:

Retail 1 $ + Retail 2 $ = Total Retail $

Markup 1 $ + Markup 2 $ = Total Markup $

Cost 1 $ + Cost 2 $ = Total Cost $

In Figure 11.3, Retail 1 would be the retail found in Group A and Retail 2 would be the retail found in Group B. Only the dollar columns can be added across products or departments. Percentage columns cannot be totaled. Each percentage must be calculated with its own dollars, including the average percentages. Average percentage is not the same as a total of percentages.

Sample Problem: Average Markup when Group 1 and Group 2 Information Is Known

In the Shoe Department, inventory is divided into two categories: dress shoes and athletic shoes. In the month of June, retail sales of dress shoes are $2,240.00 and retail sales for athletic shoes are $3,000.00. The average markup for dress shoes is 36.75% and the average markup for athletic shoes is 42.56%. What is average markup for the entire Shoe Department?

Step 1. Set up the spreadsheet.

	Dress Shoes		Athletic Shoes		Total	
	$	%	$	%	$	%
R						
− C						
= MU						

Step 2. Fill in the known information from the problem.

(Hint: Remember retail percentage is always 100%.)

	Dress Shoes		Athletic Shoes		Total	
	$	%	$	%	$	%
R	$2,240.00	100.00%	$3,000.00	100.00%		100.00%
− C						
= MU		36.75%		42.56%		

Step 3. Calculate the information for dress shoes, and add the results to the spreadsheet.

Retail $ × Markup % = Markup $
$2,240.00 × 36.75% = Markup $
$823.20 = Markup $

Retail $ − Cost $ = Markup $
Retail $ − Markup $ = Cost $
$2,240.00 − $823.20 = Cost $
$1,416.80 = Cost $

Retail % − Cost % = Markup %
Retail % − Markup % = Cost %
100% − 36.75% = Cost %
63.25% = Cost %

	Dress Shoes		Athletic Shoes		Total	
	$	%	$	%	$	%
R	$2,240.00	100.00%	$3,000.00	100.00%		100.00%
− C	$1,416.80	63.25%				
= MU	$823.20	36.75%		42.56%		

Step 4. Calculate the remaining information for the athletic shoes, and add the results to the spreadsheet.

Retail $ × Markup % = Markup $
$3,000.00 × 42.56% = Markup $
$1,276.80 = Markup $

Retail $ − Cost $ = Markup $
Retail $ − Markup $ = Cost $
$3,000.00 − $1,276.80 = Cost $
$1,723.20 = Cost $

Retail % − Cost % = Markup %
Retail % − Markup % = Cost %
100% − 42.56% = Cost %
57.44% = Cost %

	Dress Shoes		Athletic Shoes		Total	
	$	%	$	%	$	%
R	$2,240.00	100.00%	$3,000.00	100.00%		100.00%
− C	$1,416.80	63.25%	$1,723.20	57.44%		
= MU	$823.20	36.75%	$1,276.80	42.56%		

Step 5. Calculate dollar values for the total column, and add the results to the spreadsheet.

Retail 1 $ + Retail 2 $ = Total Retail $
$2,240.00 + $3,000.00 = Total Retail $
$5,240.00 = Total Retail $

Cost 1 $ + Cost 2 $ = Total Cost $

$1,416.80 + $1,723.20 = Total Cost $

$3,140.00 = Total Cost $

Markup 1 $ + Markup 2 $ = Total Markup $

$823.20 + $1,276.80 = Total Markup $

$2,100.00 = Total Markup $

	Dress Shoes		Athletic Shoes		Total	
	$	%	$	%	$	%
R	$2,240.00	100.00%	$3,000.00	100.00%	$5,240.00	100.00%
− C	$1,416.80	63.25%	$1,723.20	57.44%	$3,140.00	
= MU	$823.20	36.75%	$1,276.80	42.56%	$2,100.00	

(Hint: Check the Total Markup $ by working the following formula:

Total Retail $ − Total Cost $ = Total Markup $

$5,240.00 − $3,140.00 = Total Markup $

$2,100.00 = Total Markup $

(Hint: This markup result is the same as found by the additive method—the spreadsheet "squares" or checks.)

Step 6. Find the average markup percentage for the Shoe Department, and complete the spreadsheet.

Total Markup $/Total Retail $ = Average Markup %

$2,100.00/$5,240.00 = Average Markup %

40.08% = Average Markup %

	Dress Shoes		Athletic Shoes		Total	
	$	%	$	%	$	%
R	$2,240.00	100.00%	$3,000.00	100.00%	$5,240.00	100.00%
− C	$1,416.80	63.25%	$1,723.20	57.44%	$3,140.00	
= MU	$823.20	36.75%	$1,276.80	42.56%	$2,100.00	40.08%

Step 7. Find the average cost percentage by subtraction (R % − MU % = C %) or by the dollar and percentage combination formula (C $/R $ = C %). In either case, the cost percentage is 59.92%.

	Dress Shoes		Athletic Shoes		Total	
	$	%	$	%	$	%
R	$2,240.00	100.00%	$3,000.00	100.00%	$5,240.00	100.00%
− C	$1,416.80	63.25%	$1,723.20	57.44%	$3,140.00	59.92%
= MU	$823.20	36.75%	$1,276.80	42.56%	$2,100.00	40.08%

The average markup spreadsheet, as shown in Figure 11.1, could be used to calculate information about any of the columns or rows if information is known about at least two of the rows or two of the columns. Each individual set of columns and rows can be used to find missing information as was done for individual markup, as in Chapter 2. In addition, the entire spreadsheet can be used to find missing information about one of the product groups when information is known about the other product group and the total.

Sample Problem: Average Markup when Total and One Group Are Known

In the Shoe Department, the inventory is divided into two categories: dress shoes and athletic shoes. In the month of June, the retail sales of dress shoes are $2,240.00 and the total retail sales for shoes are $5,240.00. The average markup for dress shoes is 36.75% and the average markup for all shoes is 40.08%. What is the average markup for the athletic shoes?

Step 1. Set up the spreadsheet.

	Dress Shoes		Athletic Shoes		Total	
	$	%	$	%	$	%
R						
− C						
= MU						

Step 2. Fill in the known information from the problem.

(Hint: Remember retail percentage is always 100%.)

	Dress Shoes		Athletic Shoes		Total	
	$	%	$	%	$	%
R	$2,240.00	100.00%		100.00%	$5,240.00	100.00%
− C						
= MU		36.75%				40.08%

Step 3. Calculate the remaining information for the dress shoes, and add the results to the spreadsheet.

Retail $ × Markup % = Markup $
$2,240.00 × 36.75% = Markup $
$823.20 = Markup $

Retail $ − Cost $ = Markup $
Retail $ − Markup $ = Cost $
$2,240.00 − $823.20 = Cost $
$1,416.80 = Cost $

Retail % − Cost % = Markup %
Retail % − Markup % = Cost %
100% − 36.75% = Cost %
63.25% = Cost %

	Dress Shoes		Athletic Shoes		Total	
	$	%	$	%	$	%
R	$2,240.00	100.00%		100.00%	$5,240.00	100.00%
− C	$1,416.80	63.25%				
= MU	$823.20	36.75%				40.08%

Step 4. Calculate the remaining information for the total shoes sales, and add the results to the spreadsheet.

Total Retail $ $\times$ Total Markup % = Total Markup $

$5,240.00 $\times$ 40.08% = Total Markup $

$2,100.00 = Total Markup $

Total Retail $ − Total Cost $ = Total Markup $

Total Retail $ − Total Markup $ = Total Cost $

$5,240.00 − $2,100.00 = Total Cost $

$3,140.00 = Total Cost $

Total Retail % − Total Cost % = Total Markup %

Total Retail % − Total Markup % = Total Cost %

100% − 40.08% = Total Cost %

59.92% = Total Cost %

	Dress Shoes		Athletic Shoes		Total	
	$	%	$	%	$	%
R	$2,240.00	100.00%		100.00%	$5,240.00	100.00%
− C	$1,416.80	63.25%			$3,140.00	59.92%
= MU	$823.20	36.75%			$2,100.00	40.08%

Step 5. Calculate the dollar values for athletic shoes, and add the results to the spreadsheet.

Retail 1 $ + Retail 2 $ = Total Retail $

Total Retail $ − Retail 1 $ = Retail 2 $

$5,240.00 − $2,240.00 = Retail 2 $

$3,000.00 = Retail 2 $

Cost 1 $ + Cost 2 $ = Total Cost $

Total Cost $ − Cost 1 $ = Cost 2 $

$3,140.00 − $1,416.80 = Cost 2 $

$1,723.20 = Cost 2 $

Markup 1 $ + Markup 2 $ = Total Markup $

Total Markup $ − Markup 1 $ = Markup 2 $

$2,100.00 − $823.20 = Markup 2 $

$1,276.80 = Markup 2 $

	Dress Shoes		Athletic Shoes		Total	
	$	%	$	%	$	%
R	$2,240.00	100.00%	$3,000.00	100.00%	$5,240.00	100.00%
− C	$1,416.80	63.25%	$1,723.20		$3,140.00	59.92%
= MU	$823.20	36.75%	$1,276.80		$2,100.00	40.08%

(Hint: Check Markup 2 $ by working the following formula:

Retail 2 $ − Cost 2 $ = Markup 2 $

$3,000.00 − $1,723.20 = Markup 2 $

$1,276.80 = Markup 2 $

(Hint: This markup result is the same as found by the additive method—the spreadsheet "squares" or checks.)

Step 6.   Find the markup percentage for the athletic shoes, and complete the spreadsheet.

Markup 2 $/Retail 2 $ = Markup 2 %

$1,276.80/$3,000.00 = Markup 2 %

42.56% = Markup 2 %

	Dress Shoes		Athletic Shoes		Total	
	$	%	$	%	$	%
R	$2,240.00	100.00%	$3,000.00	100.00%	$5,240.00	100.00%
− C	$1,416.80	63.25%	$1,723.20		$3,140.00	59.92%
= MU	$823.20	36.75%	$1,276.80	42.56%	$2,100.00	40.08%

Step 7.   Find the Cost 2 percentage by subtraction (R % − MU % = C %) or by the dollar and percentage combination formula (C $/R $ = C %). In either case, the cost percentage is 57.44%.

	Dress Shoes		Athletic Shoes		Total	
	$	%	$	%	$	%
R	$2,240.00	100.00%	$3,000.00	100.00%	$5,240.00	100.00%
− C	$1,416.80	63.25%	$1,723.20	57.44%	$3,140.00	59.92%
= MU	$823.20	36.75%	$1,276.80	42.56%	$2,100.00	40.08%

Using the retail dollars formula and the percentage formulas, many combinations of information can be used to complete a spreadsheet for the average markup calculations. With simple algebraic manipulations of these formulas, a buyer could set up equations to solve for any cell in the spreadsheet. This approach uses the features of the spreadsheet for average markup so that the dollar columns can be added across (e.g., Retail 1 $ + Retail 2 $ = Total Retail $) and so that formulas can be used to calculate values down the rows in all columns (e.g., Retail 1 $ − Cost 1 $ = Markup 1 $). This strategy might be useful for a buyer who does not have complete figures for all values and needs to supplement the information in the buyer's files or to double check information obtained from other sources.

Cumulative markup calculates markup over time. The total columns represent the total for the entire period. The sets of columns within the spreadsheet might represent the first six months and the last six months of a year. The total would be the total for the year. This concept is illustrated in Figure 11.4. When the average markup is calculated for this purpose, the markup percentage for the total retail and the total markup is called the cumulative markup percentage. For example, the markup is known for the first six-month period and the markup is known for the second six-month period. The buyer wants to know the markup for the year or the cumulative markup. This markup is calculated using the spreadsheet shown in Figure 11.4. To provide control, the buyer could then compare the actual yearly total in sales, costs, and markup with the plan that was made during the profit and loss planning. Adjustments should be made if the plan and the actual are found to vary. Cumulative markup is markup averaged over time. The periods for this calculation could be by day, week, month, or any planning period for the business. As with average markup, the averages can be calculated across two periods, three periods, or any multiple period phase.

Figure 11.4

	1st 6-Month Period		2nd 6-Month Period		Yearly Total	
	$	%	$	%	$	%
R						
− C						
= MU						

Average Markup over Time for a Year with Six-month Periods.

Open-to-Buy from Planned Purchases

Unit control consists of a variety of situations for calculating totals and averages. When averages for units are calculated and comparisons are examined, adjustments can be made. Comparisons can be made between a current period and the planned total. The amount of dollars available for **planned purchases** is found through these control calculations. Once the buyer is within the month, merchandise is probably on order and must be considered as part of the planned purchases. The spreadsheet for calculating planned purchases, including the periods for BOM, planned purchases, and total plan, is shown in Figure 11.5.

Figure 11.5

Planned Purchases, Using BOM.

	BOM		Planned Purchase		Total Plan	
	$	%	$	%	$	%
R						
− C						
= MU						

The formulas for the **planned purchases** calculations include the following:

BOM Retail $ + Planned Purchase Retail $ = Total Plan Retail $

BOM Markup $ + Planned Purchase Markup $ = Total Plan Markup $

BOM Cost $ + Planned Purchase Cost $ = Total Plan Cost $

This type of spreadsheet can also be used to compare the **to-date** amount with the planned amount. To-date includes the time from the beginning of the period to the current date. For example, if the day of the calculations is May 10 and the period is a month, the to-date amount includes all the retail sales, the costs, and the associated markup from the BOM to May 10. The difference between the to-date amounts and the plan amounts is the remainder left from planned purchases. This amount becomes the OTB for the remaining period. (See Figure 11.6.) The buyer can use this tool to adjust the buying plan or to encourage the sales associates to increase sales. The evaluation of point in time to the plan may also be used to chart the progress of sales

Figure 11.6

Open-to-Buy, Using To-Date.

	To Date		OTB		Total	
	$	%	$	%	$	%
R						
− C						
= MU						

associates toward a sales goal. Planned promotions must also be examined to determine whether they are effective and need adjustment. The markup associated with the total values is usually the planned markup or the maintained markup from the Profit and Loss statement. The markup is the target for the buyer and the sales associates.

When the buyer deletes from the planned purchases what is on order, the **open-to-buy (OTB)** is remaining dollars that a buyer will have for using in new purchases in upcoming markets or for replenishment purchases during the season. OTB must be carefully examined. Although OTB is how new merchandise, including the latest fashion, is placed in the store, over-purchasing in the market can result in too much stock in the store. OTB can also be used as a control for under-purchasing of merchandise. Under-purchasing of merchandise, or not buying enough stock, can result in stock outs and stale or old stock. If the buyer can determine this situation before the stock outs occur, corrective action can be initiated. If the unit control period is a month, this unit control calculation can be used with beginning of the month (BOM), open-to-buy (OTB), and end of the month (EOM). Spreadsheets are most useful in calculating these markups because each set of items or periods is recorded in columns of dollars and percentages.

Sample Problem: OTB Markup

In the Shoe Department, the buyer made a plan for the month of June. In mid-June, the buyer wants to know if any money is available for buying some shoes that a current vendor is offering at a great discount. These shoes could be used for the summer sale. The retail sales of shoes to-date are $2,240.00, and the planned retail sales for the shoe department for June are $5,240.00. The to-date cost is $1,416.80, and the markup planned for the month of June is 40.08%. Is any OTB available for this unexpected purchase?

Step 1. Set up the spreadsheet.

	To-Date		OTB		Total Plan	
	$	%	$	%	$	%
R						
− C						
= MU						

Step 2. Fill in the known information from the problem.

(Hint: Remember the retail percentage is always 100%.)

	To-Date		OTB		Total Plan	
	$	%	$	%	$	%
R	$2,240.00	100.00%		100.00%	$5,240.00	100.00%
− C	$1,416.80					
= MU						40.08%

Step 3. Calculate the remaining information for the to-date columns, and add the results to the spreadsheet.

To-Date Retail $ − To-Date Cost $ = To-Date Markup $

$2,240.00 − $1,416.80 = Markup $

$823.20 = To-Date Markup $

To-Date Cost \$/To-Date Retail \$ = To-Date Cost %

\$1,416.80/\$2,240.00 = To-Date Cost %

63.25% = To-Date Cost %

To-Date Markup \$/To-Date Retail \$ = To-Date Markup %

\$823.20/\$2,240.00 = To-Date Cost %

36.75% = To-Date Cost %

	To-Date		OTB		Total Plan	
	\$	%	\$	%	\$	%
R	\$2,240.00	100.00%		100.00%	\$5,240.00	100.00%
− C	\$1,416.80	63.25%				
= MU	\$823.20	36.75%				40.08%

Step 4. Calculate the remaining information for the total plan for June, and add the results to the spreadsheet.

Total Plan Retail \$ × Total Plan Markup % = Total Plan Markup \$

\$5,240.00 × 40.08% = Total Plan Markup \$

\$2,100.00 = Total Plan Markup \$

Total Plan Retail \$ − Total Plan Cost \$ = Total Plan Markup \$

Total Plan Retail \$ − Total Plan Markup \$ = Total Plan Cost \$

\$5,240.00 − \$2,100.00 = Total Plan Cost \$

\$3,140.00 = Total Plan Cost \$

Total Plan Retail % − Total Plan Cost % = Total Plan Markup %

Total Plan Retail % − Total Plan Markup % = Total Plan Cost %

100% − 40.08% = Total Plan Cost %

59.92% = Total Plan Cost %

	To-Date		OTB		Total Plan	
	\$	%	\$	%	\$	%
R	\$2,240.00	100.00%		100.00%	\$5,240.00	100.00%
− C	\$1,416.80	63.25%			\$3,140.00	59.92%
= MU	\$823.20	36.75%			\$2,100.00	40.08%

Step 5. Calculate the dollar values for the OTB, and add the results to the spreadsheet.

To-Date Retail \$ + OTB Retail \$ = Total Plan Retail \$

Total Plan Retail \$ − To-Date Retail \$ = OTB Retail \$

\$5,240.00 − \$2,240.00 = OTB Retail \$

\$3,000.00 = OTB Retail \$

To-Date Cost \$ + OTB Cost \$ = Total Plan Cost \$

Total Plan Cost \$ − To-Date Cost \$ = OTB Cost \$

\$3,140.00 − \$1,416.80 = OTB Cost \$

\$1,723.20 = OTB Cost \$

To-Date Markup \$ + OTB Markup \$ = Total Plan Markup \$

Total Plan Markup \$ − To-Date Markup \$ = OTB Markup \$

\$2,100.00 − \$823.20 = OTB Markup \$

\$1,276.80 = OTB Markup \$

	To-Date		OTB		Total Plan	
	$	%	$	%	$	%
R	$2,240.00	100.00%	$3,000.00	100.00%	$5,240.00	100.00%
− C	$1,416.80	63.25%	$1,723.20		$3,140.00	59.92%
= MU	$823.20	36.75%	$1,276.80		$2,100.00	40.08%

Step 6. To complete the spreadsheet, find the markup percentages needed for OTB.

OTB Markup $/OTB Retail $ = OTB Markup %

$1,276.80/$3,000.00 = OTB Markup %

42.56% = OTB Markup %

	To-Date		OTB		Total Plan	
	$	%	$	%	$	%
R	$2,240.00	100.00%	$3,000.00	100.00%	$5,240.00	100.00%
− C	$1,416.80	63.25%	$1,723.20		$3,140.00	59.92%
= MU	$823.20	36.75%	$1,276.80	42.56%	$2,100.00	40.08%

Step 7. Find the OTB cost percentage by subtraction (Retail % − Markup % = Cost %) or by the dollar and percentage combination formula (Cost $/Retail $ = Cost %). In either case, the cost percentage is 57.44%.

	To-Date		OTB		Total Plan	
	$	%	$	%	$	%
R	$2,240.00	100.00%	$3,000.00	100.00%	$5,240.00	100.00%
− C	$1,416.80	63.25%	$1,723.20	57.44%	$3,140.00	59.92%
= MU	$823.20	36.75%	$1,276.80	42.56%	$2,100.00	40.08%

Profitability

Unit control is used not only for examining markup within the business for stock balance and open-to-buy, but also for determining profitability. Maintained markup percentage (maintained markup/net sales) and average markup percentage (total markup/total sales) are the most common markups used to evaluate profitability. Other measures of profitability include stock turn (net sales/average stock), capital turn (net sales/average stock at cost), and profit percent (profit/net sales). Profitability is usually measured in a ratio format (e.g., total markup/net sales or net sales/average stock). This format allows retailers to compare the performance of their business to the performance of other businesses, although the overall sales volume or stock flow may vary across business formats and retail size.

When retailers use a set figure as a goal or a comparison point, the amount is called a **benchmark**. The benchmark may be an industry standard, a value set by the competition, or the target goal set by the retailer to provide growth or adjustment from the previous period. Industry standards can be obtained from trade organizations such as the National Retail Federation, the International Shopping Center Association, and the American Society for Quality. Benchmarks are used by companies that want to grow and improve their profitability. Retailers must be careful that this growth occurs while maintaining or improving customer service. The goals of retailing and the objectives that are established in strategic planning must be reviewed when considering unit control.

*S*ummary

The goal of retailing is customer satisfaction; however, this goal must be achieved within the realm of profitability for the retailer. To ensure both customer satisfaction and profit, the retailer must carefully plan for sales, determine merchandise to be purchased, promote the merchandise, and create sales to the final consumer. The consumer and fashion are both elusive factors in this plan. According to strategic planning procedures, a plan must be constantly evaluated and adjusted. Unit control provides a tool for this strategic evaluation.

Unit control is a method for evaluating retail sales, costs, and markups. With unit control methods such as average markup, the buyer can evaluate the markups on several products or within a department. With cumulative markup, a buyer can evaluate markup over time. Average markup can be evaluated with markup from the six-month plan to determine whether the planned markup was maintained throughout the season. The markups that are calculated over products or over time can be evaluated relative to the markups that were planned in the Profit and Loss statements and in the six-month plans. The techniques of OTB and to-date can be used to determine the progress of retail sales and to help keep stock in balance.

When these unit control calculations are used in comparison to plan, to previous seasons, or with other businesses, the buyer can benchmark the progress for product classifications, for departments, or for individual store units. Benchmarking provides the retailer with a goal for future growth and planning. In this way, benchmarks are effective tools when used in a context of strategic planning and unit control.

Key Terms

Average markup
Benchmark
Cumulative markup

Open-to-buy (OTB)
Planned purchases

To-date
Unit control

Discussion Questions

1. What is the purpose of unit control?
2. In a retail business that must be fashion forward, ever changing, and fast paced, what is the need for unit control?
3. How does unit control relate to the strategic planning process?
4. What benefits does unit control have for the buyer?
5. How can unit control be used to obtain new merchandise for the retailer?
6. Why is average markup part of unit control?
7. How could a retailer use average markup as a benchmark against other stores?
8. How is average markup and cumulative markup similar?
9. What can a buyer do if the "to-date" markup does not equal the planned markup?
10. If the markup calculated at a midpoint in the season is lower than the target or planned markup, which is at fault? Why?

Exercises

General Directions

Markup can be figured on one item, a set of items, or groups of items. The groups can be a collection of sets at one time, a collection of departments, or sets of inventory at various periods. The calculations of groups of markup start with the relationship of cost, markup, and retail in one column. This relationship is repeated in additional columns. Finally, totals are calculated across the rows for all markups, all costs, and all retail.

Sample

	Group A $	Group A %	Group B $	Group B %	Total $	Total %
Retail						
– Cost						
= Markup						

Markup Over Groups—Average Markup

1. The dress buyer purchased $42,500.00 worth of sun dresses (at cost). The dresses carried a 52.50% markup. A shipment of slip dresses was bought at $28,000.00, with an expected markup of 56.30%. What was the average markup for the department?

2. The shoe buyer purchased 200 Nebbe Sneakers at $56.00 each and 140 Zandi Sneakers at $42.50 each. The expected markup on the Nebbe Sneakers is 76.50% and 65.00% for the Zandi Sneakers. What were the projected net sales?

3. The retail sales of white dress shirts were $289,540.00. The retail sales of patterned shirts were $197,650.00. The total amount spent on purchases for shirts was $255,500.00. If the white shirts had a 45.70% markup, what was the markup on the patterned shirts?

4. A buyer purchases 72 cowboy hats at $540.00 per dozen and retails them for $102.60 each. A shipment of ball caps cost $1,200.00 and had a 45.70% markup. What was the average markup for the combined stock?

5. A suit department had retail sales of $1,558,600.00 and costs of $780,000.00. The purchase cost of the three-piece suits was $189,500.00. The other suits had a markup of 48.60%. What was the markup for the three-piece suits?

6. The buyer for the Sportswear Department purchases denim coordinates at cost for $28.50 per pant and $42.50 per jacket. The departmental markup is 45.00%. The buyer purchases 100 pants and sells them at $52.90 each. The buyer also buys 60 jackets. To make department markup target, what is the necessary retail price of each jacket?

7. A buyer purchases 80 sweaters. The lot includes 30 hand-knit sweater vests costing $28.00 each, and 50 cardigan-style sweaters costing $35.00 each. Overall, sweaters need a 46.00% markup. The buyer thinks vests will retail for $52.00. What will be the retail price for a cardigan?

8. A buyer plans a big Fourth of July event. A shipment of 200 bathing suits will be featured at a retail of $25.00 each. An average department markup of 48.60% must be maintained. The first purchase consists of 80 suits costing $14.00. For the remaining purchases, what is the maximum average cost?

9. The buyer for the department purchased four dozen shirts for $15.50 each and put a $30.00 retail price on each shirt. The department also needs 100 ties, which will be retailed at $14.00 each. If the departmental markup is 47.00%, what is the maximum cost of each tie?

Markup Over Time—Cumulative Markup

1. On June 30, the store had sold merchandise worth $45,980.00 at retail, which had a cost of $24,000.00. During the second six months, the store sold another $56,890.00 worth of merchandise (retail), which was purchased by the buyer at $37,600.00 (cost). What was the cumulative markup for the year?

2. The buyer did a year-end report on December 31. The buyer knew that, in the first six months, the purchases of blouses were $15,450.00 (cost), which had carried a 45.00% markup. The buyer also had purchased blouses during the second six months at a cost of $25,900.00, and a markup of 52.00% had been recommended. What was the cumulative markup that the blouses maintained?

3. A buyer had an inventory on April 1 that cost $4,464.76 and was scheduled to retail for $8,812.00. Additional purchases were $16,279.87 at cost during May and June and a 46.50% markup was attained. What is the cumulative markup for the month for second quarter?

4. In November, purchases were $58,000.00 at cost with a 47.33% markup. In December, planned purchases were made that had a retail value of $50,000.00, and a 51.25% markup was achieved on those items. What is the cumulative markup for the two months combined?

5. To prepare for December, the buyer purchased stock costing $48,500.00 and placed a 42.00% markup on these items. During December, goods were purchased that were worth $38,000.00 at cost. A 46.45% markup was placed on the items purchased during December. What is the cumulative markup planned for the department?

6. On May 1, the buyer placed an order for 1,000 summer suits that cost $88.00 each. These suits will carry a 54.00% markup. For the remainder of the month, merchandise was purchased that was worth $62,000.00 with a planned 58.00% markup. If everything sells at the planned markups, what will be the department markup at May 31?

7. A linens buyer has had retail sales of $5,000.00 for March. A markup of 44.00% was obtained. At the end of April, the monthly invoices at cost and retail are $2,000.00 and $3,500.00, respectively. On April 30th, what is the cumulative markup at this point in the spring?

8. The buyer for picture frames and pillows purchased $4,400.00 worth of stock at cost for January and applied a 35.50% markup. All the merchandise was sold in January. The merchandise was replenished in February with stock worth $6,400.00, and the buyer applied a 36.50% markup. If all this stock was sold by the end of February, what would be the cumulative retail amount and the cumulative markup thus far in the year?

9. To prepare for a big July sale, a buyer wanted to sell 400 shorts, which will retail for $20.00 each. To prepare for the sale, the buyer, in June, placed an order of 300 shorts at a cost of $9.90 each to arrive on July 1. A second order was placed on July 2 for the remaining 100 shorts to arrive on July 10 and the price was $11.00 at cost. Retail price will remain constant. What is cumulative markup?

Markup Compared with Plan—Open-to-Buy

1. The BOM for August is $191,304.35 at retail. Total retail sales are planned at $338,923.40. The current inventory has a 46.00% markup. The remaining OTB is $62,000.00 (cost) with a 58.00% markup. What will be the departmental markup?

2. The men's outerwear buyer needs to maintain a 51.00% department markup. The buyer plans to buy $9,800.00 worth of merchandise at retail for June. An order had already been placed for 80 jackets costing $28.50 each with plans for a 53.00% markup. What markup percent is needed on the OTB to reach the target markup?

3. The BOM for August is $4,600.00 at retail and $2,300.00 at cost. The EOM for August is planned at $4,600.00 at retail and $2,300.00 at cost. What is the OTB for August?

4. The BOM for October is $56,000.00 at cost and a 45.00% markup is planned. The total planned retail for October is $100,000.00 and the department markup is expected to be 50.00%. What is the OTB for October?

5. March's total plan is $66,600.00 for retail with a markup of 60.00%. The buyer has already ticketed $12,000.00 worth of merchandise at $26,000.00 (retail). What is the OTB markup needed to complete the month? Is this realistic and why?

6. A buyer sets a goal for tops to be $4,000.00 in retail sales for the week with a markup of 52.00%. By Tuesday, the retail on tops is $1,500.00. What remaining sales are needed for this week? If the cost of the remaining tops to be sold is $1,200.00, what is the remaining (OTB) markup? Can the buyer make the target markup? Why or why not?

OTB

1. The planned sales for August are $49,800.00, the planned EOM for August is $180,000.00, the planned reductions are $4,000.00, and the August BOM is $89,000.00. No goods are on order. What is OTB?

2. The planned purchases for June are $55,800.00. The EOM for May is $46,000.00. Goods on order are $10,000.00. What is OTB?

3. The planned sales for September are $120,650.00. The BOM for October is $435,800.00. The EOM for August is $230,980.00. A big Back-to-School Sale is planned for September, and reductions will be equal to 10.00% of planned sales. The goods on order are $14,000.00. What is OTB?

4. After a slow month, merchandise available for March is $245,000.00. The merchandise needed is $269,000.00. What is OTB?

5. The March BOM is $16,880.00, and the planned sales are $10,000.00. The merchandise on order equals $3,500.00. The April BOM is $12,000.00. What is OTB?

6. The planned sales are $26,000.00, the planned reductions are $2,600, the planned BOM is $30,000.00, the planned EOM is $34,500.00, and the goods on order are $8,500.00. What is OTB?

7. The total sales for the department are expected to be $2,314.00 with a 45.00% markup, and the inventory on hand is valued at $934.28 cost and $1,561.00 retail. How much is left to spend on new inventory?

8. The OTB is $4,800.00 at retail. If Initial Markup is 55.50%, what is OTB at cost?

9. The stock on hand is $36,000.00, and no goods are on order. The planned sales are $26,000.00, the planned EOM is $30,000.00, and the planned reductions are $2,000.00. If the BOM is $30,000.00, what is OTB?

10. The planned sales are $234,560.00, the planned EOM is $1,500,000.00, the reductions are expected to be $22,500.00, and available merchandise is $765,430.00. What is OTB?

Computer Exercises

General Directions

Use the sample spreadsheet shown.

1. Enter your name.
2. Enter the date.
3. Enter the Title.
4. Set up the spreadsheet as follows (center or align headings for appropriate spacing):

Title						
	Group 1		Group 2		Total	
	$	%	$	%	$	%
Retail						
– Cost						
= Markup						

Create spreadsheets for the markup problems that follow.
Be certain that each spreadsheet fits on only one page (no run on's).

Markup Over Groups of Merchandise—Average

1. The Sporting Goods Department has three lines of sweatshirts from the Randuff Corporation. They want to know the combined impact (the average markup) for the three groups. Forty shirts were ordered for the Randuff Group at $10.50 each and retailed at $25.00. Sixty shirts were ordered for the Ran-dy group at $6.50 each and retailed for $12.90. Twenty Upper-Cotton shirts were ordered at $12.00 each and retailed for $28.00. What was the average markup percent for the Randuff Corporation products?

2. The Designer Department consists of two subgroups: Name Designers and Private Labels. The Name Designer subgroup has a 48.00% markup and has sold at retail $4,800.00 worth of merchandise. The Private Label subgroup has sold $6,600.00 worth at retail and normally carries a 55.00% markup. What is the average markup for the Designer Department?

3. The Menswear Department consists of two subgroups: Clothing and Furnishings. At the end of September, the Clothing subgroup has a 48.00% markup and has sold at retail $8,800.00 worth of merchandise. The Furnishings subgroup has sold $1,600.00 worth at retail and normally carries a 55.00% markup. What is the average markup for the Menswear Department for the month of September?

Markup Over Time—Cumulative

1. The shoe department had a 42.00% markup for the first six months and sold $6,000.00 (at cost). In the second half of the year, it purchased $4,500.00 worth of merchandise that sold at $9,230.00 (retail). What was the overall (average) markup for the year?

2. The housewares department had an opening inventory for May 1 of $85,000.00 at cost with a markup of 44.00%. During the month, the buyer for the department purchased additional merchandise with a retail value of $60,000.00 with a 47.00% markup. Calculate the potential cumulative markup percent for that department for May.

Markup for Plan Purchases—OTB

1. A menswear buyer needs 84 ties to retail at $18.00 each and 48 jackets to retail at $230.00. He needs to average for the department a 46.50% markup. If he pays $9.50 for each tie, how much can he pay for each jacket and still achieve the planned department markup percent?

2. A buyer plans to purchase a total of $53,000.00 (retail) worth of junior's coats for the winter season. He has already purchased 190 coats that cost $66.00 each and will retail for $88.00 each. What markup percent must be obtained on the balance of the coats (OTB) in order to average a 45.50% markup for the season?

3. A shoe buyer plans to spend a total of $23,000.00 to purchase dress shoes for the winter season. He has already purchased 390 pairs that cost $45.00 each and will retail for $72.00 each. What markup percent must be obtained on the balance of the shoes (OTB) in order to average a 45.50% markup for the season?

Relating Average Markup to Other Markups in P & L Statement

The total cost of goods is $23,000.00, the EOM cost of goods (as measured by invoice) is 54.50%, transportation is 5.00%, alterations are 8.50%, reductions are 7.20%, and no cash discounts were taken. Set up a Profit and Loss statement with this information, and calculate the Gross Margin %, Maintained Markup %, and Initial Markup % for the department.

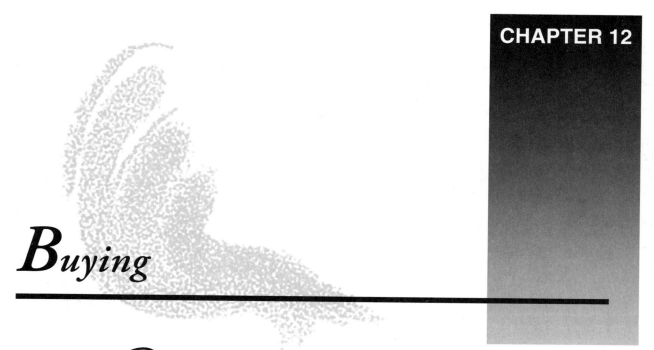

CHAPTER 12

*B*uying

*O*bjectives

After completing this chapter, the student will be able to

- identify the role of the buyer
- discuss the corporate location of the buyer
- discuss the geographic location of the buyer
- describe the buying tasks
- explain the skills and personality traits possessed by the buyer

The buyer is a central figure in the merchandising of apparel and other soft goods items. The buyer acts as the intermediary in the marketplace between the vendor (e.g., wholesaler or manufacturer) and the consumer. Depending on the type of retail business, the buyer may function in various roles such as owner–manager, department store manager, corporate buyer, head buyer, or associate buyer. Within a business organization, the buying function may be subsumed under one of several other functions and may be geographically dispersed in numerous locations. Regardless of the organizational or geographic structure of the business, the buying function is critical to sales. Many retailers and other merchandisers consider that goods that are well bought are already half-sold. The importance of good buying is also critical to the goal of customer satisfaction. A customer who enters the store and sees no appealing merchandise will leave without buying, and a lost sale is never replaced.

To ensure that the right merchandise is available for customers, the buyer performs a number of merchandise-related tasks across retail functions. Some buyers consider their tasks to be in three separate areas: planning, buying, and selling. Others would consider planning as part of buying. Typical **planning tasks** are as follows: (a) determine target consumer needs and wants, (b) project seasonal sales figures, (c) forecast product and color trends, (d) determine specific merchandise needs for departments, (e) develop seasonal merchandise plans (e.g., six-month plans), (f) establish markup and retail price for merchandise, (g) review and adjust current merchandise plans, and (h) work with manufacturers for new product development. These planning tasks are covered in Chapters 5–11.

The typical **buying tasks** include the following activities: (a) perform buying activities within the market, (b) establish and maintain partnerships with vendors, (c) negotiate terms of purchase and arrange for shipment of the merchandise, (d) complete procedures for orders, (e) supervise flow of merchandise from vendors to the customers, (f) handle returns of merchandise, (g) facilitate transfer of merchandise between stores or retail units, and (h) maintain inventory records and control for the merchandise. These buying tasks are covered in this chapter and in Chapter 13.

The buyer is always responsible for maintaining the image and other merchandising policies of the company. In a large organization, the merchandise coordinator or the senior buyer is responsible for coordinating the work of all other buyers. Head buyers are responsible for the supervision of their associate and assistant buyers and for the instruction of their staff. Care must be taken to unify efforts, to keep a clear store image, and to provide continually a merchandise assortment that is pleasing to the customer. (Buyers must constantly be in touch with the promotions staff, operations personnel, and other employees to keep the merchandise in harmony with the other store activities.)

Selling tasks for the buyer include the following activities: (a) work with promotions function to determine merchandise needs for promotional activities, (b) purchase merchandise as needed for promotions, (c) recommend use of media types, (d) ensure accuracy of merchandise information in promotions, (e) evaluate sales response to promotions, (f) recommend plans for merchandise promotions including layout of merchandise space, (g) provide information and training for sales associates, and (h) participate in special events. The selling tasks for the buyer are covered in Chapters 14, 15, and 16. Depending on the organizational structure of the retail business, the buyer may have selling tasks that involve merchandising of the department and supervising of sales associates and other personnel. In every activity, the buyer must work as a **team member** with many other employees.

Buying functions must be closely aligned with promotions, distribution, sales, and inventory functions to ensure that the retail image is maintained and supported throughout the business. For example, the promotions manager may determine that in May the retailer will highlight clothing for mothers. Throughout the entire month, merchandise promotions will feature clothing items appealing to women. The first week is to feature dresses, the second week features hats and handbags, the third week features lingerie, and the last week will feature cosmetics. The promotions manager is anticipating special shipments in April and May to provide extra merchandise for displays and sales. These shipments are planned, selected, and ordered by the buyer. The buyer must know exact dates that merchandise will arrive in the warehouse and when it will be delivered in the stores. Each item must be tracked and arrive on time or the display workers will have no merchandise for window and tabletop displays that are planned. In addition, newspaper and television coverage is planned, and merchandise featured in the media must actually be in the stores when a customer arrives. If the store features a Web site, this outlet must also be updated and coordinated with the warehouse manager, the promotions manager, and the buyer. A team approach is necessary to coordinate this "simple" promotions idea.

Organizational Location of Buying Function

Buying can be performed by general management personnel or by a specialist in buying. The buying function, as seen in the traditional retail organization, is a task within merchandising and is combined with selling. The buyer in a small retail business is often the owner or partner in the business. The position of buyer ranges from the owner–buyer, who is both buyer and seller, to a buyer with a very narrow merchandise class for a large multi-store company. Organizational structures and the placement of the buying function within the organization were introduced in Chapter 1. The traditional Mazur plan describes buying and selling as one function; however, the location and function of buying has evolved as retailing has changed. With the growth of organizations and the increase in multi-outlet retail businesses, buying frequently is split from merchandising and is a separate function. With this split, the buyer is often located in a corporate office instead of in a store. This buyer is a buying specialist and is often called a **corporate buyer**.

Small, independent retailers are usually organized traditionally with the buying function and the store management function closely related. In fact, many owner–managers are also the buyers. As described in Chapter 1, this organizational structure is called line organization. If the retail business is owned by two partners, the two partners may share or split the tasks of running the business; for example, one partner does much of the daily operational tasks while the other partner does the buying and merchandise handling tasks. Many people become retail storeowners because they like to work with the merchandise. The thrill of seeing the new fashions, the excitement of changing merchandise, and the interaction with the customer are the attraction that many retail owners feel for their business.

In contrast, the job of an owner–manager is a very busy one; therefore, a small retailer without the time or interest to do the buying may depend on a buyer partner, or depend on a resident buying office or a buying agent to make merchandise purchases for the business.

A single, large store may have more administrative personnel than just an owner–manger. Such a store may have an owner, a store manager, a buyer, and department managers. For this reason, a **single, large store buyer** may work alone or with several other buyers or assistants. The buyer for a large store may have limited selling responsibilities or may still be responsible for supervising sales associates. Overall, the size of the buying function and the number of personnel involved in the buying activities depend on the volume of the merchandise sold in the store.

The decision to divide the buying function may be made as the business is opened or may occur as the business grows. If a retail business grows and opens branch stores, the buyer, who was originally located in the first store, tends to remain located in the main store and buys for both the main store and the branches. For this reason, buying for the branch store may become an added responsibility for this **main store buyer**. This organizational structure, called brood-hen and chick, may present difficulties for the buyer depending on task allocation and on the customer profile across the stores. The buyer who remains at a main store may find that going to the branch stores is time consuming; however, depending on the main store customer to provide all the customer feedback is dangerous. The main store of a growing business is typically located in an area that has customers that are very different from the branch stores. For instance, the main store may be the major anchor store in a large mall, with the branch stores located in small suburban shopping centers. The stores may serve very different customers. For example, the target customer for a department may be female, twenty-five to thirty-five and married. The customer who shops in the anchor store may work as a lawyer in a large firm located in a corporate park near the mall. The woman who shops in the branch store in the suburbs may commute into the city every day to a corporate center, or she may have two small children and stay at home. Depending on their lifestyles, women may be similar or very dissimilar in their preference for apparel. A buyer must know the customer for each location. Sitting in an office or walking the floor in one store cannot reveal everything about all branches' customers.

If the buyer in the brood-hen and chick organization retains management duties for selling functions while located in the main store, then the buyer will have to plan carefully how to allocate time to the diverse duties of the job. Buying tasks for each store and selling tasks for the main store must each receive attention. No one store can be considered more important than the other stores. Buying cannot be thought of as more important than selling; instead, both tasks are vital to the profitability of the business. In theory, the buying and selling functions are intertwined and **interdependent functions**: That is, sales cannot happen without merchandise, and merchandise cannot make money without sales.

In some businesses and in some situations, the buying and selling functions must be divided. Large retail stores or businesses with more than one door have too much volume in merchandise for the buyer to take care of buying and supervising the selling of the merchandise. High numbers of SKUs are the result in apparel and home fashions retailing, when an item must be carried in "every color of the rainbow," in four fabric types, and in every size for all customers. The SKUs for one subclassification can reach as many as 60 to 100 pieces. (One blouse can result in 500 SKUs.) When the retail business is too large for one person to manage adequately all functions, the retailer may separate the buying function from the selling function. In these cases, the buyer becomes a "specialist" in buying or purchasing only.

A business that has many doors, such as chain stores, will have numerous buyers, called corporate buyers. Also, in businesses where buyers function separately from selling, the buyer may still have too many duties, even without the sales duties, and several buyers may be hired. The buyers then further specialize and divide the buying function according to merchandise classifications. Each buyer is assigned one classification of merchandise for buying and becomes a **buying specialist** with a **split of responsibilities**. This concept of a buying specialist is appealing to some retailers regardless of the size of the business. Buyers need many special skills including an in-depth knowledge of the product and the markets. Focusing on these aspects of the business may help the buyer to find the best buys in the market, to keep up-to-date with the latest fashions, and to maintain strong partnerships with the vendors. A large organization will have buyers who specialize in coats, women's better dresses, or men's suits. An even larger organization may have several buying specialists: one for casual coats, one for dress coats, and one for leather, fur, and specialty coats. On the other hand, some buyers may work only with one or two vendors. For example, a buyer in designer sportswear buys only two or three brands directly from the designer and the manufacturer's merchandisers.

In large organizations, buyers may have **associate** and **assistant buyers** who help them with their buying tasks. In fact, in very large organizations, many buyers may work within the buying functional area. For a large corporate chain with many doors, the manager of the entire buying division is often called the **Vice President of Merchandising** and the groupings of merchandise classifications are headed by **divisional merchandise manager (DMM)**. Each Divisional Merchandise Manager will be responsible for supervising buyers who buy merchandise within one or several merchandise classifications. For example, the Divisional Merchandise Manager for Boys' Wear will supervise buyers who buy boys' school clothing, boys' dress clothing, boys' coats and other outerwear, and boys' furnishings (e.g., socks, ties, and pajamas). If the volume within each merchandise classification is large, then each buyer may supervise one or more buyers, associate buyers, or assistant buyers. The head buyer for boys' school clothing may supervise two buyers: one who is responsible for boys' shirts and one for boys' pants. Each of these buyers may have an assistant.

Geographical Location of Buying Function

Buyers who are also owners or managers must be located in the store. These buyers usually have selling and other functions within the store that require their daily supervision. To best supervise selling, a buyer needs to be on the floor to see the customers, to meet with sales associates, and to observe the movement of merchandise. This allows the buyer time to gather information about what merchandise is selling, what customers are seeking, and what items are missing from the selling floor. Many buyers, regardless of where they have an office, want to spend time on the selling floor to "get the pulse of the customer." Reading the daily trade journals and reviewing the computer printouts of sales are important, but buyers still say that nothing replaces the time that they spend on the selling floor.

Buyers who are located in the store may be in small towns, rural communities, suburbs, or major cities. These buyers, who live and work in neighborhoods similar to their customers, will have excellent contact with customers and should have special insights into the needs and wants of these customers. These buyers may face a challenge in determining new trends and in finding new merchandise. For example, a buyer who is located in a small southern U.S. city may need to travel long distances to markets. Travel for this buyer may be a financial burden for the company and may prohibit frequent market trips. In this manner, closeness to the customer often is offset by distance from the markets.

Some buyers are located at the **corporate headquarters** or main business offices of their retailer. These offices may be in any city in the world. Offices for Wal-Mart are located in Bentonville, AR. Offices for K-Mart are located in Troy, MI. The selection of these geographic locations is usually tied to the original location of the first store, the hometown of the founder, or some other reason related to the history of the company. An international retail business usually has a world headquarters, but also has offices in the other countries where they have stores. For example, Benetton is an international company and has a world headquarters in Milan, Italy, but major corporate offices are located in other countries including the United States.

When retailers place their buyers in corporate offices, they are located near planners and top-level management. Buyers who are located in corporate headquarters have the benefit of meeting regularly with promotions managers and planners and with corporate administration who make strategic decisions related to image or customer targets.

One of the business's retail stores may be located in the city where the corporate offices are located. This store is often called the **flagship store** and can be the store that has the best merchandise, gets the newest merchandise arrivals first, and has the test merchandise for new products. A store with that level of activity can provide the buyer with information about customers and merchandise. The buyer must be careful to evaluate the consumer profile of this flagship store to determine whether the profile is similar to or different from the consumer profile of the customers at other stores. Some variation in customer preferences may be noted if the stores for a retailer are in diverse geographic locations.

Some buyers are located in market cities, either at general corporate offices or in **corporate buying offices**. To promote efficient buying, some companies locate their buyers in market cities where the buyers have ready access to vendors' showrooms.

A buyer who is located in a market city can easily visit a vendor in person, comparison shop at several vendors, and visit permanent showrooms throughout the year. In addition, this buyer is often located near small workshops and factories. This ease of entry can aid a buyer in developing a partnership with a vendor that is more trusting than adversarial. The buyer has more time to look at merchandise, discover new merchandise, and find merchandise in mid-season. This prevents the buyer from having to travel long distances and leave the office for several weeks to look at merchandise. For this reason, being located in a market city seems ideal when considering the importance that the merchandise has for the buyer.

In contrast, a buyer who is located in a market city may have no access or personal contact with the consumer who buys the merchandise. This buyer is dependent upon sales reports, inventory lists, and reports from store management to know the consumer. Although located in the very heart of the industry, buyers with offices in market cities can be very isolated. Good teamwork with store management and excellent communication is needed for this buyer.

Buyers who are located at corporate headquarters may find that they are distanced geographically and emotionally from the customer, and that they are a long distance from the markets. Many corporations are choosing to locate away from major metropolitan areas and, in particular, many U.S. companies are moving out of New York City. Buyers are being relocated from market cities to cities with lower rent prices and other small town amenities. For this corporate buyer, travel to stores throughout the region, corporate districts, or other geographical areas, becomes more important. The buyer should also maintain close relations and have good team work with store managers and sales associates to ensure that the customer is truly understood.

The need to locate in a market city to be "in the center of it all" has lessened with improvements in communication. Some vendors have Web sites where the buyer can shop and see all of the new merchandise. This type of shopping can actually be more efficient because the buyer can "visit" several vendors at the same time and make comparisons on one computer screen. Vendors can also provide videotapes and catalogs to assist a buyer who does not come to the showroom. Faxes, cell phones, and other rapid communication devices are allowing buyers and vendors to communicate from any world location. With this level of communication technology, some retailers think that a buyer does not need to be located in a market city and would rather have the buyer located closer to the customer and in a lower rent district.

Buying Tasks

The buying tasks can be grouped into three functional activities: the selection of the merchandise, the placement of orders, and the supervision of the merchandise flow. The buyer starts the buying process armed with all the information developed in the planning process. As a result of careful planning, the buyer will have a list of merchandise needed for the retail business that will include information about style, color, and size. The buyer will have listed suggested brands and specific vendors if already known, especially true for rebuys and for very new or high-demand merchandise. **New buys** are items that are selected that the store has never sold. **Rebuys** are items that the store currently sells and the buyer's main function is to place orders for more of the same items. In addition, the buyer will have a budget that notes the number of items to be purchased in each merchandise class, in a subclass, and by vendor along with the suggested wholesale price, which must be obtained to ensure that profit margins and the company's price points can be maintained.

With all of the background information prepared, the buyer is ready to shop, and then **select the merchandise**. Shopping can be done in a market city, through catalogs and videos, with a sales representative in the office, or on the Internet. The buyer looks for merchandise that fits the needs and wants of the target customer, is compatible with the company's image, and provides interest and excitement to the merchandise mix. New buys may require the buyer to do extensive shopping, and find vendors who carry the new merchandise.

For several reasons, the buyer may need to find additional vendors: new merchandise may require new vendors, current vendors may not remain satisfactory sources of the rebuy merchandise, and current vendors may not keep price structures that are workable for the buyer. Establishing trade with a new vendor may require additional research to determine the **viability of the vendor** in regards to financial stability, quality of work for the merchandise, and delivery record. A buyer must be able to depend on the delivery of the new merchandise and the product being delivered in the condition that was promised. If high quality manufacturing is important to the retail business and to the retailer's customers, then the buyer needs assurance that the new vendor will deliver the desired quality of merchandise. (At the same time, vendors evaluate buyers for viability of credit and ease of operation based partly on letters of credit and evidence of business licensing.)

The buyer may ask to see actual manufacturers' samples, which may be different from showroom samples. **Showroom samples** are often made in the design workrooms by a combination of hand and machine techniques. Seams may not be finished and hems may not be bound by the same technique as those done in the manufacturing plant. A buyer can use a showroom sample for judging the product only when the vendor assures the buyer that the sample is made to manufacturer's specifications, if the buyer has a **specification sheet** for the product, or if the buyer has previously ordered merchandise from the vendor and knows the quality of the products. A specification sheet would contain details about fabric quality, seam type, durability of construction, shrinkage, and other manufacturing information. (See Figure 12.1.) These specification sheets can be used to compare similar merchandise from several vendors.

Some vendors do not own their own manufacturing facilities and source manufacturing from a variety of companies. This contracting procedure is called outsourcing and may be used for part or all of the manufacturing process. **Outsourcing** is the process of finding other sources or companies to do part or all of the manufacturing processes. A vendor who participates in outsourcing often contracts with multiple manufacturers if the size of the order is large or if the vendor supplies many retailers. When working with these vendors, the buyer must be very careful to obtain information about the fabric and manufacturing quality of the product and to have a guarantee that the products will arrive as specified.

As part of shopping, the buyer may also be looking for ideas, information, and new merchandise. Part of every budget, six-month plan, monthly plan, or other budget plan, is reserved for unspecified merchandise. In addition, the buyer may have identified specific colors or styles, which are needed, but may not have identified actual items to purchase. For this category of merchandise, the buyer will need to keep an open mind and spend time perusing the racks and displays of many current and new vendors. Talking with vendors is also important for selecting this type of merchandise. The buyer will want to hear the vendor's descriptions and options about the new merchandise. If a buyer is unsure about the selection, a small amount of merchandise might be ordered with a contract for more orders in the future. (Some vendors will allow this type of test order and others may not.)

	Vendor A		Vendor B		Vendor C	
Store Name:	Season:		Merchandise Classification:			Date:
Item Description:					Buyer Code:	
Vendor Style Number						
Price						
Fiber Content						
Fabric Type						
Seam Type						
Seam Widths						
Hem Depth						
Care Instruction						
Country of Origin						

Figure 12.1   Specification Sheet Used for Selecting and Evaluating Merchandise.

A buyer may find that not every item on the buying list may be found in one market trip. Therefore, the buyer should be prepared to search in other markets or through other resources (e.g., catalogs and Internet) to find the products that are needed. Buyers must also be prepared to make adjustments in the buying plan. (Adjustments should be made with great caution because overall budget amounts, budget amounts for classifications, company image, and consumer preferences cannot be abandoned.) The buyer must constantly evaluate each item during merchandise selection for its contribution to the company image, the merchandise policies, and the profit margins. Every item that is selected by the buyer must be sold by the sales associates. With this in mind, the buyer should refrain from selecting frivolously any merchandise that is not specified in the buying plan.

The second general buying task is **placement of orders**. Once the buyer has selected the merchandise, orders are placed with the vendors. The buyer is the retail company's representative in the market. The buyer must place orders for merchandise following set order procedures by determining the specific items, the number of items, and the terms of the purchase. Terms of the purchase include price, discounts, shipping, and payment dates. In addition to terms, the buyer will need to negotiate services that the vendor will provide. Services can include many activities and items: promotions material, training for sales associates, informational materials, display equipment, and packaging. (Assistant buyers may help by writing the purchase orders with the information that the buyer has provided.)

The final buying task is the **supervision of the merchandise flow**. The buyer must coordinate the flow of merchandise from the vendor to the warehouse, the stores, and the consumer. Depending on the type of outlets that the company maintains, the buyer may have all merchandise delivered directly to the store. Or the merchandise may be delivered to a central warehouse or distribution facility and then sent to the stores. Some companies, especially those that have catalogs and Web sites, may also have some items sent directly to the consumer. A multi-store company may also have merchandise transferred between stores to **balance stock**, by moving stock from a store where it is not selling to a store where the merchandise is selling rapidly. For example, a blouse may sell well in one store and not sell well in a second store. The blouses in Store 2 may be removed from inventory in that store and shipped to Store 1. This decision must be made quickly to avoid stale merchandise in Store 2 and to ensure adequate stock in Store 1. If the buyer waits too long to make these transfers, the peak selling period may pass even in Store 1. Removing the merchandise too early in Store 2 can result in vacant shelves in that store and may move the merchandise before the demand for the merchandise is realized. The decision to balance stock, as many others in merchandising, depends in part on examination of selling information and in part on the merchandising insight of the buyer.

In a large business, assistant buyers often help with the tasks in the flow of merchandise process by completing follow-up with vendors to encourage prompt delivery, re-establish delivery times for late deliveries, prepare returns to vendors, and complete the transfer of merchandise that the buyer has authorized. If an order does not arrive as scheduled, the assistant buyer is often the person to track the status of the order, by phone or with the assistance of electronic communication. Assistant buyers or clerical support staff may also check-in merchandise upon delivery, communicate with branch stores about transfers, and perform other tasks to ensure good flow of merchandise.

The **flow of merchandise** must be timed to provide a steady stream of new and fresh merchandise to all company doors. Each door must look fresh, have adequate inventory to fill the spaces and still maintain an open and not crowded floor space. Placement of the merchandise is dependent upon the selling of the previous merchandise. The ideal situation would call for a constant flow of merchandise from vendor through the retailer to the consumer. The merchandise that is sold would be quickly replaced by new merchandise. This constant flow is an ideal, but in practice is not often possible. A constant flow of merchandise would require a constant flow of paperwork and expenditures. Many vendors will not ship very small quantities of products because of the cost of shipping. Shipping a large quantity of merchandise is cheaper per unit than shipping a small quantity of merchandise. Decisions about shipment sizes and timing must be determined with order placement. A retailer may have a set procedure for shipments and may try to make all vendors agree to that procedure. A buyer needs to be aware of any shipment policies that the company may enforce. Merchandise flow affects the levels of inventory within the retail company. Too little inventory results in stock outs and lost sales. Too much inventory results in crowded conditions in the store and in the distribution center and reduces cash flow within the company. Once the buyer has determined the inventory turn and the replacement rates of the merchandise, the plan for turnover and stock levels must be executed by directing the actual flow of the merchandise.

Delivery times and procedures at the store or at the distribution center are also part of the terms that must be negotiated for the proper flow of merchandise. Some retailers will only take deliveries on certain days or at certain times to ensure that personnel are available to receive and process these shipments.

The use of bar codes, package coding, electronic invoices, and other aspects of **Electronic Data Interchange (EDI)** is important to the flow of merchandise. Some vendors have their own EDI systems and require retailers to adhere to the system. Alternatively, some retailers may have in-house systems that are forced upon the vendor. If a retailer or vendor does not have the equipment to process EDI transactions, the company may need to consider how to finance this equipment. Many companies are changing to an electronic approach to merchandise flow, and the industry is continuing to upgrade industry standards and improve the total industry commitment to EDI.

The trucking industry and other suppliers are also important factors in the flow of merchandise. Some vendors and some retailers have their own trucks and trucking systems. Other retailers and vendors contract with outside sources for shipment. Some major shipping firms service the retailer in a global market and other smaller firms are used in regional shipping. An advantage of using domestic vendors is the reliance on more local forms of shipment.

If a vendor permits small lot shipments, the time and expense of a constant flow of merchandise needs to be evaluated against the stock shortages, stale merchandise, and overcrowding that may occur from single large shipments. Constant flow of merchandise also requires constant activity of sales associates for stocking. Most buyers try to achieve some midpoint of flow that balances expenses against merchandise freshness. Some merchandise is particularly well suited to a constant flow system. Basic goods that remain steady in their selling volume and similar in their styling can be placed on an **auto-replenishment system.** With an auto-replenishment system, the buyer places in the computer a plan for the model or desired stock assortment, including sizes, styles, and numbers of items. The buyer encodes minimum levels that are needed to prevent stock outs. When these minimum levels are reached, the computer system automatically places a reorder with the vendor. The vendor ships the order upon receipt of the request. Some auto-replenishment systems are established and maintained by the vendor who has more knowledge of the product and its saleability. The timing of the reorder and the shipment must be coordinated to ensure that a stock out will not occur while the order is being processed. Again, the flow of the merchandise from the vendor to the retailer and on to the consumer must be carefully orchestrated.

In addition to the three major buying tasks of merchandise selection, order placement, and flow of merchandise, the buyer performs numerous related tasks to ensure the smooth operation of the buying function. A major aspect of every buyer's job is the maintenance of records relative to the **merchandise control system.** The buyer, whether on paper or with a computer, must keep accurate and detailed records of the planning, buying, and selling for all merchandise. Some of this information may be directly supervised by the buyer and additional information may come from other parts of the retail team. For example, buying information is overseen directly by the buyer, but payments to vendors may be made by accountants, and selling information may be maintained by store managers. The volume of paperwork for a large retailer will be large. Some buyers report that more than one-half of their time is spent dealing with paperwork. The tasks performed include: keep records on sales and stock, prepare purchase orders, keep inventory figures, determine and track information about reductions, track merchandise transfers back to vendor and to other stores, and record the movement of merchandise from shipping to receipt in warehouse and distribution to retail locations. Many buyers report that computerizing the information makes it easier to access, sort, and share; however, computerized information often requires as much if not more work than what is required with old-fashioned paperwork.

From the information that is maintained in the merchandise control system, a buyer can identify fast and slow selling merchandise, and use that information to maintain or adjust stock levels, determine open-to-buy needs for new or replacement merchandise, and evaluate the basic stock programs including those controlled by auto-replenishment systems. From the merchandise control system, the buyer will obtain information needed for the next buying trip. In addition, the buyer can use the information to generate reports for other functions within the retail business. Reports are made regularly, daily, or otherwise, to management about best sellers and slow sellers, returns to vendors, profit margins and style and color trends. For example, the promotions staff will need information about selling trends to determine what stock to highlight in regularly changing promotional display space.

For some retailers, the buyer is also responsible for the **maintenance of stock**. This job may also be performed by store personnel, separately, or under the supervision of the buyer. The stock activities include keeping the stock area organized, initiating stock counts for inventory control, arranging for special orders, supervising the movement of stock from warehouse to backroom to floor, and marking stock.

Stock may have to be prepared for the floor. Some buyers will purchase **floor ready stock** that includes prepriced and tagged merchandise. Floor-ready stock may also be bagged in custom packages or prefolded to specifications. The costs of these services must be weighed against the time that is saved for sales associates and the image that is generated by the look of the merchandise.

Sometimes the buyer may have difficulty in determining the value of some services. Promoting sales and maintaining or improving image are difficult to measure in terms of dollars generated in sales and even more difficult to measure in terms of goodwill or satisfaction among customers. Again, the judgment or merchandising insight of the buyer will become an important factor in a financially dependent situation. The condition of the stock when it arrives at the retail business is part of the terms and services that must be negotiated with the vendor when the buyer places the order for the merchandise. Other buyers will have to supervise the preparation and attachment of tags for merchandise. In addition, special hangers may be used by the retailer. Stock may also require unpacking, steaming, or pressing prior to its placement on the floor.

In large businesses, assistant buyers have many tasks within the merchandise control system. Assistant buyers review inventory records, replenish basic stock—when not using an auto-replenishment program, and complete maintenance records and reports. Assistant buyers perform many of the tasks associated with inventory control, especially in stores using hand entry of data instead of using bar-coded items. In stores with EDI, the assistant buyer is still responsible for the supervision of the data entry and for the review and maintenance of the inventory data. In some large organizations, a staff person with information systems training may have direct responsibility for the computer systems and maintaining databases, but this responsibility is for the quality of the data and the efficient running of the system. Knowledge of the data contents is still a responsibility of the buying function. Information systems tasks may be outsourced by some retailers. For specialized skills needed only once or on a periodic basis, some businesses find that contracting for the service is a wise expenditure. Inventory specialists may also be part of the team who supervise the stock. Regardless of size of organization and number of staff, the buyer is ultimately responsible for the merchandise control system.

Many **miscellaneous activities** are also completed by many buyers. Buyers provide training sessions for sales associates, review customer complaints, supervise clerical staff, and constantly use the telephone, fax, or computer to check on the status of merchandise on order. Handling customer complaints, returns of merchandise, and special requests are buyer responsibilities because these activities all involve the merchandise. If buyers supervise the sales associates, then they may be responsible for scheduling the sales associates' time on the floor and for providing relief periods for these associates if other personnel are not available. The buyer, in the role as a promotions team member, may notify sales associates about ads, check on advertised items for sales and stock, and initiate and secure signage for sales items. Always, the buyer will have office chores that include answering and returning telephone calls, checking and acting on email, and reviewing postal and internal mail. The buyer must find time to shop the market, review sales forecasts, and visit stores. As recommended by the strategic planning process, the buyer must also spend time evaluating current procedures and planning for future improvement in the buying process. In addition, the buyer will review procedures and make plans for adjustments and improvements to the buying office. Ultimately, and finally, the buyer is responsible for achieving goals in sales, markup, markdowns, gross margins, profits, and turnover.

Types of Buying

Buyers who buy for one store or for several stores and who have sole responsibility for obtaining the merchandise buy similarly to the consumers who shop in their stores. Based on their buying plans, buyers make a list, shop the markets, select merchandise, and place orders. In other words, they perform the buying tasks with the assistance of their staff and supervise the delivery of the merchandise to the stores. Chain stores, and buyers who work for these organizations, may use several other methods of **centralized buying**: central merchandising plan, central purchase plan with merchandise requisition, and price list agreements. Buying by a **central merchandising plan** is performed by buyers who are located in a centralized location called the buying office, located in or near a market city or corporate office. Separate buyers are hired for each major merchandise category with each buying one classification of merchandise for all the stores and planning the distribution of merchandise to the stores. Merchandise is shipped directly to stores as allocated. A retailer who uses this method can save money because most vendors will provide discounts for purchases made in volume, although additional charges may be added to break the shipments and send them to separate locations. This plan should provide a steady flow of merchandise throughout the business. Advanced planning and related training is eliminated for store-level staff. With one person directly responsible for all stock, control of stock allocation is usually improved over systems with unit control procedures. On the other hand, adjustment and knowledge of local conditions is often difficult with this system, and the sales associates may have no sense of responsibility for the merchandise. This method provokes the attitude among sales associates that "I don't know why the buyer got this stuff. I didn't order it, so I don't have to sell it."

The **central purchase plan with merchandise requisition** is similar to the central merchandising plan, but uses a central warehouse. This method is sometimes called the **warehouse and requisition plan**. Central or corporate buyers plan the merchandise and place the initial orders. With this merchandise, the buyers stock the warehouse for the entire business. The stock list is sent to all the stores or doors. Store or department managers can select merchandise from the warehouse stock. Merchandise that sells well in one store can be transferred through the warehouse to that store and away from stores where the stock is slow selling. This plan gives the store manager some responsibility in selection of merchandise and provides for individualization of the merchandise to fit the customers. Certain minimum merchandise assortments are assured for the stores. With merchandise available from the warehouse, reorders can be filled promptly and quickly sent to nearby stores. If the organization is very large with many doors, the company may need to have several warehouses to provide more localized service for regional stores. The buyer should be able to obtain good discounts for volume without additional service charges for breaking distribution; however, the company will need to maintain transportation modes to move merchandise from the warehouse to the stores. Overall, this plan requires a very well-defined warehouse control system or an imbalance of inventory can occur in the warehouse, which will affect the inventory in the stores. Unless some controls or guidelines are provided, the buyer has little control over the composition of the merchandise selection within each store. Maintaining the company image and well-balanced stock requires the buyer to extend supervision over store managers.

Price list agreements or list agreements are partnerships made between buyers and vendors. The buyers determine categories of merchandise that can be purchased and the terms of the purchases. The commitment with the vendors includes total volume of the order, the color and size ranges, and terms of shipping. The buyer makes the commitments with the vendors. Buyers prepare lists, catalogs, videos, or Web sites for viewing by store and department managers. Store or department managers can select (or order) from the buyers' lists. The merchandise is shipped directly from the vendors to the doors. This plan provides local managers with a feeling of responsibility in merchandise selection. The plan reduces the expense of a warehouse because the vendor retains all merchandise until it is ordered by the manager or the excess merchandise is stocked in the stores depending on space. This savings may be offset by high transportation costs charged by the vendors. Additional problems may occur with tardy deliveries, which could result in stock outs and lost sales.

Model stock plans with auto-replenishment from the manufacturer are available as a buying method for any retailer who has a computer and modem. The buyer contracts with the manufacturer for merchandise and the service. The manufacturer will advise the buyer on the assortment of merchandise that the buyer should purchase. Model stock is established with styles, units, maximums, and minimums. Sales are POS recorded and sent electronically between manufacturer and individual stores. Reorders and new purchases will be initiated by the manufacturer depending on the sales transactions. Manufacturers will automatically ship new stock when store levels reach pre-established levels. The buyer or managers may suggest new purchases and may advise the manufacturer of adjustments, but the major responsibility for this buying method resides with the manufacturer.

Vendors may also act as rack jobbers or leasees. This method is technically not a buying situation because the vendor, not the retail bussiness, owns the merchandise. For this situation, there is no buyer. The vendor controls the floor space, selects the merchandise, and ships directly to each door. The vendor's representatives or merchandise managers arrive at the stores to set out the merchandise and train sales associates. The merchandise managers who are employed by the vendors will return periodically to check stock and determine reorders. Fixtures such as racks or shelves may also be provided by the vendor. The vendor pays a fee or a rent to have the stock in the store. Overall, the retailer may find this a cost-efficient method because the retailer does not have to buy the stock; however, the retailer has very limited control over the assortment, condition, or other features of the stock.

Competencies of the Buyer

A good buyer must possess the personality, knowledge, and skills for the job. The buyer must be able to function in a variety of activity areas related to the planning, buying, and selling of merchandise. Personal characteristics of a buyer include discerning taste, sensitivity to the wants of others, high energy level, diplomacy, team spirit, organization, self-motivation, creativity, and leadership. The buyer must be a person who can make decisions quickly, be flexible, and work under enormous pressures from time and people constraints. The knowledge base for the job requires a diverse background from art to science.

The fashion aspects of the job are very important. Most merchandise is fashion merchandise; even basic underwear comes in colors, styles, and fabrics. The buyer must know all aspects of the product. If the buyer is buying fur coats, the buyer must know about furs: their origins, the manufacturing process, related legislation, costing procedures, and countries of origin. If a buyer is purchasing swimwear, the buyer must know about color fastness, ultraviolet rays, stretch fibers, techniques for sewing on stretch fabrics, and other specialties of the product. Each merchandise classification will have its own unique product characteristics and manufacturing processes. A buyer who buys across multiple classifications will need depth and breadth of product knowledge.

Buyers also need to know about the cyclic and seasonal nature of the business. Styles, trends, and fashion aspects of the business are as important as the construction and performance of the product. To understand this aspect of the business, the buyer needs to know consumer behavior, psychographics, promotions, and image. Finally, much of the buyer's time is spent working with numbers: costs of the merchandise, sales prices, markups and markdowns, inventory, and other financial matters. Specific skills must include mathematical calculations, computer literacy, negotiations, and written and verbal communication.

Many buyers travel frequently and are away from their home and offices as much as 60 percent of their time. To be a buyer, a person must be willing to travel, to be positive with outlook, and to enjoy change. To advance in the profession, a buyer must be mobile and willing to change buying classifications, change locations, and sometimes to change companies. When traveling, as with all aspects of the job, the buyer is the retailer's representative in the business and must be a professional in all aspects of the job. Vendors and other suppliers may never meet a store manager or other administration from the business so they will base their entire opinion about the business on their impressions of the buyer. With this perception, the buyer has many bosses: the vendors, the managers, the sales associates, and the consumers, and must balance the many and varied responsibilities of the job.

The buyer has a very large responsibility to the financial success of the retail business and becomes a pivotal figure with all merchandise-related activities. In many decisions, the buyer must determine what is the most cost efficient and the most effective way to get the job done. Selecting the right merchandise requires merchandising insight and financial "shrewdness." Cost comparison charts may need to be created to make a comparison between alternative processes. When considering costs, the buyer will have to examine a range of items including the costs of time, capital investment for equipment, transportation, personnel, and other expenses. Financial numbers may not be the only basis for a decision. Understanding the customer and knowing what merchandise will sell is also dependent on understanding the fickleness of the customer and the fascination of new merchandise. The right merchandise is needed for sales to occur. These sales generate money to buy more merchandise and to pay other expenses, and, with the proper margins, result in profits; therefore, getting the right merchandise for the target customer and ensuring the success of the business requires the right person as the buyer.

*S*ummary

Buying is the second stage in the three-stage retail process of planning, buying, and selling. Buying includes three major steps: selecting the merchandise, placing the orders, and controlling the merchandise. Buyers can be located in stores, in offices within market cities, or in corporate offices. Buyers may plan for and place orders for merchandise for an entire retail business or for one subclassification of merchandise within a much larger buying system. Some buyers are in offices that are devoted entirely to the buying function, while other buyers are more closely integrated into the daily selling activities of the retail business.

Buyers who work for retailers who own multiple stores and other outlets may buy according to several centralized plans. Buyers, using auto-replenishment plans and model stock systems, may also depend on the vendor or manufacturer for the selection of the merchandise. Many buyers are also responsible for the flow of the merchandise into the stores. This responsibility requires that the buyer work with vendors, warehouse personnel, transportation services, and other inventory control persons. In a small organization, the buyer may perform many of these activities alone. The size of organization, volume of merchandise, and variety of assortment are all factors determining the exact duties of a buyer. In summary, the buyer is an important key to the profitable functioning of the retail business.

Key Terms

Assistant buyers
Associate buyers
Auto-replenishment system
Balance stock
Buying specialist
Buying tasks
Central merchandising plan
Central purchase plan with
    merchandise requisition
Centralized buying
Corporate buyer
Corporate buying offices
Corporate headquarters
Divisional merchandise manager
    (DMM)

Electronic Data Interchange (EDI)
Flagship store
Floor ready stock
Flow of merchandise
Interdependent functions
Main store buyer
Maintenance of stock
Merchandise control system
Miscellaneous activities
Model stock plans with
    auto-replenishment
New buys
Outsourcing
Planning tasks

Placement of orders
Price list agreements
Rebuys
Select the merchandise
Selling tasks
Showroom samples
Single, large store buyer
Specification sheet
Split of responsibilities
Supervision of the merchandise flow
Team member
Viability of the vendor
Vice President of Merchandising
Warehouse and requisition plan

Discussion Questions

1. Why is good buying important?
2. Why should buying and selling be considered interdependent functions?
3. Where will the buyer be located? What is the best geographic location for a buyer? Why?
4. What are the advantages and disadvantages of centralized buyers and centralized buying?
5. What are the major responsibilities of the buyer?
6. How can a buyer be close to the customer and close to the product?
7. Why must buyers have good communication with promotions and department managers?
8. What are advantages of a central merchandising plan with warehouse requisition?
9. Why does a buyer need to understand inventory procedures?
10. What computer skills does a buyer need?
11. What personal skills are needed to be a good buyer?

Exercises

Buying

1. Devise a merchandise selection plan.

   Select one merchandise classification.
   Describe 10 items that might be purchased within this classification.
   Using the Internet, find sources for each of these items.

2. The buyer must find alternative sources for one item. The previous vendor is no longer manufacturing the item.

   Select and describe an item.
   Using the Internet or other resources (e.g., trade magazines) find three sources for the purchase of the desired item.

3. The buyer needs to buy a new classification of merchandise. To prepare for this purchase, the buyer wants to do some comparison shopping.

   Identify an item.
   Go to a store, catalog, or Web site to identify three brands or manufacturers that make the item.
   Determine the major features that should be considered when buying the item (e.g., seams, fabric, trim, style features, labels, and country of origin).
   Make a chart of the features to compare the three brands.
   Observe the items and make comparisons.

4. A buyer has a list of merchandise that must be selected for a small store selling men's clothing. The buyer needs to plan a trip to Las Vegas to the MAGIC show. Plan the trip for the buyer. Include travel accommodations, transfers to the hotel, four nights in the hotel, and a sample one-day itinerary.

5. Make a "to-do" list for a buyer who has just returned from a buying trip at a major market.

6. The buyer, who uses an auto-replenishment system for infants and toddlers merchandise, finds that the department is always experiencing stock outs with white undershirts. Make a list of things that the buyer might want to check to determine the root of the problem.

7. A buyer wants to hire an assistant buyer. The new assistant will need a list of responsibilities and covering these responsibilities should provide the buyer with more time to make other decisions. Considering tasks in all three areas of buying make a list of responsibilities for the assistant buyer. Outline one typical day for the assistant buyer.

8. An assistant buyer is helping the buyer prepare for the market. Make a list of all the numerical information that the assistant buyer will need to collect for the buyer.

9. The buyer wants to computerize the merchandising control system for the store. The buyer must decide whether to contract with a temporary service to have the database established or spend time doing the job and hiring a clerical staff person to assist with other buying duties. Find the costs of both options and help the buyer make a decision.

*V*endor Relations

*O*bjectives

After completing this chapter, the student will be able to

- itemize criteria for selection of vendors
- discuss negotiations and ethical practices with vendors
- describe terms and services contracted between vendor and buyer
- calculate discounts using terms for merchandise purchase
- write purchase orders for merchandise
- discuss methods for evaluation of vendors
- explain the importance of long-term partnerships with vendors

Vendor relations include a variety of business activities: selection of the vendor, negotiations with the vendor, establishment of terms, placement of orders, and evaluation of vendors. Most of these tasks will be the duty of the buyer. The buyer will make the selection of vendors who have the desired merchandise, develop business partnerships, and analyze the final financial calculations to determine the cost of goods. Some very large organizations have preselected vendors. Someone in the company other than the buyer, negotiates a general contract with the vendor and the buyer will place the specific order and negotiate the actual terms of the contract. In some companies, the final negotiations are done jointly with the buyer and a store administrator working as a team with the vendor. The terms of the sale or contract contain many factors that will affect the final cost of the goods. Terms include discounting, dating, anticipation, loading, and transportation. Transportation includes how the goods are transported, who has ownership of the goods during transportation, and who will pay for the transportation. The buyer must also determine what services will be provided by the vendor, which will affect the promotions activities, sales associates' roles, and the management of the inventory. Return privileges and policies are also important issues to be settled before the contract is finalized.

Vendors are the suppliers or source of merchandise; therefore, shopping for the best vendor and purchasing merchandise from that vendor is often called **sourcing**.

Vendors may be **manufacturers** that are cutting and sewing the product and then selling to the retailer or "middlemen" or **wholesalers** that buy from manufacturers and sell the product to retailers at the markets. Using wholesalers provides the advantage of a wider assortment of merchandise than what is produced in one manufacturing plant or in one company's plants.

In the apparel business, **contractors** are also vendors that operate a business that contracts with various manufacturers to provide for the production of a product. The contractor owns neither the raw materials nor the manufacturing facilities. Contractors can be viewed as a traffic controller who oversees and ensures that the process is done, but does not actually complete the process.

Vendors become very important to the buyer because they are the source of the product, which will be sold in the retail business and, therefore, must be selected with great care. Often the choice of vendor will influence the style and price of the merchandise assortment and can ultimately influence the margins and the profit for the retailer.

The buyer may find vendors in several locations. The traditional method of shopping for merchandise is to attend the markets during specified weeks. Markets are held on a regular basis in selected cities. Vendors rent booths or showrooms at the markets and meet with buyers. Some vendors have permanent showrooms in the market cities and are available on a year-round basis. Vendors also prepare catalogs, videos, and Web sites to show goods to buyers. The vendor may send representatives to the buying office, the main stores, or corporate headquarters to meet with buyers. Trunk shows held in the store are frequently for consumers, but can be a source of information for a buyer, especially with new or trial merchandise. The buyer may also contact the vendor with telephone, fax, or Internet services, particularly when the order is a rebuy or if the buyer has a highly trusted partnership with the vendor. Some buyers never directly contact vendors, but use a buying service, especially when looking for new sources or new merchandise classifications.

Criteria for Selection of Vendors

Prior to placing any orders, the buyer must determine with whom to trade. Selecting the vendor is very important because the buyer will be dependent on the vendor to deliver the desired merchandise. For merchandise selection, the buyer is the retailer's agent or representative in the market. For many retailers, the buyer has total responsibility for selecting vendors, placing orders, and spending the budget. For large companies, the buyer may be spending hundreds of thousands of dollars, and the responsibility is very serious and critical to the satisfaction of the customers and the financial success of the retailer. Buyers are rewarded for their successes and often fired for their failures. Successes and failures can be seen in movement or stagnation of inventory and in the size of the profit margins. Forecasting will help the buyer determine what is the best merchandise and shopping will help the buyer find the right products, but selecting the best vendor will help ensure that the merchandise is in the stores as anticipated.

Whether the buyer is planning for a rebuy with a vendor of long-standing practice or is looking for new merchandise and a new vendor, the buyer must evaluate the potential success of trading with the vendor. Most buyers have a **criteria list** or some type of mental or actual checklist for determining the right vendor or source of merchandise. The criteria for selecting a source can be viewed in several categories: appropriateness of the merchandise, ability to meet company merchandise policies, reputation, terms and services offered, location, and price of the item and of the total order. The appropriateness of the merchandise is a measure of how closely the merchandise fits the forecast information and how well the merchandise rates in manufacturing quality. The buyer will need to determine whether the merchandise can be sold to the consumer. These considerations are part of selecting the merchandise as discussed in Chapters 9, 10, and 12.

Meeting company merchandising policies includes evaluating the vendors ability to provide exclusivity, brand identification, and fashion leadership. The aspects of these items vary from business to business, but must be compatible between vendor and retailer. A retailer who has spent many dollars developing an image cannot afford to provide merchandise that will be counter to this image. The development of private label goods can help a retailer increase exclusivity. If the vendor is designing and manufacturing certain products for a retailer, the retailer may require that those products not be sold to other businesses. Labels can be designed that are unique for a retailer. A vendor who can provide this service will be important to some retailers.

Some retailers may desire to be the first business in the area or in the mall to have a new style or a new color. This retailer should seek sources that can provide this level of fashion leadership. However, fashion leadership and private label products may require extra time, additional resources, and higher costs. The volume required for minimum orders may be an important criterion to small retailers and retailers who want fast-moving, high fashion merchandise in low volumes. Small-lot orders require additional handling and packaging for the vendor and usually involve additional fees. Associated costs may be offset by improved salability of items and larger initial markups.

The reputation of the vendor is another important factor in evaluating a new resource. The buyer should explore the guarantees, prior performances, and finances that the vendor can substantiate. Also, a consideration of ethics and treatment of other buyers is important, but often such information is not available except by word of mouth.

Location of the vendor is yet another important consideration when choosing a source. Costs of transportation, time from manufacturer to distribution centers or stores, and need for crossing international borders must be considered. For example, a vendor using overseas manufacturers may be able to offer merchandise at a discount price, but the charges for transportation and the lag time for delivery may negate the benefits of the low prices. In addition, a **commissionaire** or independent agent specializing in import goods may be needed as an intermediary when using overseas vendors. Needing to negotiate in a foreign language can be another consideration when selecting vendors with overseas activities. Finally, the buyer must also consider location when estimating the time and other resources needed to make any changes in the order or to return unsatisfactory merchandise.

Negotiations with Vendors

Once the buyer has selected merchandise, the negotiation process will result in a final and legal contract between the retailer and the vendor with the buyer acting as the agent for the retailer. Both the vendor and retailer must negotiate within legal confines and with ethical practices to the mutual benefit of both parties. The buyer must practice diplomacy during negotiations. Basic trade laws such as the Sherman Antitrust Act of 1890, the Federal Trade Commission Act of 1914, the Clayton Act of 1914, and the Robinson–Patman Act of 1936 regulate trade including contracts, competition, and pricing policies. The buyer should be aware of such international, federal, and state legislation; therefore, the retailer who seeks sources outside of the domestic arena must know about international trade including customs, quotas, and shipping regulations.

In addition to the legal aspects of negotiation, the buyer must practice ethical procedures when negotiating with vendors: "Get the best price at all costs" is not a good policy for a buyer. Although the cost of goods is very important because of its impact on retail price, the buyer should not engage in illegal or unethical activities to get this best price. ***Prima facie* duties** imply that the buyer has a moral obligation to the retailer and to the vendor to keep promises, create actions that contribute to the well-being of others, distribute rewards based on merit, and take actions not to injure self or others. A contract is a promise—the vendor promises to deliver the goods as described and the buyer promises that the represented company will pay the bill as negotiated. Guidance for **proportionality** can help a buyer evaluate by focusing and questioning actions in relation to the consequences. When negotiating with a vendor the buyer should consider the motivation for a vendor's actions, the means in which these actions will be performed, and the possible results or outcomes. Demands for services or costs by both vendors and buyers should be stated carefully and evaluated with equal care for their appropriateness to the situation. A buyer should never participate in bribery, including the offering or receiving of gifts and samples.

The final guide for ethical standards is **social justice**. The buyer should remember that people have the right to be treated equitably and that one person must not exploit a group of people to the benefit of others. This guide is used by many buyers who purchase merchandise that is made in countries where labor rates are very low and where the protection of the worker is not well established.

Terms and Services

Terms include the discounts, cash dating, delivery time and method, loading, and anticipation that may be assigned to any merchandise order. These terms affect the final cost to the retailer for the merchandise. Terms are negotiated by the buyer with the vendor. If the buyer can negotiate favorable terms (those that benefit the retailer), then the buyer is often rewarded by the retail employer with bonuses or promotions. However, any terms must be made within the scope of legal trade and must continue to provide merchandise that will sell to the final consumer. A great deal that does not sell is a financial loss for the retailer.

Services are the activities, aids, and other assistance that the vendor promises the buyer beyond the basic merchandise and cost considerations such as enhancements to the product, promotional aids, and training for sales associates. Enhancements for the product can include exclusivity, private brand labels, hangers, hang tags, and packaging. Promotional aids can include photographs ready for printing, cooperative advertising agreements, financial assistance with advertising, and in-store aids for displays and signage. The vendor may also assist the buyer with training for sales associates, including classes, videos, and plant tours.

Quantity Discounts

Discounts or **premiums** are appealing to buyers and retailers because they lower the wholesale cost of the merchandise. With lower wholesale costs, the buyer can obtain a larger margin if all other expenses remain the same. **Quantity discounts** are given when the buyer purchases a large number of units within one SKU. The manufacturer can afford to provide the discount because the per unit operating expenses on one single order is smaller than the per unit expenses in selling and shipping several small orders. For example, one telephone call can be made to one buyer to discuss 100 units instead of telephone calls to two buyers to discuss 50 units each. One mailing label will ship 100 units, but two mailing labels are needed to ship 50 units to buyer A and 50 units to buyer B. The money saved, or part of the money saved, from the reduced expenses can be removed from the manufacturer's markup and "passed on" to the buyer. Quantity discounts for the manufacturer also promote purchasing. The buyer might be encouraged to buy more units in order to get the discount than would be purchased without the discount. For example, the buyer may plan to get 100 units and would have purchased 50 from vendor X and 50 from vendor Y, but may consolidate the order with vendor X if a discount is given when the larger quantity is purchased.

The primary benefit to the retailer for a quantity discount is the reduction in the final cost of goods. This reduction can become part of the margin and ultimately part of the profit or can be used to reduce the margin and can be passed to the consumer as a savings. The buyer must be sure that the savings is combined with merchandise that will be sold. If the price for the merchandise is very low, but the merchandise is never sold or is sold with a drastically reduced markup, then the overall Profit and Loss statement will be negatively impacted. In addition, the buyer must be certain not to overspend the budget that was allocated for that buying trip (i.e., the planned purchases from the six-month plan) and not to overpurchase in one merchandise classification to the loss of a second classification. The assortment plan should be reviewed when buying to insure that balanced stock is maintained. The buyer must also evaluate the costs to the stores or the warehouse for receiving the merchandise in bulk. The bulk shipment will have to be opened, sorted, and distributed to the stores. Each phase of the activity will be a cost to the retailer, especially if the retailer does not have a central warehouse or distribution center. Storing the merchandise until it is needed may also be an added expense and may require that the retailer pay for the goods before the items even reach the selling floor.

The quantity discount is usually applied in "stair steps" of units. For each unit increase, the price is reduced. In other words, the more the buyer purchases, the more the buyer saves. For example, the vendor may offer a 5.00% discount for units that exceed 100 units. If the purchase amount exceeds 500 units, the discount may be 15.00%; and if the purchase exceeds 1,000 units, the discount may be 30.00%. To find the **total list price dollars** for the purchases, the buyer would use the formula

$$\text{Total List Price \$} = \text{Unit List Price \$} \times \text{\# of Units}$$

The list price dollars are usually called the list price or list and will be used in this text as List $ in the formulas. List price may also be called the original or the initial price. To find the **final discount price dollars**, the buyer would use the formula

$$\text{Final Discount Price \$} = \text{Discount Price \$} \times \text{\# of Units}$$

The **total discount dollars** is the difference between the list price and the discount price. This difference can be calculated both at the unit price level and at the total level with these formulas

$$\text{Discount \$} = \text{Unit List Price \$} - \text{Discount Price \$}$$

$$\text{Total Discount \$} = \text{Total Unit List Price \$} - \text{Final Discount Price \$}$$

This total discount dollars could be considered as how much the buyer saved when buying with the discount.

Sample Problem: Quantity Discount

The buyer was quoted a discount of 15.00% if 200 units were purchased. The discount price was $14.00 per unit. The list price for each unit was $20.00. The buyer decided to buy 300 units. What was the total list price? What was the final discount price? How much did the buyer save by ordering the large quantity?

Step 1. Calculate the total list price.

Unit List Price $ $\times$ # of Units = Total List Price $
$20.00 $\times$ 300 = $6,000.00

Step 2. Calculate the final discount price.

Discount Price $ $\times$ # of Units = Final Discount Price $
$14.00 $\times$ 300 = $4,200.00

Step 3. Calculate the total discount dollars.

Total Unit List Price $ $-$ Final Discount Price $ = Total Discount $
$6,000.00 $-$ $4,200.00 = $1,800.00

The buyer saved $1,800.00 by utilizing the discount.

Discounts are usually presented to the buyer as percentages of the list price. The buyer may need to calculate the dollar amount of the discount by using these percentages

Discount $ = Unit List Price $ $\times$ Discount %

To find the unit discount price dollars, the following formula is used:

Discount Price $ = Unit List Price $ $-$ Discount $

With some mathematical manipulations, these formulas can be used to determine the **discount percentage** when the list dollars and the discount price dollars are known.

Discount $ = Unit List Price $ $\times$ Discount %
Discount % = Discount $/Unit List $

The percentage may be calculated either with unit prices or with total and final prices. The percentage would be the same because the percentage represents the ratio of the two numbers, regardless of the size of the values.

Sample Problem: Discount Percentage

The buyer was quoted a unit list price of $46.00 and then was quoted a discount price of $43.30. What was the discount percentage?

Step 1. Find the discount dollars.

Unit List $ $-$ Discount Price $ = Discount $
$46.00 $-$ $43.30 = Discount $
$2.70 = Discount $

Step 2. Find the discount percentage.

Discount $/Unit List $ = Discount %
$2.70/$46.00 = Discount %
5.87% = Discount %

Trade Discounts

Trade discounts are also called **series discounts** or **cumulative discounts**. These discounts are so named because each discount is taken from the preceding net amount before applying the next discount. This type of discount is not the same as the quantity discount. A buyer will not get the same final discount total from a series discount as with a single quantity discount. The trade discount is calculated in a series because with each level of discount the retailer gets fewer services. The services that are removed with each discount include services such as hangers, hang tags, individual packaging, range of sizes, and choice of colors. For example, with the first discount, the buyer will not get hangers, and the merchandise will be folded and bagged individually. With the second discount, the buyer will not get the merchandise on hangers and the hang tags will not be attached. With the third discount, the buyer will still not receive the first two services and will get the merchandise packaged in one bulk container instead of individually wrapped items. A series discount with three levels would be quoted to this buyer and would be stated as 25.00%, 10.00%, 5.00%. No "and" is placed between the next-to-the-last and the last percentage. The first discount dollars are calculated and subtracted from the list price, and the resulting price is called the **net price** or **net 1**. Net 1 becomes the base price for the next discount and so forth until the final net price is determined. In a series discount with three discounts, the final net price is net 3. To further illustrate this concept, the **net dollars** formulas are

$$\text{Net 1} = \text{List \$} - (\text{List \$} \times \text{1st Discount \%})$$
$$\text{Net 2} = \text{Net 1 \$} - (\text{Net 1 \$} \times \text{2nd Discount \%})$$

Sample Problem: Trade Discounts

The trade discounts are offered as 25.00% (no hangers), 10.00% (no tags), 5.00% (no returns allowed). If the original (or list) price is $100.00, what is the net price?

Step 1. Find the first discount.
Step 2. Find Net 1.
Step 3. Find the second discount.
Step 4. Find Net 2.
Step 5. Find the third discount.
Step 6. Find Net 3.

Together, the six steps result in the following calculations:

List price	$100.00
−25%	−25.00
Net 1	75.00
−10%	−7.50
Net 2	67.50
−5%	−3.38
Net 3	$64.12

What is the discount amount? (Or, how much did the buyer save?)

$$\text{List \$} - \text{Discount Price \$} = \text{Discount \$}$$
$$\$100.00 - \$64.12 = \text{Discount \$}$$
$$\$35.88 = \text{Discount \$}$$

The sum of a series of discounts is not the same as the final discount amount when taken in a series. For example, in the preceding problem, the sum of the discounts would be 25.00% + 10.00% + 5.00% or 40.00%. The discount percentage for the above problem would be calculated as $35.88 for the $100.00 order or 35.88%. The two percentages do not result in the same amount of savings; however, a shortcut method similar to the quantity discount calculation does exist for finding the final discount price without calculating all of the net values. The buyer can find the trade or series discounts by the **on percent method.** This method is a shortcut method for finding the final discount price and involves finding the complements of the discounts and using them to find the final discount price. A complement of a percentage is the amount of the percentage subtracted from 100 percent. The **complement of a percentage** is

$$\text{Complement \%} = 100\% - \text{X \%}$$

Sample Problem: On Percent Method

The buyer was quoted a series discount of 25.00%, 10.00%, 5.00%. The list price of the item was $100.00. What is the discount price?

Step 1. Find the complements of the discounts.

$$100.00\% - 25.00\% = 75.00\%$$
$$100.00\% - 10.00\% = 90.00\%$$
$$100.00\% - 5.00\% = 95.00\%$$

Step 2. Find the series complement by multiplying the decimal equivalents of the complements.

$$0.75 \times 0.90 \times 0.95 = \text{Series Complement}$$
$$0.6412 = \text{Series Complement}$$

Step 3. Find the final discount price, or Net 3.

$$\text{List Price \$} \times \text{Series Complement} = \text{Net 3}$$
$$\$100 \times 64.12\% = \text{Net 3}$$
$$\$64.12 = \text{Net 3}$$

Cash Discounts

Cash discounts offer the retailer a premium or discount for paying promptly or for paying early. Late payment is a problem in the apparel industry. Payment is usually not made by the retailer until after the goods are delivered to the stores. Between the time of order placement by the buyer and shipment of the merchandise, the manufacturer of the merchandise has had to buy fabric, pay wages, and take goods to market. If the vendor is a manufacturer, the business may have expenses for over six months before a payment is received from the retailer. The manufacturer would desire to have the payment with the order. On the other hand, the retailer wants to wait to pay until the merchandise has sold in the store. Waiting for sales of the merchandise may increase the time for payment another three months beyond delivery. The manufacturer has now had nine months beyond the time the order was received, the fabric was initially purchased, and the products were designed. The operating expenses for the manufacturer have continued while waiting on the retailer to pay. The manufacturer needs money to buy new fabric and to pay designers for starting the next season's line. Cash flow is a constant worry for both manufacturers and retailers.

Although called cash discounts, many retailers do not pay in cash. In fact, if the retailer does not pay when goods are received, the vendor is actually advancing or loaning cash to the retailer. Terms for the cash discount are written as 2/10 EOM, n/30. The "2" is the percentage of discount. The "10" represents number of days from the date of the invoice or specified term and is the period of time that the discount is in effect. The EOM is the **dating** or the time when the cash discount period starts. The "n/30" is the **net period**, when the full amount is due. After the net period has passed, the bill is considered to be late or in arrears.

Types of Dating

Dating can vary and is part of the negotiation for cash discount terms between the vendor and the retailer. Dating indicates when the cash discount process will begin. The types of dating are itemized as follows:

- *COD.* This term means "cash on delivery." This dating is used when the vendor does not know the retailer or the retailer does not have a strong line of credit. The vendor may also require this term if the retailer was late in payment in previous shipments. No cash discount is possible when COD is the date because COD means payment is due in full when the merchandise is delivered. No net period or cash discount period is allowed.

- *DOI.* This term means "date of invoice." If no other dates are given, then the date of invoice is the start time for dating. This is the most common type of dating. If DOI is used, the cash discount terms will have no dating within the discount statement and is written as 4/10, n/30.

- *ROG.* This dating means "receipt of goods." The cash discount period and net period begin with the date of receipt of goods, and the term is written as 8/10 ROG, n/30. This dating allows the retailer ten days after the goods are received to begin selling the merchandise and still have time to pay with a discount. Additional time to sell the merchandise is allowed before the final payment is due.

- *EOM.* This term means "end of month." Dating starts with the end of the month and the invoice is to be paid within the specified number of days after the end of the month in which goods are invoiced. If merchandise is invoiced on or after the 25th, the date is extended to the end of the next month. EOM dating is written as 8/10 EOM, n/90.

- *X Dating.* This dating includes "extra dating" and extends credit for additional days in which to receive the discount. The X dating is written to show the bonus days beyond the standard cash discount days. The term is written as 8/10-30X. In this example, the ten days become 40 days for cash discount period. This type of dating is used to show the generosity of the vendor to a good client; for example, as a bonus for someone who has always paid on time. The extra dating is also used when the merchandise is being shipped from an overseas port and will take additional time in transit or in customs.

- *"as of."* This dating is advanced dating and indicates that the goods have been "postdated" to allow for the shipment or to allow extra time for discount. Again, this type of dating provides the retailer with extra time for making the payment. The extra time may be consumed by time in transit, for shipping and customs, and may not allow for extra time in selling the merchandise to the consumer.

If a buyer received a dating discount of 8/15, n/30, the terms would be read as an 8% discount if the bill is paid within 15 days of the date of invoice with the net or total amount due within 30 days of the date of invoice. Reading the terms is simple. The challenge to the buyer is in determining the last day to receive the cash discount and getting the controllers or accounting department to pay the bill. Of course, the cash would have to be available for the retailer to pay the bill. The last day to pay this bill and receive the cash discount would be 15 days past the date of the invoice. If the date of the invoice is May 31, the cash discount day is June 15. If the bill is paid on June 3, the amount due would be calculated as a discount, using the following **discount dollars** and **discount price dollars** formulas:

$$\text{Discount \$} = \text{Invoice or List \$} \times \text{Discount \%}$$

and

$$\text{Discount Price \$} = \text{Invoice \$} - \text{Discount \$}$$

Sample Problem: Cash Discounts

The buyer placed an order with a vendor for $46,800.00 worth of white shirts. The vendor offered the buyer the terms of 2/8, n/30. The invoice was dated June 15, and the shirts arrived at the store on June 19. The buyer paid the bill on June 20. What was the amount of the payment?

The terms of 2/8, n/30 state that the buyer can take a 2.00% discount for paying within eight days of the invoice date. The invoice date was June 15. The last day for the discount would be eight days past June 15, which would be June 23. The buyer paid on June 20; therefore, the buyer could take the 2.00% discount.

To calculate the amount of the payment or the discount price, the following calculations are made:

Step 1. Find the value of the discount.

Discount $ = Invoice or List $ × Discount %
Discount $ = $46,800.00 × 2.00%
Discount $ = $936.00

Step 2. Find the discount price or the amount of the payment.

Discount Price $ = Invoice $ − Discount $
Discount Price $ = $46,800.00 − $936.00
Discount Price $ = $45,864.00

The cash discount is a good idea for a manufacturer, but retailers may lack the cash flow or the dollars to take advantage of this discount. Without available cash to pay the bill, the retailer must wait for sales to gather money to pay for the goods. The industry has a service business called factoring. **Factoring** is the process of buying from the manufacturer (or vendor) the bills or payments due to the manufacturer. The retailer must then pay the factorer instead of the vendor. Factoring provides a service for the manufacturer because the manufacturer gets the cash immediately and has dollars to pay the operating bills for the manufacturing business. The disadvantage for the manufacturer is that the business doing the factoring charges a fee. The cash payment to the manufacturer is reduced by the fee charged by the factoring business. The factoring fee is similar to the fee, or interest, that a bank charges for a loan. The factoring fee is often negotiated in value of the prime lending rate. For example, the factoring business may charge the prime rate plus 3%. The factoring fee will always be higher than the prime lending rate because of the many risks involved in the retail business.

Anticipation

Anticipation is a discount applied if the invoice is paid before the end of the cash discount period, and is considered a bonus or allowance for early payment and as "interest" that is deducted from invoice. This process is based on the concept that the cash discount period is a time that the vendor is lending the retailer money because the retailer has both the merchandise and the money during the period. The anticipation discount is based on the number of days remaining in the cash discount (CD) period. The following **anticipation days** formula is used:

$$\text{Days for Anticipation} = \text{Days for CD} - \text{Days Used}$$

Days for CD are the days allocated for the cash discount as found in the term, and days used are the number of days that have passed since the dating for the cash discount started.

Anticipation uses an annual interest rate and the proportion of anticipation days relative to the days in a year, in the calculations for the discount. The resulting rate is considered to be the **anticipation rate or percentage.**

$$\text{Anticipation \%} = \text{\% Yearly Interest} \times (\text{Anticipation Days}/360)$$

Calculations for anticipation and other cash discounts begin with the contract price or the amount of the invoice. To find **anticipation dollars**, the following formula is used:

$$\text{Anticipation \$} = \text{Invoice \$} \times \text{Anticipation \%}$$

To calculate the **balance due dollars**, use the formula

$$\text{Balance Due \$} = \text{Invoice \$} - \text{CD \$} - \text{Anticipation \$}$$

in which the balance due is the amount of the bill that the buyer will pay if the cash discount and the anticipation discount are received. This amount can be called the discount price because the buyer pays that price when all discounts are taken. The preceding formula can be rewritten to express all of the terms of the anticipation discount as

$$\text{Balance Due \$} = \text{Invoice \$} - [(\text{CD \%} + \text{Anticipation \%}) \times \text{Invoice \$}]$$

or

$$\text{Discount Price \$} = \text{Invoice \$} - \text{Total Discount \$}$$

Sample Problem: Anticipation

The buyer placed an order with a vendor for $46,800.00 worth of white shirts. The vendor offered the buyer the terms of 2/8, n/30 with anticipation at an 8.90% yearly rate. The invoice was dated June 15, and the shirts arrived at the store on June 30. The buyer paid the bill on June 20. What was the amount of the payment?

The terms of 2/8, n/30 state that the buyer can take a 2.00% discount for paying within eight days of the invoice date. The invoice was June 15. The last day for the discount to be applied would be eight days past June 15, which would be June 23. The buyer paid on June 20; therefore, the buyer could take the 2.00% discount. The buyer also could take the anticipation.

To calculate the savings from anticipation and the cash discount, the following formulas and steps were used:

Step 1. Find the days for anticipation.

$$\text{Days for Anticipation} = \text{Days for CD} - \text{Days Used}$$
$$\text{Days for Anticipation} = 8 - (\text{June 15 to June 20})$$

Days for Anticipation = 8 − 5

Days for Anticipation = 3

Step 2. Determine the anticipation percentage.

Anticipation % = % Yearly Interest × (Anticipation Days/360)

Anticipation % = 8.90% × 3/360

Anticipation % = .074%

Step 3. Find the anticipation dollars.

Anticipation $ = Invoice $ × Anticipation %

Anticipation $ = $46,800.00 × .074%

Anticipation $ = $34.63

Step 4. Calculate the cash discount amount.

Discount $ = Invoice or List $ × Discount %

Discount $ = $46,800.00 × 2.00%

Discount $ = $936.00

Step 5. Determine the balance due or the amount paid.

Discount Price $ = Invoice $ − CD $ − Anticipation $

Discount Price $ = $46,800.00 − $936.00 − $34.63

Discount Price $ = $45,829.37

Loading

Loading is an additional discount that can be negotiated. With loading, the price is adjusted upward above the regular price, and large cash discounts are offered to the buyer, which reduce the price back to original or slightly lower price. Loading is used because some buyers get credit for the size of the cash discounts that they can negotiate. In the Profit and Loss statements, as discussed in Chapters 3 and 4, the cash discount amount may be considered as part of the maintained markup and is not part of the cost of goods. This accounting procedure would improve the size of the margins, and the cash discount can be used by retailers as income and not as adjustments to price. The following formula is used to calculate the **loaded cost dollars**:

Loaded Cost $ = Initial Cost $ + Initial Cost $ × Loading %

Through algebraic manipulation, this formula can be rewritten as

Loaded Cost $ = Initial Cost $ × [(100% + Loading %)/100]

The **loaded cost** becomes the invoice cost. Loading is calculated before the merchandise leaves the manufacturer's warehouse. The loaded invoice would arrive at the retailer and would be paid. If the retailer paid within the cash discount time, the invoice cost (or loaded cost) would be reduced by the cash discount; therefore, the formula to use for the **discount price dollars** is

Discount Price $ = Loaded Cost $ − (Loaded Cost $ × CD %)

and can be rewritten as

Discount Price $ = Loaded Cost $ × [(100% − CD %)/100]

Sample Problem: Cash Discount with Loading

A buyer placed an order for white shirts at $46,800.00. The vendor offered the buyer terms of 4/8, n/30 and a loading of 3.00%. The invoice was dated June 15, and the shirts arrived at the store on June 30. The buyer paid the bill on June 20. What was the amount of payment?

Step 1. Find the loaded cost.

Loaded Cost $ = Initial Cost $ × (100.00% + Loading %)/100

Loaded Cost $ = $46,800.00 × (100.00% + 3.00%)/100

Loaded Cost $ = $46,800.00 × 1.03

Loaded Cost $ = $48,204.00

Step 2. Find the amount that the retailer pays.
The buyer can take a 4.00% discount for paying within eight days of the invoice date. (The invoice was dated June 15. The last day for the discount would be eight days past June 15, which would be June 23. The buyer paid on June 20; therefore, the buyer could take the 4.00% discount.)

Step 3. Calculate the discount price using the cash discount.

Discount Price $ = Loaded Cost $ − (Loaded Cost $
     × Cash Discount %)

Discount Price $ = Loaded Cost $
     × [(100.00% − Cash Discount %)/100]

Discount Price $ = $48,204.00 × 0.96

Discount Price $ = $46,275.84

Purchase Order

Purchase orders contain a variety of information. Much of this information is based on the model stock plan and the six-month plan, only it is written in a format acceptable with the vendor. In other words, purchase orders are order forms that are used for writing the actual listing and itemization of merchandise that is to be ordered from a vendor. To write the purchase order and leave it with the vendor is to **drop paper** with the vendor. Purchase orders are legal contracts between vendors and retailers. Both parties must agree to the terms and conditions of the contract. The buyer offers money in payment for merchandise, and the offer is accepted by the vendor. Both the retailer's representative (the buyer) and the vendor's representative must be legal agents for their businesses, meaning that the persons who sign the contract or acknowledge the order must have the authority to commit the money or the resources to fulfill the contract. In addition, for the contract to be legal, both parties must be able to enter into a contract, which in most U.S. states requires that the persons be over 21 years of age and mentally competent.

Many vendors and some retailers will have their own forms. Companies who have their own forms will have the forms printed with standard information, such as the name and address of the company, merchandise classifications and inventory numbers, shipping addresses, contact personnel, and terms of the sale that must always be met. For example, a retailer's purchase order may contain information about penalties for late delivery or specifications about shipping cartons that they expect for every shipment. Some companies are using EDI and transmitting these forms electronically. Standardized forms of EDI shipments are specified by some industry organizations or may be specified by vendor or retailer. Computerized orders are also useful when basic merchandise is ordered frequently with very little change in the order from time to time. Purchase orders typically contain information about the quantity, style, color, sizes, and cost for each item or groups of items. The terms of payment, shipping information, and the **cancellation dates**, which note when the shipment will be refused because it is too late in delivery, are written on the purchase orders. Cancellation dates are important for the retail business because late deliveries cause stock outs and lost sales. If the items are fashion items or seasonal items, the delay in delivery can mean that the items, when or if they finally arrive, have no selling value for the retailer. For example, sweaters with teddy bears, green wreaths, and red stockings have no value to a retailer if they arrive at the stores in mid-January instead of mid-November. Also, any merchandise tied to a promotional campaign must arrive in correlation to the media ads for the promotion to be viable.

The purchase order is written by the buyer after selecting merchandise. The buyer may have a clerical assistant or assistant buyer who can do the paperwork associated with the purchase order. Regardless of who completes the order, exactness is very important because the style numbers refer to specific items. One transposition of a number could result in the delivery of the wrong items or the delivery of 21 dozen items instead of 12 dozen.

Ultimately, the buyer is responsible for the accuracy of the purchase orders and must remember that the order is a contract that requires acceptance of delivery and payment for the merchandise. After careful forecasting and budgeting, the buyer must spend equal care with the preparation of the order. This care is often difficult because orders may be written in showrooms, in hotel rooms, and at café tables because the vendor is waiting for the order and may not wish to wait too long. In addition, when the merchandise is popular and the vendor has many other customers, the buyer may lose the order if the purchase order is not placed promptly. A manufacturer with limited production capacity and a popular product can only take a limited number of orders; therefore, the buyer must act quickly, decisively, and carefully when placing orders, while adhering to any merchandising policies for the retail company. For example, some companies have policies that require multiple signatures for the approval of an order form.

Evaluation of Vendors

After the merchandise is received and sold and the season has passed, the buyer must evaluate the sale of the merchandise not only for styles, colors, and sizes, but also for the profitability of the merchandise by vendor. Merchandise from each vendor must be evaluated to determine how well the merchandise sold and how much markup was maintained. Returns from unsatisfied consumers are certainly a consideration in this evaluation. Merchandise that was sold, but then returned will reduce profit margins and will cost the retail business in terms of using sales associate's time, cleaning and repackaging of the items, restocking, and returning undesirable items to the vendor. In addition to the appropriateness of the merchandise, the buyer should evaluate the vendor for the terms and services that were promised and then those that were provided.

Some buyers use spreadsheets to make evaluations of vendors. Topics for evaluation include purchase or wholesale price, retail price, overall net sales, sell-through percentage, markdown dollars, markdown percentages, return dollars, and return percentages. Percentages are useful for making comparisons across items. Total dollars such as net sales and

Vendor	Product	Purchase $ at Retail	Net Sales $	Sell-Through % (ns/p)	Markdown $	Markdown % (md/ns)	Return $	Return % (r/p)

Figure 13.1 Vendor Evaluation Spreadsheet.

markdowns are important because of the contribution that each item makes to the total sales, total markdowns, and overall profit margins. On time delivery is also important. A vendor evaluation sheet could be made such as shown in Figure 13.1.

In such a spreadsheet, the vendors would be listed by vendor code or by name depending on the accounting system of the retailer. The style number, SKU number, or other product code would be used to identify the items. By using the spreadsheet format, the buyer can evaluate similar items, compare performance of products by vendors, or look for high and low performers. A spreadsheet can also be sorted by rows or columns, providing the buyer with different views of the information. Using the spreadsheet, the buyer can determine which vendor has the highest sell through for the merchandise, what merchandise contributes the most to the total net sales, and what items are responsible for markdowns. The information for the spreadsheet can be obtained by clerical encoding or can be linked to other databases and information within an overall computerized inventory system. When selecting or establishing such a computerized system, a buyer must know what information is needed and should not depend on the computer specialists to dictate the information and format of evaluation sheets and other report forms.

As with many other decisions by the buyer, the final decision about vendor performance is made among alternatives. A vendor may have great services and on-time delivery, but 65% of the merchandise does not sell at the initial markup. The merchandise from this vendor, when analyzed, has the highest markup percentage among all the vendors. The buyer must decide what is most important for the business. The buyer can also determine that the markup expected on the merchandise is too high, or the buyer can decide that the markup is to be expected and can plan for the markup when setting the budget for the six-month plan. An evaluation process is very important to provide the buyer with information, but the final decisions and the "weighting" in importance of the various variables depend largely on the buyer's judgment, knowledge of the retail business, and merchandising insight.

Partnerships with Vendors

Questions to be asked when deciding on vendors include the following: "How will you evaluate your sources?" "Where do you find new sources?" "Will the vendor–retailer relationship become a partnership?" "How do you treat your partners?"

Traditionally, buyers took a "mine-and-theirs" approach to contact with vendors; however, this approach is no longer beneficial in a competitive business environment. Vendors should not be considered as adversaries, but as partners in the retail business. Vendors can provide buyers with information to aid in forecasting, assist buyers with suggestions about merchandise selection, and definitely ease the process of placing orders and obtaining dependable deliveries. Buyers need this assistance from a vendor, and vendors need the orders that buyers place. This mutual dependency is best served by partnerships.

Causes of friction between vendors and buyers may be directly related to price issues, such as the vendor raises prices that seem unreasonable to the buyer or does so without advanced notice to the buyer. Alternatively, the issues may be only indirectly related to price through failure of the vendor to provide satisfactory merchandise. This situation could occur because the vendor did not ship the order in time to meet the retailer's deadline, the vendor substituted merchandise without prior approval by the buyer, or the order was incorrectly filled. **Cancellations** by actions of the vendor occur because of problems with raw materials, lack of labor, or overselling. Cancellations can also occur because the buyer changed the order or did not receive full authorization for the order or shipping problems prevented a timely delivery. Shipping problems are common problems for merchandise coming from overseas locations. In addition, issues of fashion piracy, special orders, required minimums, and returns and adjustments can cause friction between buyers and vendors. Buyers want the right merchandise at the right time to sell to their customers. Vendors want to provide this merchandise but are restricted by costs and availability of labor and raw materials; time, distances and costs with shipping; and their own need to make a profit. A partnership where the partners respect and understand the needs of each other is important for the competitive survival of all parties. After all, everyone needs to continue to sell products at a profit to stay in business.

*S*ummary

Vendor relations are an important link between selecting the merchandise and having the merchandise in stock to sell. The buyer needs to find vendors who have the merchandise that is forecast to be right for the retailer's customers, and the buyer must obtain this merchandise at a price that will allow for the profitable sale of the merchandise. To obtain the desired markup and to cover the costs, the buyer must negotiate a contract with the vendor that is advantageous to the retailer and that is agreeable to the vendors. Both parties must be satisfied with the contract, which is written on a purchase order specifying the merchandise and the terms of the sale. Terms can include the dating of the bill, the potential for discounts such as quantity or cash discounts, and the last days to make payments. Merchandise can be dated with a variety of methods including ROG, X dating, and as of dating. These dates can provide the buyer with additional time to pay the bill and still get a cash discount. In addition to terms, the buyer will also negotiate for services that the vendor will offer, such as selling aids, training for sales associates, promotional materials, and special packaging. Loading and anticipation are other techniques that the vendor can use to assist the buyer with justification of the cost of the merchandise.

The buyer must work with the vendor to establish a purchase order that is agreeable to both the vendor and the retailer. Partnerships can be developed between vendors and retailers, which can be enhanced through electronic communication. Buyers can use computer systems for other aspects of their vendor relations including selection of vendors and evaluation of vendor performance.

Ultimately, buyers must judge the outcome of their purchase orders to determine how the merchandise sold, what contributions the merchandise made to net sales and markdowns, and how much of the merchandise was sold but returned. Merchandise is bought to satisfy the customer both in the style of the items and the price of the items, and the decision about who is the best vendor is more than where to get the lowest price merchandise.

Key Terms

Anticipation
Cancellation dates
Cancellations
Cash discounts
Causes of friction
Commissionaire
Contractors
Criteria list
Cumulative discounts
Dating
Discounts

Drop paper
Factoring
Loaded cost
Loading
Manufacturers
Net 1
Net period
Net price
On percent method
Premium
Prima facie duties

Proportionality
Purchase order
Quantity discounts
Series discounts
Services
Social justice
Sourcing
Terms
Trade discounts
Wholesalers

Discussion Questions

1. When would a source for merchandise be a contractor instead of a manufacturer?
2. What information should a buyer gather before writing a purchase order with a vendor for the first time?
3. What are the criteria that a buyer may use to determine whether the vendor is the right vendor?
4. Why would a buyer find that the merchandise from one vendor is made in several different countries?
5. Explain how an action can be legal, but not ethical.
6. A vendor offers a buyer a 35.00% discount on each item if the buyer will take on a new product in the line. Is this ethical? Is this legal?
7. To get a bigger promotional allowance, the buyer spends time talking with the vendor and takes the vendor to lunch. The buyer explains the marketing strategy for the store at lunch. Is this legal? Ethical?
8. The retail store receives a shipment of blouses. The retailer is short of cash and does not pay the bill on time. The vendor calls the buyer every day and demands payment, but the buyer will not answer the phone and lets the phone service take a message. Who is legal? Who is ethical?
9. Why is the lowest price merchandise not always the best buy for the retailer?
10. How can the buyer save money by negotiating and contracting with a vendor that has higher prices than other vendors do?
11. How can the buyer use the terms to improve cash flow for the retail business?
12. What information can be found on a purchase order?
13. Why would a buyer refuse to receive the merchandise from a vendor when it arrived at the store?
14. Why would a buyer continue to buy from a vendor who always has higher prices than any other vendor does?
15. What is the advantage of having a partnership arrangement with a vendor?

Exercises

Quantity Discounts

1. A manufacturer offers the following quantity discounts:

   100–150 shirts $4.40 each

   160–250 shirts $4.00 each

   250–300 shirts $3.80 each

   The retailer places an order for 10 dozen t-shirts. What is the total cost?

2. A shoe manufacturer provides a 10.00% discount on all orders of 100 to 200 pairs of shoes. A 15.00% discount is offered on all orders over 200. If 342 pairs of shoes are ordered this month at an initial cost of $8,980.00, what is the net cost?

3. An invoice for baby booties is $433.00. The buyer was expecting a cost of $450.00. What was the discount percentage?

Trade or Series Discounts

1. A belt manufacturer offers the buyer a line of belts for $12.50 each. The manufacturer normally offers a discount of 10.00% for end of the season. An additional 15.00% discount will be allowed if the retailer will take the order without pre-ticketing from the vendor. The buyer orders 182 belts and agrees to the above terms. What is the invoice?

2. The Tex_Rex Manufacturer always lists the retail price at market. Discounts are then used to determine the final invoice price to the retailer. Abby Retailing is offered trade discounts of 30.00% and 20.00%. The buyer orders merchandise that has a total list price of $1,987.00. What will be the final amount of the invoice?

3. A hosiery buyer places an order for 14 dozen pairs. Each pair lists for $22.00. The trade discounts for this buyer are 30.00%, 20.00%, 5.00%. What is the payment due on this order?

4. What is the "on percent" for the discount in number 3?

5. A buyer for a large store is offered a series discount of 25.00%, 15.00%, 10.00%. A buyer at a small store is offered a series discount of 32.00%, 16.00%, 4.00%. Which buyer got the bigger discount?

6. A manufacturer offered a discount of 30.00% and 20.00% to Buyer 1, who wanted a broken shipment and individual bagging of the items. A second order was placed by Buyer 2, that was bulk shipped. Buyer 2 received 30.00%, 15.00%, 5.00%. Both orders were for $1,500.00 worth of merchandise. Who paid more?

Dating

1. What is the last date to receive the cash discount (cash discount date) for the following invoices?

Invoice Date	Merch. Rec.	Terms	CD Date
May 2	May 10	5/10	S-may 2 / e-may 12
April 10	April 21	3/10 ROG, n/30	S-April 216 / e-may 1st
July 5	July 12	3/10	
June 10	June 16	8/10 EOM	S-June 30 / e-July 10
May 10	May 16	3/10 EOM	
June 27	July 27	3/10 EOM, n/60	S-July 31st / e-aug 10
October 2	November 7	4/10-30X	
January 4	March 5	2/10-60X	S-Jan 14 / e-march 15
May 30	June 15	3/10 EOM	
April 15	April 25	5/10 as of May 1	S-may 1st / e-may 11th
May 12	May 21	4/10 EOM, n/90	
December 2	December 21	6/10 n/30	S-Dec 2 / e-Dec 12
August 17	September 5	3/10 EOM, n/30	
February 27	March 10	4/10 EOM	S-march 31st / e-april 10
December 19	December 30	5/10 ROG	

2. Hats costing $3,838.00 with terms of 2/10-60X, n/90, were received by Hatto Co on August 30 with invoice dated August 26. The accounting office paid the bill on October 31. What was the dollar amount of the payment?

3. An order was placed for 20 skirts at $42.50 each. The invoice was dated May 15. The terms were 4/10, n/30. The merchandise arrived on May 20. What was the payment if it was paid on

   a. May 24   b. June 11   c. June 25

4. The invoice was dated March 26. The goods arrived April 15. What is the payment due if the merchandise invoice was $56,850.00 with terms of 3/10 EOM when the bill was paid on

   a. April 10   b. April 30   c. May 30

5. Merchandise was ordered on May 2. The order was filled and shipped on May 4. The invoice was dated upon shipping. The merchandise was received May 8. The invoice was $30,900.00, 3/10 ROG. What was the last day to receive the cash discount?

Anticipation

Interest rate is 7.50% annually.

1. The invoice was dated March 26. The goods arrived April 15. What is the payment due if the merchandise invoice was $56,850.00 with terms of 3/10 EOM? What is the payment if the bill was paid on

   a. April 10   b. April 30   c. May 30

2. On October 12 the order was filled, shipped, and invoice dated. The cost of the merchandise was $14,980.00 with terms of 2/10-40X, anticipation permitted. If the bill was paid on November 3, what was the amount of the payment?

3. The invoice was for $42,840.00 with terms of 6/10 EOM, anticipation permitted, dated September 28. How much is paid if the store pays the bill on October 12?

4. An invoice is dated May 16. The merchandise arrives on May 28. The bill is paid June 6. The terms are 3/10 ROG. If anticipation is permitted, what is the anticipation rate?

5. An invoice of $14,567.00 is dated November 12. The terms are 3/10-40X, anticipation is permitted, and discounts of 40.00% and 10.00% are allowed. If paid on December 1, how much should be paid?

Loading

1. A buyer placed an order for plaid shirts at $66,800.00. The vendor offered the buyer terms of 4/8, n/30 and a loading of 3.00%. The invoice was dated June 15, and the shirts arrived at the store on June 30. The buyer paid the bill on June 20. What was the amount of payment?

2. A buyer placed an order for plaid shirts at $66,800.00. The vendor offered the buyer terms of 8/10, n/30 and a loading of 5.00%. The invoice was dated June 1, and the shirts arrived at the store on June 30. The buyer paid the bill on June 10. What was the amount of payment?

3. A buyer placed an order for coats at $288,800.00. The vendor offered the buyer terms of 6/12 ROG, n/30 and a loading of 3.00%. The invoice was dated June 5, and the shirts arrived at the store on June 10. The buyer paid the bill on June 20. What was the amount of payment?

4. An invoice reads $4,500.00, 3/10, n/90. Load the price for 6/10.

Computer Exercises

Cash Discounts

• Create a spreadsheet with the following information:

Invoice	CD $	Net Inv	Terms	CD Date	Net Pymt Date	Inv Date	Rec'd
$12,245.00			2/10 EOM, n/30			2/1	2/22
$11,952.00			6/10 ROG, n/60			3/16	3/26
$11,250.00			7/10, n/30			2/10	2/22
*		$5,678.00	5/10 EOM, n/90			3/26	4/1
*		$890.00	3/10, n/60			4/6	4/27
*		$766.00	4/10 ROG, n/60			6/10	6/28
$10,000.00			2/10 EOM, n/30, as of 4/10			2/15	2/22

*Note: These calculations require the manipulation of the net invoice formula. The algebraic manipulation is as follows:

$$Inv - (Inv \times CD\%) = Net\ Inv$$
$$Inv \times (1 - (CD\%/100)) = Net\ Inv$$
$$Inv = Net\ Inv/(1 - (CD\%/100)) \quad \textit{(Hint: Use this format of the formula.)}$$

- Complete the missing information.
- Use formulas for calculating dollar amounts.
- Save and print spreadsheet (one page).

Anticipation

Interest rate is 6.85% annually.

- Copy the preceding spreadsheet for the following anticipation problem:
  Add four columns: # of anticipation days, anticipation %, total discount %, and total discount $.
- Insert a column for Payment Date following the Net Payment Date. Payment Dates for the invoices are 2/22, 3/30, 2/28, 4/20, 4/19, 6/30, 5/01, respectively.
- Calculate the new values. Use formulas when possible.
- Recalculate the net invoice values—use formulas.
- Save and print the spreadsheet (one page).

Purchase Order A

- Copy the spreadsheet into the computer. Use formulas to calculate the missing values. Print the spreadsheet.

			PURCHASE ORDER				NO:		
			VENDOR:				FREIGHT ALLOWANCE:		
			ADDRESS:				FOB PT:		
							SHIP VIA:		
							TERMS:		
	SKU #	UNITS	Cost EACH	Retail EACH		Retail TOTAL	MU %	MU $ EACH	
Blouses	234	326	$15.00	$35.00					
Skirt	235	400	$25.00					$35.00	
Sweater	236	126	$20.00				61.30%		
Coat	237	57	$96.00	$196.00				$100.00	
Belt	238	600	$6.20	$15.00			58.70%		
Scarves	239	300	$14.24				51.30%	$15.00	
Dresses	999	276	$5.75				52.60%		
Dresses	100			$17.50		$175.00	61.40%		
Dresses	120	231	$19.50				48.70%		
Dresses	130	368	$9.69	$19.50			50.30%		
Total	—		—	—				—	

Purchase Order B

Develop a spreadsheet for purchase orders by percentages from a Model Stock Plan using the store data.

1. Heading or Title area. Arrange the following information in readable format (use the form for Purchase Order A as a sample guide):

   a. Your Name and Date, Store Name
   b. Total Sales for Fall: $1,488,600.00
   c. Title for the Spreadsheet: Purchase Order Checksheet Spring Season
   d. Other information: Vendor, Dept, Order Date, Freight Allowance, Terms, and Ship via

2. Chart Area.

   a. Labels for columns: Classification, SKU #, Total Units, Cost Each, Cost Total, Retail Each, Retail Total, MU %, and MU $ Each.
   b. Labels for rows: Dresses, Suits, Sweaters, Blouses, Coordinated Groups, and Separates.
   c. Provide lines and spacing as needed.

3. Data for the chart.

   a. You may assign style numbers as you wish.
   b. From the model stock plan spreadsheet in Chapter 10, Computer Exercise 1, retrieve the numbers from Total Units, and Retail Each (or Unit $).
   c. Markup percentages will be dresses 55.00%, suits 45.00%, sweaters 56.00%, blouses 42.00%, and sportswear 44.50%.

4. Calculate the remaining cells. Use formulas to calculate Markup $ Each, Retail Each, and Cost Each for all classifications. Calculate Retail Total for each classification.

5. Total columns. Use the sum function to find the totals for Retail Total, Cost Total, and Total Units.

Vendor Analysis

General Directions

- With a computer spreadsheet, set up the following spreadsheet format. Create columns and rows as needed. Type in the given information. Calculate with formulas the missing information: Sell-Through %, Markdown %, and Return %.
- Use the data sort feature to rearrange the data for the following situations. Examine the database when correctly sorted to find the answers for each question.
- Continue to reuse the spreadsheet by copying for all four questions.
- Label a spreadsheet as appropriate for each question.
- Sort to arrange the data according to the needed field of inquiry.

  (Note: Subtotals will need to be calculated for some questions. Insert rows or columns when needed for subtotals.)

- Type the response to the question at the bottom of the sorted spreadsheet.
- Print the sorted spreadsheet with label and response, one printed page per question.

1. How many vendors are used by this buyer?
   (Sort by vendor, then do a manual count or use the count function.)

2. What is the value of the remaining inventory?
   (Use [Total Purchase $ − (NS $ + MD $ − Returns $)] for subtotal.)

3. Which vendor had the lowest return rate (highest return percentage)?
   (Sort by vendor, then subtotal to average return % per vendor.)

4. Which product classification had the most returns (highest return $)?
   (Sort by product, then subtotal to sum return $ per vendor.)

Option: To examine questions 3 and 4, bar charts can be created for the subtotal data.

Vendor	Product	Purchase $ at Retail	Net Sales $	Sell-Through % (ns/p)	Markdown $	Markdown % (md/ns)	Return $	Return % (r/p)
Starry	Dress	$25,000.00	$24,800.00		$200.00		$150.00	
BrownK	Dress	$48,800.00	$40,000.00		$2,800.00		$480.00	
Starry	Jacket	$54,000.00	$52,900.00		$1,000.00		$100.00	
Adam Rib	Dress	$4,500.00	$3,000.00		$1,000.00		$40.00	
Jack O	Jacket	$92,000.00	$50,000.00		$5,000.00		$1,500.00	
Jack O	Sweater	$25,000.00	$24,500.00		$0.00		$500.00	
Starry	Dress	$42,000.00	$40,000.00		$2,000.00		$0.00	
Starry	Dress	$15,000.00	$8,000.00		$3,000.00		$1,000.00	
Adam Rib	Slip	$6,800.00	$6,400.00		$0.00		$50.00	
Adam Rib	Shell	$3,300.00	$1,600.00		$1,000.00		$20.00	
Adam Rib	Shell	$1,200.00	$400.00		$800.00		$0.00	
Suiter	Suit	$29,950.00	$20,840.00		$2,000.00		$0.00	
Suiter	Jacket	$24,500.00	$18,400.00		$0.00		$0.00	
Suiter	Jacket	$12,890.00	$12,800.00		$0.00		$90.00	
Suiter	Slacks	$33,890.00	$30,000.00		$2,800.00		$80.00	
NitNow	Sweater	$22,200.00	$22,000.00		$0.00		$0.00	
NitNow	Vest	$18,450.00	$17,900.00		$0.00		$500.00	
B&B	Vest	$6,000.00	$2,000.00		$2,000.00		$1,000.00	
Apple P	Slip	$980.00	$400.00		$0.00		$0.00	
BrownK	Dress	$4,440.00	$1,000.00		$3,000.00		$0.00	
Jack O	Vest	$3,600.00	$3,400.00		$0.00		$100.00	
Emila	Sweater	$4,400.00	$2,800.00		$1,200.00		$0.00	
Emila	Vest	$1,110.00	$1,110.00		$0.00		$0.00	
ALP	Slacks	$25,680.00	$20,000.00		$5,000.00		$0.00	
NitNow	Leggings	$8,930.00	$8,800.00		$0.00		$70.00	
ALP	Slacks	$46,330.00	$25,000.00		$10,000.00		$6,000.00	

*I*nventory

*O*bjectives

After completing this chapter, the student will be able to

- determine levels of inventory
- identify methods of retail tracking for inventory
- describe methods of inventory valuation
- calculate book inventory
- determine stock shortages and overages
- discuss ways to maintain balance and freshness in inventory

Inventory can be classified into three categories: merchandise, equipment, and supplies. Merchandise refers to all of the goods that are within the retail system for a business and of which the retailer has taken possession. By this definition, inventory includes the merchandise that is in transit from the vendor (if owned by the retailer), merchandise in a retailer's warehouse or distribution center, the backup or **reserve stock** that is in backrooms at stores, the **forward stock** that is hidden on the sales floor and the merchandise that is on the floor. (Stock is generally considered to be items that are not on the floor, which is the greatest part of inventory.)

Location of Inventory

The merchandise that is on display or in other methods shown to the consumer is the merchandise that is actively used for selling. The rest of the inventory is waiting to be "moved forward" or moved to the selling floor for showing to the consumer. Most merchandise for which the retailer has taken possession is merchandise for which they have paid. This merchandise represents cash for the retailer only if the merchandise is sold. The value of the merchandise includes both the cost of the goods and the markup that is needed to cover reductions, expenses, and profit. Merchandise that is just sitting somewhere in a warehouse may serve the purpose of backup stock and help the retailer reduce stock outs, but this merchandise is not making money for the retailer. In fact, holding inventory could cost the retailer money if money must be borrowed from a bank or other lending organization in order for the retailer to have cash to pay bills. The buyer is usually responsible for the maintenance of merchandise inventory although much of this inventory may never be seen or touched by the buyer. Other retailers may have someone who controls inventory of all varieties within the business.

Movement of stock from a slow selling location to a fast selling location may result in additional savings and in increased actual sales because the merchandise will be where a customer is wanting the merchandise instead of in another store or in the warehouse. Many customers are not willing to ask about merchandise they do not see and are not willing to wait to have merchandise transferred to the store or to their home.

Inventory also includes equipment and supplies that are owned by the retailer in order to maintain business. Equipment can include cash registers, counters, racks, mannequins, tables, and other display fixtures. When the retailer has much display space and an active promotions division, much equipment may be housed for this function. Displays for clothing require a variety of **mannequins**, dress forms, or other body shapes to use for the best showing of the clothing. These body forms are also subject to changes in fashion. Forms are often very expensive and require careful handling to preserve their features and parts.

Inventory of equipment can be the responsibility of the buyer, the store manager, or a separate inventory manager. Other display fixtures can include hangers, props, racks, tables, and many household items. Storage of this inventory can become a serious issue within a retail business. Storage space near or at the retail selling floor may be better utilized by placing selling merchandise in the space that can be seen and touched by the consumer. Storage offsite can require the renting of a warehouse and may present problems with transportation. Storage space, like merchandise, requires an investment of cash.

Supplies are also counted in inventory. Supplies include everything that is consumable beyond the merchandise and when itemized can represent a large investment. Bags and boxes, which must exist in a variety of sizes to accommodate most purchases; tapes, ribbons, and cartridges to equip the cash registers and computers; and basic office supplies such as paper, order forms, credit forms, and pencils are all supplies.

Levels of Inventory

Each item in the inventory for a retail business should be evaluated for its contribution to the satisfaction of the consumer and the profitability of the retailer and for the costs that are required to purchase or retain the item in inventory. Levels of inventory are important considerations for retailers. Most apparel and home furnishing goods are **shopping goods**, meaning that consumers need to look at merchandise to make decisions about what to buy. Retailers need to have an assortment of merchandise in the store, in their catalogs, or on their Web sites to ensure that consumers have plenty of options to interest them, to make the store look exciting, and for comparisons to other merchandise.

Retailers also want inventory in reserve to prevent stock outs and to ensure a steady flow of new merchandise into the stores. Depending on vendors for this steady stream of merchandise can require high transportation charges, and efficient transportation may not be possible from some vendors. Retailers must take batch shipments from some vendors to obtain merchandise; and in addition, they must take large shipments to obtain quantity discounts. Both of these practices will result in high levels of inventory within the retail business. Many business pressures can force the level of inventory to be high within the retail business.

On the other hand, pressures exist, which force the retailer to keep lower levels of inventory. For example, the retailer must pay for merchandise when possession is taken. Everything that the retailer owns must be bought. Inventory represents money whether sitting in the warehouse or in the store. For example, a pen or pencil may be needed to complete a credit transaction. If a writing instrument is not found, then the consumer may become tired of waiting for someone to search for the pen and leave the store without completing the transaction. Computerized credit systems are available but, of course, require an investment in equipment and in the computer service to activate the system. Someone must determine what are the costs to the retailer and the benefits to the customer for the choice of credit system. Buying pens and keeping them stocked at the registers cost money. On the other hand, investing in new computer equipment, contracting for the service, and training personnel to use a new credit system also have costs. The costs are not all dollar investments. Costs for the computer system may also be measured in time savings, satisfaction or dissatisfaction of the consumer, and reduction of bad credit cards because the new system can more accurately verify the card.

In addition to the issue of the cost of inventory and the restriction of cash flow, the retailer must consider the issues of space and inventory freshness. Inventory takes up space. If this space could be used for selling instead of storing, then the volume of inventory may be high. The retailer may choose to keep most of the merchandise inventory forward from backroom space. This may make the merchandise accessible to the consumer, but may make the selling space look crowded and allow the merchandise to become damaged or soiled.

Lower levels of merchandise inventory can be kept fresher (as was discussed in Chapter 7). The same issue is true for display inventory and other equipment. A certain level of merchandise is needed to display the merchandise and to help the retailer function in selling, but too many display materials and too much equipment can crowd the selling space. The exact level is not a formula, but rather a merchandising decision. Levels of stock or merchandise relative to sales was discussed in Chapter 7, but exact levels of any type of inventory is more an estimate of retailer functionality than an exact measurement.

One benefit of catalog retailing or Web retailing is the reduced need for any type of inventory. Store equipment and promotional devices are not needed because there is no physical store. Instead, the retailer would need office space, computer equipment, and telephone equipment. Merchandise does not need to be kept in the same space as the sales offices. In fact, catalog and Web retailers keep warehouses of merchandise in regional locations to aid distribution, while other retailers contract with vendors to keep merchandise until it sells. Either way, the vendor is responsible for storing and shipping the inventory instead of the retailer.

Tracking Inventory

Regardless of the levels of inventory and where it is housed, the retailer must keep track of the inventory. Merchandise inventory represents the potential sales for the company. It must be safeguarded. At any moment, a retailer should know where every item on the inventory list is housed. The traditional way of tracking inventory was with a hand count and a paper and pencil list. As inventory entered the warehouse or backrooms, the items were checked against the purchase order and were added to the inventory list. The list could be kept in a bound ledger for safe tracking of all pages or in a loose-leaf notebook for easier organization.

Legally a bound book is more solid and consistent evidence because pages are numbered and cannot be replaced. The inventory is itemized on a line in the **ledger** upon entering the business. The listing stays in the book and is marked as sold, transferred, or returned. Any change is noted in the ledger and is described as being **on the books**. Opening cartons and checking packing slips against purchase orders is an important step in tracking inventory. This book method can be very dependable and accurate if the person who keeps the books is dependable and accurate. The skill and fortitude of the person who is responsible for the inventory determines the accuracy of this method.

The process of hand checking cartons of merchandise and hand entering the listing of the items into a ledger can be very time consuming and can be fraught with errors created by human mistakes. Computerized versions of inventory listings or **computer inventory systems** are now used by many retailers. The entries into the computer can be made by hand from the carton or packing slips and the purchase orders. The systems that use bar coding on cartons, packing slips, and individual items are even more efficient and are rarely subject to human error once the system is devised and tested. In addition, these computerized inventory systems are dependent on the use of bar coding at all stages of the buying and selling process from manufacturer to retailer to consumer purchase. If the computer is connected to the cash register and bar codes are used, the retail manager is able to calculate inventory levels at any point in time.

Although many retail and manufacturing companies are keeping some aspect, if not all, of their inventory records on a computer, the apparel retail business is far from being totally computerized. Standards for software, bar codes, code readers, computer operating systems, and other equipment in the system are not in place for all retailers and manufacturers. Many small retailers still keep hand inventory systems or keep their inventory on personal computers that are stand-alone units with no capacity to share the data. Some major retailers and manufacturers have their own proprietary systems. A partnership with one of these large companies would require the partner to purchase the software and hardware in order to be compatible.

A retailer or manufacturer again must make decisions about the trade-off costs with the investment in computer equipment. Some computer vendors say that the removal of human errors by converting to a computerized inventory system can result in large savings. Numbers vary but some estimates are that a computerized inventory system when connected to the cash registers can result in 7 percent to 10 percent savings because of the removal of human error in all the financial and inventory transactions. These savings (both direct and indirect) could provide the retailer with the money to pay for the system.

Computerized inventory systems have additional advantages. The inventory becomes a giant database. Information such as source of the item; date the item entered the store; wholesale and retail values of the item; features of the item including sizes, colors, and styles; and sales information including number, date, and sizes sold can be included in the database. A useful part of this computer inventory is the ability to examine any aspect of the database. Depending on how the database is developed, sales of specific items can be analyzed. For example, the buyer can determine how many items of a red color were sold among all the items that were sold. The buyer can also determine how many size 5 items and how many size 20 items were sold.

These **search and sort** features can be very important in inventory systems. This information can be very useful for a buyer when forecasting for new merchandise; for managers and buyers when they are evaluating vendor, store, or department performance; and for a buyer or manager for determining stock levels and in trying to balance stock through the company.

Regardless of the method used to track inventory, the retailer must be certain that the method provides an accurate, permanent record of the inventory that enters and leaves the business. Tracking inventory is relative to establishing a basis for sales, is critical to the valuation of the business, is necessary for insurance purposes, and is important in assessing taxes. Selling merchandise to consumers is the business. Equipment and supplies are vital to selling; therefore, all aspects of inventory are vital to financial health and, ultimately, the survival of the retailer.

Inventory Valuation

Inventory must not only be tracked, but must be valued. In other words, a value or a price must be noted for the inventory. A value is necessary for inventory for assigning a value to the business, determining replacement costs for insurance, and applying tax rates. When trying to sell a business, the retailer would want a high value for the inventory because that value will represent the dollars that the retailer will receive. A low value for inventory might be desired when the retailer has to pay taxes on inventory. In contrast, if the retailer would have to replace inventory because of a fire or theft, the value must be accurate to represent what costs would be incurred to repurchase the inventory. Equipment inventory will need to be valued and depreciated as the equipment is used and ages. Merchandise inventory should not stay in the business long enough to lose value, or it may never be sold. However, some unsold merchandise may remain and provide the retailer with additional valuation problems. For example, what is the value of a bathing suit when the weather outside the store is 45 degrees and a cold north wind is blowing in the month of November? The bathing suit might have had a retail price of $58.00 in July, but with every passing month, the potential to sell the suit lessens and the value should lessen.

With a retail business, the value of the inventory varies according to the stage in the buying–selling process. The merchandise is purchased from the vendors at a wholesale price, which retailers call the cost or the **cost price**. The cost price is obviously different from the **retail price**, which is the value at which the merchandise is priced when selling to the consumer. The relationship between these two prices is established in the Profit and Loss statement using markups.

Choosing the **merchandise valuation** method is dependent on the choice of the retailer but must be consistent across the system. The retailer usually decides to keep the value on the same base, either cost or retail, through the inventory system. The **value base** is the beginning value or standard used for affixing a price or value on the merchandise. The dollar values for inventory are either all in cost or in retail. Once the value of an individual item of merchandise is established, the value can be adjusted through markups and markdowns.

When the merchandise is purchased, the dollar amounts on the purchase order will be the selling price for the vendor and the cost price for the retailer. At that point, the retailer must determine how to value the merchandise. The wholesale or cost price of the merchandise may be the value base for the inventory. In the **cost price method**, the retailer uses the invoice costs or the cost prices that are assigned by the vendor as the value base for the inventory. This valuation is used for all inventory listings and would carry some notation about the initial markup and the final sales price of the item. When the merchandise is priced for the retail floor or for viewing by the consumer, the merchandise would have the markup added to the value and would show only the retail price to the consumer. Adjustments to the value of the item would be made as additions in varying amounts, but the actual cost value would be the same because that is the amount that was paid for the item. The retailer using this cost method views the merchandise according to the cost or what was paid to the vendor.

Net sales and other terms used in the inventory formulas for calculations would be adjusted to the cost price base. For example, if net sales were valued at $45,000.00 and the average markup for the period was 45.50%, the net sales figure in cost valuation would be $45,000.00 multiplied by the retail percentage of 100% minus the cost percentage of 45.50% (or the complement of the cost). In cost valuation, the net sales would be $24,525.00. This calculation is based on the basic relationship of cost, markup, and retail that was discussed as the foundation of merchandising finance in Chapter 2. The average markup percentage is used because it represents the markup for the period just as net sales represents sales for a period. With a computerized inventory system, each item sold could be associated with the exact markup for the item. However, tracking individual SKUs requires a rather advanced computer inventory system and much computer storage space and calculation ability.

Sample Problem: Cost Valuation

The buyer purchased merchandise for a six-month period that totaled $456,780.00. The net sales for that period were $987,670.00. The average markup was 45.34%. What was the value of the net sales based on cost price method?

Step 1. Set up the retail price spreadsheet and insert the known values.

(Hint: Remember that retail is assumed to be 100%.)

	$	%
Retail	$456,780.00	100%
− Cost		
= Markup		45.34%

Step 2. Determine the value of the cost percentage.

Cost % = Retail % − Markup %

Cost % = 100% − 45.34%

Cost % = 54.66%

Step 3. Determine the cost value of the retail.

Cost $ = Retail $ × Cost %

Cost $ = $456,780.00 × 54.66%

Cost $ = $249,675.95

The alternative method of valuation is the **retail price method**. This method is used most often by retailers, especially when markups, markdowns, and other percentages are based on retail sales. In the retail price method for inventory, the retailer uses the retail price or the selling price as the value base for the inventory. When the merchandise is originally ordered, the retailer would have a set initial markup for the items. This markup would establish the initial, or first, retail price and the value for the inventory. The item could receive price adjustments, which would normally be in the form of decreases or markdowns, but could be increases in price depending on the shelf life and demand for the item. In general, the retail price method of valuation adds value to the merchandise beyond its cost. This method views the merchandise as potential retail sales, and the retail value denotes the faith that the retailer has in the salability of the items. Some retailers think that this method inflates the value of the merchandise because no sales are assured in retail. After all, if the buyer or other forecasters predict inaccurately, then the value of the item may be much less than the initial retail price.

With the retail price method, all values must be based on retail value. For calculations of inventory, the cost of items must be converted to retail value. For example, if the invoice totals for a period sum to $350,980.00, the retail value of those invoices must be calculated to have the invoices' equivalent valuation to the sales (i.e., everything is based on retail values). The invoice values or the cost must be converted to retail. Initial markups are used for this calculation because that is the markup that is first placed on the merchandise. The calculation for this would again be based on the retail–cost–markup relationships. The invoice total of $350,980.00 would be divided by the complement of the markup. If the initial markup is 53.55%, the complement would be 100% minus 53.55%, or 46.45%. The value of the invoices at retail would be $755,608.18.

Sample Problem: Retail Valuation

The buyer purchased merchandise for a six-month period that totaled $258,880.00. The net sales for that period were $537,670.00. The initial markup was 53.41%. What was the value of the purchased merchandise based on retail price method?

Step 1. Set up the retail price spreadsheet and insert the known values.

(Hint: Remember that retail is assumed to be 100%.)

	$	%
Retail		100%
− Cost	$258,880.00	
= Markup		53.41%

Step 2. Determine the value of the cost percentage.

Cost % = Retail % − Markup %
Cost % = 100% − 53.41%
Cost % = 46.59%

Step 3. Determine the retail value of the cost.

Retail $ × Cost % = Cost $
Retail $ = Cost $/Cost %
Retail $ = $258,880.00/46.59%
Retail $ = $555,655.72

The retailer must also decide whether inventory is to be tracked individually or in conglomerate groupings. The retail price method and the cost price method can be used with either tracking method. The **individual SKU method** tracks each individual SKU with an entry value and accounts for every price change. The individual SKU method of inventory valuation and tracking is extremely accurate. It also requires a large database, room for storage, and a method of retrieval for the data. Quicker methods of valuation may be desired by a retailer who does not have a computer system and does not have automatic inputs from bar coding and cash registers. The **quick method** for valuation uses the total retail sales for a period as the value base of the inventory. Cost or value of the inventory is calculated based on a percentage of the retail sales. Average markup is used to determine the complement of the cost because individual markups would vary across items and over time. This method is extremely quick for an inventory base, but is not as accurate as tracking individual SKUs.

The other situation that must be addressed in inventory valuation is the changing value of inventory over time. The potential to sell an item of fashion apparel lessens as time passes. The theories of fashion innovation are based on the idea that a fashion forward item is more valuable at the beginning of the fashion curve than later in the fashion curve. If merchandise remains in inventory for some length of time, the value should be depreciated to allow for wear and fashion obsolescence. For example, a new sweater is received at the store during the first week of November. This style of sweater has been in all the fashion magazines, seen on models appearing on several talk shows, and is featured on a celebrity in a photo shoot. The sweater has a retail price of $450.00, and the retailer paid $200 at cost for the sweater. Fourteen of the sweaters are sold during the month of November. The retailer has 40 more sweaters in stock. During the month of December, the retailer sells five of these sweaters. On January 15, the retailer is reviewing sales and stock figures. None of the sweaters has sold in the past two weeks. The retailer speculates that the sweater is no longer a fashion forward item. No one wants the sweater when its retail price is $450.00. The retail price is lowered to $300. Ten more sweaters are sold at this reduced price. Not only the price, but also the value of the sweater has changed. The sweaters now appeal to the consumers at $300.00, but not at $450.00. The consumers with their spending patterns demonstrated to the retailer that they do not value the sweater as high as $450.00. If the retailer is using the retail price value base, the value of the sweater has changed for the consumer so it has changed for the retailer. If the retailer is using the cost price base, the value of the sweater is still the same.

Two methods of tracking valuation can be used: **first in, first out (FIFO)** and **last in, first out (LIFO)**. These methods for tracking value change use values for merchandise based on the age of the inventory and on estimations or accurate measures of price changes over time. With FIFO merchandise valuation, the merchandise that arrived first in the store is considered the first that is sold, even if similar merchandise is received after the first merchandise is received, but before all the first merchandise is sold. This method is important if there is a rapid rise in the cost of the merchandise. Varying the value of the inventory is very important in periods of rapid inflation. The first merchandise is the less-expensive merchandise and should be sold before the retail price needs to be adjusted upward to accommodate the rising cost. With FIFO, the merchandise is sold in the order that it is received. Although the actual dollars that are spent and taken in will be the same, the FIFO method provides the more consistent profit picture for the company.

Sample Problem: Inventory Valuation

A jacket department had a shipment of jackets at the first of the month. The jacket, style 345, costs $34.00 each. In the shipment that arrived at the end of the month, the same jacket had an invoice cost of $38.00. Twenty jackets arrived in the first shipment, and fifteen jackets arrived in the second shipment. Using FIFO and LIFO, what is the value of the merchandise?

FIFO

Step 1. Determine the value for one jacket.

(Hint: With FIFO, the value is based on the first cost.)

Cost $ per item is $34.00.

Step 2. Determine how many jackets were purchased.

> Total # of Jackets = # in Shipment 1 + # in Shipment 2
>
> Total # of Jackets = 20 + 15
>
> Total # of Jackets = 35

Step 3. Determine the value of the merchandise.

> Total Value $ = # of Jackets × Cost $ per Jacket
>
> Total Value $ = 35 × $34.00
>
> Total Value $ = $1,190.00

LIFO

Step 1. Determine the value for one jacket.

> *(Hint: With LIFO, the value is based on the last cost.)*
>
> Cost $ per item is $38.00.

Step 2. Determine how many jackets were purchased.

> Total # of Jackets = # in Shipment 1 + # in Shipment 2
>
> Total # of Jackets = 20 + 15
>
> Total # of Jackets = 35

Step 3. Determine the value of the merchandise.

> Total Value $ = # of Jackets × Cost $ per Jacket
>
> Total Value $ = 35 × $38.00
>
> Total Value $ = $1,330.00

With FIFO, the merchandise is valued at $1,190.00, and with LIFO, the merchandise has a value of $1,330.00. The FIFO underestimates the value of the merchandise, and LIFO overestimates the value.

During periods of inflation, the retailer must realize that rising retail prices may change the profit amounts for the company, but that replacement of stock will be more costly and the long-term rise in profits will not be sustained. To determine the method for valuation, a retailer should consider several factors. The business practices of the company may be established, and managers and buyers must simply enforce policies that are in place. The advice of the accountant or the philosophy of those persons who establish policy may be overruling factors. Companies that are publicly traded and are dependent on stockholders for their survival may have considerations for the profitability of the company. The tax bracket of the company may also be considered. A company in a higher tax bracket may wish to have lower valuations and show less profits than companies in lower tax brackets show. In addition, depreciation and some other aspects of inventory valuation are also governed by the Internal Revenue Service; therefore, some choices may be legislated and not selected.

Book and Physical Inventory

Regardless of the method, the procedure of keeping a running listing of inventory in ledgers is from where the term **book value** comes. The book value is the value of the inventory as kept in the handwritten ledgers or computer system. By noting any changes in value of the inventory in the books, a **perpetual inventory** can be kept. With a perpetual inventory, the exact value of the inventory can be determined at any point in time. The price of each individual item can be adjusted, and then sums can be totaled to produce an exact inventory value; however, a method of calculating inventory value can be used, especially for systems where hand entries and hand calculations are needed.

The first step is to calculate the value of the merchandise that is available for sale to the consumer. The value of the merchandise that is available to sell starts with the merchandise that was in the store or warehouse at the beginning of the period, often the beginning of the month (BOM). The BOM value is added to the value of the merchandise that has been purchased since the beginning of the month. Purchases include merchandise for which the retailer has paid, and any merchandise that was ordered and has been taken into physical possession by the retailer (even if not paid). If the retailer has taken possession of the merchandise, the retailer is responsible for this merchandise and will have to pay for it regardless of the sales. The **merchandise available** represents all the merchandise that is on hand, in the store, or warehouse, to sell to the consumer. This **merchandise available** formula is calculated as

$$\text{Merchandise Available \$} = \text{BOM \$} + \text{Purchase \$}$$

The second step is to determine the book value of the merchandise. The available merchandise during the period is reduced by the sales that were incurred and the markdowns and employee discounts that were allowed. Sales dollars represent merchandise that was sold to the consumer and has left the store. Employee discounts and markdowns represent devaluation or reduced value for the merchandise. The same merchandise may be physically on the rack, but when it is marked down, its value is reduced. This change must be noted in the value of the inventory. For both the merchandise available formula and the book value formula, the values of the components in the formula must be stated in either cost or retail dollars, but all components must be the same. The **book value** formula is

$$\text{Book \$} = \text{Merchandise Available \$} - \text{Net Sales \$} - (\text{MD \$} + \text{ED \$})$$

Sample Problem: Book Value

In October, the manager had a retail value of BOM at $45,000.00 for the Shirt Department. During October, the buyer has purchased $12,000.00 of merchandise, valued at retail. For October, the net sales during this period are $34,000.00, markdowns were $2,200.00, and employee discounts were $140.00. What is the book value of the merchandise at the end of October?

Step 1. Determine merchandise available.

Merchandise Available $ = BOM $ + Purchase $

Merchandise Available $ = $45,000.00 + $12,000.00

Merchandise Available $ = $ 57,000.00

Step 2. Determine the book value.

Book $ = Merchandise Available $ − Net Sales $ − (MD $ + ED $)

Book $ = $57,000.00 − $34,000.00 − ($2,200.00 + $140.00)

Book $ = $57,000.00 − $34,000.00 − $2,340.00

Book $ = $57,000.00 − $36,340.00

Book $ = $20,660.00

This book value can also be used to determine stock **shortages** or **overages**. When the book value is compared to the actual value that is generated by a physical count of the inventory, a determination can be made as to whether there is a shortage or overage in the inventory. At some point during the year, a **physical inventory** should be taken to determine whether any shortages or overages are occurring. Physical inventory comes from the counting of all the items on the floor in the stock rooms and in the warehouse or other storage places. Along with counting every item, the current retail price of the item is noted. Every inventory system can have errors; even computers make errors or at least the information entered into the computer can contain errors. In addition, shortages can occur from loss, theft, misplacement, and damage. The physical count of all merchandise in the possession of the retailer is the only way to verify the book value of the inventory. Even with computerized systems, physical counts of inventory are recommended for verification of inventory. Physical inventory is taken at least once and often twice a year. During the first part of February, the inventory levels within the business should be at the lowest levels. This time is after the large movement of merchandise before and after the holiday selling season. The lower level of inventory will reduce the time needed for physically counting all items in stock.

Once the physical count is taken and the total value of the physical count is determined, the value of physical count can be compared to the value of the book inventory. The difference is a shortage or overage. If book value is bigger than physical value, then a shortage has occurred. The finding indicates that the merchandise is registered in the books but does not physically exist. Theft or other errors can be the reason for the shortage. An overage is found when the book value is smaller than the physical inventory value. This occurs when the physical count and its valuation results in more merchandise value than what is shown on the books. Overages usually occur from a clerical or accounting error. Mistakes are made in data entry. Mistakes can also be made in calculating retail price from the cost price and in noting prices changes for markdowns and other price adjustments. The **shortage or overage dollars** formula for the calculation is

$$\text{Shortage \$ (or Overage \$)} = \text{Book \$} - \text{Physical Count \$}$$

Sample Problem: Inventory Shortage

For the month of October, the book value is calculated to be $20,660.00. The manager closes the store for October 31 and has all personnel assist with a physical count of the inventory in the store. The count includes all the merchandise in storage and on the floor. The manager has each person complete inventory charts that include SKU numbers, units, and retail prices. The physical count results in an inventory value of $19,840.00. Is there a shortage? If yes, what is the value?

Step 1. Compare the book value with the physical value.

The book value ($20,660.00) is larger
than the value from physical count ($19,840.00).
A shortage has occurred.

Step 2. Calculate the value of the shortage.

Shortage $ = Book $ − Physical Count $

Shortage $ = $20,660.00 − $19,840.00

Shortage $ = $820.00

Shortages are usually indicated as percentages so that they can be compared to other periods, departments, or stores. To find the percentage for a shortage value, the shortage is compared to net sales. This formula was mentioned when the Profit and Loss statement was reviewed. The use of net sales as a basis is important to keep a standard with other percentages in the company. The **shortage or overage percentage** formula is

$$\text{Shortage \%} = \text{Shortage \$}/\text{Net Sales \$} \times 100$$

Sample Problem: Shortage Percentage

In February, the manager had a retail value of BOM at $156,000.00 for the Shoe Department. During February, the buyer has purchased $322,000.00 of merchandise, valued at retail. For February, the net sales during this period are $434,000.00, markdowns were $16,800.00, and employee discounts were $660.00. A physical inventory was taken and valued at the end of February. The value of the physical inventory was $58,980.00. What was the shortage percentage?

Step 1. Determine merchandise available.

Merchandise Available \$ = BOM \$ + Purchase \$

Merchandise Available \$ = $156,000.00 + $322,000.00

Merchandise Available \$ = $478,000.00

Step 2. Determine the book value.

Book \$ = Merchandise Available \$ − Net Sales \$ − (MD \$ + ED \$)

Book \$ = $478,000.00 − $434,000.00 − ($16,800.00 + $660.00)

Book \$ = $478,000.00 − $434,000.00 − $17,460.00

Book \$ = $478,000.00 − $416,540.00

Book \$ = $61,460.00

Step 3. Determine the shortage value.

Shortage \$ = Book \$ − Physical Count \$

Shortage \$ = $61,460.00 − $58,980.00

Shortage \$ = $2,480.00

Step 4. Determine the shortage percentage.

Shortage \% = Shortage \$/Net Sales \$ × 100

Shortage \% = $2,480.00/$434,000.00 × 100

Shortage \% = 0.57%

Errors do occur; however, every effort should be made to keep an accurate inventory system. When the error is large, especially when calculated on a percentage base, the reason for the error should be investigated. A shortage percentage of 2–3% is often common in retail. Percentages that are higher than this amount could indicate a major problem for the retailer. A miscount in the physical inventory, a mathematical error, or a persistent theft problem could be occurring. The retailer should take corrective action to find the root cause and prevent a reoccurrence of the error. This action could include auditors who visit the store to verify the physical count, to review the backroom, stock room and dressing room procedures, and to critique theft-control processes. The shortage of inventory is a serious problem for a retailer. The inventory is a major portion of the value of the business. Lost inventory is a loss to the value of the business.

Balance and Freshness in Inventory

Inventory can become stale, worn, and a detriment to the business. Equipment that is old, dirty, or scarred will affect the consumer's image of the store. Dirty equipment implies to the consumer that the retailer is uninterested in the business. The consumer may also think that the retailer has dirty and uninteresting merchandise. The consumer will not find this type of business appealing and in the competitive environment will find many other places to spend money. Display materials including mannequins and props have a fashion look and should be replaced or repaired as needed. Old mannequins can imply to the consumer that the merchandise is also old. Almost everything in apparel and home furnishings retail must change to represent new fashions or new ideas to be of interest to the consumer. Even shelves that stock basic items such as pantyhose, socks, and t-shirts should be renewed periodically. They should be painted as color popularities change or be replaced as new construction materials and styles of shelving are available. The retailer needs a schedule to renew equipment for the business. With a schedule, the business will have a fresh and clean look on a frequent basis, and the retailer can plan for payments to afford the changes. The retailer will also need a replacement schedule for supplies. The sales associate who goes to the supply shelf and finds no credit forms will lose the retail sale if the consumer is made to wait or is told that the credit card cannot be processed because no forms are available. No consumer wants to wait while the sales associate replaces a cash register tape, especially if the associate must leave the sales station and hunt for a new tape. A replacement schedule will assist the retailer in keeping the necessary inventory on hand for store operations and will prevent stockpiling of supplies, which restricts cash flow and encourages theft.

The retailer will also need a system to maintain balance and freshness in merchandising inventory. The use of model stock plans, as discussed in Chapter 7, and the use of auto-replenishment systems can assist the retailer with inventory levels. **Model stock plans** provide an outline or guide sheet of the optimum stock types and levels that should be maintained. The plan is developed over time and with experience. The retailer can establish a plan and use it with periodic adjustments to check levels of inventory. The inventory for apparel and home furnishings is both fashion cyclic and seasonal. As fashion changes, the merchandise must change to reflect the fashion. As the seasons change, the merchandise changes in fiber content, fabric weight, and color. Traditionally, light colors and white are worn and used in the summer months, while darker colors are worn in winter months, although some fashion colors transcend these rules. Cotton tends to be a summer fiber and wool is a winter fiber. This rule also has exceptions; however, a change by seasons and over time must be observed in the retail business.

Inventory must change too. Inventory, even if it is not out of fashion, will get old, worn, and damaged with time. Inventory that remains on the shelves is not being sold and is not generating money to pay for its cost. For many reasons, the retailer must ensure that inventory is flowing through the business. An auto-replenishment system that has minimum inventory levels, which trigger reorders, can be used when the flow of merchandise is consistent and the style of the merchandise is basic.

Auto-replenishment systems are agreements between vendors and retailers for type, number, and replacement of merchandise. These systems are usually tied to a computerized cash register, using bar codes, and a computerized ordering system, using EDI. The introduction of merchandise into the inventory is registered with bar codes and code readers at the loading docks, warehouse, or backrooms where the merchandise enters the business. The sale of merchandise is registered at the cash register. When inventory levels are adjusted in the computer by the sale of an item, the inventory level is checked by the computer against a preset minimum level. If the sale results in the inventory level dropping below the expected preset minimum, a purchase order is generated and forwarded by the computer to the vendor. (The generated order may need to be approved by a buyer or manager, or in some systems, the order is sent without human approval based on the preset agreements of the contract between the vendor and retailer.) This automated system of inventory is an excellent way to keep inventory levels low and to keep merchandise constantly flowing in and out of the business. Effective operation of the system has several requirements. The retailer and the vendor must have a clear and detailed agreement about orders, shipping, and payment. Each member of the partnership must truly be a partner in the contract. The retailer must pay as contracted, on time, and in the full amount. The vendor must provide the products as specified, on time, and in the expected condition. The vendor must have adequate quality-control systems to ensure that the merchandise will meet the manufacturing specifications of the retailer and will not need additional inspection upon arrival at the retailer's business. Each partner must fulfill the contract or the system will not work. Other requirements for the system are compatible computer equipment and software. Both partners must have computer systems and software that can communicate, and the systems must have the ability to read or scan the bar codes that are used on packaging. Industry standards or proprietary agreements must be used so that the information that is shared is legible by both computer systems.

Although auto-replenishment systems are an excellent method for keeping inventory low but in supply, no system is completely automatic. The retailer should periodically review the system for needed changes. The system may not be adequate for handling emergency situations, such as a failure at the manufacturing plant or an extremely large purchase by a consumer at retail. In addition, even basic stock changes and shifts in economic conditions or other environmental factors may necessitate changes in stock levels or styles.

Model stock plans and auto-replenishment systems are excellent tools for assisting the retailer in the maintenance of the merchandise inventory. Yet, not all merchandise is appropriate for these systems. Much of the merchandise sold in apparel and home fashions retailing is not basic, replacement type stock. Often the retailer carries items that, once sold, will not be reordered. For this type of merchandise and for merchandise that has limited reorder possibilities, the retailer and the vendor may find that the effort to establish an auto-replenishment system is not cost effective. A variation or **modified auto-replenishment system** is being implemented by some retailers. The retailer contracts with the vendor for a dollar or unit amount of merchandise for a merchandising period (e.g., six month or four weeks). The retailer agrees to order a maximum number of units with the units being shipped in small lots throughout the period. The retailer reserves the right to change color, styles, and sizes during the period. This method provides the retailer with the opportunity to adjust the merchandise for changes that are forecast by consumer purchases. The method also assures the vendor of a steady order of merchandise and can allow the vendor to plan the manufacturing volume that is needed to meet the retailer's order. Neither of the partners will have to warehouse inventory for long periods of time, which will improve cash flow and merchandise assortment available for the consumer.

Summary

Inventory includes equipment, supplies, and merchandise. Equipment and supplies are necessary to keep the retail business operational and must be maintained and replaced. The retailer must determine where inventory is to be stored and what levels of inventory are to be kept. Too much inventory restricts cash flow because the inventory must be bought and, if unsold, replacement cash is not entering the business. Too much inventory also requires storage space and reduces the retailer's opportunity to provide new merchandise to the consumer. If inventory amounts are too low, sales associates will not have supplies for making sales transactions, employees in the promotions division will not be able to make new displays, and merchandise will not be available for shopping by the consumer and for sale. In addition to storage and levels, the retailer must identify the value of the inventory and track its location.

Equipment inventory may remain in place for long periods, but merchandise inventory should move quickly through the business resulting in many sales. Inventory may be valued at the cost price or the retail price, but the valuation method must be consistent. Individual SKUs may be tracked, or conglomerate methods may be used for quick valuation. Book inventory represents the count and value of the inventory as noted by the entry into ledgers or a computer database. Physical inventory results from an actual count of the inventory. The difference between the value of book and physical inventory can indicate whether shortages are occurring in the inventory. Inventory must be reviewed and maintained to keep the inventory in balance and fresh. Equipment-replenishment plans, model stock plans, and auto-replenishment systems can be used to encourage optimum levels of inventory and replacement of inventory.

Key Terms

Auto-replenishment system
Book value
Computer inventory systems
Cost price
Cost price method
First in, first out (FIFO)
Forward stock
Individual SKU method
Last in, last out (LIFO)

Ledger
Mannequins
Merchandise available
Merchandise valuation
Model stock plans
Modified auto-replenishment system
On the books
Overage
Perpetual inventory

Physical inventory
Quick method
Reserve stock
Retail price
Retail price method
Search and sort
Shopping goods
Shortage
Value base

Discussion Questions

1. Why is inventory an important issue for a retailer?
2. How is equipment inventory different from merchandise inventory?
3. Why should a retailer keep an inventory of supplies?
4. What is the best method for inventory valuation?
5. Why does the inventory need a consistent value base?
6. What changes to the inventory value may occur?
7. Why are employee discounts subtracted from merchandise available when calculating book inventory?
8. If the book value of inventory is smaller than the value from a physical count, what type of errors have occurred?
9. Why is shortage percentage a better tool for comparison than the shortage dollars?
10. Why would a retailer agree to an auto-replenishment system?

Exercises

Inventory Valuation

1. The invoice cost of a shipment of sweaters was $34,678.00. The initial markup is 52.34%. What is the retail value of the merchandise?

2. The initial markup on an invoice is 54.78%. The value of the invoice is $123,456.00. What is the retail value of the invoice?

3. Net sales were $345,890.00. The average markup is 42.35%. What is the cost value of the net sales?

4. The initial markup is 55.55%. The cost of the merchandise is $44,440.00. What is the retail value of this merchandise?

5. The net sales for a department were $1,456,000.00. The average markup is 38.90%. What is the cost value of the net sales?

6. The average markup for the Boy's Department in the past six months is 33.50%. The net sales for the same period in the department was $429,880.00. What is the cost value of the merchandise that was sold?

7. A shipment of Brand X shoes was received on May 15. The shipment contained 25 pairs of shoes with a cost of $24.67 per pair. On May 30, a second shipment of Brand X was received that had a cost of $31.87 per pair and contained 12 pairs of shoes. With FIFO valuation, what was the cost value of Brand X shoes?

8. A shipment of scarves was received on December 1. The shipment contained 25 scarves that cost $4.00 per scarf. On December 30, a second shipment of scarves was received that had a cost of $4.13 per scarf and contained 10 scarves. With LIFO valuation, what was the cost value of the scarves?

9. A shipment of picture frames was received on June 15. The shipment contained 15 frames with a cost of $4.50 per frame. On May 30, a second shipment of frames was received that had a cost of $3.00 per frame and contained 20 frames. With FIFO valuation, what was the cost value of the frames?

10. A shipment of tank tops was received on May 5. The shipment contained 250 tops with a cost of $6.40 per top. On May 30, a second shipment of tops was received that had a cost of $6.00 per top and contained 200 tops. With FIFO valuation, what was the cost value of the tops?

Book Inventory and Shortages

1. The book inventory for a store is $456,890.00. The value of the physical inventory is $567,800.00. What is the overage?

2. Net sales are $653,880.00, and shortage is $78,000.00. What is the overage percentage?

3. Net sales for the month were $235,000.00 for a department. No markdowns or employee discounts were given during the month. Available merchandise was $789,520.00 for the same month. The physical inventory was $543,000.00. Is there a shortage? Justify responses with a calculation.

4. A tie department has the following figures for the six-month period from Aug 1 to Jan 31:

BOM August	$14,400.00
Purchases at Cost	$10,800.00
Net Sales	$12,380.00
Markdowns	$1,884.00
Employee Discounts	$620.00
Initial Markup	56.00%

   a. What is the book inventory?
   b. The value of the physical inventory is $25,890.00. What is the shortage in dollars?
   c. What is the shortage percentage?
   d. If the value of the physical inventory was $16,500.00, what is the situation?

5. A gift department has the following numbers:

BOM August	$23,400.00
Purchases at Cost	$22,800.00
Net Sales	$56,680.00
Markdowns	$5,660.00
Employee Discounts	$1,520.00
Initial Markup	64.00%

   Determine the book inventory and the shortage percentage.

6. A shipment of tank tops was received on April 15. The shipment contained 240 tops with a cost of $6.40 per top. On April 25, a second shipment of tops was received that had a cost of $6.00 per top and contained 180 tops. Use FIFO valuation for the cost value of the tops. The net sales were $4,660.00, and the initial markup was 55.55%. No markdowns or employee discounts were taken in May. The BOM for May was $3,500.00. What was the book value of the inventory?

7. A shipment of shorts was received on June 15. The shipment contained 40 shorts with a cost of $16.00 per item. On June 28, a second shipment of shorts was received that had a cost of $17.00 per item and contained 80 shorts. Use LIFO valuation for the cost value of the shorts. The net sales were $5,576.00 and initial markup was 51.00%. Markdowns were 10.00% of net sales, and employee discounts were $500.00. The BOM for June was $4,234.00. What was the book value of the inventory?

Computer Exercises

Inventory Database

1. Create a spreadsheet with columns for merchandise information and rows of merchandise classifications. The columns should be as follows: item, stock number, vendor, date ordered, date received, number received, cost, markup, retail, and markdown.

2. Create a row for each classification of hosiery in the hosiery classification Exercise 5 in Chapter 10.

3. Use the brands as vendors, and create your own stock numbering system and dates. Determine a percentage for spread of units similar to the model stock plan and allocate units based on a total budget of 10,000 units. Create costs appropriate for the products. Markup will vary between 35.00% for the house brands and 66.00% for the designer brands.

4. Save and print the spreadsheet in several forms (using the data sort method to create the various forms): Form A—alphabetical by vendor, Form B—numerical by cost, and Form C—alphabetical by merchandise classification.

Book Inventory

The women's department had the following inventory for August:

Vendor	Product	Purchase $ at Retail	Net Sales $	Markdown $	Employee Discounts $
Starry	Dress	$25,000.00	$24,800.00	$200.00	$0.00
BrownK	Dress	$48,800.00	$40,000.00	$2,800.00	$0.00
Starry	Jacket	$54,000.00	$52,900.00	$1,000.00	$0.00
Adam Rib	Dress	$4,500.00	$3,000.00	$1,000.00	$10.00
Jack O	Jacket	$92,000.00	$50,000.00	$5,000.00	$10.00
Jack O	Sweater	$25,000.00	$24,500.00	$0.00	$0.00
Starry	Dress	$42,000.00	$40,000.00	$2,000.00	$0.00
Starry	Dress	$15,000.00	$8,000.00	$3,000.00	$0.00
Adam Rib	Slip	$6,800.00	$6,400.00	$0.00	$5.00
Adam Rib	Shell	$3,300.00	$1,600.00	$1,000.00	$0.00
Adam Rib	Shell	$1,200.00	$400.00	$800.00	$0.00
Suiter	Suit	$29,950.00	$20,840.00	$2,000.00	$0.00
Suiter	Jacket	$24,500.00	$18,400.00	$0.00	$0.00
Suiter	Jacket	$12,890.00	$12,800.00	$0.00	$0.00
Suiter	Slacks	$33,890.00	$30,000.00	$2,800.00	$12.00
NitNow	Sweater	$22,200.00	$22,000.00	$0.00	$0.00
NitNow	Vest	$18,450.00	$17,900.00	$0.00	$5.00
B&B	Vest	$6,000.00	$2,000.00	$2,000.00	$1.00
Apple P	Slip	$980.00	$400.00	$0.00	$0.00
BrownK	Dress	$4,440.00	$1,000.00	$3,000.00	$0.00
Jack O	Vest	$3,600.00	$3,400.00	$0.00	$2.00
Emila	Sweater	$4,400.00	$2,800.00	$1,200.00	$0.00
Emila	Vest	$1,110.00	$1,110.00	$0.00	$0.00
ALP	Slacks	$25,680.00	$20,000.00	$5,000.00	$0.00
NitNow	Leggings	$8,930.00	$8,800.00	$0.00	$7.00
ALP	Slacks	$46,330.00	$25,000.00	$10,000.00	$40.00
Totals					

The BOM for August was $147,654.00. At the end of August, a physical inventory was taken. The value of the physical inventory was $220,000.00.

1. What was the value of the available merchandise?

2. What is the value of the shortage?

3. What is the shortage percentage?

4. In the BOM, $12,300.00 worth of merchandise was inventory for Adam Rib merchandise. What is the book inventory for the Adam Rib merchandise?

5. If the BOM for dresses was $22,300.00, what is the book inventory for dresses?

Price Adjustments

Objectives

After completing this chapter, the student will be able to

- identify the effects of markdowns
- discuss the importance of planning markdowns
- explain the reasons for planned markdowns
- identify reasons for unplanned markdowns
- calculate markdowns
- calculate markdown cancellations
- discuss additional price adjustments

Pricing is a fundamental activity for any retailer. Merchandise must be priced for the initial retail sale. This price is generally determined as the merchandise is ordered and is considered in conjunction with retailer image, policies, and customers. The **initial retail price** or initial price is established by placing the initial markup on the cost of the merchandise. The selection of the initial price and any subsequent prices is critical to the sale of the item. Overpricing will prevent the sale, and underpricing will encourage sales, but will reduce profitability. For a variety of reasons, prices may need to be adjusted throughout the selling period. Price adjustments, particularly downward price adjustments, are needed in the merchandising of fashion products to generate excitement and customer attraction and to increase sales. Downward price adjustments can move stock. Putting merchandise "on sale" can create an event that will draw customers to the store and will entice customers to buy. The judicious use of downward price adjustments or **markdowns** can also help induce buying by customers. The overuse of markdowns or sales can actually retard buying because the consumer will wait for the sale in order to purchase items. If every item sells at the markdown price, the overall markup will be very different from the planned or initial markup.

Other markdowns may be taken to remove errors in pricing or buying. In addition, markdowns can be used to move merchandise that is past the peak of the fashion cycle. These markdowns may be planned or unplanned. Occasionally, upward price adjustments are needed. Markups or price changes to increase price may be needed when the incoming merchandise has increased in price and the increased costs must be passed to the consumer. The retailer can decide when to adjust the price. The price adjustment may occur immediately although old merchandise still exists or the new price may be placed in effect when the new merchandise is placed in front of the consumer. However, consumers do not like to see merchandise with retail price changes that show upward changes, and the reprinting of new retail price tags could add additional expenses that offset the retail price increase. In addition, the upward price adjustment is used for markdown cancellations—that is, when merchandise has been marked down and the retail price is readjusted to the original or a higher retail price. The initial decision for the retail price of an item should be made with great care and concern for the reaction of the consumer and for the effect on the business. The same care should be taken when adjusting the price of an item.

Effect of Markdowns

Markdowns result in a reduction of the initial markup. When examining the Profit and Loss statement, the interrelationship between all types of reductions including markdowns can be seen. Markdowns and other reductions reduce the value of gross sales. In turn, this reduction reduces the size of the maintained markup and, ultimately, can reduce the profit. Planning of markdowns is important because the initial markdown must be large enough to result in the desired maintained markup when markdowns are taken. This relationship can also be noted in the formula used to calculate the initial markup percentage. The formula for **initial markup percentage** is

$$\text{Initial Markup \%} = \text{Operating Expense \%} + \text{Transportation \%}$$
$$+ \text{Profit \%} + \text{Reductions \%} - \text{Cash Discount \%}$$

For example, an initial markup of 56.00% is established to cover a profit percentage of 5.50% and operating expenses and transportation of 41.00%. The reduction value would be planned as 9.50%. If the markdown portion of the reduction percentage were larger than planned, the size of the initial markup would not be large enough to provide for the extra markdowns without some adjustment in other aspects of the Profit and Loss relationship. The initial markdown can rarely be adjusted after it is applied because that is the retail price that is placed on the merchandise when the merchandise is shown to the consumers. An upward price change will usually result in a drop in sales, which will affect the overall dollars for sales and may necessitate additional markdowns to move the merchandise. The cost of transportation will also be a cost that is fixed early in the season because the transportation is priced when the merchandise is shipped from the vendor. The operating expenses contain many fixed expenses that are budgeted and encountered early in the period. The only item in the formula with some flexibility is profit. Most often, the profit will be reduced if markdowns are larger than anticipated. In fact, if the unplanned markdowns are too large, they may absorb all of the profit and result in a loss. Increasing sales through markdowns must be carefully balanced against the reduced profit margins that are created by the markdowns. Some markdowns increase sales so the increase in volume of business may offset the reduced margins, but a "point of no return" can be passed where the overall volume of sales will not cover the expenses.

Sample Problem: Effect of Markdown on Profitability

For a shipment of pillows, the buyer plans the initial markup to be 54.00%. The transportation for the pillows was 2.30%. Toward the end of the month, the operating expenses are estimated to be 34.52%. Loss or shrinkage is usually about 2.50% for the department. No employee discounts are taken during the month. Reductions were planned to be 12.50%, but the merchandise did not sell well and the buyer would like to take additional reductions. Cash discounts are not taken. What happens to profit if reductions become 20.00%?

(Hint: Reductions = Stock Shortage + Employee Discount + Markdowns.)

Step 1. Determine the value of the planned profit.

Initial Markup % = Operating Expense %
                    + Transportation % + Profit % + Reductions %

Profit % = Initial Markup % − (Operating Expense %
            + Transportation % + Reductions %)

Profit % = Initial Markup % − (Operating Expense %
            + Transportation % + SS % + ED % + MD %)

Profit % = 54.00% − (34.52% + 2.30% + 2.50% + 0% + 12.50%)

Profit % = 54.00% − 51.82%

Profit % = 2.18%

Step 2. Determine the actual profit.

Initial Markup % = Operating Expense %
                    + Transportation % + Profit % + Reductions %

Profit % = Initial Markup % − (Operating Expense %
            + Transportation % + Reductions %)

Profit % = Initial Markup % − (Operating Expense %
            + Transportation % + SS % + ED % + MD %)

Profit % = 54.00% − (34.52% + 2.30% + 2.50% + 0% + 20.00%)

Profit % = 54.00% − 59.32%

Profit % = (5.32%)

(Note: Everything remains fixed except for the markdowns because the transportation, operating expenses, and initial markup have all been applied or expended by the end of the month. The profit is the only remaining variable that can be adjusted. A loss occurs when the markdowns are 20.00%.)

Markdowns and other retail price adjustments are also related to the image of the business. The initial pricing of merchandise is established to promote the sale of the merchandise and to create an image of the merchandise and the business in the mind of the consumer. This image, once established, can be altered through retail price adjustments. Creating or changing an image of a business may take a long period or a major event, but the image can be altered. Often, the change from a good image to a bad image is more rapid. A business that has an image of quality merchandise for a fair price can damage this image with too many markdowns. The consumer will begin to associate discounts, lower quality merchandise, and an unstable business with repeated markdowns. Consumers may stop shopping during regular price periods and shop only during markdown events if the markdowns are consistent and often. Too many markdowns can also deplete stock below adequate shopping levels and create stock outs when the markdowns move the merchandise out of the store faster than the merchandise is replaced. With planned markdowns, stock must be available to satisfy the consumers' demands for the merchandise that was generated through promotions. For these reasons, the retailer must carefully plan markdowns and other retail price adjustments to be consistent with the business's image, to move merchandise in synchronization with replacement merchandise, and to create the appropriate level of change and excitement in the business.

Planned Markdowns

Planned markdowns are used to create excitement for consumers and to move stock. Part of planned markdowns are related to promotional planning and part of planned markdowns are related to adjustments to stock levels. In practice, these functions are closely related because when consumers come to the store and find the merchandise to be interesting and appealing, they will purchase the merchandise. This activity provides shopping excitement for customers and does move the stock. **Moving stock** indicates that the stock is sold and the consumer pays for the items and takes the merchandise out of the store. Movement of stock with markdowns must be planned carefully and based on promotions, time in the selling period, and merchandising judgment. Promotions include activities that promote merchandise but offer no price changes, and promotions that coincide with price reductions. When the retailer decides to mark down and reprice the merchandise, the activity is called **taking a markdown**. The repricing that is done can be done at the register, with a sign on the merchandise or the price tags, or with rewritten tickets. Rewriting a price tag is called **reticketing** regardless of whether the price adjustment is up or down.

Markdowns should move the merchandise, which means that it should increase the sale of the merchandise. If the markdown is selected with careful planning, the increase in volume of sales should offset the decrease in markup. For example, a retailer may have planned to sell 100 items at a price of $16.00 with a $10.00 markup. The total markup for the 100 items would be $1,000.00. The consumer might be willing to buy more items if the price was lower. The retailer might sell more items if the price were $14.00 and had only an $8.00 markup. To receive the expected $1,000.00 markup with an $8.00 individual markup the retailer would have to sell 125 items. Since no one can exactly predict the sale of an item, the retailer would have to use previous sales data, data for similar items, recent selling trends, and personal experience to determine whether a $2.00 difference in price would result in the sale of 25 more items.

A major aspect of planning markdowns is the **timing of the markdown**. Timing of markdowns is especially critical for fashion goods that age or become less fashionable and for seasonal goods that have a consumer use that is defined by the calendar. Markdowns that are taken too early will reduce the initial markup more than is necessary. Perhaps customers are still willing to pay the initial retail price for the items, but when marked down they are glad to get the reduced price. They will buy at the reduced price but would have been willing to buy at the initial price. In such a case, the retailer might have gotten a 55.50% initial markup on 10 more of the items, but reduced the items early in the selling period and only received a 45.50% markup. On the other hand, if markdowns are taken too late, lost sales will occur because customers will see the merchandise, think that the price is too high for the age of the fashion, and will not buy.

Unfortunately, the point in time to take a markdown is not clearly defined. Consumer demand can be tracked with POS data, but this information is past sales rather than forecast sales. If the POS data indicate that sales have been steadily rising for three weeks, the retailer cannot tell from these past sales what tomorrow's sales will be. One slow day of sales could be the beginning of the drop in demand or it could be related to weather or other functions. Three days later, the sales could jump upward again, or three days could pass with no increase in sales. By the time the retailer sees that drop in sales with POS data, the retailer has probably experienced lost sales and should have dropped the price. Experience, past sales history, awareness of fashion trends, and conversations with sales associates can assist the retailer in the decision of when to take a markdown.

Planning promotional events with price adjustments must also be carefully done. The overuse of promotional events with markdowns can create a discount image and can affect the shopping patterns of the consumers. Too many markdown events can diminish the impact of the individual events. Promotional markdowns are often done at the end of a season, during a slow selling period, or as an annual or semi-annual event. These events are designed to draw customers to the store and to increase sales volume. Sometimes additional merchandise is purchased for these events. In this way, the price reduction and planned promotional events are not used to reduce or clear stock but to increase sales volume.

The second consideration for price adjustments is the **size of the markdown** to be taken. This consideration is extremely important with markdowns. The downward price adjustment will reduce the margins for the Profit and Loss statement. The loss in margin must be anticipated. Some increase in volume in sales will create an overall increase in sales, but this increase may or may not offset the amount of the price reduction. The loss of income is one part of the consideration. The second aspect of consideration for how much reduction is the motivation that the reduction should incite within the consumer. Some markdown percentages are not large enough to assure the purchase of the item. Consumers expect large reductions, and small reductions may create interest, but not generate a sales transaction. Traditionally, a markdown of 10.00% to 20.00% would be considered a good reduction by consumers. More recently, a markdown of 25.00% or more is needed to really motivate consumers to purchase. The retailer must realize that markdowns will be compared by consumers to other retailers with markdowns, to discount stores with low prices on a regular basis, and to outlet stores that also have consistently low prices. In addition, discount retailers and outlet retailers have price reductions below their normally low prices. In a competitive market, the size of the markdown is carefully evaluated by many consumers.

The timing of the price reduction is also related to the size of the reduction. Consumers expect reductions to be large if the merchandise is highly seasonal. Early in the season, the merchandise is new and will have the maximum initial markup. In midseason, the retailer may have a small markdown on seasonal merchandise to generate some interest or to draw consumers into the store. By the end of the season, the retailer would take the largest markdowns to ensure that the merchandise is cleared from the store. For example, on the day after Christmas, consumers expect large reductions on Christmas cards. The cards cannot be sent immediately and would be held by the consumer after purchase for eleven months before sending. The consumer would expect a large price reduction, 50.00% or more, on merchandise that is past the user's definition of the season. This markdown should help the retailer to remove all of the past-seasonal merchandise from the stock. The retailer needs to regain the money that was used to pay for the merchandise and does not want to hold the merchandise for the next usable season. Holding the merchandise requires storage and often leads to loss or damage. These additional costs would erode any markup that the retailer might think could be retained.

Slowly adjusting the price downward can have a negative effect on sales. The consumer who shops often may notice that the price is dropped in stages over time. Some consumers will wait for the next or final price reduction. They may want the merchandise, but are willing to wait and are willing to suffer the loss of the merchandise if it sells before the price is adjusted to their preferred low level. In this manner, a progression of price reductions can retard sales instead of increasing sales; therefore, the retailer must carefully plan price adjustments. A system for the adjustments should be developed and implemented. Reactions by consumers to the price adjustments should be noted and the effect the price adjustments have on sales should be examined.

Seasonal goods traditionally get larger price reductions than do more staple goods that are sold throughout the year. Staple goods sometimes never receive a price reduction. If a retailer finds the retail price that steadily moves the staple merchandise, the retailer may never need to do a downward price adjustment. Not every item needs to have a price adjustment. For example, merchandise that is part of an auto-replenishment plan is controlled for stock levels. Reorders are only placed when sales reach a predetermined level. The method should not require price reductions to assist in moving stock to balance the levels. In contrast, some merchandise is purchased especially for the price reduction. The buyer may be offered merchandise at a reduced price if the size of the order is large or if the buyer is willing to take additional unplanned items. This price reduction could be used to increase the profit margin, or it could be passed on to the consumer.

Unplanned Markdowns

Unplanned markdowns should not occur, but may be necessary. A variety of reasons can instigate the need for an unplanned markdown: weather, pricing errors, buying errors, and selling errors. Actually, even unplanned markdowns can be tentatively planned. The buyer may know from experience that a certain volume of markdowns will occur that were not part of the promotional plan or merchandise clearance plans. The buyer may estimate a percentage of the markdowns to be allocated as needed. Although the unplanned markdown is anticipated, it is not to be encouraged and is usually called unplanned.

Weather can create an unplanned markdown. For example, the buyer plans for the fall merchandise and includes a large shipment of sweaters. If the weather is unusually warm in the fall, then no one wants to buy a sweater or even wants to try on a sweater, and the sweater merchandise sits untouched on the shelves for a month. The retailer needs to pay the vendor's bill for the sweaters, and money must be made available through the sale of merchandise. The retailer decides that the sweaters are better sold with a small margin so that the invoice cost can be regained rather than defaulting on the bill. Hoping that a lower price will make the sweaters sell in the warm weather, the retailer takes a downward price adjustment. The sweater stock also needs to be moved because the stock for the next month is arriving and no space exists in the warehouse, in the stock room, or on the selling floor to place the newest merchandise. If the retailer must rent additional storage space, additional costs will be incurred, and if the merchandise is forced into crowded stock rooms loss and damage will happen, which will also result in loss of sales.

Calculation of Markdowns

Markdowns are an adjustment to the retail price. The initial retail price is often called **Retail 1**. The retail price after the markdown is the **sales price** or **Retail 2**. The difference between the initial price and the sales price is the markdown; therefore, the **markdown dollars** formula is

$$\text{Markdown \$} = \text{Retail 1 \$} - \text{Retail 2 \$}$$

Sample Problem: Markdown Using Retail 2

A dress remained in stock at the end of the season. The initial retail price of the dress was $210.00. The retailer thinks that this last dress would sell if the retail price was $140.00. What was the markdown that the retailer would take on the dress?

Step 1. Insert the known information into the formula.

$$\text{Markdown \$} = \text{Retail 1 \$} - \text{Retail 2 \$}$$
$$\text{Markdown \$} = \$210.00 - \$140.00$$

Step 2. Calculate the markdown dollars.

$$\text{Markdown \$} = \$210.00 - \$140.00$$
$$\text{Markdown \$} = \$70.00$$

This formula can be rewritten to find the sales price of an item. If the markdown is known and the retail sales price is needed, the markdown dollar formula can be used. The **Retail 2 dollars** or markdown dollar formula would be rewritten as

$$\text{Retail 2 \$} = \text{Retail 1 \$} - \text{Markdown \$}$$

Sample Problem: Finding Retail 2

A dress remained in stock at the end of the season. The initial retail price of the dress was $210.00. The retailer took an $80.00 markdown on the dress. What was the sales price of the dress?

Step 1. Insert the known information into the formula.

$$\text{Retail 2 \$} = \text{Retail 1 \$} - \text{Markdown \$}$$
$$\text{Retail 2 \$} = \$210.00 - \$80.00$$

Step 2. Calculate Retail 2.

$$\text{Retail 2 \$} = \$210.00 - \$80.00$$
$$\text{Retail 2 \$} = \$130.00$$

When the markdown is for a department, a store, or an entire classification of merchandise, the initial retail price would be the net sales value for the store unit. So, in the markdown formula, retail dollars might represent the retail price of one unit or the net sales for multiple units within a merchandise classification or a department, or for the entire store. To calculate the markdown percentage, Retail 1, or the initial retail amount, is used as the retail base. The **markdown percentage** formula is

$$\text{Markdown \%} = (\text{Markdown \$}/\text{Retail 1 \$}) \times 100$$

Sample Problem: Markdown Percentage

The buyer needs to determine the markdown percentage that was taken for a pair of shoes. The shoes were initially priced at $195.00. The shoes were marked down $56.00. What was the markdown percentage?

Step 1. Insert the known information into the formula.

Markdown % = Markdown \$/Retail 1 \$ × 100

Markdown % = \$56.00/\$195.00 × 100

Step 2. Calculate the markdown percentage.

Markdown % = \$56.00/\$195.00 × 100

Markdown % = 28.72%

This formula can be rewritten to resemble the retail dollar and percentage formulas used when determining markups and costs. The **markdown dollars and percentage** formula is

Markdown \$ = Retail \$ × Markdown %

Sample Problem: Markdown Dollars from Percentage

The department manager needs to determine the markdown dollars that can be taken for a pair of shoes. The shoes were initially priced at $195.00. The buyer sent information to the stores that said that all shoes should have a 30.00% markdown for the weekend sale. What are the markdown dollars for the shoes?

Step 1. Insert the known information into the formula.

Markdown \$ = Retail 1 \$ × Markdown %

Markdown \$ = \$195.00 × 30.00%

Step 2. Calculate the markdown dollars.

Markdown \$ = \$195.00 × 30.00%

Markdown \$ = \$58.50

When the markdown percentage and the sale price are known, the calculation can be made to determine the initial retail price. The markdown percentage is based on the initial retail price, and the dollar value of the markdown was subtracted from the initial retail price to find the sale price. Determining the initial retail price involves the use of a combination of formulas: Both the markdown dollars formula and the markdown percentage formula are needed. The two formulas are

Markdown \$ = Retail 1 \$ − Retail 2 \$

Markdown \$ = Retail 1 \$ × Markdown %

These formulas must be rewritten and combined to find the value of Retail 1 when Retail 2 and the markdown percentage are known.

Retail 1 \$ = Retail 2 \$ + (Retail 1 \$ × Markdown %)

This formula can be algebraically manipulated to become

$$\text{Retail 1 \$} - \text{Retail 1 \$} \times \text{Markdown \%} = \text{Retail 2 \$}$$

This formula in turn is refined algebraically to become

$$\text{Retail 1 \$} \times ([100\% - \text{Markdown \%}]/100) = \text{Retail 2 \$}$$

and ultimately

$$\text{Retail 1 \$} = \text{Retail 2 \$}/([100\% - \text{Markdown \%}]/100)$$

In the formula, the term, *100% − Markdown %*, is the **complement** of the markdown percentage. A complement of a percentage term is the percentage term subtracted from 100%. With the retail price relationship between cost and markup, the complement of cost percentage is the markup percentage. For the relationship among the percentages of Retail 1, markdown, and Retail 2, the complement of the Retail 2 percentage is the markdown percentage. The calculation to find Retail 1 dollars becomes the division of Retail 2 dollars by the complement of the markdown percentage.

Sample Problem: Finding Retail 1 Dollars from Retail 2 Dollars and Markdown Percentage

---

The retailer had a pair of trousers with a reticketed price of $25.00. The markdown was 30%. The original tag is no longer available, and the retailer wondered what the initial retail price was.

Step 1. Insert known information.

$$\text{Retail 1 \$} = \text{Retail 2 \$}/[(100\% - \text{Markdown \%})/100]$$
$$\text{Retail 1 \$} = \$25.00/(1 - 0.30)$$

Step 2. Calculate the value of retail 1 dollars.

$$\text{Retail 1 \$} = \$25.00/(1 - 0.30)$$
$$\text{Retail 1 \$} = \$25.00/0.70$$
$$\text{Retail 1 \$} = \$35.71$$

For most retailers, more than one item is marked down at a time. For example, markdowns could be made for all items of a brand, all items of a color, or every item within a merchandise category. For most retail businesses, merchandise is bought in multiple units. When markdowns are taken, they are taken for all of the units that remain. During a promotional event, every item in the store might receive a markdown. If multiple numbers of items receive the markdown, the markdown would be a **gross markdown**. To calculate the gross markdown or the markdown across multiple units, the unit markdown is multiplied by the number of units that is marked down. To calculate the markdown for one set of items, the **gross markdown dollars** formula is

$$\text{Gross Markdown \$} = \text{\# Units} \times \text{MD \$}$$

If multiple units are marked down and some of the units have different markdowns, then the markdowns would be calculated and summed together to get the gross markdown for a department, for a merchandise category, or for an entire store. The resulting formula for multiple units and multiple merchandise classifications is

$$\text{Gross Markdown \$} = (\text{\# Units} \times \text{MD \$})$$
$$+ (\text{\# Units} \times \text{MD \$}) + (\text{\# Units} \times \text{MD \$}) + \ldots$$

Sample Problem: Gross Markdown

The department manager was asked to calculate the markdowns for the Blouse Department. Twenty lacy blouses were to receive a $15.00 markdown. A $5.00 markdown was taken for the 30 tank tops. The satin shells got a $4.00 markdown; 25 shells were on the rack. Thirty blouses with a Peter Pan collar were marked down $12.00. What was the gross markdown for the department?

Step 1. Insert the known information into the formula.

$$\text{Gross Markdown } \$ = \text{\# Units} \times \text{MD } \$ + \text{\# Units} \times \text{MD } \$$$
$$+ \text{\# Units} \times \text{MD } \$ + \text{\# Units} \times \text{MD } \$$$
$$\text{Gross Markdown } \$ = (20 \times \$15.00) + (30 \times \$5.00)$$
$$+ (25 \times \$4.00) + (30 \times \$12.00)$$

Step 2. Calculate the gross markdown.

$$\text{Gross Markdown } \$ = \$300.00 + \$150.00 + \$100.00 + \$360.00$$
$$\text{Gross Markdown } \$ = \$910.00$$

Markdown Cancellation

A promotional event can involve the use of markdowns. In fact, entire classifications of merchandise or all the merchandise in a department or store can be marked down from the initial retail price. The gross markdown can be calculated for all of the merchandise. The retailer will then know how many markdown dollars are taken for the merchandise. In most businesses, the merchandise would be reticketed showing the sales price or Retail 2 price of the merchandise. As each item is sold, the markdown and the sales price would be noted by the accounting system used by the retailer, whether a computerized cash register or a pen-and-paper system is used. At the end of the promotional event, some merchandise may remain in the store. The retailer will determine whether the merchandise should be returned to its initial retail price or to another, third retail price or the **Retail 3** price. When the merchandise is reticketed to the Retail 3 price, the markdown is cancelled. If the Retail 3 price is the same as the Retail 1 or initial price, the markdown cancellation is the same amount as the markdown. If Retail 1 and Retail 3 are different amounts, then the markdown and the markdown cancellation are not equal in amount. **Markdown cancellation** is the amount of markdown that is not used or the difference between the sales price and the Retail 3 price. Calculation of the markdown cancellation is important because that amount of money can be returned to the total markdown amount that was planned for the business and used for other merchandise later. The **markdown cancellation dollars** can be determined with the formula

$$\text{Markdown Cancellation } \$ = \text{\# of Units for Markdown Cancellation}$$
$$\times (\text{Retail 3 } \$ - \text{Retail 2 } \$)$$

The numbers of items that have the cancellation are the difference between the numbers of items for which the markdown was taken minus the number of marked down items that were sold. The markdown cancellation is then rewritten as

$$\text{Markdown Cancellation } \$ = (\text{\# Markdown} - \text{\# Sold})$$
$$\times (\text{Retail 3 } \$ - \text{Retail 2 } \$)$$

If multiple classifications of merchandise are involved in the markdown cancellation, the individual sets of markdown cancellations can be summed together.

$$\begin{aligned}\text{Markdown Cancellation \$} = &\ (\#\,\text{Markdown} - \#\,\text{Sold}) \\ &\times (\text{Retail 3 \$} - \text{Retail 2 \$}) \\ &+ (\#\,\text{Markdown} - \#\,\text{Sold}) \\ &\times (\text{Retail 3 \$} - \text{Retail 2 \$}) \\ &+ (\#\,\text{Markdown} - \#\,\text{Sold}) \\ &\times (\text{Retail 3 \$} - \text{Retail 2 \$}) + \ldots\end{aligned}$$

Sample Problem: Markdown Cancellation

After a big promotional shirt event, the retailer had several categories of shirts left for sale and wanted to have the shirts returned to a higher price. The white shirts had a sales price of $35.00. The Retail 3 price was planned to be $38.00. The initial retail price was $40.00 per white shirt. One hundred white shirts were marked down, and 30 shirts sold. The plaid shirts were initially $45.00 and 80 of them were marked down. A $10.00 markdown was taken on these shirts for a sale price of $35.00, and 60 shirts sold at the sale price. The plaid shirts were then returned to $42.00 for the Retail 3 price. What was the markdown cancellation for the shirts?

Step 1. Insert the known information.

$$\begin{aligned}\text{MD Cancellation \$} = &\ (\#\,\text{MD} - \#\,\text{Sold}) \times (\text{Retail 3 \$} - \text{Retail 2 \$}) \\ &+ (\#\,\text{MD} - \#\,\text{Sold}) \times (\text{Retail 3 \$} - \text{Retail 2 \$})\end{aligned}$$

$$\begin{aligned}\text{MD Cancellation \$} = &\ (100 - 30) \times (\$38.00 - \$35.00) \\ &+ (80 - 60) \times (\$42.00 - \$35.00)\end{aligned}$$

Step 2. Calculate the markdown cancellation dollars.

$$\begin{aligned}\text{MD Cancellation \$} = &\ (100 - 30) \times (\$38.00 - \$35.00) \\ &+ (80 - 60) \times (\$42.00 - \$35.00)\end{aligned}$$

$$\text{MD Cancellation \$} = (70 \times \$3.00) + (20 \times \$7.00)$$
$$\text{MD Cancellation \$} = \$210.00 + \$140.00$$
$$\text{MD Cancellation \$} = \$350.00$$

After taking the markdown cancellations, the retailer will need to know exactly how much of the markdown money was used for the promotional event. The markdowns that were taken were the gross markdowns. However, if markdown cancellations are used, then the gross markdowns are reduced. The amount of markdown that was actually used is the **net markdown**. This information could be obtained from the database created from the cash register if the retailer had a very sophisticated computer system in which the computer would have identified each item that was sold and the markdown that was taken with each sale. The sum of the individual markdown for each item sold is the **net markdown dollars**. A quick way to determine the net markdown is to calculate the difference between the gross markdown dollars and the markdown cancellation dollars.

$$\text{Net Markdown \$} = \text{Gross Markdown \$} - \text{Markdown Cancellation \$}$$

Sample Problem: Net Markdown

The retailer had a promotional sale on shower curtains. A markdown was taken for 200 items. The markdown was $5.00, and the sale price was $25.00. After the sale, 98 curtains remained. The Retail 3 price was $27.00. What was the net markdown for the shower curtains?

Step 1. Find the gross markdown dollars.

$$\text{Gross Markdown \$} = \#\,MD \times MD\,\$$$
$$\text{Gross Markdown \$} = 200 \times \$5.00$$
$$\text{Gross Markdown \$} = \$1,000.00$$

Step 2. Find the markdown cancellation dollars.

$$\text{Markdown Cancellation \$} = (\#\,MD - \#\,Sold) \times (\text{Retail 3 \$} - \text{Retail 2 \$})$$
$$\text{Markdown Cancellation \$} = (200 - 98) \times (\$27.00 - \$25.00)$$
$$\text{Markdown Cancellation \$} = 102 \times \$2.00$$
$$\text{Markdown Cancellation \$} = \$204.00$$

Step 3. Find the net markdown dollars.

$$\text{Net Markdown \$} = \text{Gross MD \$} - \text{MD Cancellation \$}$$
$$\text{Net Markdown \$} = \$1,000.00 - \$204.00$$
$$\text{Net Markdown \$} = \$796.00$$

The net markdown can also be measured in percentages. A percentage is useful for comparison purposes when the volume of sales is not equal. The net markdown dollars represent the dollars for a promotional event or other price reduction, which would occur for a specific period. The net markdown dollars would then be compared to net sales for the period when determining the net markdown percentage. This calculation is similar to the reduction and net sales relationships that are found in the Profit and Loss statements as discussed in Chapters 3 and 4. To determine the **net markdown percentage**, use the formula

$$\text{Net Markdown \%} = \text{Net Markdown \$/Net Sales \$}$$

Sample Problem: Net Markdown Percentage

The net markdowns that were taken for May were $25,000.00. The net sales during that period were $81,000.00. What was the net markdown percentage?

Step 1. Enter the known values into the formula.

$$\text{Net Markdown \%} = \text{Net MD \$/Net Sales \$}$$
$$\text{Net Markdown \%} = \$25,000.00/\$81,000.00$$

Step 2. Calculate the value of the net markdown percentage.

$$\text{Net Markdown \%} = \$25,000.00/\$81,000.00 \times 100$$
$$\text{Net Markdown \%} = 30.86\%$$

The information about net markdowns and markdown cancellations will assist the retailer in determining how many markdown dollars remain for later use. These dollars are part of the initial markup. Additional or unplanned markdowns should not be taken because of the impact on profit. Markdown cancellation is important because these dollars can be used for other merchandise.

Additional Price Adjustments

Markdowns and markdown cancellations are not the only price adjustments that are taken by a retailer. The initial markup from cost to initial retail price is the initial price adjustment. The retail price may receive a markdown more than once while the merchandise is on the floor, until the merchandise finally sells. A **clearance policy** may be followed by the retailer to continue to markdown merchandise until it is all sold or cleared from the business. The size and timing of markdowns are part of a clearance policy.

Upward price adjustments are needed in times of inflation and if an overly high demand for the product manifests itself. In times of inflation, the cost of the product may rise rapidly. The retailer may decide to adjust the prices of the same items in the stock when new merchandise is added to the stock. This action would be compatible with the inventory valuation strategy of LIFO. The retailer may also decide that with inflation, the operating costs of the business are rising and that some upward adjustments of price are necessary to cover the operating costs. However, upward adjustment of retail prices for merchandise may be met with resistance by consumers. This resistance can be shown by refusing to buy merchandise or by buying less merchandise. The retailer will have to determine if the loss of sales or the reduced volume is offset by the increased markup.

For example, the retailer normally sells, in one week, 50 pairs of socks with a retail price of $6.30. The total retail sale on socks each week is $315.00. The retailer is notified of a price increase from the vendor and adjusts the retail price of the socks to $7.20 per pair. The retailer finds that the following week the sale of socks has dropped to 40 pairs in a week. The total retail sales for socks is now $288.00. Although the retailer raised the price of the socks, the overall sales are lower because fewer consumers were willing to buy the socks at the new, higher price. Through trial-and-error pricing, the retailer might be able to discover the exact price increase that would not affect the volume of sales; however, with several upward and downward price adjustments most consumers will become confused or irritated and will probably stop buying any socks from that retailer.

Another upward price adjustment that a retailer might make is an adjustment because of the unusually high demand for a product. Fashion products may be in high demand at the beginning of the selling season. A product that is a fad item can have a very rapid rise in demand. The retailer may find that the sale of the item is so rapid that the item continuously has stock outs. If the replenishment of the item cannot keep up with the sales of the item, the retailer may wish to increase the retail price. The increase in the price might deter a few shoppers, but for a product that has extremely strong demand, the increase in price may add a higher than expected markup for the retailer. If demand slows slightly with the rise in price, which might also benefit the retailer by making the sale of the item more steady and prevent disappointing stock outs, the retailer's image may be improved by keeping some of the popular items in stock even if the price is high.

*S*ummary

Price adjustments create upward and downward changes in retail prices. The initial markup is added to the cost of an item for the first price adjustment. The initial markup creates the initial retail price. Downward price adjustments are markdowns and are used to create interest and excitement among consumers and to move merchandise. Markdowns are used for both promotional events and to clear end-of-season merchandise. In addition, merchandise that is old, worn, or damaged should receive markdowns and be moved from the store. The first markdowns are reductions to the initial markup and should be planned carefully to control their impact on profitability. Although occasionally necessary because of pricing, selling, or buying errors, unplanned markdowns can negatively affect profitability. However, a buyer who has previous season or previous year data should be able to estimate an amount for unplanned markdowns and actually plan for the occasional unexpected markdown.

Markdowns are adjustments to the retail price starting from the initial retail price. The second price or Retail 2 may again be adjusted if the merchandise does not sell at the lower price. Markdown percentages are based on the initial retail price. If markdowns are taken because of a promotional event, the markdown may be cancelled on any unsold merchandise at the end of the promotional period. Markdown cancellations return money to the available markdown dollars and are the difference between the Retail 2 price and the Retail 3 price. Markups may be necessary to change the price upward for periods of inflation and for products with unusually high demand. The right retail price is expected to appeal to the consumer, to create the appropriate image in the consumer's mind, to bring the necessary margins to the retailer, and to move the merchandise out of the store through sales.

Key Terms

Clearance policy
Complement
Gross markdown
Initial retail price
Markdown cancellation
Markdowns

Moving stock
Net markdown
Planned markdowns
Retail 1
Retail 2
Retail 3

Reticketing
Sales price
Size of the markdown
Taking a markdown
Timing of the markdown
Unplanned markdown

Discussion Questions

1. Why are price adjustments needed?
2. Why are price adjustments important?
3. When are price adjustments a detriment to the margin?
4. Why should markdowns be planned?
5. How much of a markdown is necessary for the merchandise to be cleared by sales from the retail business?

6. How do markdowns on seasonal merchandise differ from those for staple merchandise?
7. When is the best time to take a markdown?
8. What is the optimum size for a markdown?
9. What is the relationship between markdown dollars and Retail 2 dollars?
10. When would an upward adjustment of retail price be appropriate?

Exercises

Basic Markdown

1. A line of dresses was received at the beginning of the month with transportation for the shipment of dresses equalling 1.40%. The operating expenses are planned to be 34.45%, profit was planned to be 6.56%, and planned markdowns were 12.45%. No employee discounts were taken in the month, and the average loss for the business was 3.44%. What was the planned initial markup? If the markdowns are actually 15.00%, what happens to the profit?

2. A shipment of shoes was received, and the transportation for the shipment was 0.54% of the net sales. The operating expenses are planned to be 35.00%, profit was planned to be 7.00%, and planned markdowns were 14.50%. The average loss for the business was 3.44%, and the employee discounts were planned at 1.50%. What was the planned initial markup? If the markdowns are actually 20.00%, what happens to the profit?

3. A line of lamps was received at the beginning of May. Transportation for the shipment was 0.70% of net sales. The operating expenses were planned to be 36.45%, profit was planned to be 5.66%, and planned markdowns were 24.50%. No employee discounts were taken in the month, and the average loss for the business was 4.40%. What was the planned initial markup? If the markdowns were actually 30.00%, what happens to the profit?

4. A dress had a retail price of $125.00. The sales price was $115.00. What were the markdown dollars?

5. The markdown for a pair of shoes was $45.00. The initial retail price was $200.00. What was the sales price?

6. The sales price of a shirt was $24.00. The markdown was $4.00. What was the initial retail price?

7. All scarves in the department had a markdown of 30.00%. The average scarf had a retail price of $14.00. What was the sales price of a scarf?

8. Tank tops were selling for $15.00. The department had 60 tops left in July, and a markdown of $5.00 was taken. What was the gross markdown for the total lot of tops?

9. Bermuda shorts were selling for $35.00. The department had 30 shorts left in August and a markdown of $15.00 was taken. What was the markdown percentage for the total lot of shorts?

10. At the end of the month, the Career Wear Department had a rack of suits that had retail prices of $140.00. The rack held 34 suits. A 25.00% markdown was taken. What was the gross markdown for the suits?

11. The markdown for a knit shirt was $10.00. If the sale price of the shirt was $56.00, what was the markdown percent?

12. The Coat Department had a promotional sale for the month of February. At the end of the month, they had a big closeout sale. They marked each coat down 28.00%. The sales price of one coat was $128.00. What was the initial price?

13. Plastic tote bags had a markdown of $5.00, and 20 bags were marked down. Brown leather bags had a markdown of $12.00 with 30 bags marked down. Twenty-three black leather bags had a markdown of $14.00 each. Brown cloth bags had a markdown of $8.00, and 10 bags were marked down. Gray cloth bags had a markdown of $9.00, with 14 bags marked down. What was the gross markdown?

14. White shirts had a markdown of $15.00, and 30 shirts were marked down. Plaid shirts were marked down $12.00, and 40 shirts received the markdown. Twenty-five solid-colored shirts were marked down $11.00 each. What was the gross markdown?

15. Gross sales were $432,680.00, and markdowns were $3,980.00. What were the net sales for the period? What was the markdown percent? (Use information from the Profit and Loss statement.)

Markdown Cancellations

1. A buyer purchased 30 jackets for a department and priced them at $45.00 each. For a Winter Weekend Sale, the 30 jackets were reduced to $30.00. During the sale, 18 jackets were sold. The following Monday, the remaining jackets were returned to their original price. These jackets sold by the end of the week at $45.00 each. Find the total markdown dollars, the markdown cancellation dollars, the net markdown dollars, the net sales, and the net markdown percent.

2. Twenty-four blazers were reduced from $80.00 to $60.00 for a Midnight Madness Sale. The next day, the 10 blazers that were not sold were re-marked to the original price. These blazers sold at $80.00 each. Find the total markdown dollars, the markdown cancellation dollars, the net markdown dollars, the net sales, and the net markdown percent.

3. The sportswear buyer reduced 20 belts from $20.00 to $12.00 for a Four-Day sale. Ten of the belts were sold during the sale. After the sale, the remaining belts were re-marked at $15.00 each and sold shortly thereafter. Find the total markdown dollars, the markdown cancellation dollars, the net markdown dollars, the net sales, and the net markdown percent.

4. The manager for a sportswear department received five dozen belts. Each belt cost $12.00. The initial markup for the order was 53.00%, and the expected maintained markup was 45.00%.
   a. What was the total gross sale potential?

   Twenty belts sold during the first two weeks. In the middle of the month, the manager has a planned Founders Day Sale. The remaining belts are given a 20.00% markdown.
   b. What are the gross markdown dollars?

   Thirty belts were sold during the big sale. The following Monday morning all of the remaining belts were marked back up to the original retail price.
   c. What are the markdown cancellation dollars?
   d. At this point, what are the net markdown dollars?

   The manager had a total markdown budget of $300.00.
   e. How many markdown dollars remain?

   Five more belts were sold in the three weeks after the sale. By the middle of the next month, the last belts were marked down 45.00% and finally sold.
   f. What are the final net markdown dollars?
   g. What are the net sales?
   h. What is the net markdown percent?

Overall Markdown Percentage

A buyer received 40 jackets retailing for $45.00 each. For a weekend sale, the 40 jackets were reduced to $30.00. During the sale, 28 jackets were sold. After the sale was over, the remaining 12 jackets were returned to their original price and were sold.
   Find the following:

   Total Markdown Dollars
   Markdown Cancellation Dollars
   Net Markdown Dollars
   Net Sales Dollars
   Net Markdown Percent

Computer Exercises

1. Create the following spreadsheet:

SKU #	Descr.	Units	Retail 1	Retail 2	MD	MD/Unit	MD %
582	Tie	2	2.50	1.80			
595	Scarf	15		6.78			33.00%
431	Hair Bow	22	5.50				25.00%
406	Hat	5	12.00				16.00%
479	Tam	3	1.98	1.20			
596	Scarf	10	3.20	2.99			
429	Hair Bow	3		4.50	7.00		
332	Belt	33		6.78			12.00%
330	Belt	12			5.00		11.00%
564	Tie	25	8.00		1.23		
432	Hat	5	6.40		1.50		
320	Belt	21		4.65	2.01		
					Total		

Use formulas to determine the missing values.

Calculate the total for total markdown dollars.

Use the sort feature to put in numerical order. (Find this option in the Data Menu.)

Save and print the spreadsheet.

2. Create the following spreadsheet for a Housewares Department:

SKU #	Descr.	Units	Retail 1	Retail 2	MD	MD/Unit	MD %
682	Toaster	2	25.00	18.00			
795	Dish Pan	15		6.78			33.00%
431	Brush	22	0.55				25.00%
206	Mat	5	1.20				16.00%
479	Brush	3	1.98	1.20			
596	Tray	10	3.20	2.99			
429	Brush	3		0.45	.07		
832	Coffee Maker	33		16.78			12.00%
830	Coffee Maker	12			5.00		11.00%
664	Toaster	25	18.00		12.30		
232	Mat	5	0.64		0.15		
820	Coffee Maker	21		26.50	12.01		
					Total		

Use formulas to determine the missing values.

Calculate the total for total markdown dollars.

Use the sort feature to put in numerical order. (Find this option in the Data Menu.)

Save and print the spreadsheet.

*M*arketing Communications

*O*bjectives

After completing this chapter, the student will be able to

- explain the role of the promotional division in marketing communications
- identify aspects of the promotional mix
- discuss the importance of teamwork across functional divisions
- discuss the importance of a promotional plan
- develop a promotional budget
- identify the importance of sales training
- explain the interaction between the promotional division and sell-through

The sale of the merchandise is the third and final step in the process of retail merchandising. **Selling** includes preparation of the merchandise for selling, activities the sales associates perform when interacting with the customer, and postsale activities. Much preparation work must be completed before the actual selling can occur. When the merchandise is delivered to the warehouse and then to the store, the merchandise must be handled or prepared for the floor. **Handling** of the merchandise includes inventory procedures, ticketing and reticketing procedures, and actual presentation of the merchandise. To be **floor ready**, the merchandise is entered into the inventory system, checked to assure the retailer that it meets the buying specifications for the merchandise, and ticketed (or the pretickets are checked for accuracy). The merchandise may then be steamed or pressed and hung or folded on shelves for display on the floor. The sales associates are responsible for interaction with the consumer on the sales floor, over the telephone, and through the Web. Therefore, the sales associates should be able to show, promote, and discuss the merchandise with the consumer. Finally, selling should conclude with a sales transaction. The **sales transaction** is the movement of the merchandise from the retail business to the consumer with an exchange of money. This transaction is often called the **sale**, not to be confused with downward price adjustments, which are also called a sale. In the sale, a consumer receives merchandise to take home and the sales associate receives payment for the merchandise. After the sale, the sales assistant may take returned merchandise when the consumer is dissatisfied and/or may do follow-up telephone calls or cards to remind the consumer of an advertised sale or about new merchandise. A successful sales transaction should result in the consumer's satisfied use of the merchandise and a return to the business for more new merchandise. Selling of merchandise is vital to the double goal of satisfaction for the consumer and profit for the retailer.

Overview

Retail sales usually do not just happen or occur without a concerted effort on behalf of the retail organization. As illustrated in Chapter 1, retail businesses may have many functional activities, one of which is the **promotions function**. The activities performed within this function are often called **marketing communications** because the promotions function or division, through a variety of methods, communicates or markets both directly and indirectly to the consumer. The endeavors of this function may be the first and only introduction that the consumer has to the retailer and to the merchandise. The promotions function may be represented within a retail organization by a separate division, department, or a few individuals. Through various advertising media, special events and promotions, publicity, sales personnel, or the presentation of actual merchandise, the promotions function markets not only the retailer's merchandise offerings, but also the retail image. The objectives of the promotional function are to sell ideas, products, or services; to create traffic into the retail store, catalog, or Web site in order to increase sales; to inform the customer of the merchandise selection and to facilitate the customer's shopping of that merchandise; to peak interest of the customer; and ultimately, to motivate the customer to buy. Overall, marketing communications in retail should help cut the cost of doing business and assure the achievement of sales goals and final profit.

Marketing communications are based on the marketing concept, which dictates that the retailer must identify a target consumer, establish an image that appeals to this consumer, and create promotional activities to attract this consumer. When, in the planning process, the target consumer is pinpointed, information about the consumers' values, attitudes, and behavior patterns will be identified. The promotions staff must translate this data into information about the buying habits and spending patterns of the consumer. Unique marketing techniques, including differential or segmented marketing and product positioning, can be used to reach, attract, and entice the targeted consumer. (For more information on target customers, see Chapter 5.)

Promotional Activities

The promotional function of the retail organization is responsible for planning and creating the visual merchandise presentation, planning and executing special events, and planning and implementing advertising media: all activities aimed at attracting the consumer and promoting the sale. Depending on the organization's size and store type, other duties for the promotional function include arranging for publicity events, handling fashion coordination or personal shopping and wardrobing services, and coordinating the training of sales personnel. To achieve a clear and concise image to the target consumer, the promotional staff will work with a **promotional mix**, which involves all potential promotional activities and the implementation level for each of these activities.

Not all activities are invoked at the same level at all times. The promotions manager, owner, or other responsible staff person can manipulate the mix of merchandise presentation, special events, and advertising to develop the most effective combination of promotional activities to promote a particular product or event for the business. For example, an item may look unappealing when sitting on a shelf or when hanging from a rack, but when in use the purpose and style of the product becomes immediately obvious. For this product, special events with demonstrations or modeling and visual media with live action are better to promote the item than print media or in-store displays. In addition, the types and number of promotional activities in the mix depend on the target consumer, the product classification, and the price point of the goods, plus the retail image including store type, history, and services available.

Among the three major activities of the promotions function, the merchandise presentation or visual merchandising activity is the one that is often most noticeable to the consumer and most closely associated with traditional retail stores. **Merchandise presentation** is the storing, housing, arranging, or positioning of merchandise within the shopping area of the store. For retailers who have catalog divisions and Web sites, merchandise presentation is also an important aspect. How the merchandise is shown, arranged, and otherwise presented to the consumer can affect the consumer's initial reaction to the merchandise and control the potential for a sale. This visual presentation of merchandise to the consumer also includes promoting and displaying items to achieve a total presentation of the goods.

Display is one aspect of this visual merchandising process and is the artistic or aesthetic presentation of the selected merchandise. Displays, as other merchandising activities and techniques, are used to create excitement about the retailer's merchandise assortments and to encourage consumers to buy. In **lifestyle merchandising**, displays are used to show the consumer how to use the selected goods in conjunction with other merchandise. This type of merchandise presentation that combines classifications of merchandise can stimulate add-on sales, multiple sales, and impulse buying.

The visual merchandising staff, including display personnel, often determines the merchandise presentation within the store and the display schedule for the store. In a chain store or other store type with multiple doors, the promotional staff or visual merchandisers may be located in the corporate office. Information about displays and merchandise presentation is sent to each local store in the form of a **plan-o-gram**. The plan-o-gram includes a sketch of the layout of the store drawn to scale with fixturing, merchandise, and display locations designated for each area of the store. Also, sales associates and other retail personnel, when directed by promotions staff, may be asked to participate in merchandise presentation. In very small retail stores, sales associates, the buyer, or owner may create displays based on seasonality and available merchandise without other direction.

Planning and executing merchandise presentation and displays is an important preparation for selling. Merchandise presentation includes merchandise placement, arrangement, and display of product classifications. Store layout and placement of fixtures are critical to developing targeted or differentiated merchandise presentations. The store layout, as well as a catalog layout or the mapping of a Web site, should make shopping easy, convenient, and enjoyable by providing adequate aisles, space or passage among the merchandise, and appropriate signage. Customers should be able to find the items of interest, not get lost or bored, and be alerted to other new and interesting merchandise. The layout should encourage the customers to browse through the merchandise and to purchase items throughout the entire store, catalog, or Web site. Consumers insist upon a fun, exciting, and entertaining shopping experience in an environment that showcases the product selections. In contrast, visual merchandisers must maximize floor space to build optimum sales, to create the desired turnover, and to maintain needed margins for the bottom line of profit. They must provide care and attention to both consumer and merchandise. The retailer must find a balance, which is difficult to achieve, between consumer satisfaction and retailer profit.

Several methods are used by visual merchandisers for organizing the merchandise presentation. With each method, amount of space (including walls, floors, and ceilings in a brick-and-mortar store), types and sizes of fixtures (or formats for holding the merchandise), displays, and merchandise categories must be considered. Effective merchandise presentation activities can actually foster the sale of slow-moving merchandise that was previously hidden in an out of the way location. One method that has been used traditionally and successfully in the brick-and-mortar store is the **3 × 3 method**, which segments the store or a department within the store into three sections. These sections are the **aisle**, **core**, and **top wall/vista wall**.

The most visible area of a traditional store or department is the aisle area, which consists of the front of the store or the perimeter or borders of a department. The front third of the store or department is the prime selling area. The same is true of the front pages of a catalog or the home page of a Web site. Some retailers indicate that as much as 50 percent of their sales occur, or are realized, in this area. Because of this potential to impact sales, this aisle should strongly support the image of the business and be designed to immediately attract customers. The aisle area usually houses the most recent merchandise arrivals, the current seasonal merchandise with trend emphasis, or major classifications of a retailer's important merchandise assortments. The core is the center of the store or department. It houses volume, promotional, and sales merchandise. The largest number of product classifications is usually found in the core area. Finally, the top walls/vista walls encompass the side and back walls of the store or department and are often perceived as the second most important space in the store. These walls must be interesting enough to entice the customer to wander throughout the store and to continue all the way to the back wall area. Color and lighting as well as a variety of fixtures and merchandise placement are very important when developing merchandise presentations for this area.

Retailers find that sales dollars per square foot also vary across the store parallel to the 3 × 3 grid. As more merchandise sells in the aisle area and the turnover is greater, this area can produce higher dollars per square foot than the other areas in the store. (The figures discussed in Chapter 6 indicate averages for sales per square foot within a store.) The retailer can use this knowledge of sales figures to an advantage and place items in the aisle area that have higher margins and really boost the impact of these items on the overall P & L for that store. In addition, the retailer can place items with generally lower sales per square foot or smaller margins in this area to make adjustments for their low contributions to the margins. At the same time, the retailer must be very cautious to remember that visual presentation not only affects sales, turnover, and margins, but also affects image including the attractiveness of and customer attraction to the store, the department, and the merchandise.

Other merchandise presentation methods include shop concepts or outposts, presentation by classification, presentation by size coordination, presentation by color, and presentation by vendor. The **shop concept** generates an area of emphasis and focus within a store or department. The same concept can also be simulated in catalog and Web site presentation. The shop concept is used to create a **concept shop** or area that typically holds all of the merchandise for one vendor, manufacturer, or designer brand, and the shop concept is also applied to floor space that is restricted to one classification of merchandise such as swimwear, cell phones, or oriental carpets. This method allows the retailer to highlight a popular brand or product and to gain additional sales through the dispersing of that brand popularity across a cluster of items. For example, Designer A has become very popular with a type of t-shirt carrying the designer's logo. The designer now has jeans and caps with the logo. If these items are grouped together, the retailer will have the potential to sell all three items to a customer instead of the one t-shirt, thereby increasing sales. Such a concept shop can be created by the promotions department or designed and implemented by the brand owner (i.e., vendor).

Other methods may be used together or in conjunction with the 3 × 3 method. Combining items and techniques across merchandise classifications can promote additional sales. Increase in sales of an **outpost** is a benefit of placing merchandise from one area into another area of the store or catalog. The benefit is maximized because the placement is unexpected by the consumer. A change in expected locations may attract extra attention to the item and increase sales.

Regardless of the method, the retailer desires a presentation that calls attention to all merchandise categories offered by the retailer. The negative possibility of an outpost or a concept shop is that the customer may search in a more traditional location within the store for items. Unless the retailer carries additional inventory to duplicate placement, the customer will not find the item and, when an item is not found, a sale is lost. A logical visual merchandise presentation encourages the customer to enter the store or turn the page of the catalog, stop, look, touch or read, and try the product offerings.

All major sections of the store, catalog, or Web site should be visited by the customer. Therefore, an effective merchandise presentation is planned to promote silent selling as well as to assist the buyer and other retail personnel to maintain acceptable stock–sales ratios of merchandise. Determining who will be credited with the sale of items that are placed as an outpost or in a concept shop can complicate accounting procedures. Nevertheless, creative methods of merchandise presentation must ultimately be balanced against customer expectations and potential for sales at different locations.

The promotional staff may also be in charge of determining the promotional or **special events** that occur for the retailer. In this second area of promotions, special events include, but are not limited to, fashion shows, trunk shows, benefits, and in-store demonstrations. Actually, any activity other than the advertising, personal selling, and publicity that are intended to, stimulate customer purchases could be considered a promotional event. Advertising and merchandise presentations should be prepared in conjunction with any special event to ensure that customers are aware of the event and that the merchandise associated with the event is in place in the store. Special events may highlight merchandise and product events; call attention to institutional events, such as sponsorships; or feature sales and/or price promotions. These events should help to increase sales volume, introduce new merchandise, and create excitement and interest to encourage the customer to buy, especially during periods that are normally slow for sales or during off-season periods. The events should entice customers into buying additional items and items that are not usually on their shopping lists. Keeping sales at a more even pace and preventing dips in sales are important objectives of special events. A steady level of sales and an increase in sales during slow sales periods can assist the retailer in maintaining a desirable cash flow and in keeping personnel busy and productive throughout the year.

Although special events require operational expenses for production, these opportunities often focus on nonmarkdown-related promotions or merchandise that is at the initial price stage and are helpful in maintaining the planned margins. Budgeting for special events is important in keeping control on the operational costs associated with these events. Advanced planning is very important with special events. When celebrities or other sponsorships are involved, planning for an event may require commitments at least one year in advance. The budgeting for these events is often difficult because of this long lead time, and budgeting is further complicated because the payments for expenses may be needed in periods preceding and succeeding the actual event. Financial return on an event can be determined with adequate record keeping, especially when specific classifications of merchandise are involved. Same period sales for overall and for specific merchandise can be compared to observe changes in sales.

A third area covered by the function of promotions is **advertising**. In a large organization, especially in a multi-door business, this activity would be housed in an advertising department, perhaps in the corporate office or in a major market city. Advertising includes a broad assortment of potential media including the following: newspaper, radio, television, bill inserts, direct mail, magazines, circulars, billboards, and Web sites, both owned by the retailer and cooperative with other vendors.

The combination and levels of usage of the media are called the **media mix** for the retailer. Using a variety of media is usually more effective, interesting, and attention getting in reaching the desired target consumer and in building and maintaining a repeat customer following. When planning advertising, the retailer will want to allocate advertising funds in the most effective manner to assist the merchandising staff in reaching sales goals and the operations function in maintaining profit margins. The retailer will use previous research about the targeted consumer to determine what is the most effective media mix for the business, the product, and the season.

At times, vendors or manufacturers will collaborate on the payment for the advertisement of selected merchandise. This type of advertising is called **cooperative advertising** and is advantageous when it benefits both the vendor and the retailer; however, vendor stipulations about the ad content or layout may prohibit the retailer from utilizing the monies that can be derived from this opportunity. Advertising personnel, other promotional personnel, and merchandisers and buyers must work as a team to select and produce advertising that is targeted to the consumer and contains a message about wanted merchandise to produce maximum sales.

Although advertising is very costly, it is an essential expense for the retailer because it is one of the main methods of communicating with the consumer outside of the physical store. Few retailers can survive on word of mouth or drive-by attention to sustain business. For this reason, advertising becomes a necessary operating expense for the retailer, and the advertising budget is included in the total promotional budget that is a line item in the expenses on the P & L statement.

A fourth activity that is often assigned to the promotions function, but involves many people assigned to another function is the **training of sales associates**. Sales associates are often viewed as the bottom of the organizational chart (see Chapter 1 for details of organizational charts), but these workers are actually a most important link to the consumer. When planning a customer-centered strategy, the customer is the center of all activities and the sales associate is the immediate contact with the customer and the linkage between the customer and all other business activities. Training of sales associates is vital for maximum sales with maximum markups and must be planned and budgeted. Although the return on the investment of training is often difficult to measure, the importance of training should not be diminished. Customers need assistance with sales, customers do not like to wait when a purchase is imminent, and merchandise needs to be tended. In general, sales increase when sales associates have improved training, and shrinkage decreases when sales associates are active, alert, and productive on the sales floor. When observing the P & L statement, increases in sales and decreases in reductions can be seen as offsets to the expenses of training. All of these reasons provide valid incentives for training sales associates appropriately.

Teamwork in Retail Functions

The promotions function may be performed by the owner/buyer and sales associates in a small retail organization, or in a very larger organization this function may be represented by a large division that is staffed with a vice president of promotions, promotions managers, special events coordinators, an advertising manager, a visual merchandising manager, a public relations manager, and a Web site manager. Each of these managers may have a staff of merchandisers, merchandising assistants, technical staff, and clerical staff to assist them with their duties. When the staff of the promotions function is multi-numbered, these people must work as a team to present a clear, concise picture of the retailer's offerings and services. They are responsible for maintaining the image of the business.

Promotions personnel must adhere closely to the guidance for image as developed in the planning processes for the business. (For more information on image, see Chapter 5.) If the image is not maintained and the message about the store, the catalog, the Web site, and the merchandise is not consistent and clear, customers become confused. Without coordinating efforts, the promotional staff can actually hamper the sale of merchandise and create problems for the merchandising staff. If sales goals are not met, inventories can become higher than expected and higher markdowns than planned may be needed to sell the merchandise. All of these results affect margins and eventually the bottom line in the P & L statement (i.e., profit) for the retailer. (For more on the interrelation of the P & L components, see Chapter 3.)

To achieve and maintain the retail image and to promote the sale of merchandise, these staff members must also interact smoothly with staff in the other functions in the organization. The activities of all functions of the retail organization must be a team effort. To be competitive, a retailer must ensure that the functions of promotions, merchandising, operations, and control are coordinated. For example, sales associates are housed in the operations function, but are a critical key to successful selling. They are the personnel who have the direct and face-to-face communication with the customer. The buyer, who is part of the merchandising function, performs duties that directly impact the promotions activities. The promotional staff must work closely with merchandising personnel to create and maintain a consistent merchandise environment and retail image to attract and keep a repeat customer.

An example of this necessary teamwork is the introduction of a new item into the merchandise assortment. The purchase of that item begins with a buyer who spots a new item in a trip to Asia. Knowing the image of the business, the preferences of the target customer, and the new fashion trends based on extensive research, the buyer identifies the item as important to the next season's assortment. The buyer places an order for the item. As an adjunct to the order, the buyer must inform the promotions manager that the new item is coming and provides the manager with pictures of the item and a summary of the background information and trend research that prompted the buyer to place the order. The promotions manager will need to do similar research to identify any trends that may surround the presentation, use, or care of the item because promotions change, have trends, and become obsolete similar to other fashion items. (See Chapter 5 on fashion cycles.) Promotional activities will need to be planned to alert the target customer of the charm and attraction of this new item. When scheduling the timing for delivery of the item, the buyer will check with the promotions manager to determine the appropriate time for delivery in order to coincide with the promotional schedule. The buyer will also need to inform the operations manager of the introduction of the new item because sales associates will need to receive training about the item and on the care and use of the item. Of course, staff in the control function will be needed to establish new accounts with the vendor of the item and to prepare to pay the bills, which may include specialized techniques needed for foreign currency, exchange rates, and overseas banks. As illustrated, a team approach is definitely needed to bring this item to the attention of the customer, facilitate the sale of the item, and ensure that the customer is satisfied with the item after the sale.

Promotional Plan

The **promotional plan** for a retail business includes the types and timing of activities that are used to highlight the merchandise and the store for a specific customer. The promotional staff will work with the buyer and store management to develop a promotional plan for the period, usually the buying period. (That is, a business that operates with a six-month buying plan would have a six-month promotional plan.) The buyer may develop the promotional plan when no promotional staff is used. Or, in the case of a very small retail business with few functional employees, the store manager may make all promotional decisions.

The plan starts with the defining of the objectives of the promotion, usually completed as part of the strategic planning process. The second step of developing a plan is the establishment of a theme for the period, the season, or the events that are planned. The third step, done simultaneously with step two, requires the identification of the consumer to be targeted with the promotions. For the fourth step, the methods for promotion implementation are detailed. This outline includes the activities that are needed to stage the promotion and that are appropriate to reach the targeted consumers. In step four, a timeline and a schedule of responsibilities for each activity must be constructed, and duties are assigned to various promotional personnel or other staff members. Finally, as a fifth step, the retailer must see that each plan contains a method of evaluation.

To be effective, a promotional activity must be evaluated as to its degree of successfulness. In relationship to objectives, the retailer will decide upon desired results of the promotion. For example, a special event can be staged to increase sales. If that were the objective, then the evaluation would be measured in terms of increased sales from a previous period. If the promotion is designed to move or increase sales of slow-selling merchandise, then the measure might be an increase in the units sold. If a markdown is part of the promotion, actual increase in sales may be offset by the reductions in price; however, the number of units would indicate exactly how much merchandise of a specific category was sold.

Although sales figures, numbers of units sold, and turnover are excellent measures of promotional activities, the exact and complete effect of a promotional activity may be very difficult to measure. Placing an exact dollar value on a specific promotional activity may be almost impossible because of the after-effects of the promotion. Although the after-effects of the promotion are difficult to measure, they are the important added benefits of promotions. For example, the retailer will have a difficult time measuring the effects of a fashion show. Many customers may buy no items on the day of the show, but will return to the store six months later to buy because they were impressed by the glamour of the show, the pleasantness of the sales associates, or the fashion level of the merchandise. To further complicate measurement, these customers may not even buy merchandise that was shown in the show.

Although results are difficult to measure, each promotional activity should be carefully monitored and evaluated against the planned objectives. Promotional activities are usually very costly to the retailer and must be part of the operating expenses of the store. For this reason, the retailer must control carefully the type and cost of all promotional activities. Any activity that does not result in a positive benefit to the retail business should be closely analyzed because a promotion that does not achieve desired results could actually reduce the profit to the retailer.

All promotional activities must be included in the promotional plan. Some promotional activities involve price adjustments, and other promotional activities involve advertising or promotion, but no price adjustments. For these and other reasons, the promotional plan is made in conjunction with the buying plan. The buyer must know what events are planned, what merchandise is needed, how much merchandise is needed, and what price adjustments are expected to determine the assortment and volume of merchandise and to plan the initial markups. The buyer usually selects merchandise for the promotions while shopping in the market for all merchandise assortments for the upcoming season or seasons. Selecting merchandise for promotions that are planned six months to a year in advance allows ample time for the buyer and the visual merchandiser to plan for a successful promotion.

Extra merchandise or merchandise with markups different from the usual initial markup are needed to accommodate the promotional events. For example, a Father's Day sale may promote ties. Ties may have a consistent sales volume for 10 months during the year, but in May and June the sale of ties may triple in men's departments. Extra merchandise may be needed for floor stock and backroom stock to prevent stock outs. In addition, the retailer may wish to have a large price reduction for ties. To prevent erosion of the profit margin, ties may be purchased that ideally have a lower cost so that they can be sold at a lower price point to provide the consumer with the illusion of a large markdown for the ties. In contrast, some promotions are made with inventory that is pulled from the standard floor stock that was bought at regular price. The price is then reduced for the promotion. The retailer may find that the promotions result in increased sales during the event, extra traffic in the store, and favorable comments from the customers; however, this increase in sales through the depletion of inventory can result not only in reduced margins and increased markdowns, but also in stock outs at a later date.

These stock outs could ultimately result in loss of sales and even higher markdowns because of leftover merchandise and broken stock assortment. When the buyer is forced to use floor stock for a promotion, the best sizes, colors, silhouettes, and styles usually sell at the reduced price and only unwanted stock is left in inventory until replenishments arrive. In this manner, a promotion that is not well planned, especially one that is dependent on floor stock, may result in loss of profit for the retailer instead of increased profit. With the potential for loss instead of gain from a promotion, teamwork and coordination between buyer and promotions manager become very important for planning any promotional activity.

Promotional Budget

Promotional activities regardless of how well planned and controlled require expenditures; therefore, for each promotional plan, a budget should be diligently developed and carefully followed. A **promotional budget** covers financial plans for expenditures related to promotions and identifies the price adjustments that will be involved with the promotional events. Planning for the promotional activities and the money needed to carry out the activities is important. Expenditures for promotions must be determined financially as part of operating expenses and as part of reductions. If the promotional activity involves price adjustments, the promotional budget would identify the markdowns, markups, and expected merchandise sales. Planning and controlling markdowns are important to maintaining the expected maintained markups and profit margins.

The promotional budget has two parts: (a) allocations for the expenses involved in preparing and staging promotional events and (b) the markdowns and markdown cancellations that will be used when the promotion has a price adjustment. The two aspects of the budget may be planned or administered by two separate managers. The promotions manager or other administrator for the business may plan the actual promotions. This person would need to detail all expenses such as labor to build displays, equipment to furnish displays, printing for promotional materials including flyers and signs, and other labor or supplies needed for all promotional events. These expenses are actually part of the operating expenses and would be determined by the promotions staff in coordination with management. In fact, some large firms have planners who make long-range plans for business activities and related budgets.

Promotional Expenses

Supplies, labor, and equipment that are needed for promotional events can be budgeted for a year if a yearly promotional plan is made. Many promotional events are done only once a year; for example an Anniversary sale, a Founder's Day sale, the day after Christmas sale, Mother's day, or Father's day. The best planning for these events would be a yearly plan in order to determine how the events are spaced throughout the year. The promotions that are clearance sales and other price reduction sales (e.g., end of the month or end of the season) can be planned on a six-month or single-month basis, once the annual events are determined. Several methods can be used to determine the overall promotions budget, such as all-you-can-afford, incremental, competitive parity, objective and task, event, or annual allocation or percentage of sales method. Alternatively, the retailer may choose to use a combination of methods. The method selected may depend on the retailer's training, organizational policy, store type, merchandise characteristics, or availability of financing. For example, the **event method** is useful when new events are planned or when a new manager is determining the budget. With the event method, each promotional event is budgeted separately and then an annual budget needed for promotions can be determined.

Sample Problem: Event Method

The promotions staff is planning events for the next year. They decide to have five major events, one for each major season. An objective is set for each event and a theme is planned. The individual activities are listed for each event. At the end of the planning, the staff determines the supplies, labor, and equipment that will be needed for each event. For these items, Event 1 is determined to cost $400.00, Event 2 costs $1,000.00, Event 3 costs $1,500.00, Event 4 costs $650.00, and Event 5 costs $2,350.00. In addition, advertising will be needed for each event and is budgeted as 10.00% of each event cost. What is the total budget needed to cover each event during the year?

Step 1. Set up a spreadsheet to provide a worksheet for the budget.

	Event 1	Event 2	Event 3	Event 4	Event 5	Total
Costs						
Advertising						
Total						

Step 2. Place the appropriate values into the cells.

	Event 1	Event 2	Event 3	Event 4	Event 5	Total
Costs	$400.00	$1,000.00	$1,500.00	$650.00	$2,350.00	
Advertising (10.00%)						
Total						

Step 3. Calculate the advertising costs for each event, and place them into appropriate cells.

Advertising $ = Event Cost $ × Advertising %

For Event 1,

Advertising $ = $400.00 × 10.00%

Advertising $ = $40.00

	Event 1	Event 2	Event 3	Event 4	Event 5	Total
Costs	$400.00	$1,000.00	$1,500.00	$650.00	$2,350.00	
Advertising (10.00%)	$40.00	$100.00	$150.00	$65.00	$235.00	
Total						

Step 4. Find totals for each event and the annual total, and place the figures in the appropriate cells.

(Hint: Add columns for the event totals, and add rows and final column for the annual total.)

	Event 1	Event 2	Event 3	Event 4	Event 5	Total
Costs	$400.00	$1,000.00	$1,500.00	$650.00	$2,350.00	$5,900.00
Advertising (10.00%)	$40.00	$100.00	$150.00	$65.00	$235.00	$590.00
Total	$440.00	$1,100.00	$1,650.00	$715.00	$2,585.00	$6,490.00

Another method that the established retailer commonly uses is the **annual allocation** or **percentage of sales method**. This method requires that an annual amount for promotions be determined and allocated throughout the year. With this method, the retailer provides funding for promotions in proportion to the planned or expected sales volume. Past financial history and percentages are useful when a retailer chooses to use this method.

With the annual allocation or percentage of sales method, the retailer bases the promotional budget on the annual merchandise budget or on planned sales for the upcoming year. Most retailers allow 1–4% of the annual sales volume for promotional budget dollars. If no percentages are available from successful promotion activities in previous periods, the retailer may chose to use a rule-of-thumb measure that allocates monies across the promotional mix in the following percentages: advertising 50.00%, merchandise presentation 20–25%, special events 15.00%–20.00% (with an additional 5.00% for fashion shows alone), and publicity (if different from other activities) 5.00%. These percentages represent ranges that must be adjusted to equal 100.00%. After calculating the annual dollar budget, promotions personnel teaming with staff from other retail functions must decide on what types and how many promotions are needed to meet the planned sales goals. Expenditures for promotions are then calculated from the total annual promotion budget and are allocated among the various components of the promotional mix. The formulas needed to make these calculations are the increase in sales formula from Chapter 6, namely,

$$\text{Planned Sales \$} = \text{Base Year Sales \$} + (\text{Base Year Sales \$} \times \text{Increase \%})$$

and the basic **dollars and percentage** formulas from Chapter 2—that is,

$$\text{Component \$} = \text{Base \$} \times \text{Component \%}$$

Therefore, the **promotions dollar** formula is

$$\text{Promotions \$} = \text{Sales \$} \times \text{Promotions \%}$$

Sample Problem: Sales Percentage Method

An established retailer wishes to plan his promotional budget based on the annual allocations method or percentage of sales method. The following information is available:

a. The retailer's annual sales volume last year was $5,600,000.00. Next year this retailer plans for a 10.00% increase in sales volume.

b. Each year this retailer plans his annual promotional budget based on 3.50% of total yearly sales volume. Calculate the annual promotional budget for this established retailer based upon sales volume for next year.

c. This same retailer usually spends 48.00% of the total promotional budget on advertising and the remainder on special events, display, fashion shows, and publicity.

Calculate the dollar allocations for the promotional mix of advertising, special events, merchandising presentation, fashion shows, and publicity.

Step 1. Calculate the planned sales for next year.

Planned Sales $ = Base Year Sales $ + (Base Year Sales $ × Increase %)

Planned Sales $ = $5,600,000.00 + ($5,600,000.00 × 10.00%)

Planned Sales $ = $5,600,000.00 + ($560,000.00)

Planned Sales $ = $6,160,000.00

Step 2. Calculate the annual promotional budget for next year.

Promotional $ = Sales $ × Promotional %

Promotional $ = $6,160,000.00 × 3.50%

Promotional $ = $215,600.00

Step 3. Calculate the dollars for advertising.

Advertising $ = Promotional $ × Advertising %

Advertising $ = $215,600.00 × 48.00%

Advertising $ = $103,488.00

Step 4. Using basic algebra functions, find the remaining percentages for the rest of the promotional mix.

Remaining Promotional % = 100.00% − 48.00%

Remaining Promotional % = 52.00%

Each of the remaining mix activities receives an equal share of the remaining promotional percentage. Percentages would be determined in planning.

Activity % = 52.00%/4 activities

Activity % = 13.00%

Step 5. Find the dollars allocated to each remaining activity.

Activity $ = Promotional $ × Activity %

Activity $ = $215,600.00 × 13.00%

Activity $ = $28,028.00

To spread the monies for each promotional mix activity across the months in a year, the retailer will need a method to allocate dollars per month per activity. The retailer may determine that equal percentages of the promotions allotment or an equal allotment in dollars can be used each month. If past history of the retail organization is available with records on promotions, the retailer may determine that some months need more promotional activities and the percentages would vary depending on the month. In that situation, the monies can be allocated to each month depending on an established percentage as discussed in the preparation of the six-month plan. (See Chapter 8.) The allocations by monthly percentage usually make promotions monies parallel to the sale volume curve or in proportion to the expected sales volume.

Regardless of the method of determining markdown dollars for promotions, the retailer must determine the allocation of the dollars through the year and allocations of the budget to the various components of the promotions mix. In addition, appropriations of promotional monies must be made for each merchandise division, department, or other segment of the retailer's business. Traditionally, retailers have used advertising primarily for promotion and have disregarded the importance of special events, visual presentation and display, and sales training. Vendors or designers, with their own retail establishments to showcase their total product lines have forced retailers to concentrate on exciting promotional events and unique merchandise presentations. Regardless of the method used to plan the budget, the promotions planning staff must ensure that the promotions that are planned can be implemented within the budget. This control may cause the staff to evaluate and reshape the promotions plan; however, a balance is always sought between the goals of meeting the sales plan and the necessity to stay within the budget.

Promotional Markdowns

The second aspect of a promotional budget is the part of the budget that will directly alter the initial markup (i.e., a markdown). The markdowns, as part of reductions, must be planned when the initial markup is determined. In fact, reductions are a line on the spreadsheet for the six-month plan, usually made by the buyer. The buyer would have to work closely with the promotions manager or whoever plans promotions to ensure that the initial markup is large enough to accommodate the price adjustments for promotions. For example, the buyer plans an initial markup of 55.50%. The markup is designed to cover the costs of transportation of merchandise and cash discounts if taken. The buyer would know this information because of the negotiations made with the vendor. From management, the buyer would need information about operating expenses, employee discounts, profit, and average loss.

The last component of the initial markup is the markdowns. Markdowns are planned by the buyer for clearance of merchandise, but in some retail organizations, markdowns may be requested by the promotions staff to coordinate with a promotional event. The buyer will also have to order additional merchandise to prevent stock outs when the promotional events increase the sales for specific items.

Someone will also have to determine the amount of markdowns that will be allocated to promotional events and the amount of markdowns that are planned for clearing merchandise out of the store. The amount of markdowns for each category is determined by a number of factors. As discussed in the section on determining the initial retail price in Chapter 2, the retail price can be determined by (1) establishing price points for merchandise and for the business that are satisfactory to the consumer or (2) setting a price based on market value. These methods of pricing set a maximum price; the cost of goods, the expenses, the profit, and the reductions must be accommodated within that retail price. If the cost of the merchandise is relatively fixed, the retailer will have to adjust operating expenses, profit, or reductions to fit within the available margin or initial markup. Cash discounts may also be included in the **initial markup dollars** formula, which shows the relationship of these budget items

$$\text{Initial Markup \$} = \text{Operating Expense \$} + \text{Transportation \$} + \text{Profit \$} + \text{Reduction \$}$$

When reductions are viewed as individual budget items, the formula is

$$\text{Initial Markup \$} = \text{Operating Expense \$} + \text{Transportation \$} + \text{Profit \$} + \text{Employee Discount \$} + \text{Stock Shortage \$} + \text{Markdown \$}$$

When the initial markup is applied to the cost of merchandise, the retail price is determined with

$$\text{Initial Retail \$} = \text{Cost \$} + \text{Initial Markup \$}$$

The retailer, when using these formulas, can evaluate the impact that reductions will have on the initial retail price or can determine the limitation that initial retail price will have on the size and components of the initial markup.

Sample Problem: Markup Dollars for Promotions by Price Point Method

---

The retailer planned to sell $34,000.00 worth of merchandise during a Labor Day sale that would last one week. Employee discounts would not be allowed during the sale. Average loss was expected to be 7.00% during the sale. A week's worth of operating expenses averaged $13,000.00. Merchandise was special ordered for the sale and transportation was $500.00, with no cash discounts allowed. Profit for the business is always expected to be 5.50%. The retailer wanted to have a large markdown for all merchandise sold during the week. Initial markup for the business was usually 52.80%. How many markdown dollars could be allocated to this sale and what was the markdown percentage?

Step 1. Rewrite the formula to solve for markdown dollars.

$$\text{Initial Markup \$} = \text{Operating Expense \$} + \text{Transportation \$} + \text{Profit \$} + \text{Employee Discount \$} + \text{Stock Shortage \$} + \text{Markdown \$}$$

$$\text{Markdown \$} = \text{Initial Markup \$} - (\text{Operating Expense \$}$$
$$+ \text{ Transportation \$} + \text{Profit \$}$$
$$+ \text{ Employee Discount \$} + \text{Stock Shortage \$})$$

Step 2. Convert the percentages to dollars for compatible items in the formula.

Initial markup \$ = Net Sales \$ × Initial Markup %

Initial markup \$ = \$34,000.00 × 52.80%

Initial markup \$ = \$17,952.00

Profit \$ = Net Sales \$ × Profit %

Profit \$ = \$34,000.00 × 5.50%

Profit \$ = \$1,870.00

Stock Shortage \$ = Net Sales \$ × Stock Shortage %

Stock Shortage \$ = \$34,000.00 × 7.00%

Stock Shortage \$ = \$2,380.00

Step 3. Enter known information into the markdown dollars formula.

$$\text{Markdown \$} = \text{Initial Markup \$} - (\text{Operating Expense \$}$$
$$+ \text{ Transportation \$} + \text{Profit \$}$$
$$+ \text{ Employee Discount \$} + \text{Stock Shortage \$})$$

Markdown \$ = \$17,952.00 − (\$13,000.00 + \$500.00
+ \$1,870.00 + \$2,380.00)

Markdown \$ = \$17,952.00 − \$17,750.00

Markdown \$ = \$202.00

Step 4. Determine the markdown percentage.

Markdown \$ = Net Sales \$ × Markdown %

Markdown % = Markdown \$/Net Sales \$

Markdown % = \$202/\$34,000.00

Markdown % = 0.59%

In the sample problem, the markdown percentage that is allowed by the initial markup and other items from the Profit and Loss statement is less than 1%. As stated previously, this size markdown would not be large enough to motivate the consumers to buy. The retailer would have to adjust the plan to allow for a larger markdown. The typical answer for this situation is to buy merchandise that is below the average cost of merchandise so that a larger initial markup can be taken, while keeping the same price points, and then offering the excess markup as the markdown. This strategy is not possible when current merchandise is marked down; therefore, the retailer must plan very carefully so that expenses, markups, and markdowns can coincide harmoniously to achieve the desired profit.

The second method of pricing is to build the price by starting with the cost of the merchandise and adding markup to the cost until a retail price is achieved that is large enough to accommodate the needed markdowns and all other expenses for the retail business. This method can be applied to the previous sample problem.

Sample Problem: Markup Dollars for Promotions by Build Method

The retailer planned a Labor Day sale that would last one week and should result in $34,000.00 in net sales. Employee discounts would not be allowed during the sale. Average stock shortage was expected to be 7.00% during the sale. A week's worth of operating expenses averaged $13,000.00. Merchandise was special ordered for the sale, transportation was $500.00, and the cost was $15,000.00, with no cash discounts allowed. Profit for the business is always expected to be 5.50%. The retailer wanted to have a large markdown for all merchandise sold during the week and planned to take $15,000.00 in markdowns. What is the initial markup percentage needed to achieve these plans?

Step 1. Convert the percentages to dollars for compatible items in the formula.

Profit $ = Net Sales $ $\times$ Profit %

Profit $ = $34,000.00 $\times$ 5.50%

Profit $ = $1,870.00

Stock Shortage $ = Net Sales $ $\times$ Stock Shortage %

Stock Shortage $ = $34,000.00 $\times$ 7.00%

Stock Shortage $ = $2,380.00

Step 2. Enter known information into the initial markup dollars formula.

Initial Markup $ = Operating Expense $ + Transportation $ + Profit $
      + Employee Discount $ + Stock Shortage $
      + Markdown $

Initial Markup $ = $13,000.00 + $500.00 + $1,870.00
      + $2,380.00 + $15,000.00

Initial Markup $ = $32,750.00

Step 3. Determine the initial markup percentage.

Initial Markup % = Initial Markup $/Gross Sales $ $\times$ 100

Initial Markup % = Initial Markup $/(Net Sales $ + Reductions $)
      $\times$ 100

Initial Markup % = Initial Markup $/(Net Sales $ + Employee Discount $
      + Stock Shortage $ + Markdown $) $\times$ 100

Initial Markup % = $32,750.00/($34,000.00 + $2,380.00
      + $15,000.00) $\times$ 100

Initial Markup % = $32,750.00/$51,380.00 $\times$ 100

Initial Markup % = 63.74%

As shown in the preceding sample problems, careful planning is needed to ensure that operating expenses are covered by the sale of the merchandise and that the expectations of profitability are met. Therefore, promotions, as with other aspects of the retail business, must be planned prior to the buying and selling periods.

Regardless of the method for determining the size and contents of the budget, the promotional budget is closely related to the six-month plan. (The six-month plan is the buyer's plan for spending related to the merchandise needs for the business.) The six-month plan is composed of dollar values for sales plan, EOM needs, BOM, stock needs, reduction plan, and goods to be purchased. This relationship is seen in two points of the six-month plan. The sales plan and other merchandise indicators (EOM, BOM, and stock) are used by the buyer to determine the amount of merchandise that will be ordered and the amount of merchandise that will be moving through the business during the month and during the entire six-month period. The buyer will also need to know the promotional plans because increased promotions will require increased stock. The ratio of stock to sales may need to be altered during a promotional period to increase the available merchandise to satisfy a sharp increase in consumer demand. The specific merchandise that is needed will be determined by the context of the promotional plan. In addition, if the promotional plan includes a markdown, the buyer will need to include an adjustment to the reductions part of the six-month plan to reflect the projected gross markdown for the promotional events. If the buyer is using the six-month plan for merchandise planning, the promotional staff will need to have plans that are based on a monthly system to coincide with the buyer's monthly plan.

Sales Associates and Promotions

The promotional activities of a business will also have an effect on the activities of the sales associates. Sales associates are the customers' direct contact with the store. Their availability, skill in selling, and knowledge of the product are important for the successful implementation of any promotions activities.

The sales associate for most retailers is responsible for a variety of activities. Specifically, these activities may include receiving of new stock, validating that it is floor ready, preparing stock for placement on the floor, placing stock on the floor, and preparing merchandise presentations. Once the merchandise is on the floor, the associate is responsible for showing merchandise to the customers, assisting customers with trying on the merchandise, making sales transactions, and straightening stock on the floor. In addition, the sales associates may be asked to do physical inventories, clean the selling space, reticket merchandise, unload merchandise from trucks, and perform other activities related to stock movement. Some expenses for a retailer will not have a direct correspondence to increased revenues, but will have effects on the business's image and the satisfaction of the consumer, which will increase sales in the long term.

The purpose of promotions is to increase sales activities for the business. This increase is associated with more merchandise moving through the business and more customers interacting with the business and the available sales associates. Although sales associates are normally classified as belonging to the operations function within retail, their performance is critical to the promotional function.

Scheduling of Sales Associates

Depending on the sales transactions resulting from a promotion, a business may need more associates on the floor, on the telephone, and on the Web. (Some brick-and-mortar stores include sales catalogs and Web sites in their promotional information.) Traditionally, the best customers, those that held the store's private charge cards, were offered promotional sales first through telephone sales before the sale was offered in the store. Every aspect of the business will be heightened prior to and during a promotional event. Sales associates should not only see more customers, but also handle more merchandise during the promotional period. Merchandise handling may include reticketing, stocking and restocking the floor, and straightening merchandise after customers have shopped.

Part-time help may be hired during peak promotional periods to assist with sales transactions and stock activities. Increased numbers of sales associates will affect operating expenses. Hiring of extra sales associates is needed during promotional events and should be planned carefully. Within the P & L statement, an increase in operating expenses will be balanced against an increase in sales volume so that increased revenues are available to cover the expenses of the promotional event. The retailer must also consider that the sales associates are necessary to increase consumer satisfaction. Sales associates on the floor can promote sales, finalize sales transactions, and straighten merchandise.

For example, a retailer plans an anniversary sale for one week that will promote selected merchandise, but will have no markdowns. Net sales are expected to increase from the average weekly volume of $189,000.00 to $195,000.00. The retailer decides to hire additional sales associates to assist with the increased customer traffic and to handle the increased sales transactions. Eight sales associates are hired for the period with salaries of $3,200.00. The increase in sales of $6,000.00 will easily cover the cost of the additional sales associates. Although this explanation is a bit simplistic, it shows the interrelationship among sales and expenses as introduced in Chapter 3 with the Profit and Loss statement. The retailer must always remember that any money spent in one area of a business will be related to all other aspects of the business. When financial planning is done on a spreadsheet with a computer, various financial scenarios can be investigated and outcomes can be evaluated easily.

Sample Problem: Increase in Sales and Expenses

The retailer plans a promotional event to highlight the arrival of some new designer merchandise. The promotional event should result in an increase in customer traffic and, therefore, an increase in sales transactions. The net sales of the designer merchandise are expected to rise 3.00% from the average net sales for the month of $158,500.00. The retailer would like to hire some sales associates to work in the designer department for the month. The retailer wonders how many hours of sales associate time could be hired without a loss. The sales associates will be paid $12.00 per hour.

Step 1. Determine the increase in net sales that is predicted.

Increase in Net Sales $ = Net Sales $ $\times$ Increase %

Increase in Net Sales $ = $158,000.00 $\times$ 3.00%

Increase in Net Sales $ = $4,740.00

Step 2. Determine the number of hours that could be purchased for this increase.

\# of Hours = Increase in Net Sales $/$ per Hour

\# of Hours = $4,740.00/$12.00

\# of Hours = 395

Although in the previous problem, the retailer had many hours of sales associate time available, every promotional event or retail activity will not increase net sales enough to hire additional sales associates. Some days the net sales may not cover the salaries of the sales associates who are working that day. The retailer must remember that some expenditures are for long-term investments in customer satisfaction and business image. Some promotional events increase the visibility of the business, improve consumer knowledge of the business, and attract shoppers to the store, but not consumers who buy. Sales associates that assist a shopper who does not buy may have assisted someone who will return another day to buy. The satisfaction of consumers is more than just satisfaction with the merchandise. For the retailer, direct return on every expenditure may not be obvious or possible.

Training of Sales Associates

An important aspect of the sales associate's job should be training. The sales associate should be knowledgeable about the business, consumers, selling procedures, and the merchandise. To be effective with increasing sales and maintaining customers, the retailer must communicate product knowledge as well as effective selling techniques to the sales associates who will use this information in their encounters with customers. Many vendors provide printed materials, videos, and other formats containing product information to assist the retailer in the training of sales associates on specific product offerings. Additionally, retailers with a training staff or training division may conduct seminars, stage fashion shows, or develop printed materials to assist sales associates in gaining product knowledge. Associates should develop an understanding not only of the product, but also of selling techniques in order to present new trends, new brands, and new merchandise classifications to the customers.

Without training, a sales associate may attempt to make a sales transaction based on a personal selling philosophy instead of trying to understand the needs and wishes of the customer. Some customers are very methodical, utilizing logic, when making a purchase. Other customers may shop in a hurry or may choose things on a whim or based on emotions or relationships. All customers must be serviced with kindness and given the appropriate time to make decisions based on their own shopping timeframe and not that of the sales associate. With training, the sales associates benefit by understanding the shopping style of the customer and the retailer benefits because when the shopping style and preferences of the customer are recognized and matched, the likelihood of a sale is greatly increased.

Training is an activity that has specific expenditures in terms of sales associate time, the time for the trainer, materials for training, and space for training and may not have direct returns in terms of increased sales. Training costs money and removes sales associates from the sales floor, which will in the short term, reduce profitability including a potential reduction in net sales; however, trained sales associates who are knowledgeable will create more satisfaction among the customers, which in turn will increase sales in the long term. Training of employees is a good investment for the retailer. In addition to increased sales transactions and improved consumer satisfaction, the well-trained sales associate is more likely to stay as an employee. Reduced turnover among employees will also result in improved profitability for the retailer.

Sell-Through

Ultimately, the retailer must be concerned with **sell-through**, or the calculation to determine how much of the merchandise that was bought was sold to the customer and did not return to the business for refunds. Sales associates should encourage the consumer to buy merchandise and should practice strong selling techniques, but should also be sensitive to the interests of the consumer. Merchandise should not be pushed on the consumer when the consumer is unwilling to buy. Merchandise that is too hastily sold will often be returned. Merchandise that is unneeded or unwanted by the consumer will also often be returned. The sales associate wants to maximize sales transactions and minimize returns of merchandise. Returned merchandise may be damaged or soiled and often cannot be sold for maximum markups. In addition, returns of merchandise take sales associate's time and require reticketing. Many returns have to be reduced in price because of the timing of the return or the condition of the merchandise; therefore, the retailer must take a loss or a markdown, in order to sell the goods. The acceptance of returned merchandise is often a burden that the retailer must take because of the need to maintain consumer satisfaction.

Sell-through is calculated as a ratio: The amount of merchandise sold is compared to the amount of merchandise purchased. Sell-through can be calculated as an average for a business, store, department, or merchandise classification. Average sell-through compares the amount of merchandise sold during a period with the amount of merchandise that was purchased during that period. This calculation will give the retailer an estimate of the sell-through for the business during a period. More accurate calculations are important to identify precisely the sell-through for a business. To determine exact sell-through, the retailer must track merchandise through the inventory system from the time it is ordered and arrives at the loading dock until it is sold to the consumer and not returned. A computerized inventory system, of course, will make this calculation swiftly. Without such a system, the retailer will have to keep very accurate records and may need to have a physical inventory taken to obtain final information for the sell-through formula. SKU numbers are useful for calculating sell-through because individual items of merchandise can be tracked with these numbers. To determine an exact measure of sell-through, the retailer would determine the exact number of items ordered and received within a specific merchandise classification. This number would be divided into the exact number of items that were sold and not returned, and the **sell-through** formula would be

$$\text{Sell-Through} = \text{\# of Items Sold}/\text{\# of Items Bought}$$

This ratio can be viewed as a percentage by multiplying it by 100 and the **sell-through percentage** formula is

$$\text{Sell-Through \%} = \text{\# of Items Sold}/\text{\# of Items Bought} \times 100$$

Sample Problem: Sell-Through Percentage

The buyer ordered 250 units of a red blouse from Vendor Y. All of the units were received. At the end of the season, only 12 units remained. What was the sell-through for the red blouses?

Step 1. Determine the number of items sold.

$$\text{\# of Items Sold} = \text{\# of Items Bought} - \text{\# of Items Remaining}$$
$$\text{\# of Items Sold} = 250 - 12$$
$$\text{\# of Items Sold} = 238$$

Step 2. Enter known information for sell-through percentage.

$$\text{Sell-Through \%} = \text{\# of Items Sold}/\text{\# of Items Bought} \times 100$$
$$\text{Sell-Through \%} = 238/250 \times 100$$
$$\text{Sell-Through \%} = 95.20\%$$

A high sell-through percentage indicates that the retailer has done a good job of planning, buying, and selling the merchandise. Every step in the process is important.

S*ummary*

The selling of the merchandise must be actively pursued to ensure that the planned net sales are achieved. Planning and buying merchandise is vital to the success of the retail business. The right merchandise must be available for customers. Although buyers say that merchandise well bought is half sold, the other half or the selling process is also important. Promotional events and sales associate training must be planned to ensure that the customers come to shop and that the merchandise is sold. Promotional events include activities that promote the business, the merchandise, and a reduction in retail price. The buyer must anticipate increased stock to accommodate increased sales of merchandise. When the promotion includes price adjustments, the buyer must be aware of these adjustments to determine the appropriate initial markup, costs, and retail prices for the merchandise. Buyers, promotional staff, and store management must work as a team to coordinate the efforts of the business to draw customers to the store and to increase sales transactions for the merchandise. Training of sales associates is another important task because a well-trained sales associate can increase sales transactions and maintain satisfaction among consumers.

Key Terms

3 × 3 method	Handling	Promotional plan
Advertising	Lifestyle merchandising	Promotions function
Aisle	Marketing communications	Sale
Annual allocation method	Media mix	Sales transaction
Concept shop	Merchandise presentation	Selling
Cooperative advertising	Outpost	Sell-through
Core	Percentage of sales method	Shop concept
Display	Plan-o-gram	Special events
Event method	Promotional budget	Top wall/vista wall
Floor ready	Promotional mix	Training of sales associates

Discussion Questions

1. Why is planning for promotions important?
2. How is promotional planning related to buying merchandise?
3. What are the major components of the promotional mix? How are these components interrelated and how do they impact marketing communications?
4. Why is merchandise presentation important?
5. What is the role of the sales associate in a promotional event?
6. What are the components of the media mix? Why are the traditionally emphasized elements no longer effective with some consumers?
7. What is the relationship between the promotional budget and the six-month plan?
8. How is pricing strategy related to promotional planning?
9. What items of information will need to be shared between the buying function and the promotional function for a retail business?
10. What should be included in a promotional plan?
11. What is the difference between planning an annual promotions budget based on the events method versus the annual allocation method?
12. What major expenses should be included in the annual promotional budget?
13. What areas should be covered in training for sales associates?
14. What expenses are incurred in training sales associates?
15. Why should the buyer have information about the activities on the sales floor?
16. How does the sales staff affect the result of buying?

Exercises

Promotional Mix

1. Select a specific retailer and observe the retailer's use of the three promotional mix activities. Document these observations with photographs of merchandise presentations, copies of newspaper and magazine advertising, video copies of television advertising, flyers about promotional events, news stories, and other evidence of promotional activity. Identify the theme and target consumer for this retailer through interviews with store personnel. Analyze the coordination of the promotional activities.

2. Select a target store and three displays within the store. Through store observations, count the number of customers who glanced at the presentation, stopped to look at the presentation, or touched the presentation. Also, count the number of customers who selected merchandise to try on or to finally purchase. Compare the activities at the three displays, and analyze any differences or lack of differences in the activities around the displays and the turnover of merchandise.

3. Select a merchandise classification within a retail store. In cooperation with the retailer, identify arrival of new merchandise for that classification. Over a period of weeks, keep a count of the number of items that are placed on the floor, and the number of items that are sold or returned. Observe how the merchandise is promoted during the research period. Analyze the effects of the promotions. Provide suggestions to the retailer for future promotions.

Promotional Budget

1. The promotions staff is planning events for six months. They decide to have three major events. An objective is set for each event and a theme is planned. The individual activities are listed for each event. At the end of the planning, the staff determines the supplies, labor, and equipment that will be needed for each event. For these items, Event 1 is determined to cost $1,400.00, Event 2 costs $2,000.00, and Event 3 costs $3,500.00. In addition, advertising will be needed for each event and is budgeted as 12.00% of each event cost. What is the total budget needed for six months?

2. The promotions staff is planning events and has decided to have two major events. Each theme is related to a major inventory reduction. The individual activities are listed for each event. At the end of the planning, the staff determines that the supplies, labor, and equipment for each event are as follows: Event 1— supplies $1,000.00, labor $2,000.00, and equipment $900.00; Event 2—supplies $2,500.00, labor $2,800.00, and equipment $960.00. In addition, advertising will be needed for each event and is budgeted as 15.00% of each event's direct cost. What is the total budget needed for the year?

3. The promotions staff decides to have five major events in the coming year. The themes will correspond to each of the five seasons. At the end of the planning, the staff determines that each event will have $4,000.00 for supplies. Labor is figured

at 30.00% of the supplies. Equipment allowances are estimated at 15.00% of supplies. The total direct costs should be calculated for each event. Advertising will be calculated as 9.00% of each event. What is the total budget needed for the year?

4. A retailer wishes to plan his promotional budget based on the annual allocations method or percentage of sales method. The retailer's planned sales for next year are $7,880,000.00.

   a. Each year this retailer plans his annual promotional budget based on 3.40% of total yearly sales volume. Calculate the annual promotional budget for this established retailer based upon sales volume for next year.

   b. From the total promotional budget, 44.00% will be allocated to advertising and the remainder of promotional mix will receive the following: special events 20.00%, merchandise presentation 26.00%, and publicity 10.00%. Calculate the dollar allocations for the promotional mix.

5. An established retailer wishes to plan his promotional budget based on the annual allocations method or percentage of sales method. The retailer's annual sales volume last year was $4,900,000.00. Next year this retailer plans for an 8.00% increase in sales volume.

   a. Each year this retailer plans his annual promotional budget based on 2.80% of total yearly sales volume. Calculate the annual promotional budget for this established retailer based upon sales volume for next year.

   b. This same retailer usually spends 40.00% of the total promotional budget on advertising and the remainder on special events, merchandising presentation, and a separate fashion show. Calculate the dollar allocations for the promotional mix.

6. Investigate the cost of advertising in the local newspaper, on the radio, on a local television station, and for development and mailing of a flyer. Using these numbers, plan a monthly budget for a retailer who wants to do one newspaper ad that runs all month, a radio spot for 30 seconds that is run 10 times, and a 15 second TV spot to air once for four days at the 6:00 pm news hour. In addition, the retailer wants to have a one-page flyer created and mailed to 20,000 customers.

Markup Dollars for Promotions

1. A retailer planned to sell $4,000,000.00 worth of merchandise next year. Employee discounts are usually at 3.00%. Average loss is expected to be 7.00%. The year's operating expenses should average $1,800,000.00. Transportation is planned at $4,500.00, with no cash discounts allowed. Profit for the business is always expected to be 5.50%. Initial markup for the business is usually 63.50%. How many markdown dollars can be allocated for this year, and what was the markdown percentage?

2. A retailer planned to sell $54,000.00 worth of merchandise during a Back-to-School Sale that would last three weeks. Employee discounts would not be allowed during the sale. Average loss was expected to be 7.00% during the sale. Three week's worth of operating expenses averaged $23,000.00. Merchandise was special ordered for the sale and transportation was $500.00, with no cash discounts allowed. Profit for the business is always expected to be 5.50%. The retailer wanted to have a large markdown for all merchandise sold during the three weeks. Initial markup for the business is usually 60.00%. How many markdown dollars can be allocated to this sale?

3. A retailer planned to sell $5,690,000.00 worth of merchandise next year. Employee discounts are usually at 5.00%. Average loss is expected to be 7.90%. The year's operating expenses should average $1,900,000.00. Transportation is planned at $3,500.00. Cash discounts are normally 1.50% of sales. Profit for the business is planned for 4.50%. Initial markup for the business is planned as 61.00%. How many markdown dollars can be allocated for this year, and what was the markdown percentage?

4. The retailer planned a Valentine's Day sale that would last one week and should result in $44,000.00 in net sales. Employee discounts would be allowed at 25.00% during the sale. Average loss was expected to be 8.00% during the sale. A week's worth of operating expenses averaged $23,000.00. Merchandise was special ordered for the sale and transportation was $1,500.00, and the cost was $28,000.00, with no cash discounts allowed. Profit for the business is always expected to be 4.50%. The retailer wanted to have a large markdown for all merchandise sold during the week and planned to take $25,000 in markdowns. What is the initial markup percentage needed to achieve these plans?

5. The retailer planned a big sale to last for one week that would start with a fashion show and should result in $14,000.00 in net sales. No employee discounts would be allowed during the sale. Average loss was expected to be 6.00% during the sale. A week's worth of operating expenses averaged $2,000.00. No special transportation was needed, and the cost was $7,000.00, with no cash discounts allowed. Profit for the business is always expected to be 4.50%. The retailer wanted to take a 30.00% markdown. What is the initial markup percentage needed to achieve these plans?

6. The retailer planned a Founders Day sale that would last one week and should result in $144,000.00 in net sales. Employee discounts would be allowed at 30.00% during the sale. Average loss was expected to be 8.00% during the sale. A week's worth of operating expenses averaged $46,000.00. Merchandise was special ordered for the sale and transportation was $1,000.00, and the cost was $60,000.00, and cash discounts were $3,000.00. Profit for the business is always expected to be 6.00%. The retailer wanted to have a large markdown for all merchandise sold during the week and planned to take $7,200.00 in markdowns. What is the initial markup percentage needed to achieve these plans?

Increase in Sales and Expenses

1. The retailer plans a promotional event to highlight the arrival of some new merchandise. The promotional event should result in an increase in customer traffic and, therefore, an increase in sales transactions. The net sales of the merchandise are expected to rise 4.00% from the average net sales for the month of $200,000.00. The retailer would like to hire some sales associates to work in the department for the month. The retailer wonders how many hours of sales associate time could be hired without a loss. The sales associates will be paid $8.00 per hour.

2. The retailer plans a promotional event to highlight the arrival of some new designer merchandise. The promotional event should result in an increase in customer traffic and, therefore, an increase in sales transactions. The net sales of the designer merchandise are expected to rise 3.00% from the average net sales for the month of $300,000.00. The retailer would like to hire some sales associates to

work in the designer department for the month. The retailer wonders how many hours of sales associate time could be hired without a loss. The sales associates will be paid $9.00 per hour.

3. The retailer plans a promotional event for the Anniversary Sale. The net sales in the store are expected to rise 8.00% from the average net sales for a day, which is $100,000.00. The retailer would like to hire some sales associates to work in the designer department for the month. The retailer wonders how many hours of sales associate time could be hired, still leaving some money from the sales increase. The sales associates will be paid $8.00 per hour.

Sell-Through

1. The buyer ordered 50 units of a home furnishings item from Vendor X. All of the units were received. At the end of the season, only 2 units remained. What was the sell-through for the item?

2. For a new video item, the buyer ordered 1,250 units. All of the units were received. At the end of the season, 600 units remained. What was the sell-through for the item?

3. The buyer ordered 150 units of a red blouse from Vendor Y and 100 units of a blue blouse from Vendor X. All of the units were received. At the end of the season, only 12 units remained for the red blouse and 8 units remained for the blue blouse. Which item had the better sell-through?

4. The buyer ordered 150 units of a new color of towel from Vendor Y and 100 units of the same color of shower curtains from Vendor X. All of the units were received. At the end of the season, 5 towels remained and 8 shower curtains remained. Which item had the better sell-through?

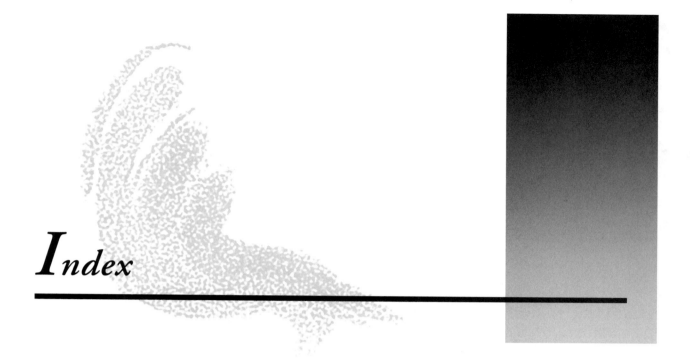

I*ndex*